Stimulating Economic Growth Through Cultural and Societal Transformations

Lina Salim
Atma Jaya Catholic University of Indonesia, Indonesia

Haider Ali Abbasi
Universiti Teknologi Petronas, Malaysia

IGI Global
Scientific Publishing
Publishing Tomorrow's Research Today

Published in the United States of America by
IGI Global Scientific Publishing
701 East Chocolate Avenue
Hershey, PA, 17033, USA
Tel: 717-533-8845 | Fax: 717-533-7115
Website: https://www.igi-global.com E-mail: cust@igi-global.com

Library of Congress Cataloging-in-Publication Data

Names: Salim, Lina, 1966- editor. | Abbasi, Haider Ali, 1987- editor.
Title: Stimulating economic growth through cultural and societal transformations / [edited by] Lina Salim, Haider Ali Abbasi.
Description: Hershey, PA : IGI Global Scientific Publishing, [2026] | Includes bibliographical references and index. | Summary: "This book aims to explore how cultural values, societal shifts, and policy reforms can serve as powerful drivers of economic growth. By addressing an often-overlooked area in economic research, it examines the transformative role of cultural and social factors in shaping resilient and inclusive economic progress"-- Provided by publisher.
Identifiers: LCCN 2024061646 (print) | LCCN 2024061647 (ebook) | ISBN 9798337306032 (hardcover) | ISBN 9798337306049 (paperback) | ISBN 9798337306056 (ebook)
Subjects: LCSH: Economic development--Social aspects. | Social change--Economic aspects.
Classification: LCC HD75 .S774 2025 (print) | LCC HD75 (ebook) | DDC 338.9--dc23/eng/20250228
LC record available at https://lccn.loc.gov/2024061646
LC ebook record available at https://lccn.loc.gov/2024061647
British Cataloguing in Publication Data
A Cataloguing in Publication record for this book is available from the British Library.

Table of Contents

Preface ... xiii

Chapter 1
A Study of Factors Affecting Intention to Use Sugar-Free Drinks of Vietnamese Youth ... 1
Tran Nguyen Gia Han, FPT University, Vietnam
Trinh Ngoc Quy, FPT University, Vietnam
Le Hoang Khang, FPT University, Vietnam
Mai Van Tien, FPT University, Vietnam

Chapter 2
Enhancing Motivation for Proactive Career Behaviours of Private University Students in Ho Chi Minh City ... 33
Nguyen Thi Truc Linh, FPT University, Vietnam
Duong Thanh Quynh Giang, FPT University, Vietnam
Tran Nguyen Hoang Anh, FPT University, Vietnam

Chapter 3
Farmers' Right to Seed at the Intersection of Intellectual Property and Human Rights: A Critical Analysis in Socio-Cultural Context ... 57
Ananya Pandey, Christ University, Bangalore, India
Achyuta Nanda Mishra, Christ University, Bangalore, India

Chapter 4
Generation Green: Navigating ESG in Generation Z's Job Search Landscape ... 83
Jing Yi Yong, Taylor's University, Malaysia
Yusliza Mohd Yusoff, Universiti Malaysia Terengganu, Malaysia
Yudi Fernando, Universiti Malaysia Pahang, Malaysia & Binus University, Indonesia
Woon Leong Lin, Taylor's University, Malaysia
Siong Choy Chong, Taylor's University, Malaysia
Chuen Khee Pek, Taylor's University, Malaysia

Chapter 5
Heritage and Culture: Conservation in the Age of Cosmopolitanism - A Case of Kampong Ayer (Brunei Darussalam) ... 101
Izni Azrein Noor Azalie, Universiti Brunei Darussalam, Brunei

Chapter 6
Individual Differences in Intentional and Unintentional Exposure to Sexual Content Among Vietnamese Students 131
Le Thi My Danh Danh, FPT University, Vietnam
Do Hoang Anh, FPT University, Vietnam
Le Nguyen Khanh Minh Minh, FPT University, Vietnam
Huynh Nguyen Yen Minh Minh, FPT University, Vietnam
Tran Hoang Bao Chi Chi, FPT University, Vietnam
Dinh Thi Thuy Hoa Hoa, FPT University, Vietnam

Chapter 7
Integrating TAM and UGT to Explore Motivations of Using Social Media for Watching Sport Contents Among a Private University's Students in HCM City 153
Le Thi My Danh, FPT University, Vietnam
Huynh Ngoc Minh Thu, FPT University, Vietnam
Nguyen Le Bao Ngoc, FPT University, Vietnam
Do Thi My Linh, FPT University, Vietnam
Pham Huu Xuan Nhi, FPT University, Vietnam
Tran Duy Hung, FPT University, Vietnam

Chapter 8
Nurturing Future-Ready Talent by Understanding the Role of Talents' Sustainable and Professional Digital Persona on Hiring Decisions 177
Nur Atikah A. Rahman, Universiti Sains Malaysia, Malaysia
Sharifah Nadiah Syed Mukhiar, Universiti Sains Malaysia, Malaysia
Rani Ann Balaraman, Universiti Sains Malaysia, Malaysia

Chapter 9
Poverty Eradication via Sustainable Human Development: A Human Security Approach 197
Jipson Joseph, Christ University, India
Achyutananda Mishra, Christ University, India

Chapter 10
Smart Technology and Indian Journalism: Progress, Problems, and Prospects 225
Nihaz Anvar, Lovely Professional University, India
Neha Sah, Lovely Professional University, India

Chapter 11
Streamlining Vaccination Process Through Innovative Solution: Bakunako - A Rewards-based Health Record Platform 241
Leah O. Pelias, University of Southeastern Philippines, Philippines
Francis O. Sale, University of Southeastern Philippines, Philippines
Carl Christian M. Capon, University of Southeastern Philippines, Philippines

Chapter 12
The Effect of Human Capital on Economic Growth: The Case of Türkiye....... 277
Burak Çanakci, Firat University, Turkey
Izzet Taşar, Fırat University, Turkey

Chapter 13
The Supply Chain Risk Analysis Using the House of Risk (HOR) Method: Integration of the Supply-Chain Operation Reference (SCOR) Model and the Fuzzy Logic 313
Aisyah Larasati, Universitas Negeri Malang, Indonesia
Ahmad Danial Ubaidillah, Universitas Negeri Malang, Indonesia
Abdul Muid, Universitas Negeri Malang, Indonesia
Anik Dwiastuti, Universitas Negeri Malang, Indonesia

Compilation of References 341

About the Contributors 391

Index 395

Detailed Table of Contents

Preface xiii

Chapter 1
A Study of Factors Affecting Intention to Use Sugar-Free Drinks of Vietnamese Youth 1
Tran Nguyen Gia Han, FPT University, Vietnam
Trinh Ngoc Quy, FPT University, Vietnam
Le Hoang Khang, FPT University, Vietnam
Mai Van Tien, FPT University, Vietnam

Sugar-free drinks, though often less tasty, provide a healthier alternative to sugary beverages. The market includes various options like teas, coffees, yogurts, juices, and detox drinks, catering to health-conscious consumers seeking low-sugar, low-calorie choices. This study applies the Theory of Reasoned Action (TRA) to explore Vietnamese students' awareness and intent to consume sugar-free drinks. An online survey of over 300 students at a Ho Chi Minh City university was analyzed using SPSS. Findings revealed that perceived awareness, functional congruity beliefs, subjective norms, self-concept beliefs, weight concerns, and enjoyment influence their consumption intent. Businesses can leverage these insights for product development and marketing, while health and educational organizations can promote reduced sugar intake and healthier lifestyles

Chapter 2
Enhancing Motivation for Proactive Career Behaviours of Private University Students in Ho Chi Minh City 33
Nguyen Thi Truc Linh, FPT University, Vietnam
Duong Thanh Quynh Giang, FPT University, Vietnam
Tran Nguyen Hoang Anh, FPT University, Vietnam

While the Vietnamese labour market is extremely competitive, little is known about the factors affecting students' prospects of having a successful career after graduation. The employment demands-resources model and goal-setting theory served as the cornerstones for the theoretical model of undergraduate students' employability that Andrew James Clements and Caroline Kamau (2018) constructed. This study investigates how motivational processes influence students' proactive career actions within the context of Vietnamese private colleges using this model. According to our research, students who are highly dedicated to their professional objectives are more likely to take proactive steps toward their careers, which is necessary for their success in the competitive job market. This research provides valuable insights for educational institutions in designing training programs and supporting students in developing essential skills needed to thrive in a competitive environment.

Chapter 3
Farmers' Right to Seed at the Intersection of Intellectual Property and Human Rights: A Critical Analysis in Socio-Cultural Context 57
Ananya Pandey, Christ University, Bangalore, India
Achyuta Nanda Mishra, Christ University, Bangalore, India

The interplay between farmers' Intellectual Property Rights (IPRs) and Human Rights is significant in socio-cultural transformations. Farmers in traditional and indigenous communities hold centuries of knowledge about biodiversity, sustainable agriculture, and seed management. However, the rise of commercial agriculture, globalization, and stringent IPR regimes—often favoring corporate interests—pose challenges to preserving and recognizing this knowledge. This chapter critically examines the intersection between farmers' IPRs and human rights, exploring how evolving frameworks impact cultural identities, societal structures, and the rights of communities to food security, self-determination, and participation in decision-making processes. It discusses the tension between the patenting of genetic resources and the traditional knowledge of farmers, emphasizing the need for equitable benefit-sharing mechanisms. By bridging legal and socio-political perspectives, this chapter aims to highlight policies that uphold farmers' and human rights amidst ongoing socio-cultural transformations.

Chapter 4
Generation Green: Navigating ESG in Generation Z's Job Search Landscape ... 83
Jing Yi Yong, Taylor's University, Malaysia
Yusliza Mohd Yusoff, Universiti Malaysia Terengganu, Malaysia
Yudi Fernando, Universiti Malaysia Pahang, Malaysia & Binus University, Indonesia
Woon Leong Lin, Taylor's University, Malaysia
Siong Choy Chong, Taylor's University, Malaysia
Chuen Khee Pek, Taylor's University, Malaysia

As the workforce evolves, Generation Z (Gen Z) prioritises Environmental, Social, and Governance (ESG) factors in career decisions. This chapter explores how ESG commitments shape employer attractiveness, using Signaling Theory and Social Identity Theory to explain Gen Z's job pursuit intentions. It examines the implications for employers, educators, and policymakers, providing strategies for ESG-driven workforce engagement. Future research should focus on empirical validation, cross-industry analysis, and policy impacts to enhance understanding. As ESG principles redefine workplace expectations, organisations integrating sustainability and ethical governance will gain a competitive edge in attracting and retaining Gen Z talent. This chapter contributes to the discourse on ESG in human resource management, highlighting evolving job market trends and the need for businesses to embed ESG principles into their long-term strategies.

Chapter 5
Heritage and Culture: Conservation in the Age of Cosmopolitanism - A Case of Kampong Ayer (Brunei Darussalam) 101
Izni Azrein Noor Azalie, Universiti Brunei Darussalam, Brunei

This chapter explores the intricate relationship between culture, heritage, and globalization in Brunei Darussalam, with a specific focus on Kampong Ayer (KA), a historically significant water village. The analysis highlights the cultural and economic challenges faced by KA, rooted in its past as the epicenter of trade and the Bruneian Sultanate, which has been undermined by modernization and globalization since the 1960s.. While recent heritage tourism efforts have been made, challenges such as poverty and poor infrastructure remain obstacles to sustainable development. By referencing the Sustainable Development Goals (SDGs), particularly SDGs 1, 8, 11, and 12, the chapter highlights how cultural heritage can guide urban revitalization. Using concepts such as cosmopolitanism, sense of place, placemaking, and place branding as part of developing the culture and heritage industry, it advocates for a comprehensive approach to preserving cultural identity while promoting local economic growth and community well-being, providing actionable strategies for policymakers and urban planners.

Chapter 6
Individual Differences in Intentional and Unintentional Exposure to Sexual Content Among Vietnamese Students 131
Le Thi My Danh Danh, FPT University, Vietnam
Do Hoang Anh, FPT University, Vietnam
Le Nguyen Khanh Minh Minh, FPT University, Vietnam
Huynh Nguyen Yen Minh Minh, FPT University, Vietnam
Tran Hoang Bao Chi Chi, FPT University, Vietnam
Dinh Thi Thuy Hoa Hoa, FPT University, Vietnam

This study investigates how university students (aged 18–22) at a private university in Ho Chi Minh City are exposed to sexual content online—both intentionally and unintentionally—amid Vietnam's technological transition. Using Gender Schema Theory and Social Bonds Theory, and adapting a Hong Kong study, it explores how gender and religious beliefs influence these experiences. A quantitative online survey guides the research, with eight hypotheses examining patterns of exposure. The findings aim to inform educators, parents, and policymakers in developing effective digital literacy and sex education programs to ensure a safer online environment for Vietnamese youth.

Chapter 7
Integrating TAM and UGT to Explore Motivations of Using Social Media for Watching Sport Contents Among a Private University's Students in HCM City 153
Le Thi My Danh, FPT University, Vietnam
Huynh Ngoc Minh Thu, FPT University, Vietnam
Nguyen Le Bao Ngoc, FPT University, Vietnam
Do Thi My Linh, FPT University, Vietnam
Pham Huu Xuan Nhi, FPT University, Vietnam
Tran Duy Hung, FPT University, Vietnam

This study examines the factors influencing private university students' consumption of sports content on social media. As digital sports media rapidly expands, we integrate the Technology Acceptance Model (TAM) and Uses and Gratifications Theory (UGT) to form a comprehensive framework. TAM assesses how perceived ease of use and usefulness shape engagement, while UGT explains how cognitive, social, and emotional needs drive content consumption. Key motivations include information seeking, social interaction, and emotional gratification. Data is collected and analyzed using SPSS. The study fills a gap in Vietnamese sports media research and offers insights for improving digital engagement strategies among youth.

Chapter 8
Nurturing Future-Ready Talent by Understanding the Role of Talents' Sustainable and Professional Digital Persona on Hiring Decisions 177
Nur Atikah A. Rahman, Universiti Sains Malaysia, Malaysia
Sharifah Nadiah Syed Mukhiar, Universiti Sains Malaysia, Malaysia
Rani Ann Balaraman, Universiti Sains Malaysia, Malaysia

Social media has become an essential source for hiring professionals to screen and cybervet potential employees. However, talents in Malaysia are unaware of this practice and how negative content can impact their career prospects. This study focuses on leveraging talent's identity to create sustainable and professional digital persona. It aims to investigate the reasons why sustainable and professional digital persona of job seekers impacts the decision-making process of recruiters when selecting candidates. Through qualitative interviews, this study found significant impact of a job candidate's digital persona on recruiters' selection decisions, emphasising the importance of character assessment, communication skills, cultural fit evaluation, consistency, and the use of LinkedIn as the primary platform for professional networking. Understanding on the need of sustainable and professional digital persona in job hunting can further contribute towards the improvement of digital recruitment process for productive employment and sustainable economic growth in Malaysia, in line with SDG8.

Chapter 9
Poverty Eradication via Sustainable Human Development: A Human Security Approach 197
Jipson Joseph, Christ University, India
Achyutananda Mishra, Christ University, India

Poverty has been one of the major human insecurities throughout history. It became more evident in the aftermath of the Industrial Revolution. Though economic growth was suggested as an effective mechanism for poverty eradication, it severely increased inequality together with poverty. Realizing the importance of poverty eradication for human well-being, the United Nations initiated many policies and programs including Millennium Development Goals (MDGs) and Sustainable Development Goals (SDGs). Based on the framework of MDGs, the SDGs was moving towards the achievement of 'no poverty' by 2030. But the Covid-19 pandemic slowed this pace, demanding more earnest effort from the international community. This chapter, in this perspective, using critical analytical method examines the possibility of human security approach's sustainable human development model for the realization of SDG1. The chapter advances human security's all-inclusive and comprehensive human-centered sustainable development model as an effective mechanism for poverty eradication in the entire globe.

Chapter 10
Smart Technology and Indian Journalism: Progress, Problems, and Prospects 225
Nihaz Anvar, Lovely Professional University, India
Neha Sah, Lovely Professional University, India

Historically, the term "smart" was mostly used to describe human intelligence and wit, but in the last twenty years, it has also come to describe advanced technologies. Smart engineering, including artificial intelligence (AI), the Internet of Things, and cloud computing, provide widespread data availability, connectivity, and information aggregation. These advancements have significantly impacted journalism globally, including in India, where the media sector is valued at over a trillion Indian rupees. The shift from print to digital news has transformed how news is accessed, produced, and consumed. AI-driven tools now automate content creation, distribution, and audience interaction, introducing new practices like data journalism and drone journalism. This study examines the current use of smart technology in Indian journalism, its benefits, and the challenges to full integration. By analyzing these aspects, the paper intends to provide a clear and comprehensive understanding of the disruptive effects of smart technology on Indian journalism and media organizations.

Chapter 11
Streamlining Vaccination Process Through Innovative Solution: Bakunako - A Rewards-based Health Record Platform 241
Leah O. Pelias, University of Southeastern Philippines, Philippines
Francis O. Sale, University of Southeastern Philippines, Philippines
Carl Christian M. Capon, University of Southeastern Philippines, Philippines

BakunAko is a platform designed to address the challenges of infant vaccination with scheduling and integrated features. A needs assessment in the methodology provides the parents and guardians a relevant tool to keep updated and responsible for the immunization of the infant. The voucher reward system allows incentivization points to be earned. Automated scheduling, digital immunization records, and SMS reminders are the features to combat stigma on vaccination for infants. The platform incorporates innovative solutions through a unique vaccination timetable, addresses financial barriers, and promotes adherence to local health sector programs. It empowers end-users to ensure seamless immunization through its user-friendly interface and comprehensive features. Aiming to improve immunization rates, protect public health, and offer incentives. Pilot testing was conducted to ensure functional and non-functional attainment of the objectives. The result underpins facilitation of faster and effective prevention of infectious diseases, especially among infants in the underserved community.

Chapter 12
The Effect of Human Capital on Economic Growth: The Case of Türkiye....... 277
Burak Çanakci, Firat University, Turkey
Izzet Taşar, Fırat University, Turkey

The concept of human capital emerged with the realization that economic growth cannot be explained solely by changes in physical capital. In this context, human capital is directly related to factors such as education, health to increase the productivity of individuals and their contribution to the economy. Economic growth is defined as the increase in the production of goods and services over time. However, the fact that this increase is sustainable and increases the welfare of the society shows the importance also investments in human capital. TDenison, Mankiw-Romer-Weil, Becker-Schultz and Jorgenson approaches from neo-classical growth models and Barro, Lucas and Charles Jones approaches from endogenous growth models are examined as economic approaches that focus on the effect of human capital on economic growth. In this study, which is specific to Türkiye, the long-term relationship between human capital and economic growth is examined in Türkiye with the GDP and human capital index between the years 2000-2022.

Chapter 13
The Supply Chain Risk Analysis Using the House of Risk (HOR) Method: Integration of the Supply-Chain Operation Reference (SCOR) Model and the Fuzzy Logic 313
Aisyah Larasati, Universitas Negeri Malang, Indonesia
Ahmad Danial Ubaidillah, Universitas Negeri Malang, Indonesia
Abdul Muid, Universitas Negeri Malang, Indonesia
Anik Dwiastuti, Universitas Negeri Malang, Indonesia

The object study is a sugar factory. During the milling period, several obstacles occur, such as delays in raw materials and machine damage. This can be anticipated with mitigation actions, which are the main output of the House of Risk (HOR) and are mapped based on the Supply-Chain Operations Reference (SCOR) model. However, the HOR method has an extensive range in its assessment, so it needs to be integrated with fuzzy logic to provide firm values. This research aims to analyze what risks arise, the risk agents, priority risk agents, and the steps to handle them in sugar production. This research uses the SCOR model and the Fuzzy House of Risk method. The research instruments include interviews, closed questionnaires, and brainstorming with the experts. Based on the interview results, 17 risk events and 19 risk agents were obtained. Based on the nine priority risk agents, several mitigation actions were formulated, such as mentoring sugar cane care for partner farmers, improving farming business management, weather prediction, and analysis of transport routes.

Compilation of References 341

About the Contributors 391

Index 395

Preface

INTRODUCTION

Economic growth in contemporary societies is increasingly shaped by complex interactions between culture, social behavior, institutional structures, and technological innovation. Traditional economic indicators alone can no longer capture the full range of forces influencing development outcomes, particularly in rapidly transforming societies across Asia and other emerging regions. Cultural norms, individual motivations, digital practices, legal frameworks, and human-centered policies now play a decisive role in shaping productivity, labor markets, consumer behavior, and long-term sustainability. *Stimulating Economic Growth Through Cultural and Societal Transformations* brings together scholarly contributions that reflect this broader, interdisciplinary understanding of economic progress.

This edited volume emphasizes the role of people—especially youth, workers, consumers, and communities—as active agents of economic transformation. Many chapters focus on how attitudes, motivations, education, health, digital engagement, and ethical considerations influence economic participation and opportunity. From career motivation and digital personas to ESG-driven employment preferences and health-related consumption behavior, the book highlights how individual choices, shaped by cultural and social contexts, aggregate into wider economic outcomes. These perspectives underscore the importance of investing in human capital and aligning development strategies with societal values.

At the same time, the volume addresses structural and institutional dimensions of economic growth, including governance, legal protections, technological systems, and supply chain resilience. Issues such as blockchain adoption, farmers' rights, poverty eradication, media transformation, and risk management illustrate how economic systems must adapt to balance efficiency, equity, transparency, and sustainability. Together, the chapters present a multifaceted exploration of how cultural and societal transformations can both enable and constrain economic growth in an era defined by rapid change and global interdependence.

CHAPTER OVERVIEW

Chapter 1 examines factors influencing Vietnamese youths' intention to consume sugar-free drinks, applying the Theory of Reasoned Action to understand how awareness, self-concept, social norms, and health concerns shape consumer behavior. The chapter provides insights for businesses and public health stakeholders seeking to encourage healthier consumption patterns while responding to evolving market demands.

Chapters 2 focuses on career motivation and proactive career behaviors among private university students in Ho Chi Minh City. Drawing on goal-setting theory and the employment demands–resources framework, these chapters highlight the importance of motivation, dedication, and proactive engagement in enhancing employability within a highly competitive labor market. The findings offer practical implications for higher education institutions and workforce development initiatives.

Chapter 3 critically analyzes farmers' rights to seed at the intersection of intellectual property and human rights. Situated within a socio-cultural context, the chapter highlights tensions between traditional knowledge systems and commercial agricultural practices, emphasizing the need for equitable legal frameworks that support food security, cultural identity, and community participation.

Chapter 4 investigates how Environmental, Social, and Governance (ESG) considerations shape Generation Z's job search behavior. Using signaling and social identity theories, the chapter demonstrates how sustainability and ethical governance increasingly influence employer attractiveness, offering guidance for organizations aiming to engage and retain younger talent.

Chapter 5 presents a case study of Kampong Ayer in Brunei Darussalam, examining heritage conservation amid globalization and cosmopolitanism. By linking cultural preservation to the Sustainable Development Goals, the chapter illustrates how heritage-based development strategies can support local economic growth, urban revitalization, and community well-being.

Chapters 6 and 7 address digital media consumption among Vietnamese university students. Chapter 7 explores intentional and unintentional exposure to sexual content online, highlighting implications for digital literacy, youth protection, and education policy. Chapter 8 integrates the Technology Acceptance Model and Uses and Gratifications Theory to examine motivations for consuming sports content on social media, offering insights for digital engagement strategies and media development.

Chapter 8 examines the role of sustainable and professional digital personas in hiring decisions within the Malaysian context. The chapter highlights how online identity, communication skills, and platform use—particularly LinkedIn—affect employability and recruitment practices, with implications for human capital development and sustainable economic growth.

Chapter 9 adopts a human security approach to poverty eradication, critically evaluating global development frameworks such as the MDGs and SDGs. The chapter advances a human-centered sustainable development model as a pathway toward achieving SDG 1 and addressing persistent inequalities exacerbated by global crises.

Chapter 10 analyzes the impact of smart technologies on Indian journalism, examining how artificial intelligence, data-driven practices, and digital platforms are transforming news production, distribution, and consumption. The chapter discusses both the opportunities and challenges associated with technological disruption in the media sector.

Chapter 11 presents *BakunAko*, a rewards-based digital health platform designed to streamline infant vaccination processes. By integrating digital records, automated scheduling, and incentive mechanisms, the chapter demonstrates how technological innovation can address public health challenges and contribute to broader social and economic well-being.

Chapter 12 investigates the relationship between human capital and economic growth in Türkiye, drawing on both neo-classical and endogenous growth theories. Using long-term empirical data, the chapter demonstrates the critical role of education and health investments in achieving sustainable economic development.

Chapter 13 applies the House of Risk method integrated with fuzzy logic to analyze supply chain risks in the sugar industry. By identifying priority risks and mitigation strategies, the chapter provides practical tools for improving operational resilience, productivity, and supply chain sustainability.

CONCLUSION

The chapters in this volume collectively demonstrate that economic growth is not merely the outcome of financial investment or technological advancement, but a process deeply embedded in cultural values, social behavior, institutional design, and human well-being. By foregrounding perspectives on youth, education, health, ethics, and governance, the volume highlights the central role of human capital and social systems in shaping sustainable economic trajectories.

A key contribution of this book lies in its interdisciplinary and regionally grounded approach. The empirical focus on Southeast Asia, South Asia, and Türkiye offers valuable insights into how emerging and transitional economies navigate globalization, digitalization, and social change. At the same time, the themes explored—such as ESG, digital identity, heritage conservation, and poverty eradication—resonate globally, making the findings relevant to a broad international audience.

We hope that *Stimulating Economic Growth Through Cultural and Societal Transformations* will serve as a meaningful resource for scholars, policymakers, educators, and practitioners seeking to design development strategies that are inclusive, ethical, and culturally informed. By bridging theory, empirical evidence, and practical application, this volume aims to contribute to ongoing discussions on how societies can foster economic growth that genuinely enhances human and social well-being.

Chapter 1

A Study of Factors Affecting Intention to Use Sugar-Free Drinks of Vietnamese Youth

Tran Nguyen Gia Han
https://orcid.org/0009-0001-7903-2763
FPT University, Vietnam

Trinh Ngoc Quy
FPT University, Vietnam

Le Hoang Khang
FPT University, Vietnam

Mai Van Tien
FPT University, Vietnam

ABSTRACT

Sugar-free drinks, though often less tasty, provide a healthier alternative to sugary beverages. The market includes various options like teas, coffees, yogurts, juices, and detox drinks, catering to health-conscious consumers seeking low-sugar, low-calorie choices. This study applies the Theory of Reasoned Action (TRA) to explore Vietnamese students' awareness and intent to consume sugar-free drinks. An online survey of over 300 students at a Ho Chi Minh City university was analyzed using SPSS. Findings revealed that perceived awareness, functional congruity beliefs, subjective norms, self-concept beliefs, weight concerns, and enjoyment influence

DOI: 10.4018/979-8-3373-0603-2.ch001

their consumption intent. Businesses can leverage these insights for product development and marketing, while health and educational organizations can promote reduced sugar intake and healthier lifestyles

I. INTRODUCTION

In recent years, the global and Vietnamese markets have witnessed a significant shift toward healthier dietary choices, with sugar-free and low-sugar beverages gaining increasing favor among health-conscious consumers. This trend reflects growing awareness of the adverse health effects associated with excessive sugar consumption, coupled with a desire for products that maintain flavor while offering nutritional benefits. In Vietnam, consumers are increasingly prioritizing foods and beverages that support weight management, enhance satiety, and preserve natural taste, aligning with broader global health movements. According to a 2022 survey by Cimigo, Vietnamese consumers are particularly concerned with reducing disease risk (58%), boosting immunity (52%), improving cardiovascular health (50%), enhancing digestive health (44%), and promoting mental well-being (52%). These priorities have driven the steady rise in demand for functional beverages, such as herbal-infused drinks that promote sleep, from 2018 to 2023. Major brands have responded to this shift, with Vinamilk launching low-sugar products like Probi Light drinking yogurt and Green Farm low-sugar milk, Nestlé introducing low-sugar Milo, and Coca-Cola and LaVie expanding their portfolios with sugar-free and flavored sparkling water options.

The market for sugar-free beverages is experiencing robust growth both globally and in Vietnam. According to Market Research Future (2022), the global sugar-free beverage market was valued at approximately USD 7.9 billion in 2022 and is projected to reach USD 10.9 billion by 2031, with a compound annual growth rate (CAGR) of 7.23% from 2024 to 2031. Segments such as sugar-free soft drinks, energy drinks, and teas are leading this growth, driven by demand for low-calorie options that support weight control. In Vietnam, the non-alcoholic beverage market, which includes sugar-free products, is expected to reach USD 9.06 billion by 2029, with a CAGR of 5.51% from 2024 to 2029 (Statista, 2024). Urbanization, rising disposable incomes, and heightened health awareness, particularly post-COVID-19, have fueled this expansion. A Kompa report (2020–2022) noted 1.55 million social media discussions on low-sugar products, predominantly on Facebook (96.8%), reflecting a cultural shift toward healthier consumption patterns. The pandemic amplified this trend, as reports highlighted higher mortality risks for diabetic COVID-19 patients, prompting consumers to seek "healthier" alternatives.

The health implications of sugar consumption underscore the importance of sugar-free beverages. The World Health Organization (WHO) recommends limiting free sugar intake to less than 10% of daily energy consumption, ideally below 5% (approximately 25 grams per day), to optimize health benefits. Excessive sugar intake is associated with non-communicable diseases, including obesity, type 2 diabetes, cardiovascular disease, dental caries, and certain cancers (WHO, 2015). The PubMed Central report (2023) correlates sugar with visceral fat deposition, gout, and high uric acid levels. Worldwide, sugar-induced diabetes saw an unprecedented upsurge of 108 million in 1980 versus 422 million in 2014 (WHO, 2016). On the other hand, sugar-free beverages bear a considerable set of benefits, prepared by natural sweeteners such as stevia or carrying some synthetic alternatives such as sucralose. The Food and Agricultural Organization (FAO) considers this a break for food technology, which now can provide delicious low-calorie beverages with no adverse impact on human health. These types of drinks can be instrumental in reducing calorie intake; controlling weight; preventing chronic diseases, such as cardiovascular diseases; and providing important nutrients, including vitamins, minerals, and antioxidants (WHO, 2015). However, WHO recommends moderation on the long-term use of artificial sweeteners, as it could raise the risk of type 2 diabetes and cardiovascular diseases, calling for further research (FAO, 2023).

Despite sugar-free drinks being more and more preferred, the consumer decision still involves basic considerations. There are always social pressures, advertising, and emotional benefits to be considered. Social media platforms, such as Facebook and TikTok, seem to greatly influence consumer behavior in Vietnam, especially for the younger demographic. Based on the Kompa Reports (2020–2022), discussions about low-sugar products were mostly about recipes, dairy products, weight loss, and product reviews, fueled by promotional activities and peer influence. This paper puts its focus on students in private universities in Vietnam as the changing landscape of consumption trends is strongly reflected by these students acting as trendsetters. Private university students, who are generally aged 18 to 24 and come from a middle to upper-middle-class background, constitute the crux of these contemporary consumption trends. Being Generation Z, the digital marketing and social media influences have been and still exert a strong appeal for young adults, with 96.8% of the discussions around low-sugar products being on Facebook (Kompa, 2022). Their higher household level of income demanded access to premium sugar-free beverages, which are usually set at a price higher than their conventional counterparts. These students report greater awareness of health and physical appearance, instigated by urban social pressures that emphasize fitness and beauty. Cimigo (2022) reports 52% of young consumers in Vietnam choose products that uplift their mental health and mood, a factor that sugar-free beverages address by making people less stressed and more energetic. They are decision-makers in their peer groups and age-related online communities; hence, a handful of private university students would set intent toward shaping future consumption trends within the larger demographics.

This research fills crucial gaps identified in the existing literature. Previous works such as Nguyen and De Steur (2021) examined mostly individual or economic factors for beverage consumption such as health consciousness and prices while ignoring the collective cultural factors in Vietnamese society. Being a group-oriented value system grounded in Confucian principles such as social harmony and peer pressure, this likely comes into play when beverage choices are made collectively, for example, in a social gathering where students may prefer to order sugar-free drinks to go with their group's choice. One example is that ordering a Coca-Cola Zero rather than a sugary tea might be more about conforming socially rather than health orientation. Second, according to the existing literature, urban consumers have been treated as a homogenous entity, disregarding the peculiarities of private university students who are exposed to global brands and trending topics through their studies and co-curricular activities, whose global exposure has made them inclined to respond to international advertising campaigns of these very companies-Coca-Cola and PepsiCo. Finally, few quantitative studies have been conducted concerning social media's impact on attitude and intention toward sugar-free beverage consumption in Vietnam. The rapid expansion of Facebook and TikTok clearly indicates the urgent want to study their influence on young consumers' buying behavior.

This research sets out to examine determinants underlying sugar-free beverage consumption among private university students in Vietnam, investigating the nutritional, social, and emotional factors. Filling these gaps has therefore aimed to shed more light on consumer behavior, thereby giving beverage marketers adapted marketing strategies and public health policies combating the decreasing trends in diet-related non-communicable diseases. It is ultimately very vital for stakeholders promoting healthier consumption to understand these contexts and look at both problems and prospects operating in the moments of change in the beverage trade landscape of Vietnam.

II. LITERATURE REVIEW

1. Global and Local Trends in Sugar-Free Beverage Consumption

Consumer awareness concerning health issues has brought about a paradigm shift toward sugar-free and low-sugar products in the global beverage industry. The sugar-free beverage market worldwide was valued at USD 18.12 billion in 2023 and is predicted to be worth USD 30.4 billion by 2032, operating at a CAGR of 5.92%, says Market Research Future (2024). Selling points for this market growth are obesity, type 2 diabetes, and cardiovascular diseases, all of which have led consumers to seek healthier choices. Segments such as sugar-free soft drinks, energy drinks, and teas are at the forefront, driven by demand for low-calorie options that support weight management (Market Research Future, 2024).

In Vietnam, the sugar-free beverage market is expanding rapidly, reflecting trends in urbanization, rising disposable incomes, and growing health consciousness. B-Company (2023) reports that Vietnam's sugar-free beverage market reached USD 756 million in 2023 and is expected to grow to USD 873 million by 2024. Notably, 34% of consumers under 25 prefer unsweetened or ionized water, indicating a shift toward health-oriented products (Zenodo, 2023). The doubling of childhood overweight and obesity rates from 8.5% in 2010 to over 19% in 2020, coupled with an increase in adult diabetes prevalence from 3.2% in 2011 to 6.1% in 2021, underscores the urgency of reducing sugar consumption (Vietnam News, 2024; IDF Diabetes Atlas, 2021). The Vietnamese government's implementation of a 10% special consumption tax on sugary drinks (exceeding 5g sugar per 100ml) further accelerates the transition to sugar-free alternatives (VCCI, 2024).

2. Nutritional Labeling and Consumer Behavior

Nutritional labeling plays a critical role in shaping consumer choices, particularly in reducing sugar intake. Nguyen & Tran (2020) found that 38% of urban Vietnamese consumers use nutritional labels to check sugar content, resulting in a 5.406% reduction in calorie intake from added sugars. This effect is more pronounced among adolescents, with females reducing calorie intake by 28.394% and males by 20.698%. Vietnam's per capita sugar consumption averages 46.5g daily, nearly double the World Health Organization's recommended limit of 25g (WHO, 2015). These findings highlight the potential of nutritional labeling as an effective public health intervention to promote sugar-free beverage consumption.

Consumer behavior toward sugar-free beverages is also influenced by social and cultural factors. In Vietnam's collectivist culture, subjective norms and peer pressure significantly impact consumption decisions, aligning with the Theory of Reasoned Action (TRA) (Fishbein & Ajzen, 1975). Nguyen et al. (2021) noted that 63% of Vietnamese consumers do not associate sugary drinks with obesity, indicating a knowledge gap that could be addressed through targeted education. This underscores the importance of enhancing awareness and social norms to encourage sugar-free choices.

3. Social Media and Generation Z Consumer Behavior

Generation Z, comprising approximately 15 million individuals in Vietnam by 2025, represents a key demographic for the sugar-free beverage market (Nielsen, 2018). Characterized by high digital engagement, 55% use TikTok and 79% are active on Facebook (McKinsey, 2022). Social media platforms are instrumental in shaping their consumption behavior, with pages and groups dedicated to healthy beverages attracting thousands of followers and high engagement (B-Company, 2023).

Influencer marketing is particularly effective in reaching Generation Z. Campaigns such as GrabFood Signatures have leveraged influencers to enhance brand awareness, demonstrating potential for similar strategies in the beverage industry (AnyMind Group, 2023). Coca-Cola, with its Coca-Cola Zero Sugar launched in Vietnam in 2016, has utilized digital campaigns to target this demographic (Kamereo, 2022). These strategies highlight the role of social media in driving intentions to consume sugar-free beverages, particularly in a collectivist culture where herd behavior influences individual choices (Hofstede, 1984). In accordance with Bandura's Social Learning Theory (1977), media exposure about sugar-free beverage products creates consumer attitudes and values that should be channeled toward health consciousness.

4. Theoretical Framework and Research Hypotheses

The present study is based on the Theory of Reasoned Action (TRA), which combines a vast theoretical foundation for investigating relationships between attitude, social norms, and intended behavior (Ajzen & Fishbein, 1980). The TRA assumes that an individual's behavior intention, or an individual's willingness to perform a specified behavior, is influenced by two elements: one's attitude about the behavior and subjective norms (Ajzen & Fishbein, 1975). Attitude, while capturing an individual's belief about consequences resulting from engaging in that behavior, subjective norms capture measures of social pressure arising from judgments of significant people such as family, community, or friends (Ajzen & Fishbein, 1975). This construct is very relevant in Vietnam's collectivist culture, where social pressures and community norms constrain the behavior of consumers (Hofstede, 1984). In comparison with the Theory of Planned Behavior (TPB), which incorporates perceived behavioral control, TRA simple yet sufficiently explanatory in tracing cognitive and social factors related to intentions to consume sugar-free beverages. However, TPB can complement TRA by dealing with practical barriers, such as price or product availability (Ajzen, 1991).

The main goal of this theory is to comprehend voluntary behavior by examining underlying motivations, which are tempered by behavioral intention; this intention is, in turn, influenced by attitudes and norms. The very basis of behavioral intention is the perceived result of carrying out a behavior. In this way, one would purchase sugar-free drinks to ensure the avoidance of obesity or promotion of good health. Under TRA, attitudes and subjective norms are considered the significant predictors of intention, more so in collectivist settings like Vietnam, where community expectations largely influence individual behavior (Hofstede, 1984).

In Vietnam, the sugar-free beverage trend is on the rise, especially when it comes to the student community, regarded as an extremely health-conscious, image-conscious, and fashion-conscious community. This segment of society is most susceptible to messages disseminated by media channels like television, press, social media, or the Internet. Social Learning Theory (1977) of Bandura posits that repetitive exposure to media content about sugar-free beverages such as advertisements for health benefits or celebrity endorsements mold the perceptions and behavior of consumers. Such content creates awareness about benefits like lower risks of obesity, diabetes, dental caries, and cardiovascular diseases (WHO, 2015). Besides, such advertising brings forth feelings associated with positive enjoyment and excitement and triggers the urge to consume sugar-free beverages.

In Vietnam's collectivistic culture, social norms play an essential role in the formation of consumer behavior. As Hofstede (2012) states, Vietnamese culture is mainly concerned with community harmony, limits individual freedom, and demands conformity to social norms. The consumers in Vietnam, especially youngsters, often fall prey to herd behavior, which is basically seeing other people do something and following if there is incomplete or uncertain information (Hofstede, 1984). For example, seeing peers, family members, or influencers consume sugar-free beverages might put social pressure on the students to follow in their footsteps. If one trusts the information from the media, including social media posts or influencer reviews, such positive assertions about sugar-free beverages become more credible-that they are healthy and trendily modern lifestyle choices.

The model integrates the cognitive and affective mechanisms, with behavioral intention serving as intervening behavior. Cognitive factors include perceived awareness, functional congruence, subjective norms, and self-concept congruence-for example, consumers' beliefs and evaluations of the functional and symbolic value of sugar-free beverages. Among emotional factors are the fear of weight gain and pleasure to motivate consumption. This model fits within the framework of TRA, implying that attitudes and norms predict intentions by integrating cultural- and media-specific variables relevant to Vietnam. TRA provides a strong theoretical foundation for studying sugar-free beverage consumption intentions in Vietnam's collectivist culture. Through a focus on attitudes, subjective norms, and media roles, this study places diversity upon the consumption behavior of students with respect to unique cultural and social factors. The integration of both cognitive and affective dimensions into the proposed model serves to enhance its membrane toward practical issues especially for consideration in marketing strategies and public health policies in Vietnam. The framework stresses the action of individuality, social and media powers in framing the health-conscious consumption trends of young consumers.

Cognitive factors

A consumer's perceived awareness refers primarily to the extent to which an individual may have cognizance of attributes and benefits of a product or behaviour; this awareness then impacts the beliefs and attitudes that an individual may have toward that product. Also, it deals with consumer knowledge about how sugar-free drinks work and what benefits or disadvantages they have. Eagly and Chaiken (1993) view attitude as "a positive or negative evaluation of a particular object". When perceived awareness is high, consumers will be more informed and are capable of making judgments on whether they would rather consume or not, and that affects their attitude, along with their behavioral intention.

H1: Consumers' perceived awareness of sugar-free beverages has a positive impact to their intention to use sugar-free beverages

Functional congruity refers to the alignment between consumer beliefs about product attributes and the benefits they expect. This concept suggests that consumers evaluate products based on how well these attributes meet their functional needs and expectations. In this study, perceived weight management or health benefits were linked to the functional attributes of sugar-free beverages. Consumers who believe that sugar-free beverages provide greater functional benefits, such as weight control or improved health, will have stronger usage intentions and more positive attitudes toward these products.

H2: Consumers' functional congruity beliefs of sugar-free beverages have a positive impact to their intention to use sugar-free beverages

The concept of subjective norms refers to consumers' perceptions of the approval or disapproval of their behaviour by friends, family, and colleagues. This can manifest itself through beliefs about other people's opinions about sugar-free drinks. According to Ajzen and Fishbein (1980), individuals are more likely to perform a behaviour if they perceive that people important to them think they should do so. Both positive and negative opinions are considered motivators, and the sum of these perceptions creates the overall subjective norm. Individuals assign different weights to opinions based on cultural influences, personality, gender, or age.

In this aspect, Vietnamese culture is characterised by collectivity, different from the individualistic culture in some Western countries, so the opinions of family members have a significant influence on consumption decisions. In collectivistic cultures, individual freedom may be limited, and the individual must integrate into the broader community (Hofstede, 1984). In addition, Vietnamese consumers are easily influenced by the "herd effect", when incomplete or inaccurate information forces them to observe the behaviour of others. This trend is especially evident when consuming sugar-free drinks when individuals feel more secure with the choices of those around them. Furthermore, Vietnamese family members tend to share similar views and beliefs, while younger members often must respect the opinions of their elders.

H3: Consumers' subjective Norm relating to sugar-free beverages has a positive impact to their intention to use sugar-free beverages

Self-concept congruity measures how well consumers feel a product represents their personal identity. Unlike functional fit, which focuses on how product attributes meet specific needs, self-concept congruity involves consumers choosing products that reflect or enhance their self-image (Rosenberg, 1979). According to Sirgy's congruity theory, the more consumers identify with the personality of sugar-free drinks or see themselves as "the health-conscious," the stronger their intention to consume these beverages. Therefore, consumers who opt for sugar-free beverages may perceive that these products help them project a desired image, thereby boosting their self-confidence and improving their self-perception. They are likely to view sugar-free drinks as value-expressive products that can convey significant personal meaning to others. By aligning their consumption choices with their self-concept, these consumers feel that they are not only making healthier choices but also reinforcing a positive and health-conscious identity that is visible to those around them. This dual benefit of personal enhancement and social signaling increases their appreciation for sugar-free beverages. Rapaport and Orbell (2000) emphasize that higher identification with a product leads to stronger intentions and more positive attitudes towards its use. Therefore, it is hypothesised that:

H4: Consumers' Beliefs about self-concept congruity relating to sugar-free beverages have a positive impact on their intention to use sugar-free beverages

Emotional Factors

Emotions have frequently been viewed as a crucial element of attitudes. The emotional factors outlined in the suggested model consist of concerns about fear of gaining weight and enjoyment. Fear has been conceptualised as "a negatively-valenced emotion, accompanied by a high level of arousal, [...] elicited by a threat that is perceived to be significant and personally relevant" (Easterling & Leventhal, 1989; Lang, 1984; Ortony & Turner, 1990 in Witte, 1992). Fear can prompt behavioural changes, especially when linked to specific personal negative outcomes (Beck, 1987). In this context, the fear of gaining weight acts as a negative reinforcement, often used in fear-based advertising. Consumers believe that sugary drinks can lead to weight gain, and to avoid this, they should use sugar-free beverages instead. This aligns with the Health Belief Model (HBM), indicating that the more consumers fear weight gain, having seen or heard about others gaining weight from sugary drinks, the more likely they are to choose sugar-free options. Rogers (1975) and Witte (1992) in the Extended Parallel Process Model suggest that fear plays a crucial role in shaping attitudes and that fear appeals can drive attitude change. Hence, consumers with a greater fear of weight gain are expected to have stronger intentions to consume sugar-free drinks.

H5: Consumers' Fear of gaining weight has a positive impact on their intention to use sugar-free beverages

Consumers' enjoyment of sugar-free beverages is expected to influence their consumption intention. Consumers will tend to choose sugar-free drinks if they like the taste and don't have to worry about calories. Holbrook and Hirschman (1982) proposed that pleasurable and emotional consumption experiences can strongly influence consumption behaviour. Similarly, Celsi and Olson (1988) suggested that when consumers engage in an activity for personal pleasure, they are more likely to perform that behaviour regularly. Consumers desire low-calorie beverages that are both enjoyable and help them avoid worrying about negative health consequences.

H6: Consumers' enjoyment of using sugar-free beverages has a positive impact to their intention to use sugar-free beverages

Figure 1 shows the theoretical model that tests the relations between six constructs and the construct of intention to use sugar -free drinks.

Figure 1. Theoretical Model of Factors Influencing Sugar-Free Beverage Consumption Intention (source by authors).

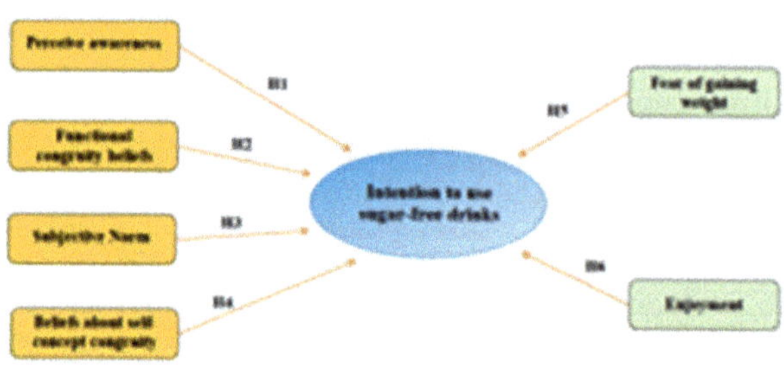

5. Research Gaps

Despite extensive research on sugar-free beverage consumption, several gaps remain. First, studies in Vietnam, such as Nguyen et al. (2021), have primarily focused on individual and economic factors, neglecting the influence of collectivist culture and social pressures, which are prominent in Vietnamese society (Hofstede, 1984). Second, private university students, who exhibit unique consumption patterns due to exposure to global trends and digital media, have not been adequately explored. Finally, the role of social media, particularly TikTok and Facebook, in shaping Generation Z's consumption behavior in Vietnam lacks quantitative analysis. This study addresses these gaps by examining the cognitive, emotional, and social factors influencing sugar-free beverage consumption intentions among private university students in Vietnam.

III. RESEARCH DESIGN AND METHODS

1. Sampling and data collection

Research on the intention to use sugar-free beverages begins with determining the goals and scope of the research. We have selected images of sugar-free drinks from big companies such as Pepsi and Coca-Cola. We will ensure this data during the research process. We are committed to privacy practices and ensure the confidentiality of data sharing during research. The study will involve private university students aged 18 to 25. This selection of ages and education levels is carefully done to ensure appropriateness to the research question and understanding. Young people's views may be more positive about the use of sugar-free drinks. The participants in this study are students from a private University in Ho Chi Minh City, Vietnam. We will invite them to participate in the study voluntarily and based entirely on their opinions. When participating in research we will commit to maintaining transparency and participant privacy.

2. Measures

Both direct and modified versions of prior research were used in the selection of the measuring items in the questionnaire. The survey's questions were adapted to the Vietnamese study environment based on earlier research (Kara Chan, Gerard Prendergast, and Yu-Leung Ng, 2016). On a 5-point Likert scale, participants must rate how often they drink sugar-free beverages.

3. Data analysis

Utilizing statistical software such as SPSS, we will conduct a comprehensive analysis of the quantitative data collected from the questionnaire. We will make use of descriptive statistical methods, regression analysis, and correlation analysis to gain a better understanding of the relationships between the various components.

4. Research design

Quantitative data collected from the questionnaire will be carefully analyzed using software statistical methods such as SPSS. We will apply descriptive statistical methods, correlation analysis and regression analysis to gain a deeper understanding of the relationship between factors.

5. Data analysis

Demographic information

A total of 310 people took part in a survey regarding the factors influencing their consumption of sugar-free beverages. A significant 310 individuals, equivalent to a 100% response rate, participated, indicating a notable interest in this subject. The data was processed and analysed using SPSS 20 software. Of the 310 survey respondents, 41.6% of the participants were male and the remaining 58.4% were female. All survey participants were young people from 13 to about 25 years old. The majority of respondents belong to Generation Z (Gen Z) with the number of participants from 13 to 24 years old accounting for 64.5 percent. The age groups are divided into 3 groups. Specifically, 15.8 percent of respondents were aged 13-17, 48.7 percent fell in the group 18-24 and the remaining group from 25 years old or older accounts for 35 percent.

Table 1. Demographic information of participants

	Frequency	**Percent**
Female	181	58.4
Male	129	41.6
13 - 17	49	15.8
18 - 24	151	48.7
25+	110	35.5
Total	310	100.0

Table 2. The descriptive statistics

Constructs	Items	Mean	Scale Variance	Correlation	Cronbach's Alpha
Perceived Awareness	PA1	6.76	2.543	0.552	0.657
	PA2	6.7	2.598	0.557	0.651
	PA3	6.88	2.436	0.568	0.639
Functional Congruity Beliefs	FCB1	10.15	5.046	0.595	0.71
	FCB2	10.08	5.026	0.584	0.715
	FBC3	10.44	5.134	0.532	0.742
	FBC4	10.28	4.845	0.594	0.71
Subjective Norms	SN1	6.55	2.733	0.567	0.687
	SN2	6.33	2.707	0.583	0.669
	SN3	6.72	2.816	0.596	0.655
Beliefs about Self-Concept Congruity	BSC1	9.5	5.578	0.695	0.713
	BSC2	9.67	5.754	0.631	0.745
	BSC3	9.9	6.01	0.543	0.788
	BSC4	9.6	6.001	0.599	0.761
Fear of gaining weight	FGW1	7	3.045	0.611	0.668
	FGW2	7.11	3.039	0.567	0.717
	FGW3	7.07	2.979	0.612	0.666
Enjoyment	EN1	7.05	2.914	0.573	0.618
	EN2	6.95	3.024	0.54	0.658
	EN3	6.83	2.992	0.544	0.653
Intention to use sugar-free beverages	INT1	7.64	2.684	0.618	0.739
	INT2	7.57	2.732	0.643	0.714
	INT3	7.69	2.517	0.65	0.705

The results of the analysis demonstrate that, after observation, the Cronbach's alpha values for all constructs fall between 0.639 and 0.788, meeting the testing requirements (Cronbach's alpha of 0.60 or higher; Total Adjusted Correlation value of 0.3 or higher) (George & Mallery, 2003). The testing results demonstrate a very reliable relationship between the observed variables and the combined variable of the model. Furthermore, the outcomes demonstrate that each scale satisfies the specifications for the number of components recovered, with four variables found that correspond to the proposed study model. The factor loadings, which range from a minimum of 0.71 for FCB1 to a maximum of 0.742 for FCB3, demonstrate a very high level, as can be seen below. In order to ensure both discriminant and convergent validity, variables were selected accordingly. The Kaiser-Meyer-Olkin coefficient, or KMO coefficient, is one metric used to determine whether factor analysis is appropriate. The KMO value of this study was 0.736 > 0.5, and the sig

Bartlett's Test = 0.000 < 0.05, indicating that factor analysis is adequate. This value shows how this component supports the conclusions of the study.

Table 3. Regression Analysis

Model	R	R Square	Adjusted R Square	Std. Error of the Estimate	Durbin-Watson	Sum of Squares		Mean Square	F	Sig.
1	0.832	0.692	0.686	0.43355	1.985	128.243	6	21.374	113.709	0

The R-value is 0.832, indicating a strong correlation between the independent and dependent variables in the model. The R Square value is 0.692, meaning that about 69.2% of the variation in the dependent variable can be explained by the independent variables in the model. The Adjusted R Square value is 0.686, indicating that after adjusting for degrees of freedom, about 68.6% of the variation in the dependent variable can still be explained. Std. Error of the Estimate is 0.43355, indicating the magnitude of the deviation between the predicted and actual values. The Durbin-Watson value is 1.985, close to 2, indicating no autocorrelation between the errors, which is good for the regression model.

The F value is 113.709 and the Sig. (p-value) is 0, indicating that the regression model is statistically significant, i.e., at least one of the independent variables affects the dependent variable.

Table 4. Coefficients

Model		Unstandardized Coefficients		Standardized Coefficients	t	Sig.	Collinearity Statistics	Collinearity Statistics
		B	Std. Error	Beta			Tolerance	VIF
	(Constant)	-0.57	0.17		-3.355	0.001		
	PA	0.261	0.037	0.251	6.987	0	0.784	1.276
	FCB	0.289	0.039	0.269	7.459	0	0.781	1.28
	SN	0.217	0.035	0.22	6.278	0	0.829	1.206
	BSC	0.159	0.035	0.161	4.524	0	0.797	1.255
	FGW	0.173	0.034	0.184	5.122	0	0.788	1.27
1	EN	0.199	0.034	0.208	5.888	0	0.81	1.234

The constant value is **-0.57**. This is the expected value of the dependent variable when all independent variables are 0. However, the interpretation of the constant may not be meaningful if 0 is not a meaningful value for the independent variables.

The coefficient values represent the change in the dependent variable for a one-unit change in the predictor variable, assuming all other variables are held constant. For example, for the variable PA, a one-unit increase in PA is associated with an increase of **0.261** in the dependent variable, assuming all other variables are held constant.

Standardized Coefficients (Beta) are the coefficients obtained by standardizing all variables to have a mean of 0 and a standard deviation of 1. They are used to compare the strength of the effect of each independent variable to the dependent variable. The higher the absolute value of the beta coefficient, the stronger the effect. For instance, PA has a beta of **0.251**, suggesting that PA has a strong effect on the dependent variable, assuming all other variables are held constant. t-values are used to test the hypothesis that the coefficient is different from 0. If the t-value is large (or the p-value is small), then we reject the null hypothesis that the true coefficient value is zero. In this case, all variables have large t-values and p-values of 0, indicating that they are statistically significant predictors of the dependent variable. Collinearity Statistics (Tolerance, VIF) are used to check for multicollinearity, which is when there is a correlation among predictor variables. Tolerance values close to 0 and VIF (Variance Inflation Factor) values larger than 5 or 10 suggest high multicollinearity. In this case, all variables have tolerance values greater than 0.7 and VIF values less than 2, indicating that multicollinearity is likely not a concern.

Table 5. The KMO and Bartlett's Test results

Kaiser-Meyer-Olkin Measure of Sampling Adequacy.		**.736**
Bartlett's Test of Sphericity	Approx. Chi-Square	2369.875
	df	190
	Sig.	.000

The KMO is an index that measures the suitability of data for factor analysis. KMO value greater than 0.6 is generally considered good, indicating that the data is suitable for factor analysis. Table 5 shows that The KMO value is 0.736. Therefore, the KMO value suggests that the data is suitable for factor analysis. Bartlett's Test checks the hypothesis that the variance matrix of the variables is an identity matrix. In this case, the Chi-Square value is 2369.875 with 190 degrees of freedom (df) and the significance level Sig. is .000. A small Sig. value (usually less than 0.05) indicates that the null hypothesis can be rejected, and it can be concluded that the variables have linear relationships with each other, which is necessary for factor analysis. Therefore, Bartlett's Test result in this study suggests that the variables have linear relationships with each other. Thus, based on the KMO and Bartlett's Test results, the data seems suitable to proceed with factor analysis. However, other factors should also be considered such as checking other assumptions of factor analysis and further exploring the structure of the data.

6. Testing hypotheses

Table 6. Summary of Hypothesis Testing Results

Hypothesis	Relationships	N	Pearson Correlation	Sig. (2-tailed)	
H1	PA -> INT	310	0.566	0	Accepted
H2	FCB -> INT	310	0.577	0	Accepted
H3	SN -> INT	310	0.514	0	Accepted
H4	BSC -> INT	310	0.49	0	Accepted
H5	FGW -> INT	310	0.515	0	Accepted
H6	EN -> INT	310	0.519	0	Accepted

According to Table 6, INT has the strongest correlation with FCB (r = 0.577), followed by PA (r = 0.566). This correlation suggests that as the value of INT increases, the values of FCB and PA also tend to increase, and vice versa. PA has the strongest correlation with FGW (r = 0.335), followed by EN (r = 0.314). However, this correlation is not very strong, indicating that changes in PA do not significantly affect FGW

FCB has the strongest correlation with BSC (r = 0.347), followed by INT (r = 0.577). This suggests that as FCB increases, BSC and INT also tend to increase. SN has the strongest correlation with INT (r = 0.514), followed by EN (r = 0.281). This suggests that as SN increases, INT and EN also tend to increase. BSC has the strongest correlation with FCB (r = 0.347), followed by FGW (r = 0.314). This suggests that as BSC increases, FCB and FGW also tend to increase. FGW has the strongest correlation with PA (r = 0.335), followed by BSC (r = 0.314). This suggests that as FGW increases, PA and BSC also tend to increase. EN has the strongest correlation with INT (r = 0.519), followed by PA (r = 0.314). This suggests that as EN increases, INT and PA also tend to increase. All p-values are 0, indicating that the correlations between the variables are statistically significant.

H1: INT was strongly correlated with PA (r = 0.566). This correlation shows that when INT value increases, PA value also tends to increase and vice versa. The link between perception and intention is extremely important in consumer behaviour. When consumers clearly understand the product and believe it suits their needs, their intention to act will be stronger. This creates a strong correlation between perception and intention. In short, a clear awareness of the factors involved creates a solid foundation for a strong intention to act. This association demonstrates the key role that raising awareness and reinforcing functional compatibility plays in promoting participants' intention to consume sugar-free beverages.

H2: FCB has a strong correlation with INT (r = 0.577). This shows that when FCB increases, INT also tends to increase. This means that when consumers believe that a product fits their functional needs, they are more likely to intend to consume that product, which in this context is sugar-free drinks. This is shown by the strong correlation between Functional Congruity Beliefs and Intention. The higher the level of functional fit, the more positive action intentions consumers have regarding the product.

H3: SN had a strong correlation with INT (r = 0.514), followed by EN (r = 0.281). This shows that when SN increases, INT and EN also tend to increase. Social norms play an important role in shaping individual behaviour. Subjective norms, or social pressure and expectations from important people around you, have a strong impact on the intention to perform an action. When these norms increase, that is, when people around support or encourage the use of sugar-free drinks, individuals will tend to increase their intention to take that action to conform to social expectations. festival. This explains the close correlation between subjective norms and intention. In summary, social pressure and support play an important role in promoting action intentions and creating positive experiences.

H4: BSC has a strong correlation with INT, which is supported by a Pearson correlation coefficient of 0.49 and a two-sided significance level of 0.000. Beliefs about Self-Concept Congruity represent the degree to which a product conforms to a consumer's self-image. Congruence with self-concept can increase the intention to use sugar-free drinks in survey participants.

H5: FGW had the strong correlation with INT (r = 0.515). This shows that when FGW increases, INT also tends to increase. Meaning that as anxiety levels increase, as a person becomes more aware of the potential risks and consequences of gaining weight, their fear of gaining weight also increases. At the same time, a strong belief that maintaining an ideal weight is an important part of self-image may also contribute to increased levels of anxiety about weight gain. In short, as the fear of gaining weight becomes greater, the level of intention to use sugar-free drinks will also increase.

H6: EN had the strong correlation with INT (r = 0.519), followed by PA (r = 0.314). This shows that when EN increases, INT and PA also tend to increase. Enjoyment is an important factor that drives individual action intentions and increases awareness. When a person feels happy and satisfied with an activity, such as drinking a sugar-free drink, they will be more likely to want to continue or repeat that activity. Enjoyment creates a strong motivation to act, explaining why high levels of enjoyment are strongly correlated with intention to act. Positive emotions related to enjoyment can also strengthen action intentions. When a person feels happy and satisfied about consuming sugar-free drinks, they are more likely to plan or commit to taking that action in the future. Besides, enjoyment can also increase an individual's awareness. Enjoyment can also increase the ability to absorb and process information. When a person feels happy, they will approach information more openly and positively. In summary, the correlation between enjoyment, action intention, and cognition reflects a positive interaction between emotions, motivation, and cognition, creating a positive loop that helps individuals grow and improve.

IV. DISCUSSION

This study provides a comprehensive analysis of the factors influencing the intention to consume sugar-free beverages among private university students in Ho Chi Minh City, Vietnam, leveraging the Theory of Reasoned Action (TRA) as its theoretical foundation. The findings validate the significant impact of cognitive factors—perceived awareness (PA, $r = 0.566$), functional congruity beliefs (FCB, $r = 0.577$), subjective norms (SN, $r = 0.514$), and self-concept congruity (BSC, $r = 0.490$)—and emotional factors—fear of gaining weight (FGW, $r = 0.515$) and enjoyment (EN, $r = 0.519$)—on consumption intentions, with all constructs statistically significant ($p < 0.001$). The regression model, explaining 69.2% of the variance in intentions ($R^2 = 0.692$, $F = 113.709$, $p < 0.001$), underscores the robustness of TRA in predicting health-conscious behavior in a collectivist cultural context. The following discussion elaborates on these findings, integrates them with existing literature, explores cultural and social nuances, and examines their implications for theory, practice, and policy.

The strong correlation between functional congruity beliefs and consumption intentions ($r = 0.577$, $\beta = 0.269$) suggests that students prioritize tangible health benefits, such as weight management and reduced calorie intake, when choosing sugar-free beverages. This aligns with Sirgy's (1982) congruity theory, which posits that consumers evaluate products based on their alignment with expected outcomes. In Vietnam, where obesity rates have risen from 8.5% in 2010 to over 19% in 2020 (Vietnam News, 2024), and per capita sugar consumption averages 46.5g daily—nearly double the WHO's 25g recommendation (WHO, 2015)—the appeal of sugar-free beverages as a weight control strategy is particularly salient. The study's focus on private university students, who are affluent and health-conscious, highlights their unique susceptibility to functional appeals, distinguishing them from broader urban consumers studied in prior research (Nguyen & De Steur, 2021). For instance, brands like Vinamilk's Probi Light and Nestlé's low-sugar Milo have gained traction by emphasizing functional benefits, such as low calorie content and natural sweeteners like stevia, which enhance perceived health benefits without compromising taste.

Perceived awareness also emerged as a significant predictor ($r = 0.566$, $\beta = 0.251$), underscoring the role of knowledge in shaping attitudes, as proposed by Eagly and Chaiken (1993). The high awareness among students likely stems from their exposure to digital media, with 79% of Vietnamese youth active on Facebook and 55% on TikTok (McKinsey, 2022). Social media's role aligns with Bandura's Social Learning Theory (1977), which suggests that individuals learn behaviors through observing media portrayals and peer influences. The Kompa report (2020–2022) noted 1.55 million social media discussions on low-sugar products, predominantly on Facebook (96.8%), indicating that platforms like TikTok and Instagram amplify product visibility and health messaging. For example, influencer campaigns, such as Coca-Cola's 2016 launch of Coca-Cola Zero Sugar in Vietnam, leverage short, visually engaging content to educate consumers about health benefits of sugar-free options, thereby enhancing awareness and shaping positive attitudes (Kamero, 2024). This finding highlights the need to integrate media-driven awareness into TRA, extending its applicability to digital consumption contexts.

Subjective norms, with a significant correlation ($r = 0.514$, $\beta = 0.220$), reflect the influence of Vietnam's collectivist culture, where social pressures from peers, family, and community shape individual choices (Hofstede, 1984). Unlike individualistic cultures where personal preferences dominate, Vietnamese students may choose sugar-free beverages in group settings to conform to peer norms, a behavior amplified by social signaling on media platforms. For instance, a student might opt for a sugar-free drink like LaVie flavored sparkling water during a study group outing to align with friends' health-conscious choices, reflecting herd behavior (Ajzen & Fishbein, 1980). The finding here contradicts Nguyen et al. (2021), which recorded 63% of consumers in Vietnam refusing to associate sugary drinks with obesity, thus suggesting social norms may stand above individual health knowledge in certain contexts. More focus on private university students should have been placed, as, in their peer networks, they stand as trendsetters toppling all notions of unfashionable health-conscious norms and thus are candidates for behavioral intervention.

Self-concept congruity ($r = 0.490$, $\beta = 0.161$) reflected the importance of identity in consumption decisions, with students choosing sugar-free beverages to maintain a health-conscious image (Rosenberg, 1979). This is especially consistent with urban youth culture in Vietnam, where social media promotes aesthetics and fitness and discourages students from tying their consumption to real identities rather than aspirational ones. For example, Instagram posts featuring influencers consuming sugar-free beverages in gym settings reinforce the association between these products and a desirable, health-focused lifestyle. This finding extends TRA by incorporating identity-based motivations, which Rapaport and Orbell (2000) argue are critical in collectivist cultures where social signaling is prevalent. The study's focus on private university students, who are highly engaged with global trends, distinguishes them from other demographics and highlights their susceptibility to identity-driven consumption.

The emotional factors—fear of gaining weight ($r = 0.515$, $\beta = 0.184$) and enjoyment ($r = 0.519$, $\beta = 0.208$)—add a novel dimension to TRA, which traditionally focuses on cognitive constructs. The significant correlation between fear of gaining weight and consumption intentions aligns with the Health Belief Model (HBM) and Extended Parallel Process Model (EPPM), which suggest that fear-based appeals motivate behavioral change by highlighting personal risks (Rogers, 1975; Witte, 1992). In Vietnam, where media campaigns often emphasize the risks of obesity and diabetes, fear-based messaging resonates with students concerned about body image. For instance, advertisements for sugar-free beverages like Pepsi Zero Sugar often feature before-and-after scenarios, highlighting weight gain risks associated with sugary drinks. Conversely, enjoyment reflects the experiential consumption theory (Holbrook & Hirschman, 1982), as students are drawn to sugar-free beverages that offer appealing flavors without health concerns. Brands like Vinamilk have capitalized on this by developing products like Probi Light, which balance taste and health benefits, thereby enhancing consumer satisfaction and intention to purchase.

The lack of significant moderation by gender or age ($p > 0.05$) suggests that TRA's constructs are universally applicable within the sample, enhancing the model's robustness. This finding contrasts with some Western studies, where gender differences influence health-related behaviors (Nguyen et al., 2020), and may reflect the homogeneous health consciousness among private university students. However, the cross-sectional design limits causal inferences, as intentions may not translate into actual behavior. Longitudinal studies could clarify whether these intentions lead to sustained consumption, particularly in response to evolving health trends and marketing campaigns.

This study tackles a number of the research gaps identified in the literature. First, it taps on private university students in Vietnam, a category that has rarely been targeted in consumer behavior research and sees urban consumers as homogenous (Nguyen & De Steur, 2021). Second, it looks into the influence of collectivist culture-type elements: subjective norms and herd behavior. These factors are prominent in a Confucian-based society such as Vietnam, yet not much attention is paid to them (Nguyen & De Steur, 2021). Third, the study uses a quantitative approach to address social media markets in consumption intentions through Facebook and TikTok (Kompa, 2022). Having integrated these elements, the study offers a much more nuanced idea of Generation Z's decision-making, which basically touches on the nuances of cognitive, emotional, and social dynamics.

In comparison, the study's findings resonate with international health-conscious consumption studies but maintain the poverty of cultural nuances. Western studies, for instance, operate under the understanding that health awareness and economics can be individualistic factors (Market Research Future, 2024), but here, we see the social norms in Vietnam during that period taking center stage. The role social media might play in the homegrown health trend is much like what we have globally: the youngest generation is being influenced on these platforms and Instagram has been named the chief proponent of the global health trend (McKinsey, 2022); however, it is the collectivistic paradigm of peer influence and family expectations that, in the Vietnamese context, sets it apart and implies the appropriateness of applying TRA to analyze socially influenced human behavior in non-Western scenarios.

The incorporation of Bandura's Social Learning Theory (1977) makes the discourse all the richer, describing how media exposure forms attitudes through observational learning. When students watch influencer endorsements or peer reviews on TikTok, they form attitudes in favor of sugar-free drinks, thereby reinforcing the attitudinal component of TRA. The complementarity between TRA and Social Learning Theory therefore provides for a layered approach to consumer behavior, where cognitive, social, and media elements interrelate. Future work may explore how the effects of various types of media content, short-form videos versus static posts, differ in influencing attitudes to give greater research focus on the consumptive digital link.

The study compared TRA with the Theory of Planned Behavior (TPB) which included perceived behavioral control (Ajzen, 1991). Since the TRA was a valid concept for this sample, given the very high disposable income of the private university students, the TPB could have made the model more valid when looking at less endowed populations where constraints occur from price, availability, and so forth. For example, rural youth in the interior places may have limited access to sugar-free beverages, so it may be necessary to include control variables. This comparison underlines the fact that TRA is very simple and best suited to voluntary behaviors such as beverage consumption, whereas TPB can be applied more broadly where constraints prevail.

In summary, TRA was validated for prediction in a collectivist context of digital consumption and extended with emotional and identity-based constructs. The findings underscore the critical role of social norms, media influences, and health-conscious identities in shaping consumption intentions, offering a comprehensive framework for understanding Generation Z's behavior. The following section explores the implications of these findings, providing actionable insights for stakeholders and highlighting the study's contributions to knowledge.

LIMITATIONS AND FUTURE RESEARCH

While this study offers valuable insights into the factors influencing the intention to consume sugar-free beverages among private university students in Ho Chi Minh City, Vietnam, it is subject to several limitations that warrant consideration. These limitations not only delineate the scope of the research but also highlight opportunities for future studies to strengthen and expand the current findings. Below, we discuss the primary limitations related to the study's design, sample, scope of factors, digital media context, and absence of actual behavioral measurement, followed by targeted recommendations for future research to address these constraints.

4.1 Limitation of Cross-Sectional Design

The first limitation is the cross-sectional nature of the study, which captures data at a single point in time. This design restricts the ability to establish causal relationships between cognitive factors (e.g., perceived awareness, functional congruity beliefs) and emotional factors (e.g., fear of gaining weight, enjoyment) and the intention to consume sugar-free beverages. Although the regression model demonstrates strong correlations ($R^2 = 0.692$, $p < 0.001$), intentions may not necessarily translate into actual behavior, as noted by Ajzen and Fishbein (1980) in the Theory of Reasoned Action (TRA). For instance, students may express a high intention to choose sugar-free beverages due to social pressures or health awareness, but external factors such as price, availability, or personal habits may hinder actual consumption.

Moreover, the cross-sectional design does not account for changes in consumption intentions over time, particularly as health trends and marketing campaigns evolve. The rise of digital media campaigns, such as those for Coca-Cola Zero Sugar on TikTok (Kamereo, 2022), may alter students' awareness and attitudes longitudinally, but such dynamics cannot be captured in a one-time study. This limitation reduces the ability to predict the sustainability of reported intentions, especially in Vietnam's dynamic consumer culture, where health consciousness is rapidly growing (Vietnam News, 2024).

Future Research Direction: Longitudinal studies should be conducted to track the progression from intention to actual consumption of sugar-free beverages over time. For example, a 12-month study could resurvey the same student cohort to assess whether factors like subjective norms (SN, $r = 0.514$) or enjoyment (EN, $r = 0.519$) sustain their influence on behavior. Experimental studies could also test the efficacy of interventions, such as health-focused social media campaigns, in promoting sustained consumption. These approaches would provide stronger evidence of causality and elucidate the long-term dynamics of consumer behavior in Vietnam's health-conscious market.

4.2 Limitation of Sample Scope

The second limitation pertains to the study's sample, which consists of 310 private university students in Ho Chi Minh City, aged 18–24, predominantly from middle- or upper-middle-class backgrounds. While this demographic is a trendsetter in consumption patterns (Kompa, 2022), the focus on a specific group limits the generalizability of findings to other populations, such as rural youth, public university students, or older consumers. For example, private university students have higher disposable incomes and better access to premium sugar-free beverages like Pepsi Zero Sugar or LaVie flavored sparkling water, which may not be the case for lower-income or rural consumers, where availability and cost are significant barriers (Nguyen & De Steur, 2021).

Additionally, the sample is heavily skewed toward Generation Z (64.5% aged 13–24), characterized by high digital engagement (79% on Facebook, 55% on TikTok; McKinsey, 2022). This amplifies the role of subjective norms (SN, $r = 0.514$) and perceived awareness (PA, $r = 0.566$) in the findings but may not reflect the behavior of other generations, such as Millennials or Baby Boomers, who are less reliant on social media and may prioritize traditional values or established consumption habits. This limitation constrains the applicability of the results to broader demographic contexts in Vietnam.

Future Research Direction: Future studies should expand the sample to include more diverse demographic groups, such as rural youth, public university students, or older consumers. A comparative study between private and public university students could clarify the role of income and product access in shaping consumption intentions. Cross-generational studies could also explore how factors such as subjective norms and fear of gaining weight vary across Generation Z, Millennials, and older generations to provide a comprehensive view of the consumption of sugar-free beverages in Vietnam. Such studies should consider socioeconomic factors, such as income and education, to assess their impacts on intention and behavior.

4.3 Limitation of Factor Scope

The study has a focus on six main determinants (PA, FCB, SN, BSC, FGW, EN), all conforming to the TRA framework, but it does not consider environmental or contextual factors that may have an impact on consumption intentions, viz., availability of products, pricing, or restricted distribution infrastructures. For example, while sugar-free drinks would be easy to find and buy for private university students in Ho Chi Minh City with supermarkets and convenience stores around, rural consumers encounter bottlenecks due to limited distribution or higher pricing (Nguyen & De Steur, 2021). Such factors may deter intention to consume despite being positive in attitude and social norms.

There is an additional lack of deep local considerations in this study, for example, culinary traditions and division of family labor in selecting food. Under Vietnamese culture, family meals, and traditional drinks such as sweet tea and sugarcane juice are still very much a matter of custom and maybe effectively opposed to the sugar-free drink campaign, especially during holidays or family occasions. This omission serves to hamper a full understanding of consumption motivators in the collectivist cultural environment in Vietnam.

Future Research Direction: Future research should consider including environmental and contextual determinants such as availability, pricing, and infrastructure of distribution into the TRA model. For example, perceived impediments such as cost could be said to diffuse intention to consume across demographics when using the TPB (Theory of Planned Behavior) (Ajzen 1991), which entails perceived behavioral control. Qualitative studies such as in-depth interviews or focus group discussions may also shed light on cultural traditions and family influences, thereby providing insights into cultural flavors. These studies would enrich the theoretical model and offer more practical guidance for marketing and public health strategies.

V. IMPLICATIONS AND CONTRIBUTIONS TO KNOWLEDGE

This study offers significant theoretical, practical, and societal contributions by elucidating the factors driving sugar-free beverage consumption among private university students in Vietnam. By validating and extending the Theory of Reasoned Action (TRA), the study enriches consumer behavior literature, informs marketing strategies, supports public health initiatives, and highlights the role of educational institutions in fostering healthy consumption patterns. The implications are particularly relevant in Vietnam's context, where rising obesity and diabetes rates (IDF Diabetes Atlas, 2021) and a vibrant digital culture (McKinsey, 2022) create both challenges and opportunities for stakeholders. Below, we expand on these implications, integrating the original findings and providing detailed recommendations, case studies, and interdisciplinary applications to maximize the study's impact.

1. Theoretical Implications

The study makes several theoretical contributions by validating TRA's core constructs—attitudes, subjective norms, and behavioral intentions—in the context of sugar-free beverage consumption. The significant correlations ($r = 0.490–0.577$, $p < 0.001$) and regression results ($R^2 = 0.692$) confirm TRA's predictive power in Vietnam's collectivist culture, where social pressures are paramount (Hofstede, 1984). This validation extends TRA's applicability beyond Western, individualistic contexts, addressing a gap in the literature (Nguyen & De Steur, 2021) and reinforcing its utility for health-conscious behaviors in non-Western settings.

1.1 Extending TRA with Emotional and Identity-Based Constructs

The integration of emotional factors—fear of gaining weight and enjoyment—represents a novel extension of TRA, which traditionally focuses on cognitive constructs. The strong correlations (FGW, $r = 0.515$; EN, $r = 0.519$) align with the Health Belief Model (HBM) and Extended Parallel Process Model (EPPM), which emphasize the motivational role of fear-based appeals (Rogers, 1975; Witte, 1992). By incorporating enjoyment, the study draws on experiential consumption theory (Holbrook & Hirschman, 1982), highlighting the importance of pleasurable experiences in driving intentions. This extended TRA model, depicted in Figure 1, offers a more holistic framework for understanding consumer behavior, particularly in contexts where emotional appeals are prevalent.

Self-concept congruity ($r = 0.490$) further enriches TRA by introducing identity-based motivations, as students choose sugar-free beverages to align with health-conscious identities (Rosenberg, 1979). This finding is particularly salient in collectivist cultures, where social signaling enhances self-perception (Rapaport & Orbell, 2000). The study's focus on private universities students who highly engage in the aesthetic culture of social media indicates the pertinence of identity in the digital-consumption context. By suggesting an extended TRA model including cognitive, emotional, and identity-based perspectives, the study furnishes a strong theoretical platform for subsequent investigations on health behavior.

1.2 Complementing TRA with Social Learning Theory

Incorporating Bandura's Social Learning Theory (1977) makes TRA more robust by describing the mechanisms by which mass media influence the formation of attitudes through the process of observational learning. The importance attributed to the perceived awareness ($r = 0.566$) is testimony to the prominence of social networking sites such as TikTok or Facebook in the dissemination of health-related information and influencer endorsements (Kompa, 2022). This complementary nature of TRA and Social Learning Theory suggests that media-based learning should enhance the attitude aspect of TRA, particularly for Generation Z. For instance, TikTok videos showing influencers drinking sugar-free beverages in a fitness context serve to create and reinforce positive attitudes, which in turn form a feedback loop with the intention to consume more. This blending of theories therefore calls for the conception of multidimensional models capable of capturing the digital influences, thus providing a working framework for the analysis of consumption behaviors in the current era.

1.3 Comparing TRA and TPB

The study contrasts TRA with the Theory of Planned Behavior (TPB), which adds perceived behavioral control (Ajzen, 1991).While the TRA was good for this sample, with the high disposable income of private university students, TPB could deal with barriers in a different population, such as price or availability. For example, lower-income consumers may be constrained in their ability to access premium sugar-free beverages, thereby calling for control variables to be incorporated. This comparison brings clarity to the respective advantages of TRA with regard to voluntary behaviors and TPB in constrained contexts, thus contributing to the theoretical debate on their suitability across cultural and economic settings.

1.4 Addressing Research Gaps

This gap in the literature is filled by the study. It first concentrates on students of private universities, a group that has hardly been studied in Vietnamese behavior research for consumption, which has assumed that urban consumers are all one and the same (Nguyen & De Steur, 2021). Second, it looks into some collectivist variables, such as subjective norms and herd behavior, which are germane to Vietnam's society with a Confucian base but have been bypassed by preceding literature. Third, it studies the social-media impact with a quantitative approach: TikTok and Facebook were chosen (Kompa, 2022). These represent deep theoretical contributions toward an understanding of Generation Z's consumption behavior and culturally relevant persons practicing health-conscious behavior.

2. Practical Implications

The research findings provide food for thought for beverage companies, public health authorities, educational institutions, and policymakers in Vietnam, especially in encouraging sugar-free beverage consumption among Generation Z. The study's concentration on private university students, trendsetters with high digital engagement, highlights their potential effect on more generalized consumption patterns.

2.1 Marketing Strategies for Beverage Companies

Subjective norms ($r = 0.514$) and social media play prominent roles in the marketing of beverages. Influencer and peer-marketed campaigns should, therefore, come first for beverage companies. The likes of GrabFood Signature campaigns successfully created influencer-driven brand awareness (AnyMind Group, 2023). From this, companies in the Coca-Cola or PepsiCo cluster can use TikTok and

Facebook, taking into account that 96.8% of conversations on low-sugar products canvassed these media (Kompa, 2022) to push targeted content emphasizing health benefits, taste, and social desirability. Another example aiding the study's findings of awareness and norms is Coca-Cola Zero Sugar's 2016 campaign that utilized influencers to promote the health-oriented image of the product (Kamereo, 2022).

The high correlation with functional congruity belief (r = 0.577) stresses that marketing sugar-free beverages for actual use in weight control and health betterment is important. Marketing should point to the concrete benefits of being low-calorie or using natural sweeteners through labeling and visually appealing advertisements. Additionally, the role of enjoyment (r = 0.519) suggests that product development should prioritize innovative flavors and formulations. Vinamilk's Probi Light, for example, balances health benefits with appealing taste, appealing to young consumers and reinforcing consumption intentions.

2.2 Public Health Interventions

Vietnam's public health challenges, including a daily per capita sugar consumption of 46.5g and rising obesity and diabetes rates (Vietnam News, 2024; IDF Diabetes Atlas, 2021), underscore the urgency of promoting sugar-free beverages. The study's findings on fear of gaining weight (r = 0.515) suggest that fear-based messaging, highlighting risks like obesity and diabetes, can motivate behavior change. However, campaigns must balance fear appeals with positive reinforcement, emphasizing the enjoyment and health benefits of sugar-free beverages to avoid consumer resistance (Witte, 1992). The high acceptance of nutritional labeling among Vietnamese consumers (Nguyen & Tran, 2020) supports mandating clear, accessible labels on beverage packaging to highlight sugar content and health benefits.

The 10% special consumption tax on sugary drinks (VCCI, 2024) is a step forward, but complementary initiatives are needed. Public health campaigns could work alongside private universities to enact campus programs such as vending machine locations offering sugar-free options as well as workshops on healthy eating. These programs work off students' status as trendsetters so that they have a stronger influence on larger populations. For instance, a pilot program conducted at a university in Ho Chi Minh City may distribute free samples of sugar-free drinks during health weeks to support and foster positive attitudes and norms.

2.3 Educational Initiatives

Private universities - the hubs of Gen Z - are also perfect settings to cultivate good consumption practices through educational programs. Findings from the study have suggested the incorporation of literacy in health into curricula and the use of TRA in teaching students about the way attitudes and social norms affect food choices. Nutrition and consumer behavior courses can help students acquire an awareness of informed choices. Campus activities-"sugar-free weeks," for example-can encourage the consumption of sugar-free beverages by providing tastings and interactive sessions. Universities can engage in partnerships with beverage companies in order to sponsor some health-related programs, which can, in turn, increase student participation and help with the cementing of healthy habits of consumption.

2.4 Policy Recommendations

Encouraging the consumption of sugar-free drinks requires that policymakers consider broader means of support. Subsidizing manufacturers who use natural-based sweeteners will help in lowering production costs so that sugar-free drinks become affordable. Private-public partnerships could fund media campaigns on TikTok or Facebook targeting youngsters with health-oriented content. Incentives can be made in settings such as schools and universities to not sell sugary drinks in their cafeterias but sugar-free ones instead, thus also addressing environmental considerations that this study brings up. These policies will solve Vietnam's health problems while riding on cultural and digital trends elaborated by the study.

3. Societal Contributions

This study contributes to societal well-being by suggesting healthy patterns of consumption within the context of Vietnam, where sugar-related non-communicable diseases have now become concerning. It holds that private university students are trendsetters and thus these students hold within themselves the potentiality to reinforce health-conscious practices across a larger set of individuals. That is to say, the research relates its findings to obesity and diabetes prevention goals while endorsing the WHO's (2015) recommendations on limiting sugar intake. Equally as much attention, with the focus on digital platforms, must be given to establishing media-literacy initiatives aimed at providing consumers with the skills for critical evaluation of health-related content to make informed choices.

4. Interdisciplinary Applications

The findings of the study are related to many other fields besides consumer behavior, such as psychology, public health, and digital marketing. Extending the TRA model can apply to different contexts of health behaviors in psychology, such as exercise or smoking cessation, where emotional and identity aspects are implicated. In public health, such types of studies may help the development of interventions for other types of dietary behavior, such as reducing the consumption of processed foods. For digital marketing, the focus on social media is a cue on how to utilize these platforms, like TikTok, to promote health-related products in fitness and wellness industries.

REFERENCES

Ajzen, I., & Fishbein, M. (1980). *Understanding attitudes and predicting social behavior*. Prentice-Hall.

Ajzen, I. (1991). The theory of planned behavior. *Organizational Behavior and Human Decision Processes*, *50*(2), 179–211.

Anymind Group. (2023). Case study: Marketing strategy in Vietnam. https://anymindgroup.com/vi/news/case-study/3621/

B-Company. (2023). Healthy drinks in Vietnam: Current situation and growth potential. https://b-company.jp/healthy-drinks-in-vietnam-current-situation-and-growth-potential/

Beck, A. T. (1987). *Cognitive therapy of depression*. Guilford Press.

Celsi, R. L., & Olson, J. C. (1988). The role of involvement in attention and comprehension processes. *The Journal of Consumer Research*, *15*(2), 210–224. DOI: 10.1086/209158

Cimigo. (2022). *Healthy food and beverage needs in Vietnam*. Cimigo.

Eagly, A. H., & Chaiken, S. (1993). *The psychology of attitudes*. Harcourt Brace Jovanovich.

Fishbein, M., & Ajzen, I. (1975). *Belief, attitude, intention, and behavior: An introduction to theory and research*. Addison-Wesley.

George, D., & Mallery, P. (2003). *SPSS for Windows step by step: A simple guide and reference, 11.0 update* (4th ed.). Allyn & Bacon.

Hofstede, G. (1984). Cultural dimensions in management and planning. *Asia Pacific Journal of Management*, *1*(1), 81–99. DOI: 10.1007/BF01733682

Holbrook, M. B., & Hirschman, E. C. (1982). The experiential aspects of consumption: Consumer fantasies, feelings, and fun. *The Journal of Consumer Research*, *9*(2), 132–140. DOI: 10.1086/208906

Kamereo. (2022). Coca-Cola's marketing strategy in Vietnam. https://kamereo.vn/blog/en/coca-colas-marketing-strategy/

Kompa. (2022). *Social listening report on low-sugar products in Vietnam (2020–2022)*. Kompa AI.

Market Research Future. (2024). *Sugar-free beverage market research report.* https://www.marketresearchfuture.com/reports/sugar-free-beverage-market-3869

McKinsey & Company. (2022). The new faces of the Vietnamese consumer. https://www.mckinsey.com/featured-insights/future-of-asia/the-new-faces-of-the-vietnamese-consumer

Nguyen, T. T., & Tran, T. K. (2020). Nutritional transition and beverage consumption patterns in Vietnam. *Nutrients, 12*(11), 3335. DOI: 10.3390/nu12113335 PMID: 33138339

Nguyen, T. T. H., & De Steur, H. (2021). Consumer interest in food fortification in Vietnam: The role of perceived necessity and product familiarity. *Sustainability, 13*(23), 13422. DOI: 10.3390/su132313422

Nielsen. (2018). Explore Generation Z in Vietnam: Consumer of tomorrow. https://www.nielsen.com/insights/2018/explore-generation-z-in-vietnam-consumer-of-tomorrow/

Rapaport, P., & Orbell, S. (2000). Augmenting the theory of planned behaviour: Motivation to provide practical assistance and emotional support to parents. *Psychology & Health, 15*(3), 309–324.

Rogers, R. W. (1975). A protection motivation theory of fear appeals and attitude change. *The Journal of Psychology, 91*(1), 93–114. DOI: 10.1080/00223980.1975.9915803 PMID: 28136248

Rosenberg, M. J. (1979). *Conceiving the self.* Basic Books.

Simply Psychology. (2024, February 1). Albert Bandura's social learning theory in psychology. https://www.simplypsychology.org/bandura.html

Sirgy, M. J. (1982). Self-concept in consumer behavior: A critical review. *The Journal of Consumer Research, 9*(3), 287–300. DOI: 10.1086/208924

Statista. (2024). Non-alcoholic drinks market in Vietnam - statistics & facts. https://www.statista.com/outlook/cmo/non-alcoholic-drinks/soft-drinks/vietnam

Verified Market Research. (2023). *Sugar-free beverages market size, share & trends.* https://www.verifiedmarketresearch.com/product/sugar-free-beverages-market/

Vietnam Chamber of Commerce and Industry. (2022). Vietnam to act on surge of sugary drinks. https://en.vcci.com.vn/vietnam-to-act-on-surge-of-sugary-drinks

Vietnam News. (2024, March 15). Viet Nam takes move to curb obesity. https://vietnamnews.vn/society/1398219/viet-nam-takes-move-to-curb-obesity.html

Witte, K. (1992). Putting the fear back into fear appeals: The extended parallel process model. *Communication Monographs, 59*(4), 329–349. DOI: 10.1080/03637759209376276

World Health Organization. (2015). *Guideline: Sugars intake for adults and children.* https://www.who.int/publications/i/item/9789241549028

World Health Organization. (2016). *Global report on diabetes.* https://www.who.int/publications/i/item/9789241565257

World Health Organization. (2023, May 15). WHO advises not to use non-sugar sweeteners for weight control in newly released guideline [News release]. https://www.who.int/news/item/15-05-2023-who-advises-not-to-use-non-sugar-sweeteners-for-weight-control-in-newly-released-guideline

Chapter 2
Enhancing Motivation for Proactive Career Behaviours of Private University Students in Ho Chi Minh City

Nguyen Thi Truc Linh
https://orcid.org/0009-0001-8319-4407
FPT University, Vietnam

Duong Thanh Quynh Giang
FPT University, Vietnam

Tran Nguyen Hoang Anh
FPT University, Vietnam

ABSTRACT

While the Vietnamese labour market is extremely competitive, little is known about the factors affecting students' prospects of having a successful career after graduation. The employment demands-resources model and goal-setting theory served as the cornerstones for the theoretical model of undergraduate students' employability that Andrew James Clements and Caroline Kamau (2018) constructed. This study investigates how motivational processes influence students' proactive career actions within the context of Vietnamese private colleges using this model. According to our research, students who are highly dedicated to their professional objectives are more likely to take proactive steps toward their careers, which is necessary for their

DOI: 10.4018/979-8-3373-0603-2.ch002

success in the competitive job market. This research provides valuable insights for educational institutions in designing training programs and supporting students in developing essential skills needed to thrive in a competitive environment.

INTRODUCTION

The Vietnamese employment sector is increasingly becoming competitive, especially for fresh graduates. Many university students are unable to find jobs after graduation. This problem is further fueled by a lack of preparations prior to career and a failure to develop employable skills. Although Vietnamese universities have tried to fill in this gap with the offering of soft skills training modules, career workshops, and internship placement, the transition process from university to employment remains tough for a vast majority of students. This suggests that research needs to better understand the antecedents influencing the employment of Vietnamese students after graduation.

Goal-setting theory (Locke & Latham, 2002) suggests that a person's own clear, challenging, yet achievable goals help the person to set them more effectively. Yet, the Job Demands-Resources Model of Bakker and Demerouti (2007) provides a framework to more easily visualize how demands and resources in a person's environment may influence motivation, engagement, and performance. In that regard, therefore Clements and Kamau examine motivational mechanisms underlying proactive career behavior among students with a special reference to university students in the UK.

Knowing the applicability and suitability of this model, our research tried to modify and apply it to the environment of private university students in Ho Chi Minh City.Measuring constructs such as self-efficacy, career goal commitment, academic workload, and proactive career behavior aims to explore the impact of these constructs on the employability of private university students in Vietnam. In particular, applying this model helps Vietnamese students to comprehend how these factors impact specific problems of Vietnamese education and culture when it was previously applied to analyze employability in the West.

To understand these motivators, one needs to examine the culture and sociology of the Vietnamese. As in other cultures, Vietnam is associated with more traditional values like social expectation and family expectation. This would impact on students' career choice and aspiration. These aspects may influence levels of motivation, which differ from Western models of career development. In contrast to Western students who focus on individual achievement, actualization, and overall personal growth, Vietnamese students are pressed to take up professional lives that are consistent with family dreams or at least provide employment security consistent with existing or perceived social norms. In so doing, integrating culture in the research will help to understand the determinants and obstacles (employability) of Vietnamese students towards more advanced career development strategies to include employability skills. This would further allow institutions to align their interventions with more aspects of their students' values and aspirations to steer their careers. It is those students most interested in their own career development who will emphasize the role – within this culture – of institutional versus non-institutional support in their early years alongside family support through organized social networks within the community to the termination of proactive career-directed behavior.

In addition, engaging employers in the education process to hotlink academic credentials with Vietnamese labor market demands is crucial. Lastly, asking industry partners to design education programs and assess learners' competencies guarantees that education quality is consistent with expectations in real life. Creating internship and co-op education programs helps expose students to experience which opens them up to marketability. Thus we can attain through effective collaborations between companies and universities to enable the transition of students into the job market. Through these collaborations, as we equip students for their working careers, we also address the mismatch of skills and enhance the quality of the workforce in Vietnam's economy for graduates and employers in equal proportions.

Universities and colleges can better prepare their plans to support students' labor market readiness through an understanding of how college students obtain jobs. This can lead to a stronger connection between academic education and labor market requirements, this would lead ultimately to a higher level of employability among graduates. Results of the study may be utilized to add and extend the model, which will benefit the overall purpose of improving education in multicultural contexts.

THEORETICAL FRAMEWORK AND HYPOTHESES

Goal-Setting Theory

Goal-Setting Theory is a prominent work motivation theory that was established in the 1990s by Locke and Latham. Based on the theory, performance is higher with challenging, clear, and specific goals than with easy goals. The theory assumes that goal difficulty, goal specificity, and goal commitment are three conditions necessary for successful goal setting. With difficult goals achievable, there will be improved performance since difficult goals make people or groups exert extra effort, be more creative, and utilize their full potential, leading to improved performance. Also, personal commitment to the task, which is established through their engagement in the task and the information that accompanies it, is necessary for performance (Locke & Latham, 2002).

Goal setting theory receives robust empirical support in a vast majority of research studies, which establishes the positive impact of clearly difficult goals on motivation and performance by creating and promoting work outcomes across a broad range of settings (Harkins & Macrosson, 1990; Schoorman & Mayer, 2008). In addition, the goal setting theory has been criticized to produce negative effects by inducing stress or over-stressing on the stated goals (Locke & Latham, 2013). But goal setting theory also has a well-planned program which can support students in preparing for all things in their career path. According to this study, having knowledge on setting specific career goals can motivate students at private universities in Ho Chi Minh City to participate more actively in career activities.

Job Demands-Resources Model

Demerouti, Bakker, Nachreiner, and Schaufeli came up with the Job Demands-Resources (JD-R) model in 2001. The model builds a process that allows students to better understand how work characteristics and work effects produce employee happiness and productivity. The assumption of the model emphasizes two job characteristics: job demands and job resources. More specifically, job resources enable goal achievement and job demands encompass continuing work that may lead to employee strain.

When employees are involved in the goal-setting process (Locke & Latham, 2002; Hollenbeck & Klein, 1987) and the implementation of the JD-R model, the authors are of the opinion that through the recognition and commitment to specific goals, employees can most effectively improve their performance and motivation.

At the same time, the model is applied in many working environments and organizations to enable the recognition of both the positive and negative elements of work (Schaufeli & Taris, 2014). In addition, studies that have employed the JD-R model demonstrate that definite, challenging goals and adequate resources will lead to proactive career behavior, such as learning new competencies and building new relationships (Tims & Bakker, 2010). In this study, whether the application of the JD-R model can improve students' career performance in the case of students at a private university in Ho Chi Minh.

Aims and Hypotheses

In this study, four hypotheses used by Andrew James Clements and Caroline Kamau (2018) to investigate motivational factors driving proactive career involvement of university students in the UK are used. According to the above four hypotheses, in this study, the above four hypotheses are used to gauge and analyze the influence of motivational mechanisms on proactive career behavior at private universities in Ho Chi Minh City:

H1: Self-efficacy positively correlates with the mastery approach.

Self-confidence refers to confidence in one's ability to create plans and take steps to execute the activities needed to produce future occurrences. Self-efficacy is a concept that has been proposed in order to strengthen mastery strategies, develop skill development, and education (Bandura, 1997). In Vietnam, where high esteem is placed on academic success and self-autonomy, autonomy plays a central role in developing a mastery-oriented orientation when students have confidence in their abilities. When they are self-assured, they strive and achieve more challenging goals. Research has identified that high-self-esteem students are able to build career strategies (Lent et al., 2002).

H2: Proactive career behaviors are a mediating factor in the relationship between the mastery approach and perceived employability.

Improving career thinking and the development of relationships are activities that are able to make thinking more forward-thinking. This assists in playing an important role in raising awareness of one's own employability. If mastery thinking helps in the acquisition of knowledge and self-improvement, it helps oneself to be able to take proactive steps in raising awareness of employability. It has been found through research that students with mastery thinking have a greater inclination to take part in the public marketplace by individual action to expand their employment opportunities (Parker et al., 2010). If you and your students possess that same attitude in Vietnam, being a market purportedly more competitive, then active student participation will render you more unique in employers' eyes and specifically in the context of more competitive Vietnamese employment these days.

H3: Goal commitment mediates the influence of the mastery approach on proactive career behaviors.

Goal commitment to set clear goals will enhance the effectiveness of the mastery approach to active behavior. Since in goal-oriented cultures like Vietnam, people with high mastery-approach are likely to translate their mastery aspirations into tangible career actions. Besides that, previous studies also suggest that setting clear goals prompts them to be active on career tasks (Locke & Latham, 2002).

H4: Perceptions of workload pressures mediate the mastery approach-proactive career behaviour relationship.

Pressure from workload may be stressful, but it can also drive some students towards performance. It is this research's contention that students' perceptions of workload pressure can either prevent or facilitate the conversion of mastery goals into proactive career actions based on their own resilience and coping mechanisms. It is in Vietnam, where academic expectations are high, that understanding this relationship is imperative. Empirical studies have come with mixed results, with some findings showing that moderate pressure levels enhance concentration and motivation (Yerkes & Dodson, 1908).

Figure 1. Theoretical framework (Source by authors)

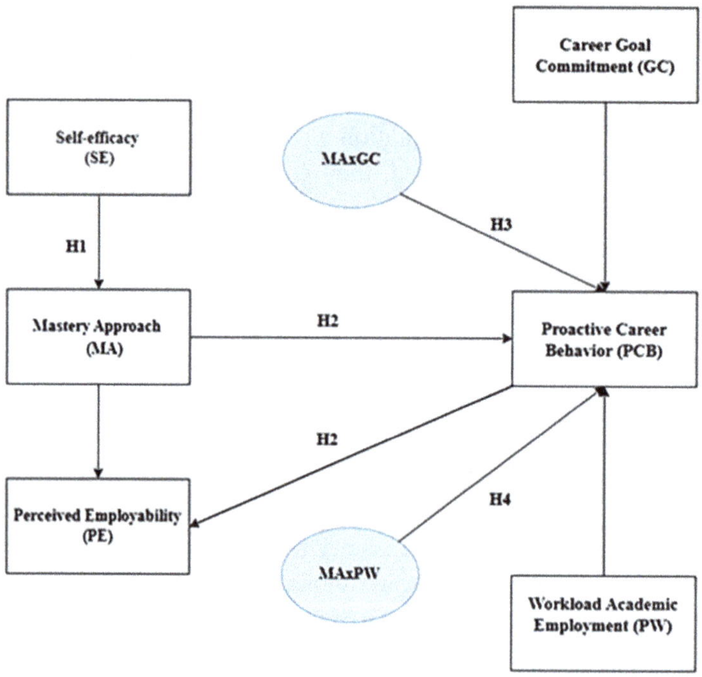

METHODOLOGY

Research Approach

An analytical framework is being applied here to examine variables that promote Vietnamese university students to be risk takers in their professional lives. To understand population trends of relationships and conclusions, apart from collecting and researching with quantitative approaches in order to examine numerical data. Students in a private school in Ho Chi Minh City provided a structured survey via Google Forms in this study. Facebook, Zalo, and Gmail social media platforms were used in the distribution of the survey. After data has been collected, the data is analyzed to find patterns in the proactive career behaviors and motivation of the students.

Sampling Design

This study utilized a four-week online survey that was designed to investigate the reasons and positive career actions of Vietnamese students aged between 19 and 24 years and comprised male and female subjects. The respondents were not selected by the researchers but volunteered to participate using an openly available online survey, which was posted on student forums in social media sites, namely Facebook, Gmail and Zalo. Although the initial objective was to obtain 385 responses, by applying the Yamane (1973) formula, with the success rate $p = 0.5$, error margin $e = \pm 0.05$, and confidence level 95% ($Z = 1.96$). The research only obtained 250 valid responses as there were certain limitations. This reduction in sample size consequently reduced the confidence level to around 89%.

Measures

Some of the previously developed measures were used in this study to measure key variables, and 34 items for the questionnaires were outlined in Table 1. All these tools measured a specific aspect of students' career motivation and behavior to ensure high reliability and completeness in data analysis and collection. The table mentioned will include the variable measurement scale, variables, variable description, variable scores to provide the reader with an overview of the use of the measurement scale with the subjects in the study.

Table 1. Variable and Survey Item Inventory in Career Behavior Study

Variable Measurement Scale	Variable	Variable Description	Likert Scale
New General Self-Efficacy Scale	SE1	1. You will be able to accomplish most of your personal goals.	5 point Likert (from 1 to 5)
	SE2	2. When faced with difficult tasks, do you have confidence that you will complete them?	5 point Likert (from 1 to 5)
	SE3	3. You think you can achieve results that are important to you.	5 point Likert (from 1 to 5)
	SE4	4. You believe that you can succeed in almost any endeavor you set your mind to.	5 point Likert (from 1 to 5)
	SE5	5. You will be able to win despite many obstacles.	5 point Likert (from 1 to 5)
	SE6	6. You are sure that you can do well in many different roles.	5 point Likert (from 1 to 5)
	SE7	7. Compared to others, you can do most jobs very well.	5 point Likert (from 1 to 5)
	SE8	8. Even when things are tough, you can still do pretty well.	5 point Likert (from 1 to 5)
Mastery Approach Subscale	MA1	1. You have listed specific goals for your career field.	7 point Likert (from 1 to 7)
	MA2	2. You believe you are capable of achieving your career goals.	7 point Likert (from 1 to 7)
	MA3	3. You have developed a specific action plan to achieve your goal.	7 point Likert (from 1 to 7)
	MA4	4. You have achieved significant success in your career by following an action plan.	7-point Likert (from 1 to 7)

continued on following page

Table 1. Continued

Variable Measurement Scale	Variable	Variable Description	Likert Scale
Unidimensional Target-free Scale	GC1	1. You have achieved good results in life.	5 point Likert (from 1 to 5)
	GC2	2. You are committed to growing and maturing.	5 point Likert (from 1 to 5)
	GC3	3. You always try your best to achieve your important goals.	5 point Likert (from 1 to 5)
	GC4	4. You value commitment and determination in pursuing your goals.	5 point Likert (from 1 to 5)
Work Pressure subscale from the Work Characteristic Measure	PW1	1. You feel pressured by the amount of work you have to complete each day.	5 point Likert (from 1 to 5)
	PW2	2. You often have to complete a lot of work in a short period of time.	5 point Likert (from 1 to 5)
	PW3	3. You often feel pressured when having to handle a large amount of work at once.	5 point Likert (from 1 to 5)

continued on following page

Table 1. Continued

Variable Measurement Scale	Variable	Variable Description	Likert Scale
Proactive Career Behavior Measure	CP1	1. You are self-motivated and can ensure progress in your work.	5 point Likert (from 1 to 5)
	CP2	2. You set clear goals and make a plan to achieve them.	5 point Likert (from 1 to 5)
	CP3	3. You manage your time and work very efficiently.	5 point Likert (from 1 to 5)
	SK1	4. You are always looking for new opportunities to learn and develop your professional skills.	5 point Likert (from 1 to 5)
	SK2	5. You are always proactive in seeking out and participating in exciting new projects.	5 point Likert (from 1 to 5)
	SK3	6. You are always looking for ways to improve your work performance and achieve better results.	5 point Likert (from 1 to 5)
	CC1	7. You give feedback and suggestions to improve the workflow.	5 point Likert (from 1 to 5)
	CC2	8. You proactively suggest and implement improvements in your work.	5 point Likert (from 1 to 5)
	CC3	9. You look for opportunities to contribute your opinions and ideas to group work.	5 point Likert (from 1 to 5)
	NB1	10. You create new and innovative opportunities in your work.	5 point Likert (from 1 to 5)
	NB2	11. You are proactive in building networks and working relationships.	5 point Likert (from 1 to 5)
	NB3	12. You are confident and determined to overcome difficulties and challenges at work.	5 point Likert (from 1 to 5)
Perceived Employability Measure	PE1	1. You believe that my abilities and skills are sufficient to be recruited in the desired field.	7 point Likert (from 1 to 7)
	PE2	2. You believe you have the ability to present yourself well in the interview process and score points in the recruitment process.	7 point Likert (from 1 to 7)
	PE3	2. You believe you have the ability to present yourself well in the interview process and score points in the recruitment process.	7 point Likert (from 1 to 7)

The New General Self-Efficacy Scale (NGSE) was used by Chen, Gully, and Eden (2001) to assess self-efficacy. The NGSE will include eight items that assess an individual's beliefs about performing tasks and achieving goals on a 5-point Likert scale ranging from 1 (strongly disagree) to 5 (strongly agree). For example, "Even in difficult situations, I can complete the task relatively well."

Baranik, Barron & Finney's (2007) Mastery Approach in Work Domains Scale assessed mastery approach. The scale has four items with 1 (not at all true of me) to 7 (extremely true of me) answers and measures to what degree a person emphasizes being skilled and learning efforts. For instance, "I often seek out ways to acquire new skills and knowledge."

Goal commitment was assessed by the unidimensional Goalless Scale developed by Klein et al. (2014). On a five-point Likert scale, where 1 equals "not at all" and 5 "very much," this four-item scale assesses the level of commitment one has toward his or her career goal. "How committed are you to [your career goal]?" is only one example.

Ten Brummelhuis et al. (2008) applied a modified version of the Work Characteristic Measure work pressure scale in measuring felt workload pressures. On a 5-point Likert scale from 1 (never) to 5 (every day), the three test items request the individual to rate the level of work-related stress. Answer, "I always have a lot of work to do," as an example. Both the paid and unpaid academic load and workload concerning the workplace were examined individually.

Proactive professional behavior was measured by the Proactive Professional Behavior Measure (Strauss, Griffin & Parker, 2012). The twelve-item measure evaluates four domains: networking, career planning, career counselling, and skill development. Respondents scored on a 5-point Likert scale ranging from "strongly disagree" (1) to "strongly agree" (5) the extent to which they agreed with the statements of their proactive activities as professionals. For example, "I am engaged in planning my career path."

The Perceived Employability Measure (Kirves et al., 2014) was used to assess how students perceive their employability. The measure has three items. Each item checks the extent to which participants agree or disagree with statements about their employability on a 7-point Likert scale, ranging from 1 (full disagreement) to 7 (full agreement). For example: "I think my skills are adequate to fulfill the employer's demands."

Data Analysis

In this study, SPSS and SmartPls 3 are employed. Data analysis methodology of the study consists of two phases in a broader sense. In the first phase, research was focused on testing the factors that affect the active role in the career of the student.

Through statistical testing on SPSS, scale reliability was tested by the consistency of data through the application of CRONBACH's Alpha coefficient. Subsequently, using SmartPls 3 structural equation modeling (SEM), average variance (AVE) and composite reliability (CR) were also investigated to obtain and test the strength of the scale. Other indicators such as: SRMR, Chi-Square and NFI are ordered for the distinct value of the model compared to the actual data, according to Fornell-Larccker's cut-offs. The final phase, seeking the influence and describing the variables within the model is looked at by association coefficients, t-values, P, R2 and F2. For analyzing, in this study it can completely comprehend and measure the determinants driving active career involvement of students in Vietnamese private universities.

RESULTS

Demographic Information

The study initially set the use of a cross-sectional survey method to investigate and ascertain influences that influence the willingness of students to participate in active career-oriented activities in Vietnamese private universities. Beneath Table 2, the survey was administered to 250 students, of whom 125 were males (50%) and 125 were females (50%), hence the genders were equal. Participants were picked from private universities in Ho Chi Minh City.

Table 2. Gender Distribution of Survey Participants

Gender	Frequency	Percent
Valid Male	125	50.0
Female Total	125	50.0
	250	100.0

The age distribution of participants varied, with most of them aged 21 years (70.4%, n = 176). The remaining ages were 20 years (17.6%, n = 44), 22 years (8.8%, n = 22), 23 years (2.0%, n = 5), 24 years (0.8%, n = 2), and 19 years (0.4%, n = 1). Demographic makeup ensures representative diversity of students, provide a well-rounded perspective of the determinants of their career motivation.

Table 3. Age Distribution of Survey Participants

Age	Frequency	Percent
Valid 24	2	.8
23	5	2.0
22	22	8.8
21	176	70.4
20	44	17.6
19	1	.4
Total	250	100.0

The demographic information, as shown in Table 3, define the gender balance in representation and participants in the age group of 20-21, which is typical of university students in the advanced levels of their undergraduate program. The selection and determination of subjects for gender balance helps the study have a more comprehensive view, limiting the imbalance between subjects. In addition, the selected subjects in this age group have a special interest in the future career that the study wants to exploit. At the same time, it is also a premise to expand the subjects and scope for future studies, in order to improve the quality of labor resources and improve more suitable educational programs in the near future.

Correlation Analysis

All vocational behavior variables are highly correlated with each other, as can be seen from the Pearson correlation table, where most of the correlations are at the 0.01 level, statistically significant. These findings highlight the importance of self-efficacy for proactive behavior and career commitment in that they demonstrate a high correlation between self-efficacy and career commitment, (SE) and proactive career behavior (PCB) of 0.732 and career goal commitment (GC) of 0.697 in Table 4.

Proactive Career Behavior (PCB) of 0.750 and Perceived Employability (PE) of 0.750 represent a positive correlation with Mastery Approach (MA), which signifies the influence of forward-looking tendencies on the ability to act and career possibilities. GC carries the strongest correlation with Proactive Career Behavior of 0.815, and that career goal commitment is what causes proactive behavior. The results showed that Work Pressure (PW) had a very weak correlation but still had a significant impact on Proactive Career Behavior (PCB) with the obtained data of 0.550 and Perceived Employability (PE) obtained as 0.434.

Table 4. Correlation matrix results between variables in occupational behavior research. (Source: Author)

		SE	MA	GC	PW	PCB	PE
SE	Pearson Correlation	1	.673	.697	.433	.732	.604
	Sig. (2-tailed)		.000	.000	.000	.000	.000
	N	250	250	250	250	250	250
MA	Pearson Correlation	.673	1	.675	.388	.750	.750
	Sig. (2-tailed)	.000		.000	.000	.000	.000
	N	250	250	250	250	250	250
GC	Pearson Correlation	.697	.675	1	.498	.815	.658
	Sig. (2-tailed)	.000	.000		.000	.000	.000
	N	250	250	250	250	250	250
PW	Pearson Correlation	.433	.388	.498	1	.550	.434
	Sig. (2-tailed)	.000	.000	.000		.000	.000
	N	250	250	250	250	250	250
PCB	Pearson Correlation	.732	.750	.815	.550	1	.743
	Sig. (2-tailed)	.000	.000	.000	.000		.000
	N	250	250	250	250	250	250
PE	Pearson Correlation	.604	.750	.658	.434	.743	1
	Sig. (2-tailed)	.000	.000	.000	.000	.000	
	N	250	250	250	250	250	250

The significant correlation coefficient is shown at the 0.01 level (2-tailed).

Overall, this table shows a strong relationship between these variables. In the process, the development of an individual's career and the demonstration of its importance are reflected in the realization of professional commitment and achievements in the labor market. Self-efficacy, mastery approach, and career-proactive behaviour are just some of them.

Reliability and Validity Analysis

As shown in Table 5, analysis table reveals that the mean values of variables under occupational behavior study are high and standard deviations are manageable, showing consistency in participants' opinions. It is clear that most of the outer loadings are above 0.7, justifying the reliability of variables in measuring the concepts. The VIF values are for the most part within the safe limit, but variable PCB6 has the highest VIF value of 4.052, which is a reflection of little chance of multicollinearity.

But it is still within the acceptable limit and has no impact on the overall analysis. For the most part, the table shows how reliable and feasible the study variables are.

Moreover, the model was also assessed on the basis of derived indices of internal reliability and average variance, which revealed that the scales ensured both convergence and reliability requirements

Table 5. Analysis of statistical indicators and suitability of variables (Author's source)

Constructs	Variable	Mean	Standard Deviation	Outer Loadings	VIF	Cronbach's Alpha	rho_A	Composite Reliability (CR)	Average Variance Extracted (AVE)
SE	SE1	3.588	0.902	0.797	2.219	0.901	0.903	0.92	0.59
	SE2	3.744	0.939	0.795	2.370				
	SE3	3.96	0.926	0.735	1.855				
	SE4	3.624	1.007	0.767	1.990				
	SE5	3.96	0.922	0.728	1.728				
	SE6	3.54	1.018	0.753	2.064				
	SE7	3.436	1.005	0.757	2.275				
	SE8	3.568	0.929	0.811	2.483				
MA	MA1	5.128	1.388	0.883	2.694	0.899	0.901	0.93	0.768
	MA2	5.18	1.309	0.885	2.696				
	MA3	4.928	1.42	0.895	2.958				
	MA4	4.828	1.47	0.840	2.218				
GC	GC1	3.708	0.922	0.690	1.428	0.834	0.848	0.89	0.671
	GC2	4.02	0.866	0.848	2.063				
	GC3	4.096	0.849	0.880	2.435				
	GC4	4.1	0.906	0.845	2.133				
PW	PW1	3.84	0.997	0.888	2.319	0.866	0.87	0.918	0.788
	PW2	3.744	0.989	0.896	2.221				
	PW3	3.972	1.007	0.879	2.196				

The findings showed that the study variables had high homogeneity, as evidenced through proof in correlation with the Composite Reliability index and Cronbach's Alpha of above 0.7. The average variance extracted (AVE) for each variable is greater than the stipulated 0.5, with the exception of the SE variable whose AVE was lower than that of the rest but was still within reasonable limits. These results satisfy the need for additional research by demonstrating the validity and reliability of the model scales.

Evaluate Variables Using The Fornell-Larcker Criterion

Table 6. Evaluation of variables via Fornell-Larcker Criterion (Sources by authors)

	SE	PW	PE	PCB	MAxPW	MAxGC	MA	GC
GC								0.819
MA							0.876	0.681
MAxGC						1	-0.164	-0.3
MAxPW					1	0.721	-0.095	-0.16
PCB				0.787	-0.183	-0.26	0.752	0.819
PE			0.897	0.745	-0.141	-0.232	0.753	0.663
PW		0.888	0.438	0.551	-0.05	-0.15	0.396	0.5
SE	0.768	0.434	0.608	0.734	0.017	-0.131	0.68	0.693

Looking at Table 6, evaluating the variables through the Fornell-Larcker criterion, the results of the discrimination test between the latent variables of the model have been determined. And the square root of the AVE of each variable is used to be able to estimate the proxy for the correlation of the variable with other latent variables, and it is found to be higher than the sum of the correlation coefficients. This shows that ensuring that each variable in the model is assessing a separate concept without overlapping with another concept, means that the variables are showing very good discrimination. Finally, this result ensures that the measurement model is valid and suitable for testing other additional constructs.

Evaluate The Results After Hypothesis Testing

Table 7. Hypothesis Testing Result (Source by authors)

Hypotheses	**H1**	**H2**		**H3**	**H4**
Relation	**SE - MA**	**MA - PCB**	**PCB - PE**	**MAxGC - PCB**	**MAxPW - PCB**
Original Sample (O)	0.680	0.346	0.411	0.025	-0.069
Sample Mean (M)	0.683	0.343	0.412	0.026	-0.068
Deviation (STDEV)	0.052	0.052	0.056	0.038	0.045
T Statistics (|O/STDEV|)	13.118	6.612	7.404	0.660	1.525
F Square	0.858	0.270	0.205	0.002	0.016

continued on following page

Table 7. Continued

Hypotheses	H1	H2		H3	H4
Relation	SE - MA	MA - PCB	PCB - PE	MAxGC - PCB	MAxPW - PCB
R Square (R^2)	0.462	0.765	0.641	0.765	0.765
P Values	0.000	0.000	0.000	0.509	0.127

The above are the results of hypothesis testing presented in detail in Table 8, which presents in detail the interaction relationship between the path coefficients, statistical significance and other important measures of each hypothesis presented in detail. Therefore, the above results provide a general sense of the relationships that need to be tested and explored in the current study.

H1: Self-efficacy is positively related to the mastery approach.

This hypothesis was proven. The path coefficient of SE -> MA is highly statistically significant, which can be observed from the findings, the path coefficient is 0.680 and whose P-value is 0.000. It proves that there is a positive correlation between an individual's work mastery approach to learning and self-efficacy.

H2: Proactive career behaviours mediate the relationship between the mastery approach and perceived employability.

This hypothesis was proven. The results demonstrated that path coefficients for the correlation between MA and PCB were 0.411 and 0.346, respectively, and that former and PE, respectively, had P-values of 0.000. In addition, the results from Fornell-Larcker Criterion table show that there is a high level of relationship (r = 0.897) and strong correlation (r = 0.753) between PCB and perceived employability and Mastery Approach, respectively. These findings are in accordance with the PCB as a mediator and career activities can increase a person's chances of being hired.

H3: Goal commitment mediates the mastery approach and proactive career behaviors relationship.

This hypothesis is not supported. Since with a path coefficient of 0.025 and a P-value of 0.509, the MAxGC -> PCB relationship is not statistically significant. This suggests that there is in fact no correlation between variables such as mastery approach, proactive professional activities and goal commitment level as hypothesized.

H4: Perceptions of workload pressure moderate the relationship between the mastery approach and proactive career behaviors.

The hypothesis was not supported. As the result of this path coefficient is -0.069 and P value is 0.127 which shows that there is actually no statistically significant relationship between MAxPW and PCB as stated earlier. According to this study, the relationship between mastery approach and proactive career involvement seems to be completely unrelated to the job stress mentioned as hypothesized.

DISCUSSION

This study contributed meaningful findings to promote students' motivation of proactive career behavior (PCB) at private universities in Ho Chi Minh City based on the Job Demands-Resources (JD-R) Model and Goal Setting Theory. Theoretically and practically, these findings impact students' career development and subsequent studies.

For starters, the research demonstrated that Self-efficacy has a strong and positive impact on the Mastery Approach (H1), proving that a significant factor supporting the mastery approach is the self-efficacy of students.Goal-setting theory holds that students with improved levels of self-efficacy are linked to more proactive learning and career development plans. Clear, well-formulated goals can enhance performance and motivation. Secondly, the study validates that Proactive Career Behaviors moderate the relationship between Perceived Employability and Mastery Approach (H2). This means that students embracing a comprehensive approach to acquiring the material will attain proactive professional behaviors, hence increasing their employability. The mediating role of the PCB is a key concept that helps explain how students may have proactive measures in their overall career development to ensure they become highly competitive.

But the influence of proactive professional behavior on mastery technique does not seem to be driven by goal commitment or perceptions of workload stress (H3 and H4). Consistent with previous work by Andrew James Clements and Caroline Kamau (2018), results of this study are very consistent. The above discussion offers new avenues and horizons to analyze the more intricate relationship between job stress and goal commitment for private university students in Vietnam.

However, these factors have less influence on the development of proactive behaviors among Vietnamese private university students than expected. Utilizing online resources in career building is also key because technology has become a central component of most businesses, and the students must be endowed with the appropriate digital competencies. The learning centers should also incorporate technology skill training into the curricula by offering access to social media platforms for the students to engage and network with entrepreneurs within school hours.

This study examines the dynamics of self-efficacy, perceived employability, and proactive career behaviors in Vietnam private universities. The findings show that the most effective self-efficacy and proactive behavior models are drawn from intra- and extra-curricular support models, including but not limited to corporate mentorship. By these measures undertaken in good time, learning institutions can prepare students in a better way for different job opportunities through adaptability skills.

CONCLUSION

With the Job Demands-Resources Model and Goal Setting Theory as a basis to explain what enables proactive career behavior (PCB) in students in Ho Chi Minh City private colleges. The findings of the study indicate that Mastery Approach improves active learning and employability among students, and it is more or less enabled by self-efficacy. The study points out that the promotion of self-efficacy and proactive learning approaches can be considered very crucial elements to enhance competitiveness within the labor market. In addition, the study depicts that proactive career behavior acts as a mediator variable between employability and mastery learning, and therefore students employing mastery learning strategies will achieve proactive career behaviors. Therefore, enhancing employability and self-development has to be reinforced and supported in the present competitive career market. Based on these perspectives and conclusions, we can see considerable results for opinions in supporting students to set goals as well as facilitating students' career progress in private universities in Ho Chi Minh City.

Besides, the results also demonstrated that Perceived Workload Pressure and Goal Commitment also did not play a significant moderation role in Mastery and proactive career habits relationship, which suggests that there are possibly other variables, such as learning environment, learning climate or individual variables, which could be further investigated to give deeper and richer insights on how these variables affect students' career activities in specific contexts like students at Private Universities in Vietnam.

On the functional level, research shows that schools need to emphasize figuring out such courses as enhancing students' confidence, co-curricular activities to more confidently make them a part of, and first and foremost, schools need to encourage them to take initiative in taking measures in their professional decisions in a precise and concise manner. In order to accomplish this, schools also gain useful skills, experience through learning or taking part in activities at schools. This can make them more adaptable in the future labor market and more successful in the future.

In addition to that, soft skill growth needs to be dealt with as well, such as communication, analytical skills, team work and adaptability, which are fundamental aspects in the modern workforce. Universities can conduct seminars, courses and out-of-class activities that can help students practice these skills. That means it contributes not only to the well-rounded development of not only knowledge but also skills and beliefs. At the same time, one's family support greatly contributes to the direction of students' careers. A supportive family can significantly push students to pursue particular goals and achieve set milestones. Parents are the most powerful individuals over their children, providing advisory services that allow them to move through the intricacies of the working world, professionally interact with it, and be aware of occupations they are interested in. The second important aspect entails modern technology together with internet sites for procuring job opportunities. Modern job applications and websites not only offer students suitable job posts, but also offer instant marketing of various skills and job requirements in addition to valuable lessons needed by businesses or employers. With such resources available on the internet, students can take initiative while searching as well as adequately prepare themselves for job interviews.

The conclusions of the research contribute to enhancing Vietnamese students' career prospects as well as revealing new directions for universities to further cultivate education and better address the demands of industries. With such outcomes, universities can make curriculum changes, develop cooperation programs with businesses, and maximize the process of workplace learning that not only benefits the students but also supports the development of socio-economic growth of the nation. In short, identifying and addressing problems of student's employability is a matter of importance not only for the universities, but for all social stakeholders. By adding such aspects as industry interaction, soft skill development, family and technical application, we can create a supporting environment to develop and succeed in the future for students. Through research and application of appropriate models, we can not only improve education but also enhance the value of human resources of Vietnam on the global labor market.

LIMITATIONS AND FUTURE RESEARCH DIRECTIONS

Further research may ameliorate the shortcomings of this study, though it provides extremely specific information. Causal relationships between work results and motivational factors are difficult to identify due to the study's cross-sectional design that is not overly comprehensive. In subsequent studies in order to improve the way in which these characteristics by influencing career behavior in future workplaces, longitudinal designs should be included and used in combination with the cross-sectional design to be able to provide a more holistic perspective on this issue. Additionally, the study may not encompass all of Vietnam's educational setting and system with only one private university in Ho Chi Minh City. Future research, with more diverse samples to other universities in different areas, may increase generalizability and power, which would be capable of expanding the study even further. In the meantime, the study only made use of self-reported data which may increase the chances of biases such as social desirability bias, so the study is still limited. To ensure a deeper understanding of the employability factors, future research needs to include more objective indicators such as skills independent assessment or labor market results. Research can expand on the impacts of digital literacy within the contemporary workplace and how it is used in business. Investigating employability alongside technology and digital skill-based competencies can be very helpful for research.

Apart from solving the mentioned issues, other new dimensions of concern like the changing world of labor through technological advancement need to be solved as well, considering that one of the challenges posed by the understanding of information technology is an issue of digital literacy. In Vietnam, where there is a shift of labor in the technology-based sectors' direction, even though all foreign players are rushing to establish modern industries requires accepting devices fast dealing with their Educational Technology on Teaching Practices forces. In addition, the insight into students and educators by way of interviews and focus group discussions conducted with employers enables appreciation for their construction narratives of the lived sociocultural phenomena makes possible working towards the examination of employability concerns. Through these strategies, researchers will have a broader vision concerning the intersection of traditional academic aspirations and outcomes brought about by practices as well as digital literacy.

The effects of digital literacy go beyond one's professional prospects and include social implications as well. The resulting inequalities in access to resources may enhance prevailing disparities. This issue is particularly sharp in Vietnam, where these disparities are most keenly felt. By addressing equity in digital literacy, policies can be informed by future research to enable all students to have access to opportunities regardless of geographical location in a digitally driven economy. In addition, schools must prioritize the integration of digital literacy into curricula to ensure teaching and learning are rendered contemporary and innovative. Researchers play a part in informing this debate by critiquing existing frameworks and their impact on social practice outcomes. Such collaborative efforts among schools, business, and government can lead to formulating comprehensive guide documents for the design of curriculum and vocational training for the students.

Moreover, this research is a starting point for determining the factors which affect employability and proposes further areas for research. Surpassing the limitations of sample diversity regarding cross-sectional research and taking a more extensive approach to digital literacy would be efficient in future research contributions, which this field needs. Acquiring knowledge of these matters would not only enrich knowledge regarding Vietnam's employability background but also equip students with knowledge in dealing with a more creative marketplace and digitally advanced working environment. This study remains applicable to education policy efforts committed to building strategically effective programming designed to cultivate critical skills in students at all age levels.

REFERENCES

Bakker, A. B., & Demerouti, E. (2007). The Job Demands-Resources model: State of the art. *Journal of Managerial Psychology, 22*(3), 309–328. DOI: 10.1108/02683940710733115

Bandura, A. (1997). *Self-efficacy: The exercise of control.* W. H. Freeman.

Clements, A. J., & Kamau, C. (2018). Understanding students' motivation towards proactive career behaviours through goal-setting theory and the job demands–resources model. *Studies in Higher Education, 43*(12), 2279–2293. DOI: 10.1080/03075079.2017.1326022

Demerouti, E., Bakker, A. B., Nachreiner, F., & Schaufeli, W. B. (2001). The job demands-resources model of burnout. *The Journal of Applied Psychology, 86*(3), 499–512. DOI: 10.1037/0021-9010.86.3.499 PMID: 11419809

Hollenbeck, J. R., & Klein, H. J. (1987). Goal commitment and the goal-setting process: Problems, prospects, and proposals for future research. *Academy of Management Review, 12*(2), 212–220. DOI: 10.5465/amr.1987.4307798

Kirves, K., Kinnunen, U., De Cuyper, N., & Mäkikangas, A. (2014). Trajectories of perceived employability and their associations with well-being at work: A three-wave study. *Journal of Personnel Psychology, 13*(1), 46–57. DOI: 10.1027/1866-5888/a000103

Lent, R. W., Brown, S. D., & Hackett, G. (2002). Social cognitive career theory. In Brown, D. (Eds.), *Career choice and development* (4th ed., pp. 255–311). Jossey-Bass.

Locke, E. A., & Latham, G. P. (1990). *A theory of goal setting & task performance.* Prentice Hall.

Locke, E. A., & Latham, G. P. (2002). Building a practically useful theory of goal setting and task motivation: A 35-year odyssey. *The American Psychologist, 57*(9), 705–717. DOI: 10.1037/0003-066X.57.9.705 PMID: 12237980

Parker, S. K., Bindl, U. K., & Strauss, K. (2010). Making things happen: A model of proactive motivation. *Journal of Management, 36*(4), 827–856. DOI: 10.1177/0149206310363732

Schaufeli, W. B., & Taris, T. W. (2014). A critical review of the job demands-resources model: Implications for improving work and health. In Bauer, G. F., & Hämmig, O. (Eds.), *Bridging occupational, organizational and public health: A transdisciplinary approach* (pp. 43–68). Springer., DOI: 10.1007/978-94-007-5640-3_4

Strauss, K., Griffin, M. A., & Parker, S. K. (2012). Future work selves: How salient hoped-for identities motivate proactive career behaviors. *The Journal of Applied Psychology*, *97*(3), 580–598. DOI: 10.1037/a0026423 PMID: 22122111

Tims, M., & Bakker, A. B. (2010). Job crafting: Towards a new model of individual job redesign. *SA Journal of Industrial Psychology*, *36*(1), 841. Advance online publication. DOI: 10.4102/sajip.v36i2.841

Yamane, T. (1973). *Statistics: An introductory analysis* (3rd ed.). Harper & Row.

Yerkes, R. M., & Dodson, J. D. (1908). The relation of strength of stimulus to rapidity of habit-formation. *The Journal of Comparative Neurology and Psychology*, *18*(5), 459–482. DOI: 10.1002/cne.920180503

Chapter 3

Farmers' Right to Seed at the Intersection of Intellectual Property and Human Rights: A Critical Analysis in Socio-Cultural Context

Ananya Pandey
https://orcid.org/0000-0002-2419-6314
Christ University, Bangalore, India

Achyuta Nanda Mishra
https://orcid.org/0000-0002-4113-0974
Christ University, Bangalore, India

ABSTRACT

The interplay between farmers' Intellectual Property Rights (IPRs) and Human Rights is significant in socio-cultural transformations. Farmers in traditional and indigenous communities hold centuries of knowledge about biodiversity, sustainable agriculture, and seed management. However, the rise of commercial agriculture, globalization, and stringent IPR regimes—often favoring corporate interests—pose challenges to preserving and recognizing this knowledge. This chapter critically examines the intersection between farmers' IPRs and human rights, exploring how evolving frameworks impact cultural identities, societal structures, and the rights of communities to food security, self-determination, and participation in decision-making processes. It discusses the tension between the patenting of genetic resources and the traditional knowledge of farmers, emphasizing the need for equitable

DOI: 10.4018/979-8-3373-0603-2.ch003

benefit-sharing mechanisms. By bridging legal and socio-political perspectives, this chapter aims to highlight policies that uphold farmers' and human rights amidst ongoing socio-cultural transformations.

INTRODUCTION

Farmers' rights have emerged as a pivotal issue in the face of a conflict between Intellectual Property Rights (IPRs) and Human Rights. Farmers are the custodians of traditional knowledge and biodiversity significantly contributing to global food security and environmental sustainability. Where agriculture continues to be essential for promoting pro-poor growth, ensuring food security, lowering poverty, and creating jobs in the rural economy, food security is a prerequisite for any country's social, cultural and economic stability (Pawlak & Kołodziejczak, 2020). Stable food supplies and healthy agricultural markets are necessary for sustainable food security. A condition where all people constantly have physical, social, and financial access to enough safe, nourishing food that satisfies their dietary needs and food choices for an active and healthy life is what the term "food security" signifies (World Health Organization, 2020). However, the upcoming technological advancements in the era of globalization, internationalization and commercialization of the intellectual property regime challenge the rights of the farmers to control, utilize and benefit from their labor, cultural heritage and traditional practices. These upgrades and enhancements often prioritize commercialization over the farmers' collective and individual rights, levitating a crucial issue of equity, justice and cultural preservation (McGuire et al., 2024).

IPRs have now been significantly allied with corporate and institutional interests, which were traditionally designed to incentivize innovation and creativity. Currently, the marginalization of farmers due to the expansion of plant patent and plant variety protection across the globe under the intellectual property regime and its protection under the international framework, such as the Agreement on Trade-Related Aspects of Intellectual Property (TRIPS), has affected the farmers considerably, particularly in the Global South (Chakraborty, 2021). The intellectual property regime fails to recognize the contribution of farmers in the agricultural domain leading to loss of their traditional knowledge and control/ownership over the seeds and plants. Due to the significant expansion, commercialization and commodification of plant varieties, farmers' rights along with the Indigenous cultural practices and community-based system of heritage and innovation, is largely affected (Gautam et al., 2012).

On the other hand, human rights principles emphasize protecting and promoting the inherent dignity and equal rights of all individuals and communities. International human rights law is based on the Universal Declaration of Human Rights (UDHR),

1948 and International Covenant on Economic, Social and Cultural Rights (ICESCR), 1966. The ICESCR concentrates on economic, social, and cultural rights, acknowledging that states must take progressive measures to realize them, whereas the UDHR declares the inalienable rights of all people. When taken as a whole, they provide a thorough foundation for preserving and advancing human dignity and welfare. Internationally, particularly in relation to farmers' rights, the United Nations Declaration on Rights of Peasants and Other People Working in Rural Areas (UNDROP) of 2007 focuses on the importance of protecting and promoting farmers' rights to seeds, land and participation in decision-making processes (Claeys & Edelman, 2020). It is a necessary declaration recognizing the mutual relationship between farmers' rights and broader human rights such as the right to health, food and cultural identity. However, these rights are in practice under the heavy burden of challenges that include inadequate enforcement mechanisms, limited legal recognition, and conflicting policy priorities (Eide, 1998).

The tension between farmers' Intellectual Property and Human Rights has intensified significantly after the cultural and societal transformation with the emerging globalization and technological advancements. Modern agricultural practices, such as genetically modified crops and seeds brought up and driven by biotechnology and corporate monopoly, marginalize traditional farming systems and knowledge. This expansion of advancement is not only a technological shift but also a cultural disruption that alters how individuals and communities relate to their land, seeds and heritage. In this perspective, safeguarding farmers' rights has not only become a matter of legal and economic concern but also has become a critical aspect of protecting human rights knitted with cultural survival and social justice. This chapter, therefore, critically analyzes the complex intersection between the IPRs of farmers' and the human rights perspective in the context of cultural and societal transformation. It also examines the legal and institutional framework governing farmers' rights in the context mentioned above. Furthermore, the author also explored the potential pathways to reconcile the competing interests between farmers' rights and human rights. Thereby, adopting and exploring the multidisciplinary lens of farmers rights in the intellectual property and human rights context, this study contributes to a more nuanced understanding of how IPRs can further sustainable development, social, cultural diversity, without affecting the human rights of the individuals and the community. Eventually, the chapter also calls for a paradigm shift that places a human right centric approach by balancing IPRs of farmers at the global level to further agricultural growth.

THEORETICAL FRAMEWORK

In general terms, intellectual property is defined as intangible property that results from creative intellectual thinking. IPRs are usually related to controlling physical manifestations or expressions of ideas, not the abstract non-physical substance itself (Drahos, 1999). By granting and upholding legal rights to create and manage tangible manifestations of an idea, intellectual property law safeguards the interest of content creators (Brown et al., 2005). There are three main ways that arguments for IPRs have been presented. Firstly, according to *Personality Theorists*, Intellectual property is an extension of a person's personality. Secondly, according to *Utilitarians*, IPRs are based on social progress and incentives for innovation (Moore, 2008). Lastly, according to *Lockean Theory*, rights are justified by considering merit and labor. Further, the intellectual property framework's recognition of farmers' contributions to the creation and preservation of plant genetic resources (PGRFA) forms the basis of farmers' rights (Merges, 2011). By acknowledging farmers' rights to preserve, use, trade, and sell farm-saved seed, it seeks to balance the interests of farmers and plant breeders while also offering incentives to breeders to create new cultivars. The International Treaty on Plant Genetic Resources for Food and Agriculture (ITPGRFA), which establishes a legal foundation for farmers' rights globally, enshrines the framework.

Concerning the human rights perspective, Intellectual Property also serves as a human right which is enshrined in Article 27 of the UDHR. The Article recognizes the right to benefit from one's individual creation while upholding the rights of all individuals to participate in cultural life and access to knowledge (United Nations Office of the High Commissioner for Human Rights, 1966). Similarly, Article 15 of the ICESCR focuses on the right to benefit from scientific progress, cultural participation which may be undermined by stringent intellectual property protection (United Nations, n.d.). Culturally, the intersection of intellectual property and human rights is clear in the protection for traditional knowledge and cultural expressions. The traditional knowledge system still lacks intellectual property recognition and is majorly vulnerable to exploitation and misappropriation. Therefore, the human rights framework further the protection of rights of farmers and indigenous communities to maintain their cultural heritage. This advocates for the need of intellectual property regime to recognize cultural diversity and enhance inclusive participation.

CONCEPTUALIZING FARMERS' RIGHTS WITHIN A MULTIDISCIPLINARY LENS

The concept of farmers' rights is rooted in the recognition of farmers' individual and their community's contribution to matters focusing on food security and biodiversity. It is surrounded by an extension of legal, social, economic and political considerations (Borowiak, 2004). Considering this perspective from a multidisciplinary lens, the rights of the farmers are subject to interaction with agriculture, law, economics, social justice and environmental sustainability (Hallett, 2016). Farmers' rights are deeply in association with the protection of traditional knowledge, conservation of biodiversity, fair distribution of seeds and access to genetic resources (Sumita, 2023). From an international perspective, the ITPGRFA of 2001 is the key legal instrument that accords farmers access to genetic resources and seeds and provides fair compensation for their contribution to conserving agricultural biodiversity (Moore & Tymowski, 2005). The right to access seeds and genetic resources often challenges the Intellectual Property laws that put forth corporate ownership and monopoly first over the community-based agricultural practices and rights. The root of farmers' rights is the need to ensure protection from exploitation of seeds and other resources from large stakeholders, industries and agribusinesses (Campi & Nuvolari, 2021). Economically, it also requires access to an equitable market and receiving fair prices for their produce. Some other practices that advocate for farmers' rights under the inclusive economic framework are access to credit, insurance and technology, along with the enjoyment of fair credit for their labor (Stringer et al., 2020).

Additionally, from the perspective of farmers, examining social justice via a multidisciplinary lens is essential to strengthening their current rights and overcoming obstacles related to their equal access to resources, work conditions, and land ownership (Yuan et al., 2022). The inequalities intrinsic to the global agriculture system, specifically related to smallholder farmers and indigenous farmers, such as the right to seed, land and other resources, are some challenges that need to be addressed (Touch et al., 2024). Environmentally, farmers' rights are in accordance with sustainable development and agricultural practices that enhance sustainability, ecological growth, soil health and climate resources. A multidisciplinary lens over the rights of farmers calls for a holistic approach that not only protects their ability to produce seeds but also enhances the quality of their life and livelihood (Borowiak, 2004).

FARMERS' INTELLECTUAL PROPERTY IN THE GLOBAL CONTEXT

Farmers' IPRs in the global context address the complex interplay between traditional knowledge, innovation, and modern intellectual property laws. These rights aim to recognize and protect farmers' contributions to agricultural biodiversity while promoting sustainable development and food security, maintaining the cultural heritage and diversity in terms of traditional knowledge, access to resources and the like. Agrobiodiversity conservation, particularly on farms, depends heavily on custodian farmers. Few farmers in communities practicing traditional agriculture have accumulated information through centuries of experience (Bisht et al., 2020). These farmers use this knowledge to promote traditional crops and seeds in their communities. They keep a variety of traditional crops and kinds, choose crops and varieties suited to the local environment, and encourage their friends and neighbors to use and preserve local diversity (Swiderska et al., 2011). They frequently stem from community pride, cultural significance, or personal passion. These farmers contribute significantly to the in-situ conservation of genetic resources by choosing and promoting crop varieties well-suited to regional conditions (Bellon et al., 2017). Custodian farmers share seeds and knowledge across their communities, are deeply knowledgeable about agricultural biodiversity, and are dedicated to conservation, which sets them apart from regular farmers (Gruberg et al., 2013).

Nevertheless, their numbers are declining, and their conservation strategies might not be scientifically sound, underscoring the necessity for institutional support to identify, encourage, and formalize their contributions. The production of high-quality seeds and the preservation of crop species and regional cultivars depend heavily on custodian farmers (Halewood et al., 2018). The Biodiversity Board, the Department of Agriculture, and other research and development organizations can take on the vital task of identifying and assisting these farmers. Custodian farmers are selected based on their professional skills, experience, and commitment to protecting indigenous resources in the area. They might be rewarded or compensated in monetary or non-monetary ways for their invaluable expertise and willingness to share genetic resources (Sthapit et al., 2013).

International Agreements

In theory, IPRs are based on sovereign nations; each has its legal system for granting IP rights and protection to promote innovation. However, to facilitate trade, investment, and innovation as well as ease dispute resolution, the new international trade system, which is founded on free markets and global competition, aims to bind individual nations through international agreements to a set of essential criteria for intellectual property protection (Ezell & Cory, 2019). The World Trade Organization (WTO) Agreement on TRIPS, the UN Convention on Biodiversity (CBD), the FAO's International Treaty on Plant Genetic Resources for Food and Agriculture (FAO-IT), the Conventions of the International Union for the Protection of New Varieties of Plants (UPOV, 1978, 1991), the Patent Cooperation Treaty (PCT) and other international agreements are crucial for agricultural research and technology transfer (Helfer, 2004).

Nagoya Protocol

In the Preamble and the operational requirements of the Nagoya Protocol, strengthening the legal protection of traditional knowledge holders under international law, which is implicitly a part of farmers' rights, is prioritized (Secretariat of the Convention on Biological Diversity, 2011). In accordance with the Nagoya Protocol, the parties must take steps to guarantee that indigenous and local communities get fair and equitable benefits from the exploitation of genetic resources and related traditional knowledge (Friso et al., 2020). More precisely, the parties will take adequate action to guarantee that traditional knowledge related to genetic resources is accessed by the indigenous and local communities that own it on mutually agreed conditions and with their prior informed permission (Tripathi, 2003). In carrying out their responsibilities under the protocol, the parties must also consider the role of community protocols and customary laws. They must also set up systems to notify prospective users of traditional knowledge related to genetic resources of their responsibilities (James & Rajasekharan, 2023). The Nagoya Protocol outlines various supplementary support measures to strengthen indigenous and local communities in access decision-making and discussions of mutually agreed terms, equivalent to the Farmers' Rights component on decision-making involvement (Prip, 2024).

UPOV

The World Intellectual Property Organization (WIPO) administers the UPOV Conventions. The main area where the two treaties diverge is protecting farmers' rights to save and sell seed or other propagative material from a registered variety. Additionally, the 1991 convention significantly limits plant breeders' ability to employ protected varieties in their development initiatives (Dutfield, 2011). Since a legal framework exists, a country's membership in UPOV, 1991 will automatically align its intellectual property system for plant variety protection with that of the TRIPS regime (Seshia, 2002). There are a few initiatives within UPOV that aim to address the issue of traditional knowledge. For example, UPOV has developed a tool called UPOV PRISMA, which helps applicants to apply for breeders' rights with all participating PVP Offices, via the UPOV website. This tool can help to ensure that traditional knowledge is not overlooked in the plant variety protection process (Brahmi et al., 2004).

CULTURAL DIMENSIONS OF FARMERS' RIGHTS

The cultural dimensions of the farmers' rights include traditional practices, seed sovereignty, participation in the decision-making process and the right to share benefits equitably. This section of the chapter explores the role of traditional knowledge in advancing agricultural innovation, the cultural transformation with globalization, and its impact on farmers' rights.

Traditional Practice and Seed Sovereignty

Traditional Practices and Seed Sovereignty are deeply connected to farmers' rights since they encompass the cultural heritage and agricultural knowledge carried through generations. The foundation and root of agrarian biodiversity, which is inclusive of the recognition, promotion and protection of farmers' rights in conserving, exchanging and utilizing seeds, is greatly emphasized by these rights (Borowiak, 2004). Traditional farming practices are intrinsically connected to the cultural identities and practices of indigenous and rural communities, and they reflect a holistic approach towards the use of land, stewardship of seeds and nature. The indigenous and rural communities consider the seeds as the symbol of their ancestral heritage and cultural continuity rather than considering it as a product of commercialization or commodity (Ba et al., 2018). Traditional methods are being resurrected in place of industrialized agriculture since they are thought to contribute to resilient farming systems (Brush, 2007). Seed sovereignty, which represents farmers' freedom and rights over their seed, free from agribusiness and limiting mechanisms like patents and IPRs, is derived from the concept of sovereignty, which refers to the independence of nation-states from outside intervention. The freedom of farmers to save, share, and reuse their seeds is the foundation of seed sovereignty (Singh, 2021). The foundation for preserving both food security and biodiversity is seed sovereignty. It is simple and inexpensive to manufacture high-quality open-source seeds, which lowers the cost of buying seeds. It enables farmers to freely exchange seeds with one another and create their seeds (seed self-reliance) (Fredriksson, 2021). In addition to preserving valuable traditional or indigenous vegetable seed varieties for future generations, seed sovereignty allows farmers to choose seeds that are appropriate for their location. Food sovereignty, or the right of people, groups, and nations to choose their own agricultural and food policy, is closely related to seed sovereignty

(Coomes, 2015). The cultural dimension of such rights reflects the relationship of farmers, the environment and their ongoing traditional heritage, which helps foster a resilient agricultural ecosystem. Therefore, protecting farmers' rights to seed is vital to maintain cultural identity and ensure food security by promoting sustainable farming practices (Gamage et al., 2023).

Role of Indigenous Knowledge in Advancing Agricultural Innovation

For ages, local communities and indigenous peoples have had to adapt to changing environmental conditions and deal with severe weather conditions. They have achieved this using long-standing customs and methods, or traditional knowledge, about sustainable resource use and adaptive ecosystem management (Swiderska et al., 2011). Ignoring the wealth of traditional knowledge that farmers hold, globalization, decentralization, and privatization all have only accompanied new developments in agriculture, just as they do in other economic sectors, ignoring the human rights perspective. To meet the demands of the private sector during the colonial era, innovation was overseen by state institutions or public-private partnerships (Robinson & Carson, 2015). A small number of scientists, planters, and representatives of multinational corporations were involved in channeling information and financial flows along commercial commodities lines. Subsistence farming and food production for domestic consumption or sale were not considered at the time (Grunert et al., 1997). Indigenous and traditional knowledge was minimally used. Following independence, new strategies were created to accomplish developmental objectives like increasing food production and decreasing dependency on imported food. Over time, technological advancements that were created via research stations did not meet the diversity of conditions local farmers had to cope with (Rowe et al., 2024). In many communities, this kind of information is transmitted orally from one generation to the next. In addition to the culture in which it develops, indigenous knowledge is valuable to planners and scientists working to enhance rural communities. Every community has a vast amount of technological knowledge derived from its natural resources and careful observation (Mundy & Compton, 1991). Every culture has systems in place whereby indigenous knowledge serves as the foundation for collective decision-making and the creation of new technologies and knowledge when discussing contemporary issues and potential solutions. Additionally, every culture has methods for sharing new knowledge and technologies, whether they are created inside or externally. In a similar agroecosystem in a different region of the world, indigenous technologies that are successfully employed by one civilization can be applied to address issues that another society faces. It could be appropriate to combine strategies and techniques from other systems (Warren, 1991).

Cultural Transformation with Globalization and its Impact on the Farmers' Rights

Globalization, a complex phenomenon, has greatly impacted many facets of our society, including food security and agriculture. Globalization is the term used to describe the growing interdependence and integration of economies, cultures, and communities across the globe (Pingali, 2007). In recent decades, globalization has significantly altered food distribution networks, production systems, and agricultural methods, eventually affecting global food security The globe is now a highly interdependent and interconnected system where social, cultural, and economic interactions take place worldwide because of globalization (Kennedy et al., 2004). National economies are now integrated into a global network of production, commerce, and investment due to the escalation of cross-border exchanges. This interconnection has brought benefits and challenges for many industries, including agriculture. Cultivating plants, rearing animals, and other endeavors to produce food, fiber, and other agricultural goods are all included in the broad category of agriculture (Schanbacher, 2010). Crop farming, raising animals, aquaculture, and other methods are examples of these practices. While livestock husbandry concentrates on raising animals to produce meat, milk, or fiber, crop farming entails the cultivation of crops like grains, fruits, and vegetables. Cultivating aquatic species, including fish, shellfish, and aquatic plants, is known as aquaculture. These varied farming methods are essential to maintaining the general economy and standard of living of communities as well as making a substantial contribution to the world's food supply (Viana et al., 2022). Agricultural environments differ in adopting precision agriculture, genetically modified organisms (GMOs), and other agricultural technology. It is influenced by socio-economic circumstances, farmer choices, and regulatory frameworks (Buiatti et al., 2013). GMOs have been shown to offer both advantages and disadvantages in empirical research. GMOs may boost crop yields, decrease the need for pesticides, and improve disease and insect resistance. Concerns exist, meanwhile, regarding possible threats to the environment, effects on biodiversity, socio-economic ramifications of IPRs and farmers' reliance on seed firms (Bawa & Anilakumar, 2013). Globalization has also resulted in changes to land use patterns. Land may be set aside for agribusiness endeavors or export-oriented crops as agricultural systems grow more integrated into international markets, which could displace small-scale farmers and encroach on natural ecosystems. One crucial factor to consider is the effects on small-scale farmers. For these farmers, globalization may bring both possibilities and difficulties. While access to global markets might give new avenues for revenue generation, it exposes small-scale farmers to market volatility and unequal power dynamics in value chains (Lambin & Meyfroidt, 2011).

HUMAN RIGHTS PERSPECTIVE ON FARMER'S INTELLECTUAL PROPERTY

The enactment of laws that forbid farmers from engaging in their long-standing practice of conserving, sharing, and using plant genetic resources or seeds; imposing and promoting IPRs or patent rights on seeds; disregarding farmers' traditional knowledge in favor of public breeding institutions researching genetically modified organisms and other destructive farming practices; permitting bio-piracy of genetic resources that are valuable to farmers by failing to closely monitor and prevent the patenting and commercialization of these resources and their by-products, thereby preventing farmers' unrestricted access to such resources; and denying farmers a voice in decisions that impact them are all examples of the systematic violations of farmers' rights (Helfer, 2004; Prip, 2024). Plant genetic resources are a substantial source of income for farmers. Farmers have generated, conserved, and sustainably utilized plant genetic resources or seeds ever since agriculture began. There would be no agricultural biodiversity without farmers. To provide a broad genetic foundation of features that enable the breeding of plant varieties resistant to climate shifts and socio-economic instability, agricultural biodiversity is crucial (Halewood et al., 2018). Farmers' human rights to their livelihood and existence are violated by recent advances imposing patent rights or IPRs on plant genetic resources, which forbid the conservation, development, and sustainable use of genetic resources or seeds (Breen, 2009). To reduce poverty sustainably, the impoverished must have access to natural resources (land, woods, water, fisheries, pastures, etc.). Rural residents lacking or having limited access to natural resources face challenges in getting food, building up other assets, and recovering from market or natural shocks or tragedies, making their livelihoods fragile (Ellis & Allison, 2004). Different approaches to rural development, such as ecosystems, people-centered development, farming systems, and participatory methods, can coexist with the livelihoods approach. A livelihoods viewpoint can be informed by all these diverse approaches, which provide insights into the connections between seeds, PGRs, and livelihoods (Scoones, 2013).

The rights of indigenous populations started receiving much attention from the UN human rights apparatus in the early 1990s. These peoples made numerous demands of nations, including the right to acknowledge and govern their culture, including traditional knowledge about agriculture, medicine, and biodiversity (Assembly, 2007). A large portion of this information was regarded as public domain from the standpoint of intellectual property, either because the indigenous tribes that produced it did not support private ownership laws or because it did not satisfy established subject matter standards for protection (Correa, 2001). However, intellectual property legislation made traditional knowledge accessible for unfettered outside appropriation by considering it essentially unowned. Many used this information as an upstream contribution for later downstream discoveries that were privatized through patents, copyrights, and plant breeders' rights. Also, indigenous populations were rarely given access to the technological and financial advantages of those advancements (Cottier & Panizzon, 2004).

CONFLICTS BETWEEN GLOBAL IP REGIMES AND LOCAL FARMERS' PRACTICES

IPRs have become one of the most contentious areas of political conflict in discussions about the global political economy and the establishment of institutions for global governance. This is especially true in the conflict over seeds, genetic and biological resources (Maskus, 2000). Since commercial agriculture and pharmaceutical interests successfully linked biological resource intellectual property with international trade in the 1980s and the WTO subsequently institutionalized IPR protection, intellectual property has become extremely important to agricultural producers worldwide (Clancy & Moschini, 2017). Signatory nations were required to protect plant varieties with property rights under a significant and contentious clause in the WTO's TRIPS Agreement. This effectively means they must give state-sponsored monopolies over the commercial distribution of seeds that have undergone scientific engineering (Helfer, 2004). A virtual seed war has arisen in the shadow of this IPR regime. For the biotechnology sector, establishing such protection—through so-called breeders' rights—offers commercial seed companies, who had inherited the responsibility for seed innovation from farmers decades earlier, much deserved acknowledgement and a fair compensation. However, extending IPRs to cover plant varieties represents a break from customs and beliefs for many farmers in developing nations, endangering their independence and long-standing lifestyles (Cabrera Cornide, 2016). Global intellectual property (IP) regimes, such as those governing patents and plant variety protection, can create conflicts with the traditional practices of local farmers. For example, farmers in many developing countries have long relied on exchanging and saving seeds from their crops, practices that are essential for their food security and cultural heritage (Filatova, 2021). However, intellectual property laws, particularly those influenced by the TRIPS Agreement, often grant exclusive rights to plant varieties to breeders or companies. This can restrict farmers' ability to save and exchange seeds, forcing them to purchase new seeds each year, which can be expensive and inaccessible. Such restrictions can also stifle innovation among farmers, as they may be hesitant to develop new varieties for fear of infringing on intellectual property rights (Buttle & Belsky, 1987; Charnley & Radick, 2013).

CHALLENGES IN PROTECTING FARMER'S INTELLECTUAL PROPERTY RIGHTS

The corporate monopoly on seeds, biopiracy, political, social, and economic restraints, as well as institutional and legal obstacles, are just a few of the numerous obstacles' farmers must overcome to safeguard their IPRs.

TRIPS

The Agreement offers protection through patents or an efficient sui generis system that each country might use regarding plant varieties (Matthews, 2003). Plant varieties protected by patents are registered under the breeder's name, giving the breeder the only right to utilize the variety for any purpose. This implies that the breeder must approve any further use of the variety and subject to a royalty payment (Sahai, 2003). Stricter IPRs on seeds brought about by TRIPS limit farmers' capacity to store, utilize, trade, and sell seeds that have been conserved on their farms. For small-scale farmers who depend on storing seeds for both income and food security is very harmful (Peter, 2017). Access to technology, including GMOs, which are frequently protected by intellectual property, are impacted by TRIPS. This makes it more difficult for farmers to implement innovative technologies that could boost production and productivity. Traditional knowledge, which is frequently held by farmers and indigenous populations, has been criticized for not being sufficiently protected by TRIPS (Watal et al., 2015). This results in the deterioration of cultural assets and the corporate theft of traditional knowledge.

Corporate Monopolies

Farmers are significantly impacted by the small businesses controlling the seed market. The cost of inputs going up, with fewer options and higher prices, is one of the most obvious consequences. These businesses have increased the cost of pesticides and seeds as they have strengthened their market dominance, reduced farmers' profits and made it harder for smallholders to compete (Michelson et al., 2023). Farmers are forced to buy new seeds every season because of patented seeds, which limits their ability to save and share seeds. In addition to increasing reliance on a small number of multinational firms, this degrades agricultural biodiversity in the marketplace and the environment, essential for food security and resilience to diseases, pests, and climate change (Sagoff, 2001). These companies also pose a legal threat to farmers, as they have been known to file lawsuits for alleged patent infringements (PepsiCo, for example, sued four Gujarati farmers in 2019 for cultivating a patented potato variety), further solidifying their dominance and control over the agricultural industry (Roy & Chatterjee, 2022). In certain areas, these methods have raised farmer debt, exacerbating social and economic hardship in rural areas. The quality of agricultural products can also be impacted by the prevalence of seed monopolies and the farming methods they encourage. The emphasis on genetically homogeneous, high-yielding crops may result in a decline in the nutritional value of food (Klümper & Qaim, 2014).

Biopiracy

The unapproved use of farming and indigenous communities' expertise and genetic resources by people or organizations aiming to obtain exclusive monopoly control through patents or intellectual property is called biopiracy, sometimes referred to as scientific colonialism (Wynberg, 2023). According to Merriam Webster, the unethical or illegal appropriation or commercial exploitation of biological elements that are indigenous to a country or territory without giving the people or government of that country or territory just recompense is known as "biopiracy". These biological substances include chemical, plant, and animal substances (Rahmah et al., 2020). Furthermore, stealing information concerning methods associated with these chemicals, such farming methods or the extraction of medicinal characteristics is also considered to be biopiracy. There have been numerous reports of actors in the agriculture sector trying to patent resources or goods from less affluent communities and areas, even though researchers in the pharmaceutical industry are thought to be among the most frequent offenders (Bhattacharya, 2014). These monopolies can increase developing countries' reliance on big businesses, in addition to denying these peoples just remuneration for their traditional knowledge and genetic resources. These incidents are seen in markets for raw materials and ingredients, as well as seeds, fertilizers, insecticides, and herbicides (Twarog & Kapoor, 2004). There is no denying the connection between colonialism and contemporary biopiracy; instances of biopiracy are frequently referred to as "neo-colonial" or "bio-colonial." The World Intellectual Property Organization (WIPO) Intergovernmental Committee on Intellectual Property and Genetic Resources, Traditional Knowledge and Folklore (IGC) is attempting to establish international legal guidelines that guarantee the preservation and payment for the use of traditional knowledge, genetic resources, and traditional cultural expressions due to the increasing global awareness of the exploitative nature of biopiracy (Yu, 2024).

Socio-Economic and Political Constraints

Farmers face significant political and social obstacles when trying to assert their IPRs. Socio-economic barriers include ignorance of intellectual property laws, costly legal proceedings, and dependence on customs that are not officially acknowledged (Braga & Fink, 1998). Poverty, illiteracy, limited access to resources, and other issues that make it difficult for farmers to comprehend intricate and occasionally elusive intellectual property frameworks are made worse by this. Politically, they are typically at a disadvantage when it comes to policy making, as laws typically favor huge corporations over smallholder farmers (De Macedo & Chino, 2002). Such models jeopardize the way people have historically performed agriculture, and seed monopolies and restrictive patents on genetically modified crops run the risk of further depriving farmers of their ability to conserve seeds and swap ratios. Furthermore, farmers who claim any benefits from their innovations face extra obstacles due to a lack of enforcement procedures and inadequate institutional assistance (Kruft, 2001). To consistently emphasize the contributions made by farmers while simultaneously preventing the exploitation of their traditional knowledge and innovations, a suitable mix of inclusive policies, capacity building initiatives, and equitable legal frameworks is required (Stringer et al., 2020).

POLICY AND LEGAL RECOMMENDATIONS

Balancing farmers' intellectual property rights with human rights requires a multi-faceted approach. Policymakers should prioritize the protection of traditional knowledge and farmers' rights to use, exchange, and save seeds, while also encouraging innovation in agriculture. This can be achieved through flexible intellectual property frameworks that allow for the recognition of traditional knowledge and the development of sui generis systems that protect farmers' rights. Additionally, promoting access to technology and information for farmers, and supporting local and regional seed systems, can help ensure a sustainable and equitable agricultural system. To assist the implementation of farmers' rights, laws and policies relating to Plant Genetic Resources, Food and Agriculture (PGRFA), seeds, and the environment, as well as the procedures associated with them, may be adopted or altered. National legislation on biodiversity conservation, genetically modified organisms, PGRFA, seeds, plant variety protection, peasant rights, and local and indigenous communities are only a few examples of the concerns that may be covered by such policies and regulations (Lawson, 2015). They can take a comprehensive approach to farmers' rights or concentrate on elements that are thought to be especially pertinent in particular circumstances. The protection of traditional knowledge pertaining to the conservation and sustainable use of PGRFA, the recognition of the efforts made by custodian/guardian farmers, local communities, and indigenous peoples, and the representation of farmers, local communities, and indigenous peoples in decision-making bodies and/or advisory boards of government institutions working on PGRFA-related issues are a few examples of such laws and procedures (Halewood et al., 2021). Farmers' seed systems and associated activities may be further protected and safeguarded by such regulations and related procedures. Participation may involve formal representation of farmers and/or their organizations in decision-making bodies and/or the development of discussion procedures, for example to jointly analyze needs or share perspectives in preparation of choices that may be taken in the future (Vernooy et al., 2023). Facilitating farmers' participation in decision-making on pertinent topics at all levels may be beneficial, as national decisions frequently depend on decisions made at other levels, such as international, subnational, or local levels. To guarantee a viable, dynamic, and efficient national institutional mechanism of IP management, inventors and innovators should receive their share in proportion to the value of a commercialized invention, while incentives should be granted to all inventions, whether they be processes or products (Ashby, 1987).

CONCLUSION

The environment, soil health, farmers, and the overall quality of agricultural products are all significantly impacted by the concentration of the seed industry. Although these businesses have helped boost agricultural output, there are growing concerns about the long-term viability of their methods. Policymakers, governments, the commercial sector, and civil society will need to work together to address these issues to save biodiversity, encourage more sustainable farming methods, and guarantee that the advantages of agricultural innovation are distributed fairly. It is not only desirable but also essential to reconsider the current course of industrial agriculture as the globe struggles with ecological degradation and declining human health and nutrition. Farmers rights are not an isolated issue but a complex interwoven concept that requires attention socially, legally, economically, environmentally and politically. The multidisciplinary approach to this ensures farmers a better and empowered system to enhance food security and promote equity in the face of global challenges.

To acknowledge the past, present, and future contributions of farmers to the preservation, enhancement, and accessibility of plant genetic materials that are crucial for food and agriculture, the ITPGRFA formally established farmers' rights. Enhancing food security, biodiversity values, and human rights all depend on farmers' rights to their intellectual property. Agricultural communities are empowered to maintain their legacy while promoting resilient food systems by acknowledging that farmers' knowledge of traditional crops and crop types bred over many generations is their property right. Since a farmer can grow and trade their seeds without being taken advantage of by companies, these rights are also included in the human right to food. In addition to acknowledging farmers' intellectual property, they address the economic disparity faced by many rural farmers who rely on information sharing and seed saving for their livelihood. Fighting the monopoly of agriculture by biotechnology corporations, which typically patent genetic resources originating from farming communities, requires reaffirming the legitimacy of farmers' intellectual property in general. Through worldwide commitments to fair access and benefit-sharing, such as the ITPGRFA, it defends these rights. In the end, the human rights concepts of supporting sustainable development, protecting indigenous methods, and uplifting historically marginalized populations are all closely related to the right to intellectual property of farmers. The social, environmental, and economic foundation required to create a fair and acceptable global food system would be strengthened by such an idea.

REFERENCES

Ashby, J. A. (1987). The effects of different types of farmer participation on the management of on-farm trials. *Agricultural Administration and Extension*, *25*(4), 235–252. DOI: 10.1016/0269-7475(87)90079-1

Assembly, U. G. (2007). United Nations declaration on the rights of indigenous peoples. *UN Wash*, *12*, 1–18.

Ba, Q. X., Lu, D. J., Kuo, W. H. J., & Lai, P. H. (2018). Traditional farming and sustainable development of an indigenous community in the mountain area—A case study of Wutai village in Taiwan. *Sustainability (Basel)*, *10*(10), 3370. DOI: 10.3390/su10103370

Bawa, A. S., & Anilakumar, K. R. (2013). Genetically modified foods: Safety, risks and public concerns—a review. *Journal of Food Science and Technology*, *50*(6), 1035–1046. DOI: 10.1007/s13197-012-0899-1 PMID: 24426015

Bellon, M. R., Dulloo, E., Sardos, J., Thormann, I., & Burdon, J. J. (2017). In situ conservation—Harnessing natural and human-derived evolutionary forces to ensure future crop adaptation. *Evolutionary Applications*, *10*(10), 965–977. DOI: 10.1111/eva.12521 PMID: 29151853

Bhattacharya, S. (2014). Bioprospecting, biopiracy and food security in India: The emerging sides of neoliberalism. *International Letters of Social and Humanistic Sciences*, *23*(12), 49–56. DOI: 10.18052/www.scipress.com/ILSHS.23.49

Bisht, I. S., Rana, J. C., Yadav, R., & Ahlawat, S. P. (2020). Mainstreaming agricultural biodiversity in traditional production landscapes for sustainable development: The Indian scenario. *Sustainability (Basel)*, *12*(24), 10690. DOI: 10.3390/su122410690

Borowiak, C. (2004). Farmers' rights: Intellectual property regimes and the struggle over seeds. *Politics & Society*, *32*(4), 511–543. DOI: 10.1177/0032329204269979

Braga, C. A. P., & Fink, C. (1998). The relationship between intellectual property rights and foreign direct investment. *Duke J. Comp. & Int'l L.*, *9*, 163.

Brahmi, P., Saxena, S., & Dhillon, B. S. (2004). The protection of plant varieties and Farmers' Rights Act of India. *Current Science*, *86*(3), 392–398.

Breen, D. (2009). *Farmers' Rights as Human Rights*. OHCR.

Brown, J. D., Tai, J. D., & June, T. (2005). Introduction: An Overview of Intellectual Property. *Biopharm International*, *2005*(2).

Brush, S. B. (2007). Farmers' rights and protection of traditional agricultural knowledge. *World Development, 35*(9), 1499–1514. DOI: 10.1016/j.worlddev.2006.05.018

Buiatti, M., Christou, P., & Pastore, G. (2013). The application of GMOs in agriculture and in food production for better nutrition: Two different scientific points of view. *Genes & Nutrition, 8*(3), 255–270. DOI: 10.1007/s12263-012-0316-4 PMID: 23076994

Cabrera Cornide, J. (2016). *The control over seeds: the confrontation between human rights and intellectual property rights* (Doctoral dissertation).

Campi, M., & Nuvolari, A. (2021). Intellectual property rights and agricultural development: Evidence from a worldwide index of IPRs in agriculture (1961-2018). *The Journal of Development Studies, 57*(4), 650–668. DOI: 10.1080/00220388.2020.1817395

Chakraborty, S. K. (2021). Genetically Modified Seeds, Intellectual Property and Agriculture: Has India Addressed the Challenges of Commodifying Plant Genetic Resources and Farmers' Right to Access Seed? *CMR University Journal of Contemporary Legal Affairs, 3*, 90.

Charnley, B., & Radick, G. (2013). Intellectual property, plant breeding and the making of Mendelian genetics. *Studies in History and Philosophy of Science, 44*(2), 222–233. DOI: 10.1016/j.shpsa.2012.11.004

Claeys, P., & Edelman, M. (2020). The United Nations Declaration on the rights of peasants and other people working in rural areas. *The Journal of Peasant Studies, 47*(1), 1–68. DOI: 10.1080/03066150.2019.1672665

Clancy, M. S., & Moschini, G. (2017). Intellectual property rights and the ascent of proprietary innovation in agriculture. *Annual Review of Resource Economics, 9*(1), 53–74. DOI: 10.1146/annurev-resource-100516-053524

Coomes, O. T., McGuire, S. J., Garine, E., Caillon, S., McKey, D., Demeulenaere, E., Jarvis, D., Aistara, G., Barnaud, A., Clouvel, P., Emperaire, L., Louafi, S., Martin, P., Massol, F., Pautasso, M., Violon, C., & Wencélius, J. (2015). Farmer seed networks make a limited contribution to agriculture? Four common misconceptions. *Food Policy, 56*, 41–50. DOI: 10.1016/j.foodpol.2015.07.008

Correa, C. M. (2001). Traditional knowledge and intellectual property. *Geneva: The Quaker United Nations Office (QUNO), 17.*

Cottier, T., & Panizzon, M. (2004). Legal perspectives on traditional knowledge: The case for intellectual property protection. *Journal of International Economic Law, 7*(2), 371–399. DOI: 10.1093/jiel/7.2.371

De Macedo, J. B., & Chino, T. (2002). *Technology and poverty reduction in Asia and the Pacific*. Development Centre of the Organisation for Economic Co-operation and Development.

Drahos, P. (1999). *The universality of intellectual property rights: origins and development. Intellectual Property and Human Rights*. World Intellectual Property Organization.

Dutfield, G. (2011). Food, biological diversity and intellectual property. *Global Economic Issue Publications Intellectual Property, Issue Paper*, (9).

Eide, A. (1998). *The Human Right to Adequate Food and Freedom from Hunger, In the Right to Food in Theory and Practice*. FAO Publication.

Ellis, F., & Allison, E. (2004). *Livelihood diversification and natural resource access. Overseas Development Group*. University of East Anglia.

Ezell, S., & Cory, N. (2019). *The way forward for intellectual property internationally*. Information Technology and Innovation Foundation.

Filatova, E. A. (2021). *Intellectual Property Rights in the Seed Industry: Barriers to Sustainable Agriculture* (Master's thesis, University of Denver).

Fredriksson, M. (2021). Open-source seeds and the revitalization of local knowledge. *Sustainability (Basel)*, *13*(21), 12270. DOI: 10.3390/su132112270

Friso, F., Mendive, F., Soffiato, M., Bombardelli, V., Hesketh, A., Heinrich, M., Menghini, L., & Politi, M. (2020). Implementation of Nagoya Protocol on access and benefit-sharing in Peru: Implications for researchers. *Journal of Ethnopharmacology*, *259*, 112885. DOI: 10.1016/j.jep.2020.112885 PMID: 32311487

Gamage, A., Gangahagedara, R., Gamage, J., Jayasinghe, N., Kodikara, N., Suraweera, P., & Merah, O. (2023). Role of organic farming for achieving sustainability in agriculture. *Farming System*, *1*(1), 100005. DOI: 10.1016/j.farsys.2023.100005

Gautam, P. L., Singh, A. K., Srivastava, M., & Singh, P. K. (2012). Protection of plant varieties and farmers' rights: A review. *Indian Journal of Plant Genetic Resources*, *25*(01), 9–30.

Gruberg, H., Meldrum, G., Padulosi, S., Rojas, W., Pinto, M., & Crane, T. A. (2013). *Towards a better understanding of custodian farmers and their roles: insights from a case study in Cachilaya*.

Grunert, K. G., Harmsen, H., Larsen, H. H., Sørensen, E., & Bisp, S. (1997). New areas in agricultural and food marketing. *Agricultural marketing and consumer behavior in a changing world*, 3-30.

Halewood, M., Bedmar Villanueva, A., Rasolojaona, J., Andriamahazo, M., Rakotoniaina, N., Bossou, B., Mikpon, T., Vodouhe, R., Fey, L., Drews, A., Kumar, P. L., Rasoanirina, B., Rasoazafindrabe, T., Aigbe, M., Agbahounzo, B., Otieno, G., Garforth, K., Kiene, T., & Nnadozie, K. (2021). Enhancing farmers' agency in the global crop commons through use of biocultural community protocols. *Agriculture and Human Values*, *38*(2), 579–594. DOI: 10.1007/s10460-020-10164-z

Halewood, M., Chiurugwi, T., Sackville Hamilton, R., Kurtz, B., Marden, E., Welch, E., Michiels, F., Mozafari, J., Sabran, M., Patron, N., Kersey, P., Bastow, R., Dorius, S., Dias, S., McCouch, S., & Powell, W. (2018). Plant genetic resources for food and agriculture: Opportunities and challenges emerging from the science and information technology revolution. *The New Phytologist*, *217*(4), 1407–1419. DOI: 10.1111/nph.14993 PMID: 29359808

Hallett, S., Hoagland, L., & Toner, E. (2016). Urban agriculture: Environmental, economic, and social perspectives. *Horticultural Reviews*, *44*(44), 65–120. DOI: 10.1002/9781119281269.ch2

Helfer, L. R. (2004). *Intellectual property rights in plant varieties: International legal regimes and policy options for national governments* (No. 31). Food & Agriculture Org.

James, T. C., & Rajasekharan, S. (2023). Access and Benefit Sharing of Biological Resources and Associated TK: A Multi-tiered Responsibility. In *Biodiversity Conservation Through Access and Benefit Sharing (ABS) Himalayas and Indian Sub-Continent* (pp. 81–102). Springer International Publishing.

Kennedy, G., Nantel, G., & Shetty, P. (2004). Globalization of food systems in developing countries: impact on food security and nutrition.

Klümper, W., & Qaim, M. (2014). A meta-analysis of the impacts of genetically modified crops. *PLoS One*, *9*(11), e111629. DOI: 10.1371/journal.pone.0111629 PMID: 25365303

Kruft, D. (2001). Impacts of genetically-modified crops and seeds on farmers. *The Agricultural Law Resource and Reference Center*, 1-11.

Lambin, E. F., & Meyfroidt, P. (2011). Global land use change, economic globalization, and the looming land scarcity. *Proceedings of the National Academy of Sciences of the United States of America*, *108*(9), 3465–3472. DOI: 10.1073/pnas.1100480108 PMID: 21321211

Lawson, C. (2015). Implementing Farmers' Rights: Finding Meaning and Purpose for the International Treaty on Plant Genetic Resources for Food and Agriculture Commitments? *Available at SSRN* 2626668.

Maskus, K. E. (2000). *Intellectual property rights in the global economy*. Peterson Institute.

Matthews, D. (2003). *Globalising intellectual property rights: the TRIPS Agreement*. Routledge. DOI: 10.4324/9780203165683

McGuire, E., Al-Zu'bi, M., Boa-Alvarado, M., Luu, T. T. G., Sylvester, J. M., & Leñero, E. M. V. (2024). Equity principles: Using social theory for more effective social transformation in agricultural research for development. *Agricultural Systems*, *218*, 103999. DOI: 10.1016/j.agsy.2024.103999

Merges, R. P. (2011). *Justifying intellectual property*. Harvard University Press. DOI: 10.4159/harvard.9780674061125

Michelson, H., Gourlay, S., Lybbert, T., & Wollburg, P. (2023). Purchased agricultural input quality and small farms. *Food Policy*, *116*, 102424. DOI: 10.1016/j.foodpol.2023.102424

Moore, A. D. (2008). Personality-based, rule-utilitarian, and lockean justifications of intellectual property. *The handbook of information and computer ethics*, 105.

Moore, G. K., & Tymowski, W. (2005). *Explanatory guide to the international treaty on plant genetic resources for food and agriculture* (No. 57). IUCN.

Mundy, P., & Compton, L. (1991). Indigenous communication and indigenous knowledge. *Development Communication Report*, *74*(3), 1–3.

Pawlak, K., & Kołodziejczak, M. (2020). The role of agriculture in ensuring food security in developing countries: Considerations in the context of the problem of sustainable food production. *Sustainability (Basel)*, *12*(13), 5488. DOI: 10.3390/su12135488

Peter, K. Y. (2017). The objectives and principles of the TRIPS agreement. In *The Regulation of Services and Intellectual Property* (pp. 255–322). Routledge.

Pingali, P. (2007). Agricultural growth and economic development: A view through the globalization lens. *Agricultural Economics*, *37*(s1), 1–12. DOI: 10.1111/j.1574-0862.2007.00231.x

Prip, C. (2024). Farmers' Rights in the Plant Treaty: Interrelations and recent interactions with other international regimes and processes. *Development Studies Research*, *11*(1), 2357095. DOI: 10.1080/21665095.2024.2357095

Rahmah, M., Barizah, N., & Blay, S. (2020). Ensuring disclosure of origin of genetic resources in patent applications: Indonesia's efforts to combat biopiracy.

Robinson, G. M., & Carson, D. A. (2015). The globalisation of agriculture: Introducing the Handbook. In *Handbook on the globalisation of agriculture* (pp. 1–28). Edward Elgar Publishing. DOI: 10.4337/9780857939838.00006

Rowe, S., Brady, C., Sarang, R., Wiipongwii, T., Leu, M., Jennings, L., Peterson, T., Boston, J., Roach, B., Phillips, J., & Conrad, Z. (2024). Improving Indigenous Food Sovereignty through sustainable food production: A narrative review. *Frontiers in Sustainable Food Systems*, *8*, 1341146. DOI: 10.3389/fsufs.2024.1341146

Roy, A., & Chatterjee, B. (2022). Evolution and Application of IPR Laws with Reference to Pepsico vs. Gujarat Farmers Case. *IUP Law Review*, *12*(3).

Sagoff, M. (2001). Biotechnology and agriculture: The common wisdom and its critics. *Indonesian Journal of Global Legal Studies*, *9*, 13.

Sahai, S. (2003). India's plant variety protection and Farmers' Rights Act, 2001. *Current Science*, *84*(3), 407–412.

Schanbacher, W. D. (2010). *The politics of food: The global conflict between food security and food sovereignty*. Bloomsbury Publishing USA. DOI: 10.5040/9798400698576

Scoones, I. (2013). Livelihoods perspectives and rural development. In *Critical perspectives in rural development studies* (pp. 159–184). Routledge.

Secretariat of the Convention on Biological Diversity. (2011). *Nagoya Protocol on access to genetic resources and the fair and equitable sharing of benefits arising from their utilization to the convention on biological diversity: text and annex*. UN.

Seshia, S. (2002). Plant variety protection and farmers' rights: Law-making and cultivation of varietal control. *Economic and Political Weekly*, •••, 2741–2747.

Singh, P. (2021). Politics of knowledge in development: Explorations in seed sovereignty. *Studies in Indian Politics*, *9*(1), 105–117. DOI: 10.1177/2321023021999179

Sthapit, B. R., Lamers, H., & Rao, R. (2013). Custodian farmers of agricultural biodiversity: selected profiles from South and South East Asia: proceedings of the workshop on custodian farmers of agricultural biodiversity, 11-12 February 2013, New Delhi, India.

Stringer, L. C., Fraser, E. D., Harris, D., Lyon, C., Pereira, L., Ward, C. F., & Simelton, E. (2020). Adaptation and development pathways for different types of farmers. *Environmental Science & Policy*, *104*, 174–189. DOI: 10.1016/j.envsci.2019.10.007

Sumita. (2023). Farmers' Rights in the International Treaty on Plant Genetic Resources for Food and Agriculture. *Part 2 Indian J. Integrated Rsch. L., 3*, 1.

Swiderska, K., Reid, H., Song, Y., Li, J., Mutta, D., Ongugo, P., ... & Barriga, S. (2011). The role of traditional knowledge and crop varieties in adaptation to climate change and food security in SW China. *Bolivian Andes and coastal Kenya.*

Touch, V., Tan, D. K., Cook, B. R., & Liu, L. D., Cross, R., Tran, T. A., ... & Cowie, A. (2024). Smallholder farmers' challenges and opportunities: Implications for agricultural production, environment and food security. *Journal of Environmental Management, 370*, 122536.

Tripathi, S. K. (2003). Intellectual property and genetic resources, Traditional Knowledge and Folklore: International, regional and national perspectives, trends and strategies.

Twarog, S., & Kapoor, P. (2004). *Protecting and promoting traditional knowledge: systems, national experiences and international dimensions* (p. 418). UN.

United Nations. (n.d.). Article 27, UDHR. https://www.un.org/en/about-us/universal-declaration-of-human-rights

United Nations Office of the High Commissioner for Human Rights. (1966). Article 15, ICESCR. https://www.ohchr.org/en/instruments-mechanisms/instruments/international-covenant-economic-social-and-cultural-rights

Vernooy, R., Adokorach, J., Kimani, D., Marwa, A., Mayoyo, A., & Nyadanu, D. (2023). On the margins: a review of policies and laws in support of farmer-managed seed systems in.

Viana, C. M., Freire, D., Abrantes, P., Rocha, J., & Pereira, P. (2022). Agricultural land systems importance for supporting food security and sustainable development goals: A systematic review. *The Science of the Total Environment, 806*, 150718. DOI: 10.1016/j.scitotenv.2021.150718 PMID: 34606855

Warren, D. M. (1991). *Using indigenous knowledge in agricultural development* (No. 127, p. 46pp).

Watal, J., Taubman, A., & Cottier, T. (2015). The making of the TRIPS agreement: Personal insights from the Uruguay round negotiations.

World Health Organization. (2020). *The state of food security and nutrition in the world 2020: transforming food systems for affordable healthy diets* (Vol. 2020). Food & Agriculture Organization.

Wynberg, R. (2023). Biopiracy: Crying wolf or a lever for equity and conservation? *Research Policy*, *52*(2), 104674. DOI: 10.1016/j.respol.2022.104674

Yu, P. K. (2024). WIPO Negotiations on Intellectual Property, Genetic Resources and Associated Traditional Knowledge. *Akron Law Review*, *57*, 23–71.

Yuan, G. N., Marquez, G. P. B., Deng, H., Iu, A., Fabella, M., Salonga, R. B., Ashardiono, F., & Cartagena, J. A. (2022). A review on urban agriculture: Technology, socio-economy, and policy. *Heliyon*, *8*(11), e11583. DOI: 10.1016/j.heliyon.2022.e11583 PMID: 36406682

Chapter 4
Generation Green:
Navigating ESG in Generation Z's Job Search Landscape

Jing Yi Yong
https://orcid.org/0000-0003-1332-4779
Taylor's University, Malaysia

Yusliza Mohd Yusoff
Universiti Malaysia Terengganu, Malaysia

Yudi Fernando
Universiti Malaysia Pahang, Malaysia & Binus University, Indonesia

Woon Leong Lin
https://orcid.org/0000-0002-6568-412X
Taylor's University, Malaysia

Siong Choy Chong
Taylor's University, Malaysia

Chuen Khee Pek
https://orcid.org/0000-0003-4376-9816
Taylor's University, Malaysia

ABSTRACT

As the workforce evolves, Generation Z (Gen Z) prioritises Environmental, Social, and Governance (ESG) factors in career decisions. This chapter explores how ESG commitments shape employer attractiveness, using Signaling Theory and Social Identity Theory to explain Gen Z's job pursuit intentions. It examines the implications for employers, educators, and policymakers, providing strategies for ESG-driven workforce engagement. Future research should focus on empirical validation, cross-industry analysis, and policy impacts to enhance understanding. As ESG principles redefine workplace expectations, organisations integrating sustainability and ethical governance will gain a competitive edge in attracting and retaining Gen Z talent. This chapter contributes to the discourse on ESG in human resource management, highlighting evolving job market trends and the need for businesses to embed ESG principles into their long-term strategies.

DOI: 10.4018/979-8-3373-0603-2.ch004

INTRODUCTION

The modern workforce is grappling with significant challenges in attracting and retaining Generation Z (Gen Z) talent. Brain drains, where young professionals seek better opportunities abroad, and persistent talent shortages within domestic labour markets, highlight the urgency for organisations to adapt. Gen Z, born between 1997 and 2012, enters the workforce with distinct career expectations and priorities shaped by digitalisation, social consciousness, and evolving workplace norms. Unlike previous generations, they are increasingly reluctant to work for employers who do not align with their values or fail to offer meaningful work experiences. This generation places a high value on purpose, flexibility, work-life balance, and ethical corporate practices, particularly concerning sustainability and social responsibility (Nguyen Ngoc et al., 2022; Popaitoon, 2022; Schroth, 2019).

The rapid advancement of technology, particularly artificial intelligence (AI) and digital collaboration tools has further shaped Gen Z's expectations of the workplace. Growing up in a digital world, they are highly proficient with new technologies and skilled at evaluating potential employers through online platforms and demand transparency in corporate commitments. This technological fluency has placed pressure on organisations to demonstrate authentic environmental, social and governance (ESG) commitments (Deloitte, 2024). According to the 2024 Gen Z and Millennial Survey by Deloitte, young professionals increasingly reject roles that conflict with their personal values. Many avoid jobs with negative environmental impacts or poor inclusivity, instead favouring workplaces that champion well-being and work-life balance. Interestingly, recent research indicates that 50% of Gen Z aspires to leave corporate jobs in favour of entrepreneurship, reflecting a broader preference for autonomy, innovation, and purpose-driven careers (Smith, 2023).

Environmental sustainability remains a major concern for Gen Z, many of whom express anxiety over climate change and advocate for stronger corporate and governmental actions. This generation demonstrates a profound awareness and commitment to ethical and environmental issues, largely fuelled by their extensive exposure to social media platforms and online resources that facilitate the widespread sharing of information (Djafarova & Foots, 2022). They take proactive steps to reduce their environmental footprint and urge businesses to enable sustainable consumer choices. Many Gen Z individuals choose career paths aligned with environmental priorities or perceived job security amid automation. Once employed, they advocate for workplace improvements, including initiatives on diversity, equity, inclusion (DEI), wellness, and environmental responsibility. Their strong emphasis on work-life balance drives their preference for flexible work arrangements, leading to increased demand for part-time roles and compressed workweeks (Deloitte, 2024).

The increasing prominence of ESG principles in Gen Z's job preferences reflects a broader shift towards sustainability-driven employment. This trend aligns with the United Nations' Sustainable Development Goals (SDGs), particularly SDG 8 (Decent Work and Economic Growth) and SDG 13 (Climate Action), which emphasise ethical employment and environmental responsibility. As Gen Z enters the workforce, they expect employers to move beyond traditional profit-driven models and actively contribute to sustainability. Companies that fail to incorporate sustainability into their long-term strategies risk not only talent shortages but also reputational challenges (Singh et al., 2023), as young professionals gravitate towards employers who align with their values. By embedding ESG principles in alignment with SDGs, organisations can build credibility and attract value-driven employees who prioritise meaningful, purpose-driven careers.

Beyond individual preferences, global trends in sustainability-driven employment are reshaping workforce expectations. The increasing regulatory pressure on ESG disclosures, exemplified by frameworks such as the European Union's Corporate Sustainability Reporting Directive (CSRD), Global Reporting Initiative (GRI), and the Task Force on Climate-related Financial Disclosures (TCFD), reinforces the urgency for businesses to uphold transparency and accountability. Well-defined regulatory policies play a crucial role in providing corporations with the necessary structure and strength to enhance ESG transparency and accountability, ensuring that sustainability commitments are not merely performative but embedded within corporate strategies (Bayong et al., 2024). These regulations not only mitigate greenwashing risks but also shape investor confidence and talent attraction, making ESG integration a business imperative rather than an optional corporate initiative.

Simultaneously, investors and stakeholders are demanding that corporations extend their focus beyond financial performance to include social and environmental impact (Baah et al., 2021). This shift underscores the growing influence of ESG as a key differentiator in employer branding. Beyond monetary incentives, Gen Z values workplaces that foster a sense of community, innovation, and inclusivity (Pandita, 2022). They seek environments that not only embrace racial and gender diversity but also acknowledge diverse identities and orientations. With their strong career aspirations and preference for flexible, independent work styles, they are drawn to employers that encourage creative problem-solving and support social causes. Organisations that proactively integrate sustainability into their operations, whether through ethical governance, green job creation, or inclusive workplace policies, are better positioned to attract and retain this generation. By aligning corporate strategies with global sustainability expectations, businesses can enhance workforce engagement, foster long-term commitment, and remain competitive in an evolving job market.

Despite indications from surveys and anecdotal evidence pointing to Gen Z's preferences, there is limited research on understanding how Gen Z's environmental consciousness impacts their job search preferences and the role of ESG principles in this landscape. While existing surveys and industry reports indicate that Gen Z places significant importance on ESG factors in their job decisions, much of the current discourse remains fragmented, relying on workforce trends rather than a cohesive theoretical framework. There is a need for a deeper conceptual understanding of how ESG commitments influence job pursuit decisions and whether they serve as critical decision-making criteria for young job seekers. Additionally, it remains unclear to what extent organisations' sustainability and ethical initiatives function as tangible differentiators in attracting Gen Z talent. Without stronger theoretical insights into these mechanisms, businesses may struggle to develop authentic, effective ESG strategies that resonate with the emerging workforce. Addressing this gap is crucial to ensuring that sustainability-driven employer branding efforts are not only strategic but also aligned with the real expectations of Gen Z candidates.

As businesses strive to attract and retain Gen Z talent, it is crucial to grasp their attitudes towards ESG issues, which are shaping how companies approach sustainability initiatives. This study proposes a conceptual framework that leverages signalling theory and social identity theory to address existing gaps by examining how organisations can strategically integrate ESG principles into their operations and culture. This understanding is vital for aligning with the values of the emerging workforce, enhancing sustainability efforts, and maintaining a competitive advantage in the evolving job market.

LITERATURE REVIEW

Environmental, Social and Governance (ESG) Principles

ESG principles have evolved from a set of responsible business practices into a core strategic priority that influences corporate sustainability and workforce dynamics. The concept of ESG is rooted in the broader framework of corporate social responsibility (CSR) and sustainable development, gaining traction as investors, regulatory bodies, and consumers demand greater accountability from corporations (Eccles et al., 2019). The United Nations Principles for Responsible Investment outline ESG across three dimensions: environmental concerns, including climate change mitigation, biodiversity conservation, and responsible resource management; social aspects, encompassing labour standards, workplace diversity, and human rights; and governance factors, such as corporate ethics, board diversity, and transparency in decision-making (United Nations Global Compact, 2021). As ESG reporting becomes more standardised, companies are expected to integrate these principles into their operational strategies rather than treating them as external compliance requirements (Eccles & Klimenko, 2019).

Increasingly, ESG is not only an external measure of corporate responsibility but also a critical determinant of employer attractiveness. The 2022 Edelman Trust Barometer reported that a significant portion of the global workforce chooses their employer based on shared values, with ESG-related aspects like business ethics and corporate culture playing a decisive role (Edelman, 2022). This trend highlights the shift from ESG being a niche investor concern to a mainstream business imperative that influences corporate reputation, stakeholder trust, and employee engagement. Moreover, studies indicate that organisations that prioritise ESG performance experience lower employee turnover, increased job satisfaction, and stronger overall workforce commitment (Alves et al., 2025).

This growing emphasis on ESG has significant implications for human resource management. Companies that integrate ESG into HR strategies can enhance their talent acquisition efforts, particularly in a labour market shaped by sustainability-conscious job seekers. Gornostaeva and Chernysheva (2023) emphasise that ESG-based HR management not only facilitates green job creation but also strengthens corporate governance by fostering a culture of accountability and ethical leadership. Similarly, Zhang et al. (2024) found that corporate ESG behaviours, particularly transparency in environmental initiatives and strong governance structures, enhance employee satisfaction and organisational trust. These findings underscore the necessity for businesses to align their values with ESG principles to remain competitive in attracting and retaining top talent.

Understanding Gen Z's Values

As the emerging workforce, Gen Z brings distinct expectations shaped by their digital upbringing and heightened social and environmental consciousness. Unlike previous generations, they place a strong emphasis on purpose-driven work, diversity, and sustainability. While they share some similarities with Millennials—such as valuing work-life balance and digital communication—Gen Z places an even greater premium on internal career development and ethical corporate practices (Nguyen Ngoc et al., 2022; Schroth, 2019). Research suggests that they actively evaluate an organisation's environmental impact when deciding on potential employers, with many prioritising businesses that demonstrate tangible commitments to sustainability (Gabrielova & Buchko, 2021).

Moreover, Gen Z's approach to work extends beyond environmental concerns to broader issues of diversity and inclusion. Coman et al. (2022) found that this generation is acutely aware of racial and gender diversity and prefers workplaces that reflect these values. They are also more likely than previous generations to engage in ethical consumption, advocate for social justice, and seek out employers that align with these priorities. This heightened awareness signals a shift in workforce expectations, where businesses must move beyond performative sustainability efforts and embed genuine ESG commitments into their organisational culture.

ESG Principles and Job Pursuit Intention

Job pursuit intention has garnered substantial attention in recent years, particularly in the context of evolving workforce demographics and shifting values. This term refers to an individual's inclination to seek employment or remain open to job opportunities (Chapman et al., 2005). Contemporary job seekers increasingly prioritise various aspects of potential employers, with ESG considerations emerging as a key differentiator. Companies that demonstrate strong commitments to social and environmental responsibility are gaining a competitive edge in attracting talent, as job seekers are more inclined to pursue opportunities with organisations that align with their values.

Studies suggest that corporate social responsibility (CSR) and sustainability initiatives significantly enhance employer attractiveness. Waples and Brachle (2020) argue that organisations with strong CSR commitments experience higher stakeholder engagement and a more favourable public image, which, in turn, makes them more appealing to prospective employees. Additionally, Yasin et al. (2023) highlight how corporate environmental and social sustainability efforts mediate the relationship between green HRM and employer branding, reinforcing the role of ESG in shaping job seekers' perceptions.

For Gen Z in particular, the appeal of ESG-aligned organisations extends beyond surface-level branding. Rzemieniak and Wawer (2021) assert that sustainable development initiatives play a crucial role in employer branding, influencing Gen Z's job search behaviour. Characterised by their digital proficiency, ethical awareness, and commitment to social justice, this generation seeks work that aligns with their personal values and contributes to meaningful societal impact (Gomes et al., 2023). In response to these generational shifts, organisations are compelled to adapt to remain competitive and attract top talent.

The Influential Effect of Environmental Responsibility

Gen Z is particularly attuned to environmental issues such as global warming and climate change, pollution, alternative energy sources and recycling, having grown up amidst climate activism and global environmental movements. They prioritise working for organisations committed to sustainability, favouring employers who actively reduce their carbon footprint, implement sustainable waste management and recycling, and invest in renewable energy. These factors are crucial in aligning with Gen Z's values and enhancing organisational attractiveness through "green employer branding" (Macalik & Sulich, 2019).

Empirical evidence suggests that Gen Z's environmental concerns directly influence their career decisions. A global study by Dell Technology (2018) found that Malaysian Gen Z respondents exhibited stronger preferences for environmentally responsible employers compared to their peers in other countries (e.g., United States, Canada, Brazil, Australia, and eight Asian countries), reflecting a heightened regional awareness of sustainability issues. Additionally, Deloitte's 2024 Gen Z and Millennial Survey found that many young professionals have either left or plan to leave jobs due to misalignment with their environmental values. When job hunting, Gen Z prioritises employers' environmental policies, emphasising the need for corporate environmental alignment to attract and retain talent (Deloitte, 2024). This reinforces the need for businesses to integrate sustainability not only into their operations but also into their employer branding efforts.

The hospitality industry provides a notable example of this trend. Goh and Okumus (2020) report that Gen Z job seekers favour hotels that implement sustainable practices such as reducing food waste and increasing social responsibility initiatives. This suggests that industries traditionally associated with high environmental impact must adopt proactive sustainability strategies to remain attractive to the next generation of workers.

The Influential Effect of Social Responsibility

Beyond environmental factors, Gen Z places significant importance on social issues in the workplace, seeking employers who actively promote diversity, equity, and inclusion (DEI) while engaging in community support and ethical labour practices (Leslie et al., 2021). ESG initiatives, which encompass diversity and inclusion efforts, offer human resource development practitioners a pivotal role as change agents in fostering socially responsible behaviours and transforming organisational culture (Cho et al., 2021). Addressing employee well-being and mental health support is equally essential, as emphasised by Deloitte (2024), reflecting Gen Z's expectation of a supportive and socially responsible workplace environment. These preferences highlight Gen Z's inclination to align their career choices with organisations demonstrating ethical leadership and a commitment to social responsibility.

Moreover, Gen Z's expectations of workplace diversity extend beyond traditional categories of race and gender to include identity, orientation, and broader social representation. Pandita (2022) highlights that financial gain is not the sole priority for Gen Z in their career development; they also value workplaces that prioritise community support and embody an innovative mindset, utilising creative approaches to achieve their goals. Insights from the 2024 Gen Z and Millennial survey by Deloitte highlight a significant trend: younger generations prioritise ESG factors as essential to the core purpose of business. Remarkably, 75% of respondents view an organisation's community engagement and societal impact as pivotal considerations when assessing potential employers. This generation perceives businesses as having the potential to tackle critical societal challenges, such as promoting equal pay, fostering transparency, creating inclusive job opportunities, and supporting educational initiatives (Deloitte, 2024). This paradigm shift underscores the importance for businesses to broaden their evaluation criteria beyond financial metrics, emphasising the long-term societal impact of their operations.

The Influential Effect of Corporate Governance

Corporate governance is another critical aspect of ESG that shapes Gen Z's job pursuit behaviour. Transparency, ethical leadership, and accountability are highly valued by this generation, with many prioritising employers that uphold strong governance standards (Mahapatra et al., 2022). They seek workplaces with clear and transparent corporate governance practices, ensuring that decision-making processes are accessible and understandable to all stakeholders. Furthermore, accountability in leadership and operations is essential, with Gen Z advocating for leaders who take responsibility for their actions and ensure that organisational practices align with ethical principles. As discovered by Chillakuri (2020), Gen Z values transparency and expects their leaders to be open in their dealings. They also desire organisations to have clear visions, values, and strategic objectives, along with providing flexible work arrangements, opportunities for career advancement, and growth.

Ethical business conduct and integrity are fundamental to Gen Z (Djafarova & Foots, 2022), who seek employers committed to upholding high standards of honesty and fairness in their operations. Strong anti-corruption measures are crucial, as Gen Z expects organisations to take proactive steps to combat unethical practices and maintain trust with stakeholders. This generation places a high value on ethical practices and transparency in the workplace. They actively research potential employers to ensure these standards are met, as evidenced by Nguyen Ngoc et al. (2022). They are strongly opposed to working for companies involved in environmental pollution or unethical labour practices, with many willing to leave such jobs immediately. Moreover, this generation is highly conscious of their ethical choices and seeks to avoid any association with unethical decisions. These governance factors reflect Gen Z's commitment to working in environments that prioritise ethical values and contribute to building trust and sustainability within the broader business community.

In sum, ESG principles are not merely corporate obligations but key determinants of employer attractiveness in the evolving job market. By aligning business strategies with Gen Z's expectations for environmental responsibility, social equity, and ethical governance, organisations can build sustainable, competitive employer brands that resonate with the next generation of talent.

Proposed Conceptual Framework

Based on the literature review, it is evident that integrating ESG principles into core strategies, significantly enhance an organisation's attractiveness to Gen Z talent. Gen Z prefers to work in environments that prioritise sustainability and transparency. Organisations that cultivate a culture of environmental stewardship and social accountability are viewed more favourably (Cho et al., 2021; Chillakuri, 2020; Macalik & Sulich, 2019). In light of this, it is recommended that organisations implement initiatives tackling environmental issues, establish mechanisms to support employee well-being and development, and adopt transparent and ethical decision-making processes. These aspects, often integrated into ESG strategies, make organisations perceived as supportive and caring more appealing to Gen Z.

Furthermore, as highlighted by Macalik and Sulich (2019) and Rzemieniak and Wawer (2021), public perception of an organisation's commitment to ESG values significantly influences Gen Z's trust and loyalty. Companies genuinely dedicated to ESG principles are more attractive to this generation. Therefore, organisations should build a brand image associated with sustainability and ethical behaviour, making them a likely employer of choice. This strategy is viable for attracting, recruiting, and retaining the youngest generational workforce.

Additionally, Gen Z seeks alignment between their personal values and the organisation's mission. According to Kuzior et al. (2022), Gen Z places high importance on values and self-fulfilment, with financial aspects playing a less significant role. They are more likely to be drawn to companies whose missions reflect their beliefs in environmental sustainability and social justice, such as company engagement in climate change, commitment to fighting hunger and social exclusion, and sustainable development. In other words, Gen Z seeks value congruence, and organisations that demonstrate commitment to these values attract talent who prioritise ESG principles in their career choices.

Given the unique characteristics of Gen Z and their role as the future workforce, a tailored recruiting strategy is essential for enhancing organisational attractiveness. This study integrates signalling theory and social identity theory to propose a theoretical model for attracting Gen Z talent. Based on a thorough literature review, it identifies ESG principles—environmental responsibility, social responsibility, and corporate governance—as effective components of a new recruitment strategy. Figure 1 presents the proposed model, which analyses the relationship between ESG principles and Gen Z's job pursuit intentions.

Figure 1. Proposed Conceptual Framework

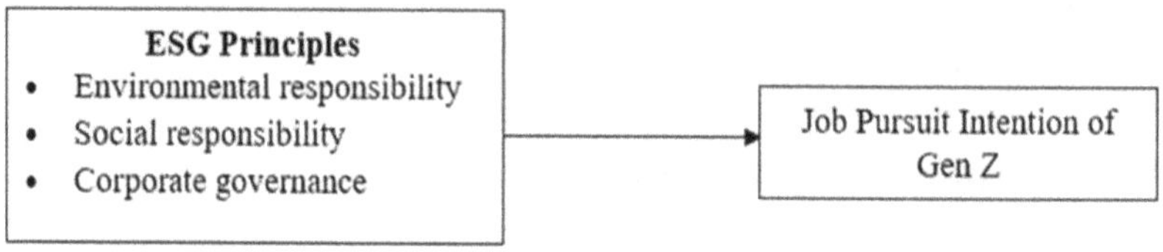

Signalling theory, as described by Connelly et al. (2011), highlights the interaction between parties who send and interpret signals over time. In the context of recruitment, organisations are the signallers with valuable but initially hidden information, communicated through signals to potential employees. ESG principles serve as potent signals of an organisation's commitment to sustainability and ethical behaviour. For Gen Z, who highly value transparency and corporate responsibility, these signals critically influence their perceptions and job pursuit intentions.

Additionally, social identity theory offers further theoretical support. This theory posits that individuals seek alignment with organisations that reflect their personal values and identity (Tajfel et al., 1982). Gen Z, prioritising environmental and social responsibility, are likely to feel a greater sense of alignment and belonging with organisations adhering to ESG principles, which in turn affects their job pursuit intentions.

By integrating signalling theory and social identity theory, this paper provides a comprehensive understanding of how ESG principles shape Gen Z's perceptions of organisational culture, reputation, and mission alignment, ultimately influencing their job pursuit intentions.

DISCUSSION OF IMPLICATIONS

The role of educators in shaping a workforce that prioritises sustainability and ethical business practices is paramount. To ensure that future professionals are well-versed in ESG principles, educational institutions must incorporate sustainability topics into business curricula. By integrating ESG considerations into coursework, students gain a comprehensive understanding of environmental stewardship, social responsibility, and ethical governance, preparing them to make informed career decisions. Moreover, equipping students with tools to assess an employer's ESG commitments is essential. This can be achieved through workshops, case studies, and practical training that familiarise students with ESG reporting and corporate sustainability strategies. Additionally, collaborations between academic institutions and industry partners can provide students with real-world exposure to ESG-driven workplace practices. Internship programs, guest lectures from sustainability professionals, and hands-on research projects can bridge the gap between theoretical learning and practical application, fostering a workforce that is both sustainability-conscious and business-savvy.

Furthermore, companies seeking to attract and retain Gen Z talent must integrate ESG principles into their corporate strategies. One effective approach is strengthening employer branding through ESG-driven initiatives. By publicly committing to sustainable business practices and ethical governance, organisations can enhance their reputation among job seekers who prioritise social responsibility. Transparency in sustainability reporting is another critical factor in engaging Gen Z workers. Companies should provide clear and verifiable data on their ESG performance, demonstrating their dedication to reducing carbon footprints, fostering inclusive workplaces, and upholding ethical standards.

Aligning corporate values with the expectations of Gen Z employees is also crucial for fostering engagement and long-term retention. Organisations should actively involve employees in sustainability initiatives, creating opportunities for them to contribute to meaningful projects that align with their values. Furthermore, implementing Green Human Resource Management (Green HRM) strategies can attract job seekers who prioritise environmental consciousness. Initiatives such as green office policies, sustainability training programs, and eco-friendly workplace incentives can make organisations more appealing to environmentally responsible candidates. Additionally, businesses should establish ESG-focused internships and talent development programs to embed sustainability into workplace culture. By offering hands-on experience in ESG initiatives, companies can nurture a workforce that is both skilled and aligned with their long-term sustainability goals.

Lastly, policymakers play a crucial role in fostering an ESG-driven labour market by creating regulations and incentives that encourage responsible corporate behaviour. One effective approach is to develop incentives that reward companies for adhering to ESG standards. Tax benefits, grants, and subsidies for businesses that implement sustainable practices can motivate organisations to prioritise ESG initiatives. In addition, establishing regulatory frameworks that mandate sustainability disclosures is essential for ensuring corporate transparency. By requiring businesses to report on their ESG performance, policymakers can hold organisations accountable for their environmental and social impact.

Another important step is the development of accreditation frameworks that recognise ESG-compliant organisations. Certification programs that assess a company's sustainability efforts can provide job seekers with a reliable benchmark for evaluating potential employers. Furthermore, promoting ESG literacy among employees through government-funded training programs can enhance workforce readiness for sustainability-driven roles. By integrating ESG topics into vocational training and professional development programs, policymakers can equip workers with the knowledge and skills needed to navigate an increasingly ESG-focused job market.

FUTURE DIRECTIONS

Future research should focus on conducting empirical studies that assess the long-term impact of ESG commitments on Gen Z's job search behaviours. While conceptual models provide valuable insights, empirical validation is necessary to determine the extent to which ESG factors influence job pursuit intentions. Longitudinal studies tracking Gen Z's career decision-making processes over time can offer deeper perspectives on how these values evolve with experience and exposure to different work environments.

Additionally, theoretical advancements are needed to integrate ESG considerations into broader work motivation and employer branding frameworks. Current research primarily examines ESG through the lenses of sustainability and ethics, but further exploration of its intersection with job satisfaction, organisational commitment, and psychological contract theory would be beneficial. Examining how ESG influences workplace engagement and productivity can expand our understanding of the role of sustainability in workforce dynamics.

Cross-sector analysis is another promising avenue for future research. The degree to which ESG impacts job pursuit intention may vary across industries, regions, and corporate structures. Comparing ESG-driven employer attractiveness in sectors such as technology, finance, healthcare, and hospitality can provide valuable insights into industry-specific sustainability expectations. Furthermore, exploring cultural differences in Gen Z's perception of ESG commitments across different countries can shed light on global workforce trends.

Practical research should also focus on assessing the effectiveness of corporate ESG initiatives in talent retention. Many organisations have implemented sustainability programs, but their impact on employee loyalty and job satisfaction remains underexplored. Understanding the link between ESG policies and workforce stability can guide companies in refining their sustainability strategies to maximise both environmental and human capital benefits.

Finally, policy-related research can explore the role of government regulations in shaping ESG practices and workforce expectations. Investigating how national policies influence corporate compliance and Gen Z's job preferences can inform policymakers on the best strategies for fostering ESG-driven economic growth. By examining government incentives and their effectiveness in promoting sustainable employment practices, researchers can contribute to a more comprehensive ESG framework that benefits both businesses and job seekers.

CONCLUSION

The growing influence of ESG principles on Gen Z's job search landscape presents both opportunities and challenges for employers, educators, and policy-makers. Organisations that proactively embed sustainability and ethical governance into their corporate culture stand to gain a competitive advantage in attracting and retaining young talent. Similarly, educational institutions must prepare students for a workforce that increasingly prioritises environmental and social responsibility. Policymakers, in turn, play a vital role in promoting ESG literacy and incentivising responsible business practices.

As ESG considerations continue to shape labour market trends, businesses that neglect these principles risk reputational damage and talent shortages. By embracing sustainability as a core business strategy, companies can align with the evolving expectations of the workforce while contributing to broader societal goals. Future research should deepen our understanding of these dynamics, ensuring that ESG remains at the forefront of workforce development strategies. Ultimately, fostering a workplace culture that values sustainability, transparency, and ethical governance will not only attract Gen Z employees but also drive long-term organisational success.

REFERENCES

Alves, I. R., Mesquita, E., Caneppele, N. R., & Martins, F. S. (2025). Beyond practicing: understanding the influence of ESG perceptions on employee retention. *Management Research*. Vol. ahead-of-print No. ahead-of-print. https://doi.org/DOI: 10.1108/MRJIAM-06-2024-1562

Baah, C., Opoku-Agyeman, D., Acquah, I. S. K., Agyabeng-Mensah, Y., Afum, E., Faibil, D., & Abdoulaye, F. A. M. (2021). Examining the correlations between stakeholder pressures, green production practices, firm reputation, environmental and financial performance: Evidence from manufacturing SMEs. *Sustainable Production and Consumption*, *27*, 100–114. DOI: 10.1016/j.spc.2020.10.015

Bayong, D., Bawuah, B., & Amoah, E. (2024). Advancing environmental, social, and governance disclosure in emerging economies: Does regulatory environment and ownership structure matter? *SN Business & Economics*, *5*(1), 11. DOI: 10.1007/s43546-024-00766-8

Chapman, D. S., Uggerslev, K. L., Carroll, S. A., Piasentin, K. A., & Jones, D. A. (2005). Applicant attraction to organizations and job choice: A meta-analytic review of the correlates of recruiting outcomes. *The Journal of Applied Psychology*, *90*(5), 928–944. DOI: 10.1037/0021-9010.90.5.928

Chillakuri, B. (2020). Understanding Generation Z expectations for effective onboarding. *Journal of Organizational Change Management*, *33*(7), 1277–1296. DOI: 10.1108/JOCM-02-2020-0058

Cho, Y., Kim, S., You, J., Moon, H., & Sung, H. (2021). Application of ESG measures for gender diversity and equality at the organizational level in a Korean context. *European Journal of Training and Development*, *45*(4/5), 346–365. DOI: 10.1108/EJTD-05-2020-0090

Coman, I. A., Yuan, S., & Tsai, J. Y. (2022). Toward an audience-centric framework of corporate social advocacy strategy: An exploratory study of young consumers from Generation Z. *Sustainability (Basel)*, *14*(7), 4099. DOI: 10.3390/su14074099

Connelly, B. L., Certo, S. T., Ireland, R. D., & Reutzel, C. R. (2011). Signaling theory: A review and assessment. *Journal of Management*, *37*(1), 39–67. DOI: 10.1177/0149206310388419

Dell Technology. (2018). Gen Z: The future has arrived. Retrieved from https://www.dell.com/en-us/dt/perspectives/gen-z.htm

Deloitte. (2024). 2024 Gen Z and Millennial Survey, Living and working with purpose in a transforming world. https://www.deloitte.com/global/en/issues/work/content/genz-millennialsurvey.html

Djafarova, E., & Foots, S. (2022). Exploring ethical consumption of generation Z: Theory of planned behaviour. *Young Consumers*, *23*(3), 413–431. DOI: 10.1108/YC-10-2021-1405

Eccles, R. G., & Klimenko, S. (2019). The investor revolution: Shareholders are getting serious about sustainability. *Harvard Business Review*. https://hbr.org/2019/05/the-investor-revolution

Eccles, R. G., Lee, L.-E., & Stroehle, J. C. (2019). The Social Origins of ESG: An Analysis of Innovest and KLD. *Organization & Environment*, *33*(4), 575–596. DOI: 10.1177/1086026619888994

Edelman (2022). *Edelman Trust Barometer 2022 – Global Report*. https://www.edelman.com/sites/g/files/aatuss191/files/2022-01/2022%20Edelman%20Trust%20Barometer%20FINAL_Jan25.pdf

Gabrielova, K., & Buchko, A. A. (2021). Here comes Generation Z: Millennials as managers. *Business Horizons*, *64*(4), 489–499. DOI: 10.1016/j.bushor.2021.02.013

Goh, E., & Okumus, F. (2020). Avoiding the hospitality workforce bubble: Strategies to attract and retain generation Z talent in the hospitality workforce. *Tourism Management Perspectives*, *33*, 100603. DOI: 10.1016/j.tmp.2019.100603

Gomes, S., Lopes, J. M., & Nogueira, S. (2023). Willingness to pay more for green products: A critical challenge for Gen Z. *Journal of Cleaner Production*, *390*, 136092. DOI: 10.1016/j.jclepro.2023.136092

Gornostaeva, Z. V., & Chernysheva, Y. S. (2023). Improving the quality of corporate governance with reliance on ESG-based HR management. In *Smart Green Innovations in Industry 4.0: New Opportunities for Climate Change Risk Management in the "Decade of Action"* (pp. 247-255). Cham: Springer Nature Switzerland. https://doi.org/DOI: 10.1007/978-3-031-45830-9_28

Kuzior, A., Kettler, K., & Rąb, Ł. (2022). Great resignation—Ethical, cultural, relational, and personal dimensions of generation Y and Z employees' engagement. *Sustainability (Basel)*, *14*(11), 6764. DOI: 10.3390/su14116764

Leslie, B., Anderson, C., Bickham, C., Horman, J., Overly, A., Gentry, C., Callahan, C., & King, J. (2021). Generation Z perceptions of a positive workplace environment. *Employee Responsibilities and Rights Journal*, *33*(3), 171–187. DOI: 10.1007/s10672-021-09366-2

Macalik, J., & Sulich, A. (2019, May). External employer branding of sustainable organizations. In *International Scientific Conference Contemporary Issues in Business, Management and Economics Engineering*, 239-250. https://doi.org/DOI: 10.3846/cibmee.2019.054

Mahapatra, G. P., Bhullar, N., & Gupta, P. (2022). Gen Z: An emerging phenomenon. *NHRD Network Journal, 15*(2), 246–256. DOI: 10.1177/26314541221077137

Nguyen Ngoc, T., Viet Dung, M., Rowley, C., & Pejić Bach, M. (2022). Generation Z job seekers' expectations and their job pursuit intention: Evidence from transition and emerging economy. *International Journal of Engineering Business Management, 14*, 1–13. DOI: 10.1177/18479790221112548

Pandita, D. (2022). Innovation in talent management practices: Creating an innovative employer branding strategy to attract generation Z. *International Journal of Innovation Science, 14*(3/4), 556–569. DOI: 10.1108/IJIS-10-2020-0217

Popaitoon, P. (2022). Fostering work meaningfulness for sustainable human resources: A study of generation Z. *Sustainability (Basel), 14*(6), 3626. DOI: 10.3390/su14063626

Rzemieniak, M., & Wawer, M. (2021). Employer branding in the context of the company's sustainable development strategy from the perspective of gender diversity of generation Z. *Sustainability (Basel), 13*(2), 828. DOI: 10.3390/su13020828

Schroth, H. (2019). Are you ready for Gen Z in the workplace? *California Management Review, 61*(3), 5–18. DOI: 10.1177/0008125619841006

Singh, K., Abraham, R., Yadav, J., Agrawal, A. K., & Kolar, P. (2023). Linking CSR and organizational performance: The intervening role of sustainability risk management and organizational reputation. *Social Responsibility Journal, 19*(10), 1830–1851. DOI: 10.1108/SRJ-07-2022-0309

Smith, M. (2023, October 31). 50% of Gen Z wants to ditch corporate jobs and run their own businesses, according to new research. *CNBC*. https://www.cnbc.com/2023/10/31/50percent-of-gen-z-wants-to-ditch-corporate-jobs-run-their-own-business-says-report.html

Tajfel, H., Turner, J. C., & Austin, W. G. (1982). Social psychology of intergroup relations. *Annual Review of Psychology, 33*(1), 1–39. DOI: 10.1146/annurev.ps.33.020182.000245

United Nations Global Compact. (2021). Principles for Responsible Investment. https://www.unpri.org/download?ac=10948

Waples, C. J., & Brachle, B. J. (2020). Recruiting millennials: Exploring the impact of CSR involvement and pay signaling on organizational attractiveness. *Corporate Social Responsibility and Environmental Management*, *27*(2), 870–880. DOI: 10.1002/csr.1851

Yasin, R., Huseynova, A., & Atif, M. (2023). Green human resource management, a gateway to employer branding: Mediating role of corporate environmental sustainability and corporate social sustainability. *Corporate Social Responsibility and Environmental Management*, *30*(1), 369–383. DOI: 10.1002/csr.2360

Zhang, T., Zhang, J., & Tu, S. (2024). An empirical study on corporate ESG behavior and employee satisfaction: A moderating mediation model. *Behavioral Sciences (Basel, Switzerland)*, *14*(4), 274. DOI: 10.3390/bs14040274

Chapter 5
Heritage and Culture: Conservation in the Age of Cosmopolitanism – A Case of Kampong Ayer (Brunei Darussalam)

Izni Azrein Noor Azalie
https://orcid.org/0000-0003-0616-3241
Universiti Brunei Darussalam, Brunei

ABSTRACT

This chapter explores the intricate relationship between culture, heritage, and globalization in Brunei Darussalam, with a specific focus on Kampong Ayer (KA), a historically significant water village. The analysis highlights the cultural and economic challenges faced by KA, rooted in its past as the epicenter of trade and the Bruneian Sultanate, which has been undermined by modernization and globalization since the 1960s.. While recent heritage tourism efforts have been made, challenges such as poverty and poor infrastructure remain obstacles to sustainable development. By referencing the Sustainable Development Goals (SDGs), particularly SDGs 1, 8, 11, and 12, the chapter highlights how cultural heritage can guide urban revitalization. Using concepts such as cosmopolitanism, sense of place, placemaking, and place branding as part of developing the culture and heritage industry, it advocates for a comprehensive approach to preserving cultural identity while promoting local economic growth and community well-being, providing actionable strategies for policymakers and urban planners.

DOI: 10.4018/979-8-3373-0603-2.ch005

INTRODUCTION

Being a country, whose history saw the rise and slow decline of a Bornean Malay Sultanate (circa the 1400s) tainted with European colonialism and Japanese occupation between the 19th and 20th centuries, Brunei Darussalam as a nation-state is known to be a crucible of diverse cultures and ethnic groups resulting from such historical phenomenon. The late independence granted to the country in 1984 from the British Empire not only helped the nation retain some of its traditional and conservative values but also indirectly assisted in sustaining the culture and heritage of the diverse groups. Despite such development, however, the forces of modernization in the 1960s (Bakar, 2018) and globalization from the late 90s onwards have slowly eroded these culture and heritage tapestry, putting pressure on the need to preserve and conserve whichever remains. Hence, the turn towards developing culture and heritage-based industries became paramount, which became more critical with the declaration of the Brunei Vision 2035 in 2007.

Using Kampong Ayer (KA) as the case study, the rationale for its focus is its historical importance in the Bruneian Empire, the center for trade and commerce, and the seat of the Sultanate. Due to this, the Europeans historically referred to the water village as the 'Venice of the East'. This is apart from the uniqueness of the water village itself, which historically was divided into wards specializing in different production activities within the traditional economy, from metal smithing (gold, silver, and brass), fishing, and shipbuilding to woven textile production (Azalie and Yong, 2022). Kampong Ayer, at present, is a shadow of its past glory, and due to its cultural significance in the memoryscapes of Bruneians, there have been attempts to revive and revitalize the area spanning 10 square kilometers through the development of culture and heritage industry as part of heritage tourism. However, issues and challenges that require addressing, such as poverty, persistent low-altitude economic activities, and infrastructural-related problems, continue to plague its development potential. Apart from the socioeconomic challenges, both tangible and intangible cultural traits relating to the Brunei Malays, their identities, i.e., what they best signify and how it is shaped and reflected in the urban landscapes of present KA, require in-depth scrutiny to make sense of their preservability or "conceivability." This is crucial to help relevant players and agencies strategize and develop a sustainable development policy that benefits the community.

Hence, this chapter will provide insights into sustainable culture-heritage-globalization dynamics based on current national research compared to those beyond the national boundary. It will also explore the direction in which this discipline area is taking shape based on the current trajectory that has moved beyond mere glocalization but also cosmopolitan. These owe to the world's emerging realities where citizens are becoming more aware, and societies are becoming more 'woke', with grassroots activities gaining traction. In the long run, how this will affect culture and heritage will be very much of interest due to the complex dynamism and relationship between individuals, communities and the environment they are living in. The declaration of the Sustainable Development Goals (SDGs) in 2017 and the diverse SDG components will also be used to reposition current strategies of culture and heritage development in Kampong Ayer by linking them to these components. The SDG identified thus far is related to SDG 1 (no poverty), SDG 8 (decent work and economic growth), SDG 11 (sustainable cities and communities), and SDG 12 (responsible consumption and production). The end of the chapter will also provide the readers with potential strategies on how culture and heritage development can be used as part of the urban revitalization and redevelopment agenda. This is crucial for urban planners, policymakers, and industrial players to stimulate and enable local development to benefit the local communities and the country.

GLOBALIZATION, COSMOPOLITANISM, PLACE AND IDENTITY: A CONCEPTUAL OVERVIEW

This chapter will address this development from the lens of cosmopolitism, also known as globalization from within, and propose some new ways in which culture and conservation can become the source of economic growth. The chapter starts by contextualizing cultural, heritage, and creative development from a global perspective, rationalizing why culture and heritage industrial development were necessary, and dismantling the existing academic theories or approaches towards culture and heritage economy development. This involves reviews of the work by cultural and economic geographers such as Allen Scott (2004, 2010) and pioneer works by Richard Florida (2003) on creative cities and theories on globalization. Globalization, both as a process and a disciplinary study, has been very transformative, particularly in the sociocultural, political, and economic realms, since its inception in the mid-1990s. Debates surrounding whether it resulted in new cultural hegemony leading to the homogenization of culture or its hybridization potentials leading to the heterogenization of cultures seem to show no signs of abatement. Instead, the processes of globalization have become so complex, multifaceted, and multidimensional that they affect national culture and heritage in diverse forms, raising new questions over its preservation and conservation potentials in tandem with or in contrast to new economic development. The changes brought about by technologies, particularly with Industrial Revolution 4.0 (IR 4) via smartphones, the expansion of global production networks (GPN) in cultural products production, the proliferation of new chic and hipster cultures as in the case of specialty coffee café culture and the urban revitalization potentials brought along with it, provides new dimension as well as challenges when addressed through the lens of sustainable development.

GLOBALIZATION AND COSMOPOLITANISM: TWO FACES OF THE SAME COIN

The discourse on globalisation reveals two primary perspectives on its relationship with nation-states. Scholars like Vásquez and Marquand (2000) categorize views into two camps: homogenizers, who argue that globalisation promotes uniformity, and heterogenisers, who maintain that globalisation enhances local identities by providing new avenues for cultural expression. Hannigan (2002) further explores this by suggesting that globalisation acts as a de-territorialising force, promoting cultural diversity through the blending of various flows—cultural, economic, and political. He emphasizes the emergence of transnational and hybrid identities within ethnoscapes.

Tomlinson (2003) expands on this by asserting that globalisation fosters rather than undermines national identities. He posits that it creates a new dynamism in nation-states, allowing for the reorientation of cultural identities. This adaptation enables localities to retain their essence while integrating new global developments. He also highlights the role of state institutions, such as law, education, and media, in constructing and maintaining national identity, coining the terms "empowerment" and "negotiated identities" to describe this process. This perspective informs research on Brunei's response to globalisation, mainly focusing on the significant influence of His Majesty in navigating these changes.

Understanding identity requires a broader lens beyond traditional nationalism, considering it as a cultural project. Paasi (2001) argues that regions are social constructs shaped by political, economic, and cultural discourses, which can wield power in governance and societal structures. Similarly, Anthias (2001) views culture as both a product and a process influencing the formation of national identity. The creation of national identity is rooted in societal symbols and practices, self-perception versus otherness, and the institutionalisation of a shared identity using state apparatuses. The emotions of nationhood, belonging, and patriotism arise from dynamic social relations and interactions within specific spaces, constantly evolving due to influences like globalisation, which renders these identities less stable and more fluid.

Hence, how important is cosmopolitanism for cultural heritage preservation and development? The binaries or intellectual discourse between globalization and localization stems from portraying the Self and Other as different, mutually diverging from one another and, therefore, highly repellent. Although this nexus results from Western imperialism's line of thought, the perception of the other and the rise of post-colonial writings used the global platforms as spaces of resistance, promotion, and empowerment by bringing forth the local into the international. In the recently edited volume on rooted cosmopolitanism in archaeological and anthropological research, Kruijer et al. (2024) have tried to unravel the nuances and multidimensionality of cosmopolitanism in heritage research. Other scholars such as Gaikwad et al (2024) reverse engineer the perspective of potential migrant workers by immersing them in training program as part of elevating their cosmopolitan outlook. Embracing vernacular cosmopolitanism (Knight, 2024) that supports cultural acceptance and openness in the age of right-wing governments is essential for any project to be successful. At times, there is also the need to exercise caution, especially in the politicization of the cosmopolitanist worldview, as evident from the study Wyer (2024) on the cosmopolitan rhetoric of Palermo. It highlighted the need to utilize the non-distorted, grounded historlcal and present knowledge of urban communities to foster such an open outlook.

Despite the extensive coverage, however, geographical concepts of place, its associated senses, and identities linked to heritage remained elusive. As will be discussed in the latter subsections, this diverse conceptualization of place senses and its convergence with cosmopolitanism and heritage conservation is hoped to create new pathways in conservation research. This includes the reinvention of a heritage industry's development strategies that address sustainability dimensions rooted in the places in which it operates. It also utilizes the positive global-regional externalities through localized constructed advantages (Cooke and Leydesdorff, 2006), borrowing the term from innovative industry to be applied to a newly consolidated place-anchored heritage and conservation industry. Through such development, further enrichment and empowerment of the communities is expected to materialize, leading to the emergence of competitive social enterprises.

SENSE OF PLACE AND PLACE-MAKING: BETWEEN EMOTIONAL ATTACHMENTS, CULTURAL ROOTEDNESS, AND A GENUS LOCI

To date, this chapter has examined the conceptual debates surrounding globalization, a term that appears increasingly outdated in academic discourse but still represents an ongoing process that shows no signs of diminishing. The rising prominence of cosmopolitanism, which highlights the celebration of local identities in the face of global influences, has served as a catalyst for multi-scalar research. In light of this development, it is pertinent to investigate how cosmopolitanism impacts the fields of place-based and landscape studies and explore the emerging synergistic relationship between these geographical disciplines in shaping innovative pathways in geography.

The notion of the locale as an embodiment and reflection of local communal culture, a crucible where the human-environment relationship can be traced or identified, has been at the core of cultural geography, particularly in landscape studies. Owing to the pioneering work of Carl Sauer (1959) on the Morphology of Landscape, he successfully addressed the geographical potentials of cultural landscape studies by transforming cultural landscapes into cultural artifacts. The locale, according to Sauer (1959) and his predecessors, such as Duncan and Levy (2013), not only allows for the reading of the landscape as a text and metaphor, but it also contains elements of it being representational of the people or communities that live and interact with it daily. According to them, derivative meanings can be acquired by understanding how humans, individuals, or even communities perceive and relate to their living environment, leading to environmental possibilism rather than environmental determinism. Hence, landscape should be approached as a collection of experiences that can be defined and interpreted (Thwaites and Simkins, 2006) that have symbols, signs, and meanings, living discourses that are constantly created and recreated and affected by spatial-temporal law (Hubbard, 2017). Hence, what role does a place then play in these cultural landscapes?

While an in-depth exploration of the literature surrounding the concept of place within landscape studies is valuable, it remains incomplete. Addressing all related dimensions is beyond the scope of this chapter. Moreover, landscape studies have significantly evolved since Saur's time, incorporating diverse perspectives and, at times, becoming more interdisciplinary. This evolution signifies a transition from merely interpreting and defining meanings in reflected landscapes to engaging with cultural shifts in cultural studies, regardless of whether they acknowledge existing structures. Additionally, development in this field now emphasizes the existence of multiple realities more than a singular, universal one. Going beyond the nomenclature hypothesis (Thompson, 2009) where interpretation of a defining feature based on shared categorical traits of other similar feature, it requires humanist or cultural geographers to approach such realities from within communities, utilizing a much more insider's approach rather than looking at things from a bird's eye point of view. Part of the reason stems from the fact that signals emanating from the research subject often are misinterpreted or mispresented in the academic discourse, skewing the real intended meanings in favor of presumptive ones. For instance, this notion of reading the landscape as a text allows researchers and scholars to define and describe the phenomenon as it unfolds. However, the meanings attached to it can only be extracted and explained by connecting deeply with those who are part of those events. Therefore, revisiting the works of Mitchell (2000), Agnew (2011), and Tuan (1979, 1991) will offer insights into the place-based concepts that connect the trinity of place, culture, and heritage with the forces of globalization, extending beyond the historical frameworks of communities as proposed in Anderson's (2022) Imagined Communities, which incorporates a geographical perspective on communities at its core.

According to Tuan (1979), places are not only comprised of a locale with known physical characteristics, but they also contain spirits and personalities that make them stand out in contrast to other places, invoking the question "Why this place but not that place?". Communities altered where they dwell and left traces or imprints, which often led to the personalization of these places and created meaning. History, communities, and their language create narratives of these spaces (Tuan, 1991), giving rise to what is later called a sense of place, a genius loci. Often, some of these places eventually turned into religious sanctuaries, as places of ancestral worship or essentially labelled as sacrilegious, resulting in different forms of senses that are only sensible from these communities' perspectives (Kinnard, 2014). Tuan's (2017) summary study on historical geography of China, how our world's and our perspectives of our landscape, community are results of the composing of the worlds, through the use of language, cultural artefacts and memories as a tool, despite facing cosmic changes in the face of globalization, imbued with it either the constructive forces of hybridization or one that erased or 'cancelled' via homogenous hegemons. Since places and their senses are temporal, how shall such places, their senses, and identities be maintained or portrayed? Such a question is imperative as place, within the culture and heritage industry, when linked with other sectors such as tourism, needs to address such genius loci, often traditional or historical, for positive reiteration of its importance and uniqueness.

According to Massey (1995), there is a need to bridge such dislocations between the past and the present of a place. A symbolic return to the past, according to Tilley (2006), is a reflection of the uncertainties that the present holds, as a means of cultural escapism for fear of addressing or facing the challenges brought about by spatial cultural inflows, often different from the localized space. Due to this contestation, any culture associated with such places should be treated as plural rather than singular (Mitchell, 2002). Whilst culture is often treated as territorial and trans-local in its evolutionary learning processes (Pieterse, 2009), our sensescapes and attachments to these places should also consider incorporating all human experiential senses beyond words and images (Bunkše, 2012). To be able to construct such positive experiences, linking the concepts of place-branding, place-making, and consumption theory is essential as the act of transmitting and sensitizing spirits of these places are none other than an act of consuming life, a term coined by Baumann with regards to the rise of high expression and taste-related industries (Childress et al, 2021).

CULTURE AND HERITAGE DEVELOPMENT FROM A CONSUMPTION PERSPECTIVE

When discussing consumption and its contribution towards the development of cultural industry, the works by Bourdieu (1990), Veblen (1899) (cited in Trigg, 2000), and Appadurai (1988) served as the classic example of cultural commodification. Whilst Veblen (1899) argued that the changing lifestyle of the upper working and middle class resulted from income surpluses leading to the change in cultural consumption patterns, particularly relating to higher-end products, Appadurai (1988) argued on the existence of the social in every cultural product that embodies cultural meanings and close relationships with human. Such social things often exist to serve a particular utilitarian function, with Bourdieu (1990) highlighting this as a symbolic value. These sociocultural traits exist in products deemed to be of specific community and heritage importance, and for it to be elevated to a heritage status, it needs to fulfill specific requirements before being classified into tangible, intangible, or living heritage.

The relationship between consumption, an individual's class associations, attachments, and division of social standings is best explained using Pierre Bourdieu's idea of habitus and cultural capital (Bourdieu, 1990; 2000). Regarding cultural products such as food intake, Bourdieu's definition of Habitus is more complex since multiple variables affect an individual's consumption. Individuals' preferences, social, cultural, political, and educational influences, gender influence, and rental influence can all determine food and beverage choices (Woodhall-Melnik & Matheson, 2017). Overall, one significant factor that affects a decision is the value put on the product and service by the customers themselves, which illustrates how people's consumption preferences shape their identity and lifestyle, representing how they behave in the world. As a result, consumers who bestow product value signify a product's standard while also creating a social framework through consumption because consumers identify themselves through the goods and purchases (Rojas-Rivas et al., 2019). Hence, culture commodification involves turning the aspects of culture into products.

Understanding cultural and economic resources concerning Habitus is essential. Cultural capital pertains to a consumer's level of education, while financial capital relates to their income (Skuland, 2015). Both are significant in shaping Habitus, as they influence a consumer's access to and consumption preferences. When it comes to food consumption, the taste of the product is also a crucial factor. Warner et al. (1985) differentiates between two taste types: luxury and necessity. The dominant class values the former, while the latter resonates with the lower class, who prioritize affordability and comfort. Similarly, when commodifying a place's culture and heritage, the industry should also consider who the target market is, the rationale behind the choice of targeting such a group, and what benefit can be achieved through such activities. A clear direction, marked by readily available social, economic, and cultural capital, is, hence, necessary to develop a new cultural economy. Capitalism capitalises on this cultural capital, which is both tangible and intangible, tacit and codified knowledge, by including it as part of the production of both material and immaterial goods through human creativity and intellectual activity (Santagata, 2002). Cultural commodification is linked closely with cultural consumption. Market decentralisation allows for further flexibility and the production of specialised products.

Such development posits an alternative towards enhancing urban development through commodifying cultural products and understanding consumers' current consumption patterns within the domestic market and beyond. Such development in tourism and hospitality services-related activities would benefit other hard industries such as manufacturing as new innovative products are required to 'enrich' and create meaningful experiences for cultural consumers such as tourists. Hence, as part of adapting to this new market dynamics, there is a need to revisit the concepts of place-making, place-branding, and place-marketing to understand their utility as the locale, which includes its unique characteristics, is now marketed or exported beyond its borders for the consumption of others.

Markussen (2006) argues that export base theory, which suggests that regional growth is driven by external sales of locally produced goods and services, is a prevailing principle in economic development practice. However, she acknowledges that the consumption base can also act as a catalyst for growth. Local investments may encourage residents to shift their spending towards local purchases, attract new and mobile residents and tourists, and revitalize aging urban centers. A consumption-based approach is not merely about import substitution; instead, it aims to meet latent demand and diversify the range of goods and services available in the local market. Markussen emphasizes the importance of investing in the performing arts and other traditional cultural sectors, noting that such investments can significantly benefit a city's economy, promoting growth from within rather than relying solely on external sources. With the development of the creative and cultural industries, there are more opportunities for job creation and income generation. These labor-intensive cultural sectors and their beneficiaries tend to spend their earnings locally. Furthermore, cultural industries are positioned to articulate their human capital and creativity needs, which could attract public investment similar to what high-tech industries have achieved in securing resources for science and engineering research.

According to Light (2014), commodifying place names or toponyms allows for the potential of reinvigorating the economy and the spirit of the place via tourism. Appropriation of place names and their commodification may, at times, help promote the place as part of a tourist destination; the production of replicas and souvenirs associated with the place denotes its position as an essential cultural marker. However, some of this approach's drawbacks stemmed from the contestation emerging from these places. Some cultural and heritage sites often mute the traditional history of these places due to the historical violence involving place-taking usually associated with colonial histories (Johnson and Oakley, 2013). At times, contestation emerges from different religious attachments (Hui et al., 2008) or commodification of places that downplay local ancestral connections to these sites (Nugraheni et al., 2023; Kinnard, 2014; Bremer, 2006), leading to irk community gazes and distrust that can affect the popularity of such places, stifling further economic growth potentials.

CURRENT APPROACHES TOWARDS HERITAGE PRESERVATION AND CONSERVATION IN SOUTHEAST ASIA AND THE NOTION OF GROWTH

Post Second World War (WWII) Southeast Asia marked a diverging development in the context of nation-building and decolonization. The West experienced renewed interest in their search for national identities, marked by the loss of the empires, destruction of pre-war architecture, monuments, buildings, and technology, and rebuilding via preserving and conserving whichever remains were crucial for posterity purposes. In the East, on the other, the creation of new identities after independence from their colonial masters towards nationhood and nation-building, as a form of creating a sense of belongingness, identities, shared political, collective future, and rights towards self-determination became the key focus of conservation and preservation. Maintaining political stability and the need to increase confidence-building measures are at the core of national prosperity and posterity. This explains why economic growth aspirations were embodied into national policies due to their stabilizing effect.

Most ASEAN Member States (AMS) are signatories to UNESCO's tangible and intangible cultures conventions regarding heritage preservation and conservation. Southeast Asia, before the coming of the Europeans, was the crucible of diverse civilizations that linked Europe and Asia (West, Central, South, and East) via the old Mainland and the Maritime Silk Route (MSR). Due to such blending, the culture and heritage characteristics took hybridized forms, making them contextually unique based on each locality. While the tangible aspects of heritage, such as architecture, buildings and monuments can be seen to co-exist in the rapidly urbanized megacities of the region, the intangible heritage, such as oral traditions, performing arts, social practices and rituals, Indigenous knowledge, and traditional craftsmanship, to name a few require a more careful treading to ensure its sustainability and cultural survival (Ruggles and Silverman, 2009).

In Southeast Asia, the growth of the culture and heritage industry linked to tourism activities has gained more traction due to the development of hospitality and other service-related industries, as well as the rise in consumerism in tourist-sending countries such as China and India. At the regional level, initiatives led by ASEAN, under the ASEAN Socio-Cultural Community pillar of the ASEAN Economic Community, such as the yearly appointments of ASEAN City of Culture as part of the Visit ASEAN tourism initiatives, also help strengthen preservation and conservation efforts. The increase in ecological awareness though highly contested within the tourism industry owing to prominent non-governmental organizations (NGOs) such as the Worldwide Foundation (WWF), the Greenpeace movement, and local NGOs also plays a particular role in expanding conservation efforts.

Despite the success of establishing or conserving some national sites into World Heritage Sites, the long-term problems of such conventions have never been discussed in depth. The challenges associated with the museumification of historical sites, buildings, and villages that lead to subservient culture (Camprag, 2017; Dellios, 2002), and the issues about existing owners or landlords' inability to revitalize such sites for present generational economic use (Ertan and Egerrcioglu, 2016), the alteration of the deathscapes such as diasporic cemetery of a particular ethnic group for modernity as in the case of the Bukit Brown Cemetery in Singapore (Tan and Yeo, 2023), hence, need to be addressed from the perspectives of the local. For some, the rapid growth in cultural tourism exposed sites such as the Angkor Wat Complex in Cambodia to newer threats such as human vandalism and sociocultural and environmental disturbances resulting from a lack of infrastructure and the inability to establish adequate surveillance and monitoring infrastructures (Chatterjee, 2021). Conventions, whilst useful, are not neutral from power politics and often serve as a space of subjugation of the needs and wants of those governed in favor of those of the standard-setters (Ponte and Gibbon, 2016). As Southeast Asia is slated to be the 4th largest regional economic bloc by 2050, the rapid ascension of some of its Third World cities into developed megacities would undoubtedly see the rise in contestations and conflict between nation-states and global convention governors. For Brunei, the rapid urbanization within the old city center of Bandar Seri Begawan (BSB) has affected much of the traditional historical sites. It begs the question on the current conservation status of Kampong Ayer in the face of these external forces and the economic potentials that it brings once KA communities connected with these global regional networks.

THE CASE STUDY ON KAMPONG AYER HERITAGE: BETWEEN PRESERVATION, CONSERVATION, AND COSMOPOLITANISM

The institutionalization of cultural heritage and its preservation has been examined in greater detail in a prior study (see Azalie and Yong, 2022). This study highlights the paradoxical roles of the British, who acted both as colonial superpowers and as guardians of Brunei's culture and heritage. They established significant cultural institutions and exhibits, such as the Brunei Museums and the Arts and Handicrafts Centre, which serve as vital nodes for knowledge and preservation. There had been attempts to restore and revive the vibrancy of the traditional KA communities through modernization, particularly from the 1960s onwards. However, as will be discussed in greater length in the next few subsections, it is evident that current 'preservation' efforts require a renewed approach should cultural heritage is to be conserved and served as the key commodity towards a new culture and heritage economy. The challenges brought about by globalization and opportunities by adapting to a more cosmopolitan outlook highlighted the multiple pathways in which cultural heritage conservation is to be made plausible.

a) Conservation, Housing, and Malay Cosmology

Previous scholarly works by McGarrigle (1994), Jones (1997), and Azman Ahmad (2013) have examined the conservation challenges and issues faced by Kampong Ayer from the early 1990s to the early 2000s. In particular, McGarrigle (1994) and Jones (1997) noted that the modernization of housing in Kampong Ayer has resulted in a decline in the aesthetic value of traditional architecture, a loss of local ambiance, and the onset of environmental degradation. The adoption of modern construction materials, shifting communal consumption patterns, and ineffective government planning have significantly impeded meaningful conservation efforts, as economic growth has been prioritized over preservation (Jones,1997). Detailed studies by local scholars such as Bakar (2018) and Mail (2018) have highlighted the linkages between national welfare policy and its effects on housing and the livelihood of communities of Kampong Ayer as modernization took hold. Hassan (2023), on the other hand, emphasizes how financial liberalization resulting from modernization and employment in Brunei altered citizens' perceptions and preferences toward homeownership value. While Bakar (2018) and Mail (2018) highlighted the rationale of modernization as part of delivering national aims and objectives, not much was mentioned concerning its effects on culture and heritage. Jones (1997) and McGarrigle (1994), on the other, primarily address the decline of traditional housing styles from the 1960s and 1970s—especially following the implementation of the resettlement programs both on land and water as seen from the Kampong Bunut and Lambak Kanan land-based resettlement and the Kampong Bolkiah resettlement scheme on water to name a few—it is critical to reconsider whether the 'traditional' architecture they reference accurately represents Kampong Ayer's authentic architectural identity. Like many historical urban centers, Kampong Ayer has been affected by various external influences, including its prominence as a regional trade hub in the 15th century, the gradual decline of the Sultanate associated with civil conflict, the impacts of colonialism, and the wave of modernization that followed the Second World War. These external forces have undoubtedly left distinct imprints on Kampong Ayer's cultural landscape, resulting in modifications to its physical materials and forms while still preserving the essence of its architectural design and layout.

This essence is often tied to the tacit or indigeneity of knowledge regarding the use of living spaces, where the arrangement of rooms, housing structures, and the orientation of buildings reflect Brunei Malay cosmology. Earlier studies by Hassan et al. (2011) and Hassan (2023) pointed out the existence of such cosmology when studying the Bruneian's approach toward vertical living and their use of space based on functionalities and justifications over their preferences. For instance, one must observe traditional conventions or convenance concerning house design and architecture. The researcher's personal experiences of growing up within the Brunei Malay community show the centrality of these practices. For example, the positioning of house roofs, particularly of the edge where the rainwater falls, should not be placed in front of the house's main entrance. This was enacted to avoid any dwellers or visitors from being exposed to the raindrops. Other conventions such as inserting gold jewelries or nuggets into the main stilts or columns of a soon to be built dwelling, the need to avoid the start of house buildings based on traditional Malay cosmology calendar marked with pictograms or words such as snakes, poison and the likes associated with ill omen and the need to avoid positioning doors to rooms precisely opposite of the other are just some of the traditional conventions which gradually become obsolete or are no longer being practiced.

As for building materials, imposing preservation mandates on traditional houses or reverting to historically utilized materials can be considered anti-development and unsustainable. Such measures may infringe upon the rights of communities to exercise self-determination and undermine their ability to live with dignity for future generations. Interestingly, the resettlement of both partial and whole communities to the land, as seen in the case of partial or different communities of Kampong Ayer resettled in Lambak Kanan, coming from various wards of KA or the whole communities of KA's Burong Pingai Ayer residence to the land-based Kampong Burong Pingai, for instance, have altered the socio-cultural dynamics and cultural landscape of these communities particularly concerning their sense of place and its subsequent effects towards place-branding or place-making which will be discussed.

b) Tourism Development and Heritage

Ahmad (2013), on the other hand, expanded further on the problems and challenges associated with developing tourism in Kampong Ayer as part of the new service economy. Environmental challenges posed by indiscriminate urban waste disposal into the Brunei River catchment from non-point origin, fire hazards, loss of authenticity, and lack of activities and services related to tourism were the profound features of his research finding. In a recent work by Amalina and Hussin (2022) on the touristication of KA, their findings found limited community involvement towards tourism development in KA despite the existence of collaboration between some Village Consultative Councils (MPK), the Brunei Tourism Board (BTB), under Ministry off Primary Resources and Tourism (MPRT) and private travel agents and firms in 2017. A visit to the Brunei tourism webpage found the existence of twenty-two travel guides, of which three were linked to the KA with a focus on Bandar Seri Begawan and the Kampong Ayer trail, Kampong Ayer Walking Trail, and Brunei River Heritage Trail. The latter two will be discussed in the following paragraphs. As for homestay, there are few currently in operation within KA, with one able to obtain recognition at the ASEAN level for meeting ASEAN's guidelines on homestay establishment and operations (Adli and Chin, 2021).

Figure 1. Kampong Ayer Walking Trail

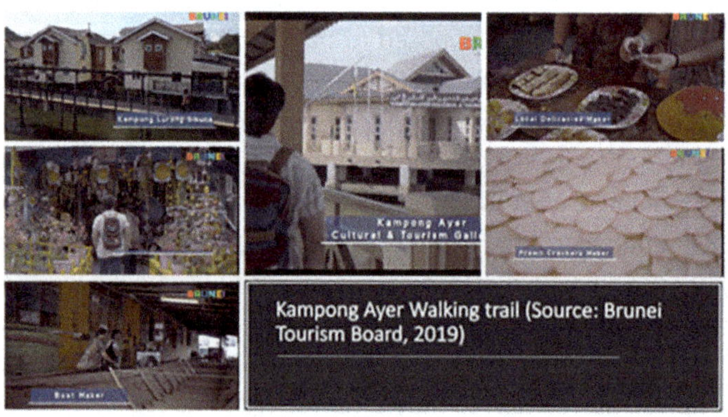

An analysis of BTB's promotional video (see Fig. 1) on the Kampong Ayer Walking Trail highlights nine key nodes or locations within Kampong Ayer (KA) presented as part of the tourist trail. These sites—including the KA Cultural and Tourism Gallery, Pottery House, the homestay Kunyitlodge 7, and various traditional artisans such as the boat maker, wood crafter, prawn cracker maker, and traditional delicacy maker—are promoted to enhance KA's cultural offerings in the context of its culture and heritage tourism development. The inclusion of newly constructed KA houses in Kampong Lurong Sikuna as part of the revitalization project along this trail aims to showcase the resilience and relevance of KA in the face of modernity and globalization. While these initiatives reflect the government's commitment to highlighting the cultural significance of local communities, the daily realities encountered by residents of KA and their involvement in the tourism industry may present challenges, as will be discussed in the later subsection.

Figure 2. Brunei River Cruise Route under Brunei River Heritage Trail (Source: www.bruneitourism.com)

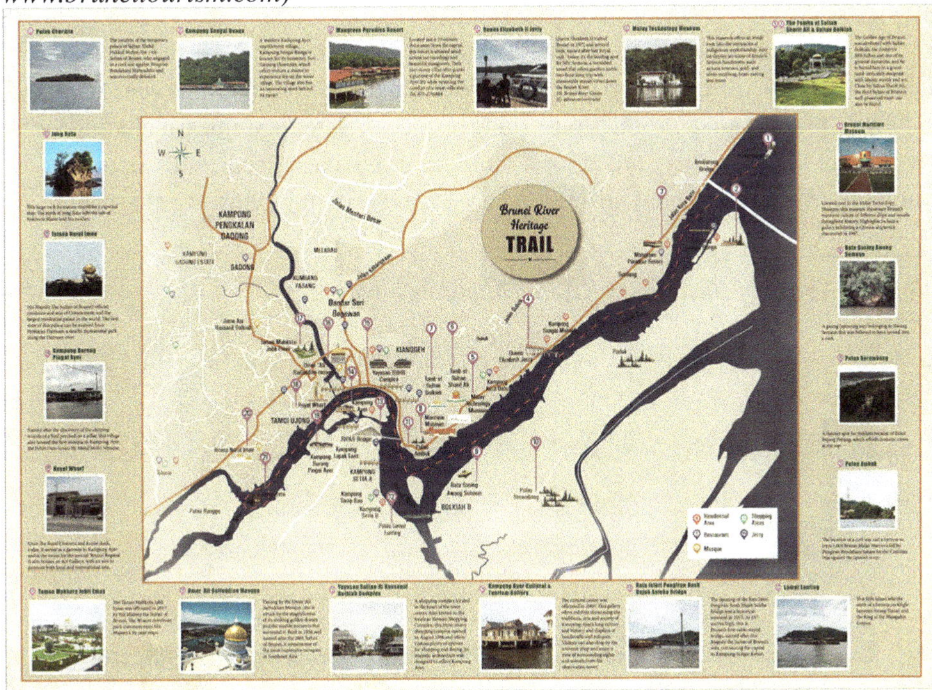

Like the KA Walking trail, BTB, in partnership with the Brunei River Cruise company, launched the Brunei River Heritage Trail (Fig. 2) in 2019 to promote the natural sights and historical tour along the Brunei River. An analysis of the brochure showed the branding of several key places along the river cruise deemed to be of particular historical importance to the Brunei Sultanate. These include sites such as Pulau Chermin that function as the last stand for one of the Brunei Sultans during the Brunei civil war, Lumut Lunting – a small stone island touted to have originated from one of the cursed roosters that fled during the cock fight in the early formation of the Brunei kingdom as well as Jong Batu. This mythical place was claimed to be a petrified front starboard of a traditional ship, the *Jong*, resulting from a woman's curse of her son who was also the vessel's captain as he denounced their maternal relation. Apart from the visual aestheticization of the natural environment within the vicinity of KA, the river cruise also provides dine-in services for their customer as part of an enriching experience. However, further evaluation of this cultural trail also proved that the commodification of such sites proved challenging with new issues identified.

c) Contemporary Cultural Economic Activities of KA: An Insight

Based on data collected from a previous study on poverty by Hassan (2022; 2024), analyzing the typologies of economic activities that KA communities were involved in showed a fascinating insight. Concerning services-related activities, including those involved in tourism, there are at least 40 types of businesses currently operating in Kampong Ayer, and their distribution can be found in the following chart (Fig. 3):

Figure 3. Types of Businesses KA communities involved in

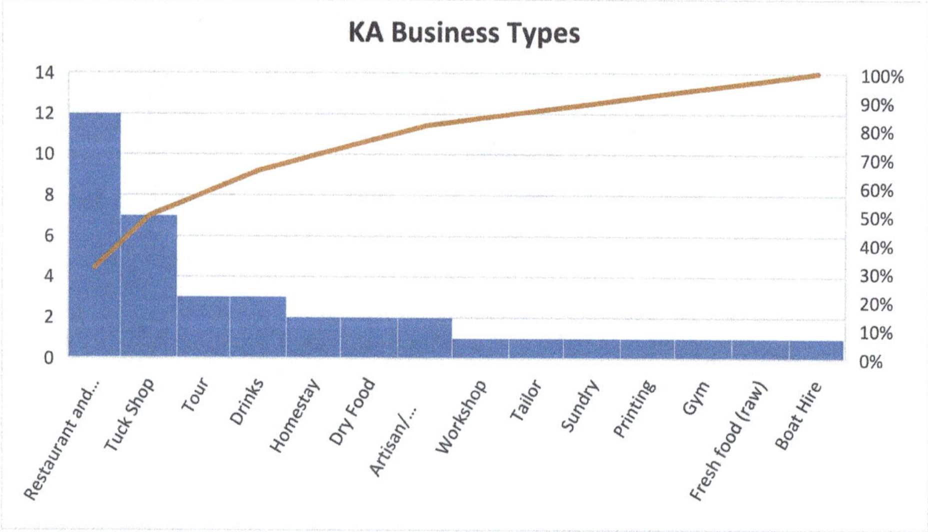

Most businesses, such as stilted restaurants and cafes, are involved in the food and beverage sector, with 12 (30%) entrepreneurs spread across multiple wards or kampong. Tuck shop operators follow this with 7 (17.5%) shops, drinks sellers, and informal tours at 3 (7.5%) each. There are also 2 (5%) homestays with multiple rooms and beddings. Two (5%) artisans are also involved in boatmaking and wood crafting. Two (5%) dry food businesses selling prawn crackers and dried seafood products are also operating. The remaining 7 (30%) operators are involved in other services ranging from boat rental or hiring, tailoring, printing services, sundry, raw food sellers, and private gyms. Interesting information regarding this finding lies in the existence of cool and chic or hipster cafes within this amalgamation of wards. Restaurants or cafes such as Adresto and homemade burger eateries showed the insertion of globalized urban subcultures setting foot in the former historical urban center. Their co-existence with other traditional food operators shows local communities' support for such operators so long as the social fabric is maintained. An earlier study by Hassan and Yong (2019) on *Bakuts,* i.e., man-made little islands or pieces of land constructed using then-now-lost technology, supported the cosmopolitan outlook of the KA communities toward new knowledge and technological innovation. Historically, the existence of Chinese merchants, living and setting up shops between 8 to 10 shops within the various wards, lasted well until the mid-1990s from the diverse Saba Wards to Pekan Lama and Peramu, to name a few, was a testament of such cosmopolitanism. Based on personal encounters of the researcher growing up within such a community, the ability of these Chinese families to adopt the use of the traditional Brunei Malay language as part of the means of communication up until the 90s was also a reflection of the importance of the KA community as the root that supports their businesses sustainability. All these Chinese families, however, ended up resettling themselves to the landed side of Brunei after the major fires that broke out well into the late 90s. From this analysis, it can be concluded that despite the lack of connection to the culture and heritage industry, the existence of all these businesses to service the tourism industry in Brunei should be applauded. The current activities were not making full use of the economic potentials and opportunities provided by this sector. Intervention from various players and stakeholders is needed to assist in further enabling the growth of the culture and heritage industry in KA as part of conservation. To date, the effects were somewhat muted and minimal. The map below (Fig.4) shows the location of these businesses:

Figure 4. Business distributions across Kampong Ayer in adjacent with Bandar Seri Begawan's Waterfront

RECURRING AND NEWLY EMERGING CHALLENGES TOWARDS KA'S CONSERVATION EFFORT AS PART OF NEW CULTURAL ECONOMY

As mentioned in this chapter, the current development of KA's cultural and heritage sector showed signs of detachment, dystopian, and fractal in its execution and implementation. The rationale behind developing this sector for tourism is mainly geared toward the prescribed or presumptive assertion that "things would fall into place" once cultural themes or activities are identified.

The evaluation of the Brunei Tourism Board's advertisement for the Kampong Ayer Walking Trail, as part of the place branding initiative implemented by KA, reveals notable deficiencies within the current framework. It is imperative for the sustainable development of any industry to comprehensively assess both forward and backward linkages that constitute its industrial structure (Scott, 2010). In the context of KA, there appears to be an absence of genuine conservation initiatives integrated into these cultural trails, particularly those that reflect the distinct identity of the Malay Islamic Monarchy.

An analysis of the existing activities and cultural products offered—such as the cultural exhibition of traditional Malay artifacts and culinary experiences facilitated by entities like the KA Cultural and Tourism Gallery, Jabal Rahmah, Kampong Tamoi's traditional Kuih (pastry) maker, and Awg Haji Ahmad's Pottery House—highlights a primary focus on cultural awareness rather than on value and wealth generation within the sector. For instance, the Pottery House showcases vibrant physical crafts composed of recycled plastics, which correlate little to traditional pottery-making practices. Most activities associated with the Kampong Ayer Walking Trail initiative are free of charge, with the notable exceptions being Terapung restaurant, Kunyit-lodge 7, and the prawn cracker producer, where charges apply to dining experiences and packaged products. The lack of an admission fee for exhibitions indicates an inadequate compensation model for labor, maintenance of exhibition spaces, and the conservation and restoration of artifacts, all of which reflect a reticence among local industry stakeholders towards fostering future growth in the sector.

This reluctance may stem from a deficiency in knowledge and competencies regarding effective pathways to development, necessitating intervention from relevant actors within academia, government, and the private sector. Moreover, the activities designated as part of the KA heritage trail, such as boat-making and wood crafting, are similarly plagued by these issues. In particular, the free nature of site visits and the tendency to perform non-authentic activities to cater to tourist expectations (Urry, 1995) further complicate the representation of genuine heritage. Current boat-making practices do not align with those of traditional vessels historically used and manufactured in the region. The establishment of the Raja Isteri Pengiran Anak Saleha (RIPAS) Bridge, which connects Bandar Seri Begawan with remote areas such as Lumapas-Kasat, has led to an increased reliance on private transportation, thus diminishing the demand for traditional boats utilized in community transport.

Similarly, observations from the activities offered by the Brunei River Cruise as part of the Brunei River Heritage Trail package showed the need for further improvement. Observations from participation in this cruise showed the minimal to low-end type of services where the aim is mainly on sightseeing, leisure, and recreation rather than conservation efforts per se. For each two to three-hour cruise, it has been found that there is a lack of interpretive tourism activity. Some areas shown from the downstream and up the Brunei River are sites of rich historical importance. Hiring proper, licensed, and knowledgeable tourist guides for each session would help elevate the cruise experiences to be more meaningful, much more so for those who possess no knowledge on the importance of the sites identified in the river cruise leaflet.

With regards to the sense of place, based on a data collection exercise carried out in 2022 by the Universiti Brunei Darussalam's Geography, Environment and Development (GED) Programme on thirty-three respondents comprising of inhabitants and former inhabitants of KA, the results of both questionnaire survey and interview showed interesting dynamics. For the current inhabitants of KA, their attachment and sense of place towards KA were mainly linked to its function as a place where food provisions for the family are readily accessible from the water bodies and surrounding physical environment. The existence of communal support, marked by the provision of advisories and guidance by fellow community members around the different wards and villages, made daily living bearable and helped ease the pressure and burden. These findings on the importance of the social fabric that holds communities together were supported by findings from other studies (see Hassan et al., 2022; Chu, 2024). The exercise also managed to uncover the acceptance that living in KA has become a generational tradition among the inhabitants, and interestingly, for both inhabitants and former inhabitants that have settled to the landed side of Brunei, they still possessed strong affections towards their respective wards or villages, with 93.9% supporting.

Apart from the sense of belongingness and sense of place, there are also changes in the spirit of KA regarding culture and heritage. Based on the data collected, most residents agreed on KA's changing energy, sights, and buzz, making the wards less lively. According to them, the vibrant atmosphere was only experienced during family events such as weddings or any official events such as visitation of foreign delegates and groups of tourists, as well as during the holidays. The sights and buzz experienced during its heydays at least 25 to 30 years ago, marked by children playing and running along the wooden walkways, the views of them chasing the stowaway kites during kite fighting, nor the view of them going to and leaving the mosques in large groups after the daily prayers and Quranic lessons, according to majority of the respondents, are dwindling with fewer numbers usually spotted. Earning income, which used to be easier, is now complicated even from simple activities such as fishing. The research on poverty by Hassan et al. (2022) and Chu (2024) uncovered how social marginalization has affected the socioeconomic structure of these communities, leading to the emergence of an alternative sense of place and place-branding, often discriminatory and derogatory (Hamdi et al., 2024), with KA being considered as a backward village with poverty, drug abused, and other social illnesses are rampant. Hence, such findings helped uncover some of the sense of place and attachments that respondents have towards KA. Whilst some challenges regarding low-end economic activities and poverty-related issues need to be addressed, developing the culture and heritage economy becomes more imperative to resolve the problems.

In a nutshell, current culture and heritage sectoral development issues are as follows. The current landscape of low-end economic activities reveals a concerning trend marked by low productivity and limited production-related endeavors. This situation is exacerbated by a lack of strong cultural connection to culture and heritage, particularly on the tangible aspect of the sector, resulting in a narrow range of product diversities. Traditional cultural products often remain cut off from the mass consumer market due to their niche nature. For example, the traditional production of woven textiles and the final product is usually priced between BND 350 to BND 10,000 and above per piece at retail. Furthermore, creative spaces and related activities are almost non-existent, leading to a highly dispersed and organic activity. This forced some of these activities, such as traditional performing arts (TPA), to remain informal and ad hoc in terms of their occurrences. While recreational, leisure, and sightseeing activities flourish, there is a marked absence of genuine conservation efforts that foster deeper awareness and a sense of attachment. This deficiency hampers the ability to achieve economies of scale and scope, ultimately questioning the degree of value creation and value capture within local village communities.

In conclusion, there is a conspicuous absence of cultural conservation and heritage-related activities within this historically significant site in Brunei. Alarmingly, the purported 'cultural' and 'heritage' activities presented are significantly detached from authentic MIB cultural practices and heritage conservation efforts as understood locally. The problems of place-branding are based on the perspectives of the BTB that tend to celebrate the past and market KA based on prima facie values of culture and heritage, which need intervention. Rather than branding places based on "what we thought there are", the act of place-making is deemed to be more fruitful as the latter involved actual grounded actions and investment into the place to elevate its position through the use of knowledge sharing, knowledge creation and co-creation and a concerted effort by diverse players within the communities to find the best way forward. This needs to go beyond mere consultation and coordination, and a model to materialize this has been proposed in another study by Azalie and Yong (2022). Hence, what potential pathways can KA take towards culture and heritage development? The following subsection will discuss this.

POTENTIAL DEVELOPMENT PATHWAYS TOWARDS CULTURE AND HERITAGE INDUSTRIAL DEVELOPMENT

The future of the culture and heritage industry lies in its innovative transformation into an experiential and immersive sector that embraces sustainability and knowledge-sharing. As we navigate the advancements brought about by the Industrial Revolution 4.0, integrating technologies such as IoT and e-commerce platforms can create new forward and backward linkages, revitalizing traditional crafts that are on the brink of extinction, like iron smithing and conventional woven textiles *(kain tenunan)*. Instead of allowing these valuable skills to fade, the focus must shift toward conserving living cultural experiences—preserving the essence of designs, oral histories, and local identities to inspire new product creation. This approach enhances urban revitalization by re-purposing existing structures for cultural exhibitions and strengthens local economies by reinventing traditional manufacturing to cater to broader markets. By fostering a comprehensive local historical and cultural trail, we can ensure inclusive community development and promote interpretive tourism that reflects the rich tapestry of local heritage, creating a sustainable future for cultural engagement.

The redevelopment of KA as part of conservation can be significantly enhanced by focusing on several key strategies. Firstly, repurposing the current river heritage trail presents an opportunity to expand visitor engagement by incorporating nearby historical sites, commodifying the experience, and adding value. Furthermore, retraining and empowering local communities to create and promote their own culture and heritage products is essential; for instance, developing a new, innovative gastronomic trail could leverage local culinary strengths. Using special effects that affect and stimulate an individual's senses and experiences would be helpful. One of the land-based restaurants in BSB managed to utilize such innovation as a way to enrich one's experience, in this case, the consumption of Brunei's traditional food, i.e., th*e Ambuyat*, as part of the dine-in customer experience (see Fig. 5). This was made possible by the new technologies brought about by globalization, to be used as a way to showcase the local domestic culture at the global level, in celebration of cosmopolitanism. KA communities should leverage from such technology through knowledge capture and enhancement. Below is a snapshot of the visual effects taken from their social media account:

Figure 5. A screenshot of the audio-visual effects used while consuming the Brunei traditional sago food, the Ambuyat (Source: MyFavoureatKopitiam Instagram)

Additionally, renewal projects that transform abandoned or derelict structures, such as concrete piles and stilts, into vibrant performance and exhibition spaces can breathe new life into the area. Finally, promoting heritage and ecotourism in Kampong Ayer could capitalize on the lush mangrove flora and fauna, inviting visitors to participate in a community-led mangrove safari that celebrates the environment and local culture. Currently, mangrove safaris are done by individual boatmen or boat rental enterprises in an informal setting and arrangement. Whilst this benefits individual boatmen, developing this as part of a project or contract-based arrangement would help expand the sector further. This contributes towards value-adding and value-creation components of the entire culture and heritage sector, with new niche and innovative sectors to be developed. Hence, a new network of industrial activities would grow from such a constructed advantage. This is on top of the need to incorporate interpretive tourist experiences, including interpretive site visits of sites with strong connections with the Bruneian Sultanate. Some studies have been written on this (see Chin et al., 2023; Azalie and Yong, 2022), and combining it with these recommendations would allow for further capitalization of the current tourism development momentum. The figure below (Fig. 6) shows the potential add-on sites to the current Brunei River Heritage Trail that truly reflect the Bruneian culture and identity, particularly those of the Brunei Malay communities of KA.

Figure 6. Proposed new sites to be included in the Brunei River Heritage Trail

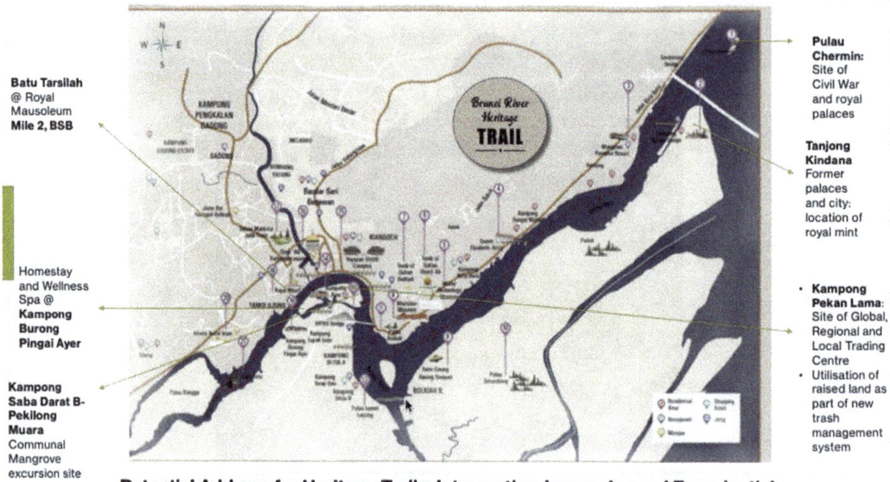

Potential Add-ons for Heritage Trails: Interpretive, Immersive and Experiential

Based on the figure above, the newly proposed sites comprised of six important sites. The historical sites of Pulau Chermin and Tanjong Kindana located at end of the Brunei estuary need to be included. It has been mentioned under the previous subsection that Pulau Chermin was proposed to be one of the sites included under the the Brunei River Heritage trail. However, the observations of the cruises showed the absence of any attempt to foretell or at least share the historical importance of these sites for the tourists or cruise ship participants. The addition of Tanjong Kindana into this list is of importance as it was also the legendary place where one of the Sultans cannoned his throne into the sea or estuary, a site of one of the former palaces during the civil war as well as the historical location of the royal mint. As previously mentioned in the research by Hassan and Yong (2019) on the *bakuts* as well as on the existence of Chinese merchants settling in the villages, the findings led to the tracing of these groups and their activities to center around the place called *Pekan Lama* (old town), one of the wards of KA and a new proposed site for the heritage trail. Not only that, this ward has linkages with the diasporic Chinese community of the Kianggeh river located at the opposite bank of the old BSB; they also have linkages with the Chinese traders of the Straits of Malacca. The potential visit to the Batu Tarsilah located in the Royal Mausoleum at Mile One, BSB, would also help enrich the cultural experiences of the visitors as the stone tablet is linked to the genealogical origins of the current Bruneian Sultanate. Linking the culture of the Bruneians and their relationship with the Sultanate showed the simple Monarch-Subject relationship between the two. But it also showed the revolving relationship between the Sultan (both historically and at present) but also concerning the other hinterland Malay communities that are linked with the downstream KA Communities via the major tributaries of the Brunei river such as the Damuan - links up to Kupang and Tutong as well as the Sengkurong-Bengkurong-Limau Manis, Terusan River in current Limbang and Lawas of Sarawak, Malaysia as well as those across the three Brunei districts i.e. Temburong, Tutong and Belait as stated in Hassan and Yong (2022) and Bakar (2018). Since it is evident that studying the culture and heritage of KA, Brunei, lies beyond the current/ present boundaries, there is a need for a concerted effort to address this. From a higher educational institution's point of view, Brunei Darussalam Universities can leverage their linkages with the Borneo Studies Network (BSN) to build up research capacity and capabilities as part of expanding the knowledge base.

In conclusion, understanding the distinction between preservation and conservation is essential when discussing cultural heritage, which encompasses more than just tradition, history, and aesthetics. It includes the dynamic cultural and heritage elements integral to our daily experiences and ongoing conversations. Recognizing the nature of these components—intended to be codified and passed down through generations—is crucial. Furthermore, the landscape embodies bodily, cultural, and symbolic meanings, utilizing signs and symbols that promote reflection and representation. It is vital to comprehend the scale, scope, and depth of activities that a nation must undertake to cultivate its cultural industry. In the case of KA, remastering and realigning its cultural and heritage sector to the rich history of the Sultanate while putting more effort into place-making and place branding of these historical sites would eventually help the socio-economic development of the communities in line with the conservation effort. Embracing cultural creativity can drive innovation, while communities' active inclusion and empowerment are pivotal for their development within this sector. Establishing value-driven services and acknowledging the significance of both forward and backward linkages are fundamental for growth. Ultimately, creating an innovative environment is necessary to leverage the opportunities presented by the fourth industrial revolution, ensuring that the advantages of this evolution are fully realized. Using the opportunities provided by IR 4, the chapter will propose the potential leeway that local communities could undertake or develop as part of empowering and socially enterprising themselves. This includes emphasizing knowledge's critical role in speeding up innovation in product offerings for tourist and local consumers alike, on top of re-examining current strategies by re-purposing current environmental functions of the water village by linking heritage and eco-tourism as part of the new development strategies. This is particularly important as Brunei Darussalam aims to achieve a more diversified economy beyond carbon-based industrialization by 2035.

REFERENCES

Adli, A., & Chin, W. L. (2021). Homestay Accommodation in Brunei Darussalam: An exploratory study. *Southeast Asia: A Multidisciplinary Journal, 21*(1), 15-29.

Agnew, J. (2011). Space and place. *Handbook of geographical knowledge, 2011*, 316-331.

Ahmad, A. (2013). The constraints of tourism development for a cultural heritage destination: The case of Kampong Ayer (Water Village) in Brunei Darussalam. *Tourism Management Perspectives, 8*, 106–113. DOI: 10.1016/j.tmp.2013.09.002

Appadurai, A. (Ed.). (1988). *The social life of things: Commodities in cultural perspective*. Cambridge University Press.

Azalie, I. A., & Yong, G. Y. V. (2022). *Heritage industry as a conservation strategy for Kampong Ayer*. The Brunei Museums Journal.

Bakar, H. T. B. H. A. (2018). Pembinaan dan Penyediaan Rumah Menaik Taraf Kampong Ayer di Negara Brunei Darussalam. *SOSIOHUMANIKA, 11*(1), 33–46.

Bakar, H. T. B. H. A. (2018). The Residents of Kampong Ayer, 1906–1940: The Activities of Pengalu, Padian, and Handiwork. *TAWARIKH, 9*(2), 151–158.

Bourdieu, P. (1990). *In other words. (Various Trans.)*. Polity Press.

Bourdieu, P. (2000). *Pascalian meditations* (Nice, R., Trans.). Polity Press.

Bremer, T. S. (2006). Sacred spaces and tourist places. In *Tourism, religion and spiritual journeys* (pp. 25–35). Routledge.

Bunkše, E. V. (2012). Sensescapes: Or a Paradigm Shift from Words and Images to All Human Senses in Creating Feelings of Home in Landscapes. *Proceedings of the Latvia University of Agriculture: Landscape Architecture & Art, 1*(1).

Camprag, N. (2017). Museumification of Historical Centres: The Case of Frankfurt Alstadt Reconstruction. In Bellini, N., & Pasquinelli, C. (Eds.), *Tourism in the City: Towards an Integrative Agenda on Urban Tourism* (pp. 165–178). Springer. DOI: 10.1007/978-3-319-26877-4_11

Chatterjee, A. B. (2021). Challenges for Cultural Tourism & Sustainability of the World Heritage Site of Angkor, Cambodia. *Journal of Heritage* [JHAM]. *Archaeology & Management, 1*(1), 30.

Childress, C., Baumann, S., Rawlings, C. M., & Nault, J. F. (2021). Genres, Objects, and the Contemporary Expression of Higher-Status Tastes. *Sociological Science, 8*, 8. DOI: 10.15195/v8.a12

Chin, S. W. L., Hassan, N. H., & Yong, G. Y. (2023). The new ecotourists of the 21st century: Brunei as a case study. *Cogent Social Sciences*, *9*(1), 2191444. DOI: 10.1080/23311886.2023.2191444

Chu, Y. (2024). The Social Landscape of Kampong Ayer: Marginalization and Modernization in a Traditional Water Village. *Journal of Humanities, Arts and Social Science, 8*(7).

Cooke, P., & Leydesdorff, L. (2006). Regional development in the knowledge-based economy: The construction of advantage. *The Journal of Technology Transfer*, *31*(1), 5–15. DOI: 10.1007/s10961-005-5009-3

Dellios, P. (2002). 'Museumification of the Village: Cultural Subversion in the 21st century. *Culture Mandala: The Bulletin of the Centre for East-West Cultural and Economic Studies*, *5*(1), 1–16.

Ertan, T., & Egercioglu, Y. (2016). 'The Impact of UNESCO World Heritage list on Historic Urban City Centers and Its Place in Urban Regeneration: The Case of Melaka, Malaysia and Tire, Turkey. *Procedia: Social and Behavioral Sciences*, *216*, 591–602. DOI: 10.1016/j.sbspro.2015.12.031

Florida, R. (2003). Cities and the creative class. *City & Community*, *2*(1), 3–19. DOI: 10.1111/1540-6040.00034

Gaikwad, N., Hanson, K., & Tóth, A. (2024). Bridging the gulf: How migration fosters tolerance, cosmopolitanism, and support for globalization. *American Journal of Political Science*.

Hannigan, J. (2002). Culture, globalization, and social cohesion: towards a de-territorialized, global fluid models. *Canadian Journal of Communication, 27(2)*, 1-9. Retrieved from http://cjc- online.ca/index.php/journal/article/viewArticle/1301/1333

Hassan, N. H. (2023). The Sociocultural Significance of Homeownership in Brunei Darussalam. In *Re) presenting Brunei Darussalam: A Sociology of the Everyday* (pp. 185–206). Springer Nature Singapore. DOI: 10.1007/978-981-19-6059-8_11

Hassan, N. H., Azalic, I. A., Ibrahim, K., Yong, G., & Maricar, H. H. A. (2011). Cultural Consideration in Vertical Living in Brunei Darussalam. 44th EAROPH Conference 'Managing Urban Growth: Challenges for Small Cities.

Hassan, N. H., Rigg, J., Azalie, I. A., Yong, G. Y., Zainuddin, N. H. H., & Shamsul, M. A. S. M. (2022). Making do and staying poor: The poverty context of Urban Brunei. *Geoforum*, *136*, 132–141. DOI: 10.1016/j.geoforum.2022.09.012

Hassan, N. H., Rigg, J., Yong, G. Y., Azalie, I. A., Muhammad Shamsul, M. A. S., & Zainuddin, N. H. (2024). Administering and encountering the poor: Poverty from above and below in Brunei Darussalam. *Singapore Journal of Tropical Geography*, *45*(2), 311–331. DOI: 10.1111/sjtg.12545

Hassan, N. H. & Yong, G. Y. V. (2019). The cultural value of bakuts in Kampong Ayer, Brunei Darussalam. *South East Asia: A Multidisciplinary Journal*, *19*, 47–63.

Hubbard, P. (2017). *City*. Routledge. DOI: 10.4324/9781315471259

Hui, L. K., & Har, W. M. (2008). Sanitising and Satanising Malaysia's Cityspaces: Cultural Power from Malay Decolonialism to Islamic Occidentalism and Beyond. *Asian Social Science*, *4*(11), 44–52.

Johnson, L. C., & Oakley, S. (2013). Place-taking and place-making in waterfront Australia. *Urban Studies (Edinburgh, Scotland)*, *50*(2), 341–355. DOI: 10.1177/0042098012452328

Jones, A. (1997). Urban conservation issues in Brunei Darussalam: The case of Brunei's water villages. *Planning Perspectives*, *12*(4), 457–475. DOI: 10.1080/026654397364627

Kinnard, J. N. (2014). *Places in motion: The fluid identities of temples, images, and pilgrims*. Oxford University Press. DOI: 10.1093/acprof:oso/9780199359653.001.0001

Knight, D. M. (2024, January). The death of vernacular cosmopolitanism. [). Routledge.]. *Anthropological Forum*, *34*(1), 135–149. DOI: 10.1080/00664677.2023.2218583

Light, D. (2014). Tourism and toponymy: Commodifying and Consuming Place Names. *Tourism Geographies*, *16*(1), 141–156. DOI: 10.1080/14616688.2013.868031

Mail, H. A. A. (2018). Yayasan Sultan Haji Hassanal Bolkiah, 1992-2012: Sejarah, Perumahan, dan Melayu Islam Beraja. *INSANCITA, 3*(2).

Markusen, A. (2007). A consumption base theory of development: An application to the rural cultural economy. *Agricultural and Resource Economics Review*, *36*(1), 1–15. DOI: 10.1017/S1068280500009412

Massey, D. (1995, April). Places and their pasts. In *History workshop journal* (No. 39, pp. 182-192). Oxford University Press. DOI: 10.1093/hwj/39.1.182

McGarrigle, D. (1994). Unsettling Brunei. *Australian Plants, 31*(3), 159–164. DOI: 10.1080/07293682.1994.9657627

Mitchell, D. (2002). Cultural landscapes: The dialectical landscape–recent landscape research in human geography. *Progress in Human Geography, 26*(3), 381–389. DOI: 10.1191/0309132502ph376pr

Nugraheni, S. A., Muljaningsih, S., Mahardika, P., & Saputra, A. (2023). Are We Being Rational? Economics Perspectives on Sacred Natural Sites Commodification. *Экономическая социология, 24*(5), 175-192.

Paasi, A. (2001). Europe as a social process and discourse: Considerations of place, boundaries and identity. *European Urban and Regional Studies, 8*(1), 7–28. DOI: 10.1177/096977640100800102

Pieterse, J. N. (2009). *Globalization and culture: global melange* (2nd ed.). Rowman and Littlefield Publishers Inc.

Ponte, S., & Gibbon, P. (2005). Quality standards, conventions and the governance of global value chains. *Economy and Society, 34*(1), 1–31. DOI: 10.1080/0308514042000329315

Rojas-Rivas, E., Espinoza-Ortega, A., Thomé-Ortíz, H., Moctezuma-Pérez, S., & Cuffia, F. (2019). Understanding consumers' perception and consumption motives towards amaranth in Mexico using the Pierre Bourdieu's theoretical concept of Habitus. *Appetite, 139*, 180–188. DOI: 10.1016/j.appet.2019.04.021 PMID: 31059761

Ruggles, F., & Silverman, H. (2009). *From tangible to intangible heritage. Intangible heritage embodied, 1-14.* Springer.

Scott, A. (2004). Cultural products industries and urban economic development. *Urban Economic Review,* 461-490.

Scott, A. (2010). Cultural economy and creative field of the city. *Geografiska Annaler. Series B, Human Geography, 92*(2), 115–130. DOI: 10.1111/j.1468-0467.2010.00337.x

Skuland, S. E. (2015). Healthy eating and barriers related to social class. The case of vegetable and fish consumption in Norway. *Appetite, 92*, 217–226. DOI: 10.1016/j.appet.2015.05.008 PMID: 25982927

Tan, S. M., & Yeo, B. J. (2023). Between life, death, and modernity at Bukit Brown Cemetery, Singapore. In *New Perspectives on Urban Deathscapes* (pp. 42–60). Edward Elgar Publishing.

Thompson, F. C. (2009). Nomenclature and classification, principles of. In *Encyclopedia of insects* (pp. 707–714). Academic Press. DOI: 10.1016/B978-0-12-374144-8.00191-0

Thwaites, K., & Simkins, I. (2006). *Experiential landscape: an approach to people, place and space*. Routledge. DOI: 10.4324/9780203462096

Tilley, C. (2006). Introduction: Identity, place, landscape and heritage. *Journal of Material Culture*, *11*(1-2), 7–32. DOI: 10.1177/1359183506062990

Tomlinson, J. (2003). Globalization and cultural identity. In Held, D., & McGrew, A. (Eds.), *The Global transformation reader: An introduction to the globalization debate* (2nd ed., pp. 268–277). Polity Press.

Trigg, A. B. (2001). Veblen, Bourdieu, and conspicuous consumption. *Journal of Economic Issues*, *35*(1), 99–115. DOI: 10.1080/00213624.2001.11506342

Tuan, Y. F. (1979). Space and place: humanistic perspective. In *Philosophy in geography* (pp. 387–427). Springer Netherlands. DOI: 10.1007/978-94-009-9394-5_19

Tuan, Y. F. (1991). Language and the making of place: A narrative-descriptive approach. *Annals of the Association of American Geographers*, *81*(4), 684–696. DOI: 10.1111/j.1467-8306.1991.tb01715.x

Tuan, Y. F. (2017). *A historical geography of China*. Routledge. DOI: 10.4324/9781315083537

Urry, J. (1995). *Consuming Places*. Routledge.

Warner, M., Bourdieu, P., & Nice, R. (1985). Distinction: A Social Critique of the Judgement of Taste. *MLN*, *100*(5), 1133. DOI: 10.2307/2905454

Woodhall-Melnik, J., & Matheson, F. I. (2017). More than convenience: The role of habitus in understanding the food choices of fast food workers. *Work, Employment and Society*, *31*(5), 800–815. DOI: 10.1177/0950017016648255

Wyer, S. (2024). 'Palermo is a mosaic': Cosmopolitan rhetoric in the capital of Sicily. *Modern Italy*, 29(4), 1–20. www.bruneitourism.com. DOI: 10.1017/mit.2024.13

Chapter 6
Individual Differences in Intentional and Unintentional Exposure to Sexual Content Among Vietnamese Students

Le Thi My Danh Danh
FPT University, Vietnam

Huynh Nguyen Yen Minh Minh
FPT University, Vietnam

Do Hoang Anh
https://orcid.org/0009-0008-6328-4123
FPT University, Vietnam

Tran Hoang Bao Chi Chi
https://orcid.org/0009-0004-0841-8097
FPT University, Vietnam

Le Nguyen Khanh Minh Minh
FPT University, Vietnam

Dinh Thi Thuy Hoa Hoa
FPT University, Vietnam

ABSTRACT

This study investigates how university students (aged 18–22) at a private university in Ho Chi Minh City are exposed to sexual content online—both intentionally and unintentionally—amid Vietnam's technological transition. Using Gender Schema Theory and Social Bonds Theory, and adapting a Hong Kong study, it explores how gender and religious beliefs influence these experiences. A quantitative online survey guides the research, with eight hypotheses examining patterns of exposure. The findings aim to inform educators, parents, and policymakers in developing effective digital literacy and sex education programs to ensure a safer online environment for Vietnamese youth.

DOI: 10.4018/979-8-3373-0603-2.ch006

INTRODUCTION

The internet has emerged as the predominant platform for engaging in digital sexual activities (Cooper, Galbreath, & Becker, 2004; Fisher & Barak, 2001; Mehta, 2004; Peter & Valkenburg, 2006). In this ever-evolving digital landscape, Vietnam's youth are facing increasing exposure to sexual content. According to Article 16 and Clause 1, Article 26 of the 2003 Vietnamese's Obscenity Crime Prevention Ordinance, "pornography" is defined as the act of using gestures, actions, images, and sounds to stimulate sexual desire, and sexual content is defined as images, language, sounds, or actions that are provocative, stimulating, and contrary to the traditional ethics and cultural customs of the Vietnamese people. This includes descriptions of genitals, nudity, descriptions of nudity that are sexually stimulating whether or not the individuals are clothed, descriptions of libido, and any form of masturbation.

It is argued that this exposure, whether intentional or unintentional, partly stems from the country's rapid digital transformation (Ashata, 2024), characterised by widespread internet access and smartphone usage. While existing studies around online pornography often pivot on moral or societal standpoints (Macleod, 2021), the angle of intentional versus unintentional exposure and how individual factors influence this is less explored (Goldstein, 2018). It is argued that two of these potentially significant determinants are gender and religious affiliations. Does a student's gender predispose them to certain types of online interactions? Does one's religious beliefs affect exposure levels?

It has become crucial to investigate this phenomenon and its impact on Vietnamese youth, considering cultural and societal factors that influence their experiences. Our research seeks to fill this critical gap, by taking into account unconscious factors that shape their experiences while exposing to sexual content online. By doing so, we aim to provide valuable insights to guide policymakers, educators, parents, and mental health professionals in developing informed strategies and support systems, filling a notable research gap in this area.

Our research particularly focuses on university students and early adulthood individuals aged 18-22. We intend to modify the research model based on a study examining individual variations in deliberate and accidental adolescent exposure to online pornography in Hong Kong Chinese by Cecilia Ma and others (2017). Our goal is to assess the applicability of these factors in the Vietnamese societal context and to determine whether we are utilising appropriate models to analyse the rate of passive exposure among Vietnamese university students. Finally, we seek to contribute valuable insights into the consequences of this exposure and its broader relevance in the context of rapidly evolving media and technology.

LITERATURE REVIEW

Previous studies of exposure to and engaging in digital sexual activities spanned over various age groups and demographic cohorts, as well as covering ethnicities from all over the world (see Ballester-Arnal et al., 2023; Solano et al., 2018). For instance, many notable researches that studied the youth aged 18-22 have been conducted (Ezzell et al., 2020; Tan et al., 2022; Lim et al., 2015). In light of literature reviewing, it was shown that these prior research focused a lot on exploring the gender aspects and its effect, while also typically utilising popular social psychology theories such as Social Bonds Theory and Gender Schema Theory. This research will also rely on those theoretical basis.

Social Bonds Theory

In addition to gender, religious affiliation emerged as a potential determinant influencing individuals' exposure to explicit content. These facets were possibly intertwined with the social bonds theory. Originating in the 1960s, Travis Hirschi's social bond theory posited that individuals, inherently driven by self-interest, upheld societal norms through the establishment of social bonds. These bonds, encompassing attachments to family, peers, school, occupational and educational commitments, academic involvement, and belief in societal rules, served as an implicit agreement fostering adherence to societal standards. It was argued that during Hirschi's initial formulation of the theory, the exploration of sexual content was limited due to the absence of extensive internet and digital platforms for content sharing, impeding comprehensive studies on the influence of religion on exposure to explicit material.

Subsequently, in the 2000s, investigations into Hirschi's theory expanded to encompass various social factors. A study on religion and social control by Cretacci (2003) challenged the efficacy of social control theory in explaining violence and highlighted gaps in understanding how religion, an agent of social control reinforcing moral behaviour, influences human conduct. Notably, the research underscored the scarcity of studies examining the intricate relationship between religiosity and explicit content consumption.

Building on this, Nelson et al. (2010) conducted a study on religious young men, revealing an association between religiosity and pornography use. Individuals who refrained from pornography demonstrated elevated levels of engagement in religious practices, both individually and within the family. They also showed higher self-worth, more developed identities in dating and family situations, and lower levels of depression. This linkage suggested that religious backgrounds and active participation in religious services correlated with reduced consumption of pornography. Similarly, Hardy et al. (2013) argued that religiousness might shield adolescents from both intentional and accidental exposure to explicit material, a finding reiterated by Cohan's (2009) study on religious communities. The collective evidence suggested that religion may cultivate conservative attitudes towards sex, serving as a protective element against adolescents' engagement with pornography.

Nevertheless, it can be argued that precedent studies examining the connection between religion and pornography consumption have predominantly concentrated on subjects from Western cultural backgrounds (Golemeeva, Elena Ivanova, 2020; Haggstrom-Nordin et al., 2006). Therefore, it remains unclear whether these findings can be generalised to non-Western settings.

To comprehend the methodology of this study, it is crucial to familiarise oneself with the cultural foundation and many religions within Vietnam. Notably, Lingaism (tín ngư ng ph n th c) forms a cornerstone of Vietnamese cultural identity amongst of the existence of other religious influences in the region nowadays such as Buddhism, Christianity, and Catholicism.

In terms of cultural foundation, it was claimed that from the very beginning, sustaining and developing life has been the most essential need for humans. In the context of agricultural culture, emerged Lingaism or tín ngưỡng phồn thực (phồn = many; thực = sprouting). In Vietnam, the Lingaism or tín ngư ng ph n th c (ph n = many; th c = sprouting) has persisted throughout history, manifesting in two forms: worship of reproductive organs and rituals related to sexual behaviour (Tran, 1999, 127).

It's important to note that individual attitudes toward sexual activities can vary widely within any cultural or religious context. Cultural beliefs and social bonds provide a framework, along with personal experiences, education, and other factors that can also play significant roles in shaping individual perspectives on sexual activities. As the Lingaism rooted in cultural and possibly religious practices, may contribute to a moral framework regarding sexual activities, promoting a set of values and norms.

Buddhism, Christianity, and Catholicism represent significant religious influences in Vietnam, each entering the country through distinct historical trajectories - ngu n. These religions have endured for centuries, becoming integral cultural elements that shape the lifestyle and thought patterns of the Vietnamese population (Do, 2016). In Vietnam, Buddhism and Catholicism emerged as the predominant religions, boasting over 26.5 million followers, constituting 27% of the nation's populace. Buddhism holds the largest number of adherents and worship facilities, followed by Catholicism (C ng hòa xã h i ch nghĩa Vi t Nam - Ban Tôn Giáo Chính Ph , 2022). Religious individuals in Vietnam, particularly those practicing Buddhism and Christianity, may indeed encounter some potential conflicts between their religious moral codes and societal expectations regarding sexual behaviour. Both Buddhism and Christianity often promote ethical guidelines and moral principles that may impact individuals' attitudes toward sexual activities. Religious values might influence broader societal attitudes towards sex, potentially creating a more conservative sexual culture within certain communities, yet the lived experiences of religious individuals in Vietnam vary considerably. Some may find a way to integrate their faith with societal norms, while others might prioritize one over the other.

The aim of this study was to explore variations in pornography consumption concerning gender and religious affiliations among FPTU students.

Gender Schema Theory

Gender Schema Theory (GST) was a psychological framework conceived by Sandra Bem during the 1980s, and offered a cognitive perspective on the development of gender (Bem, 1981). GST delved into how individuals, starting from childhood, formulate notions and hypotheses concerning the concepts of masculinity and femininity, using these mental constructs to classify information, make decisions, and govern their behaviour based on gender. Consequently, it wielded the potential to influence individuals' exposure to explicit content.

After Bem's pioneering work, scholars from the early 1980s onwards have put forward a variety of approaches to theorise about gender schemas. It's worth noting that while three seminal papers on gender schemas (Markus et al., 1982; Liben and Signorella, 1980; Martin and Halverson, 1981) exhibited some similarities with Bem's framework, they also presented significant distinctions. These scholars have harnessed the concept of schema to address inquiries of interest to social and personality psychologists. Remarkably, GST has been applied to conduct research even beyond the United States, demonstrating its potential for adaptation in diverse cultural contexts, in this instance Vietnam's.

In this text, we employed GST to understand gender segregation in exposure and investigated how pre-existing gender schemas among students can shape their attitudes and conduct concerning online pornography. Additionally, this exploration considered the influence of cultural context, particularly within Vietnamese culture, on the interplay with gender schemas, recognising that these schemas were influenced by prevailing cultural norms and values.

RESEARCH DESIGN AND METHODOLOGY

This study aims to test eight pivotal hypotheses concerning the exposure of university students to online pornography:

H1: The male gender increases the likelihood of unintended exposure to sexual content online.

H2: The male gender decreases the likelihood of unintended exposure to sexual content online.

H3: The male gender increases the likelihood of intended exposure to sexual content online.

H4: The male gender decreases the likelihood of intended exposure to sexual content online.

H5: People who have religious beliefs increase the likelihood of unintended exposure to sexual content online.

H6: People who have religious beliefs decrease the likelihood of unintended exposure to sexual content online.

H7: People who have religious beliefs increase the likelihood of intended exposure to sexual content online.

H8: People who have religious beliefs decrease the likelihood of intended exposure to sexual content online.

To address these hypotheses, the authors collected data through a survey of a representative sample of FPT a private University's students in Vietnam (354 samples), including 194 male (54.80%) and 160 female (45.20%) of young adulthood. Similar to Vietnam's populace statistics, 65% of the sample from FPTU populace were non-religious; Buddhism and Catholicism in FPTU were also the predominant religions, constituting 19.20% and 14.7% respectively.

Additionally, to assess more clearly the frequency of students' exposure to different categories of online pornographic material over the past six months, the research team categorised these materials into six sections: stories, images, videos, pornographic advertisements, websites, and chat rooms. Subsequently, we incorporated the use of the questionnaire from a study titled "Individual differences in intentional and unintentional exposure to online pornography among Hong Kong Chinese adolescents" by Cecilia Ma and others (2017) to test whether the questionnaire was applicable in the Vietnamese context. When doing surveys, participants were asked to indicate their age, gender, religion and frequency of their exposure to online pornographic content, with response options ranging from 1 (never) to 6 (daily). The survey took place from October 13 to December 5, 2023, and afterward, the collected data was then subjected to analysis by SPSS for Windows to identify whether there were any correlations between gender or religious beliefs and exposure to sexual content. Survey participants were fully informed about the research purpose and assured of the confidentiality of their information.

DATA ANALYSIS

Table 1. Frequencies of intentional exposure to online pornography

Over the past 6 months, while online, the frequency that you have intentionally been exposed to	Never (%)	Less than once a month (%)	1-3 times a month (%)	About once a week (%)	Several times a week (%)	Daily (%)
1. Perusing sensual narratives (comprising comics)	49.2	18.6	12.4	9.9	6.2	3.7
2. Observing explicit images (displaying genital regions/nude bodies)	50.8	18.9	11.0	8.8	6.8	3.7
3. Watching pornographic videos (including cartoon videos)	42.9	16.4	15.3	11.6	9.9	4.0
4. Engage in sexually explicit conversations (sex chat)	81.1	8.2	4.2	3.1	1.1	2.3
5. Watch ads with pornographic content	69.8	16.4	5.6	4.8	1.4	2.0
6. Browse websites with pornographic content	61.9	15.0	12.1	5.4	3.4	2.3

Table 2. Frequencies of unintentional exposure to online pornography

Over the past 6 months, while online, the frequency that you have unintentionally been exposed to	Never (%)	Less than once a month (%)	1-3 times a month (%)	About once a week (%)	Several times a week (%)	Daily (%)
1. Perusing sensual narratives (comprising comics)	46.9	24.6	13.6	6.5	5.6	2.8
2. Observing explicit images (displaying genital regions/nude bodies)	39.3	24.6	16.7	8.8	6.2	4.5
3. Watching pornographic videos (including cartoon videos)	38.7	24.9	15.3	10.7	7.1	3.4
4. Engage in sexually explicit conversations (sex chat)	79.9	9.3	4.8	2.8	2.0	1.1
5. Watch ads with pornographic content	50.3	22.3	12.1	5.9	5.4	4.0
6. Browse websites with pornographic content	54.8	20.1	12.4	7.6	2.5	2.5

Tables 1 and 2 demonstrated the frequency at which individuals came across online pornography passively and actively. Notably, intentional exposure tended to be consistently lower than unintentional exposure across all categories. This could be supported by a study about exposure to sexual content (Lewis et al, 2018) which found that a significant portion of the sexual content encountered by young individuals was unintentional and intrusive. This content often originated from paid pop-up advertising or appeared in the sidebars of social media sites, ranging from nude photos to explicit pornographic material. Young individuals reported encountering these ads on various online platforms, describing them as intrusive. Additionally, sexual material featured in social media 'news feeds' or pages was sourced from shared content within networks, with friends or friends of friends posting or disseminating such material. Similar to paid advertising, a considerable number of young individuals expressed a sense of limited agency regarding the unintentional and intrusive sexual user-generated content they encountered. The majority of the exposure described by young people was unintentional and intrusive, leading to frustration (Lewis et al, 2018).

Examining intentional exposure, about half of the respondents (49.20%) asserted they had never intentionally exposed themselves to erotic stories, whereas 3.70% of those who had been unintentionally exposed reported daily exposure. Similarly, for intentionally viewing pornographic pictures, 50.80% claimed never to do so, while 3.70% reported daily engagement. In the case of intentionally watching pornographic videos, the majority (42.90%) reported never engaging, but 4% did so daily. Regarding intentional engagement in sexually explicit conversations, 81.10% reported never doing so, while 2.30% reported daily involvement. Additionally, nearly 69.8% claimed to never intentionally watch ads with pornographic content, and over 60% reported never intentionally browsing websites with pornographic content.

On the other hand, examining unintentional exposure revealed that nearly half of the respondents (46.90%) reported never experiencing unintentional exposure to erotic stories, with 2.80% reporting daily exposure. Approximately 39.30% claimed never to experience unintentional exposure to pornographic pictures, while 4.5% reported daily exposure. Similar to the aforementioned groups, nearly 39% of individuals indicated that they had never encountered unintentional exposure to pornographic videos, while 3.40% reported daily occurrences. The majority (79.90%) reported never unintentionally engaging in sexually explicit conversations, with 1.10% reporting daily exposure. Half of the respondents reported never unintentionally watching ads with pornographic content. Approximately 55.90% claimed never unintentionally browsed websites with pornographic content.

Table 3. Frequencies of unintentional exposure to online pornography by gender

	F	M	F	M	F	M	F	M	F	M	F	M
Over the past 6 months, while online, the frequency that you have unintentionally been exposed to	Never (%)		Less than once a month (%)		1-3 times a month (%)		About once a week (%)		Several times a week (%)		Daily (%)	
1.Perusing sensual narratives (comprising comics)	45.4	48.8	26.8	21.9	16.0	10.6	5.2	8.1	4.6	6.9	2.1	3.8
2. Observing explicit images (displaying genital regions/ nude bodies)	50.0	26.3	25.8	23.1	13.9	20.0	6.2	11.9	3.1	10.0	1.0	8.8
3. Watching pornographic videos (including cartoon videos)	48.5	26.9	26.8	22.5	13.4	17.5	6.2	16.3	4.1	10.6	1.0	6.3
4. Engaging in sexually explicit conversations (sex chat)	84.0	75.0	8.2	10.6	4.6	5.0	1.0	5.0	1.5	2.5	0.5	1.9
5. Watching ads with pornographic content	51.5	48.8	22.7	21.9	14.4	9.4	4.6	7.5	5.2	5.6	1.5	6.9
6. Browsing websites with pornographic content	59.3	49.4	23.2	16.3	11.9	13.1	4.6	11.3	0.5	5.0	0.5	5.0

Note. F = Female; M = Male

Table 4. Frequencies of intentional exposure to online pornography by gender

	F	M	F	M	F	M	F	M	F	M	F	M
Over the past 6 months, while online, the frequency that you have unintentionally been exposed to	Never (%)		Less than once a month (%)		1-3 times a month (%)		About once a week (%)		Several times a week (%)		Daily (%)	
1.Perusing sensual narratives (comprising comics)	50.0	48.1	19.1	18.1	12.9	11.9	9.3	10.6	5.7	6.9	3.1	4.4
2. Observing explicit images (displaying genital regions/ nude bodies)	60.8	38.8	23.2	13.8	5.7	17.5	7.2	10.6	2.6	11.9	0.5	7.5
3. Watching pornographic videos (including cartoon videos)	56.2	26.9	18.0	14.4	12.4	18.8	6.2	18.1	5.7	15.0	1.5	6.9
4. Engaging in sexually explicit conversations (sex chat)	84.5	76.9	8.2	8.1	2.6	6.3	1.5	5.0	1.5	0.6	1.5	3.1
5. Watching ads with pornographic content	78.9	58.8	14.4	18.8	2.6	9.4	2.6	7.5	1.0	1.9	0.5	3.8
6. Browsing websites with pornographic content	72.2	49.4	12.4	18.1	10.8	13.8	2.6	8.8	1.5	5.6	0.5	4.4

Note. F = Female; M = Male

Gender had proven to be the primary determinant in expressing or communicating sexual arousal (Exton, et al., 2000; Janssen, et al., 2003; Mosher & Maclan, 1994; Quackenbush et al., 1995). As we delved into the gender factors, Tables 3a and 3b revealed distinct patterns in both unintentional and intentional exposure to online pornography. These patterns signified diverse preferences and habits among respondents, with exposure rates varying across different types of explicit content and gender groups.

In general, male respondents consistently reported a higher frequency of daily exposure to sexual content, whether intentional or unintentional. This observation aligned with previous studies that had indicated a higher preference among men for sexually explicit material (Janssen, Carpenter, & Graham, 2003; Lo & Wei, 2002). Furthermore, male respondents exhibited more frequent engagement across all surveyed categories of sexual content (supporting H1, H3). Conversely, female respondents generally reported higher avoidance rates in unintentional and intentional exposure across various content categories.

Analysing unintentional exposure, females reported higher instances of never encountering pornographic images, videos, and ads, in contrast to males while males reported higher rates in other levels of frequency. In the case of never engaging in sexually explicit conversations and never intentionally browsing websites with pornographic content, females exhibited significantly higher rates (84% and 59.3%, respectively) compared to males (75% and 49.4%).

Conversely, in intentional exposure, females reported marginally higher instances of never intentionally exposing themselves to erotic stories, never engaging in sexually explicit conversations, and never watching ads with pornographic content. In contrast, males reported higher frequencies in other scenarios. Regarding never intentionally viewing pornographic pictures and browsing websites with pornographic content, females (60.8% and 72.2%, respectively) exceeded males (38.8% and 49.4%). When it came to never intentionally watching pornographic videos, females (56.2%) reported more than double the rates of males (26.9%). These findings aligned with previous studies indicating a consistent gender difference, where men tended to be more psychosexually responsive to erotic videos compared to women (Koukounas & McCabe, 1997; Mosher & Maclan, 1994).

The analysis of the data presented in Table 3a strongly supports the acceptance of H1, which suggested that the gender male played a role in increasing the chances of unintentional exposure to online sexual content. Both genders exhibit high percentages of individuals who had never engaged in sexually explicit conversations, with females (84%) reporting a slightly higher percentage than males (75%). Notably, most males exposed to pornography belonged to the intentional exposure group rather than the unintentional exposure group. This is supported by a finding by Chen and partners (2013), that compared to female participants, male respondents typically disclosed a greater frequency of deliberate exposure to pornography, an extended history of exposure, and a more favourable connection with intentional pornography. The data also refuted H2, indicating that being male did not decrease the likelihood of unintended exposure to sexual content online.

The findings from analysing Table 3b data provided substantial support for the acceptance of H3, which posited that the male gender increased the likelihood of intended exposure to sexual content online, and rejected that the male gender decreases the likelihood of intended exposure to sexual content online (H4).

Table 5. Frequencies of unintentional exposure to online pornography by religiosity

	R	NR	R	NR	R	NR	R	NR	R	NR	R	NR
Over the past 6 months, while online, the frequency that you have unintentionally been exposed to	Never (%)		Less than once a month (%)		1-3 times a month (%)		About once a week (%)		Several times a week (%)		Daily (%)	
1.Perusing sensual narratives (comprising comics)	52.4	43.9	16.9	28.7	13.7	13.5	7.3	6.1	8.1	4.3	1.6	3.5
2. Observing explicit images (displaying genital regions/ nude bodies)	44.4	36.5	18.5	27.8	14.5	17.8	11.3	7.4	4.8	7.0	6.5	3.5
3. Watching pornographic videos (including cartoon videos)	38.7	38.7	22.6	26.1	14.5	15.7	12.1	10.0	6.5	7.4	5.6	2.2
4. Engaging in sexually explicit conversations (sex chat)	74.2	83.0	10.5	8.7	8.1	3.0	4.8	1.7	0.8	2.6	1.6	0.9
5. Watching ads with pornographic content	54.0	48.3	23.4	21.7	12.1	12.2	4.8	6.5	2.4	7.0	3.2	4.3
6. Browsing websites with pornographic content	59.7	52.2	17.7	21.3	11.3	13.0	7.3	7.8	0.8	3.5	3.2	2.2

Note. R = Religious; NR = Non-religious.

As per Hirschi's Social Bonds Theory, social bonds encompassed the relationships individuals formed with society, which encompassed their connections with family, educational institutions, and the workplace (Hirschi, 1969). The theory posited that when these bonds were stronger, individuals were less inclined to partake in unethical actions. This principle could also be applied to investigate how religious beliefs might have influenced individuals' proclivity for encountering sexual content (Costello & Laub, 2019). Since religion could also be seen as a factor of social bond because it served several functions for society, according to the functionalist perspective, religion provided meaning to life and inspired positive social change. In some religious doctrines, engaging in sexual activities solely for pleasure outside the purpose of reproduction, such as masturbation or consuming explicit content, was deemed sinful. The belief in the moral validity of these laws varied among individuals based on their religious affiliations. For those strongly connected to their religious beliefs, the fear of violating moral codes and incurring negative consequences, both in the spiritual and social realms, might have influenced the intent to be exposed to sex content.

Table 4a indicated that the percentage of religious individuals who reported "Never" experiencing unintentional exposure was consistently higher than non-religious individuals. Religious individuals reported lower frequencies of perusing sensual narratives, with 52.4% indicating never being exposed. In contrast, non-religious individuals demonstrated a higher occurrence, with 43.9%. Religious individuals again exhibited lower exposure rates of observing explicit images (44.4% never exposed), while non-religious individuals reported higher frequencies, with 36.5% exposed. Both groups displayed a relatively similar pattern in watching pornographic videos, with 38.7% of religious individuals never exposed, and 38.7% of non-religious individuals. A notable contrast emerged, with a substantial majority of non-religious individuals engaging in sexually explicit conversations (83.0%), compared to religious individuals at 74.2%. Both groups demonstrated varying exposure frequencies, providing insights into the nuanced online behaviours of religious and non-religious individuals. Moreover, religious individuals consistently indicated lower rates of inadvertent exposure across all categories in comparison to their non-religious counterparts, although the variance in percentages was not substantial. Hornor (2020) highlighted that the consumption of pornography was more common among youth who had lower levels of religious involvement and who believed they were less likely to face condemnation if their engagement with pornography was discovered. Religiosity could have served as a significant safeguard against risks among late adolescents, as suggested by Coie et al. (1993). These results endorsed the idea that college students who strongly aligned themselves with religious doctrines and customs were less prone to take part in risk-related behaviours, such as sexual activities. Consequently, religion might have functioned as a crucial social influence affecting late adolescents' choices to refrain from intimate relations (Cochran and Beeghley, 1991; Campbell and Stewart, 1992). The study suggested that religiousness served as a protective factor against pornography consumption for multiple reasons, including fostering a more conservative stance on pornography, promoting self-regulation, and contributing to social controls against its use. Therefore, it was suggested that religious individuals were less likely to encounter unintentional exposure to explicit content (supporting H6). Surprisingly, religious individuals demonstrated notably higher frequencies of unintentionally engaging in sexually explicit conversations than those without religious beliefs. Religious individuals' unintentional exposure to explicit images was notably twice as high as non-religious individuals daily (Religious: 6.5%; Non-religious: 3.5%). Similar trends were observed in the category of watching pornographic videos, including cartoon videos (Religious: 5.6%; Non-religious: 2.2%). This observation argued that engaging in sexually explicit conversations online may have been inherently more susceptible to unintentional exposure, regardless of an individual's religiosity.

The analysis of Table 4a data provided substantial support for the acceptance of H6, which posited that religious beliefs decreased the likelihood of unintended exposure to sexual content online. Furthermore, the unexpected observation that religious individuals reported relatively high percentages of engaging in sexually explicit conversations warrants further exploration. It also refuted H5, indicating that religious beliefs did not increase the likelihood of unintended exposure.

Table 6. Frequencies of intentional exposure to online pornography by religiosity

	R	NR	R	NR	R	NR	R	NR	R	NR	R	NR
Over the past 6 months, while online, the frequency that you have unintentionally been exposed to	Never (%)		Less than once a month (%)		1-3 times a month (%)		About once a week (%)		Several times a week (%)		Daily (%)	
1.Perusing sensual narratives (comprising comics)	53.2	47.0	15.3	20.4	11.3	13.0	12.1	8.7	3.2	7.8	4.8	3.0
2. Observing explicit images (displaying genital regions/nude bodies)	57.3	47.4	15.3	20.9	9.7	11.7	8.9	8.7	4.0	8.3	4.8	3.0
3. Watching pornographic videos (including cartoon videos)	41.1	43.9	13.7	17.8	16.1	14.8	13.7	10.4	10.5	9.6	4.8	3.5
4. Engaging in sexually explicit conversations (sex chat)	77.4	83.0	9.7	7.4	5.6	3.5	4.0	2.6	0.8	1.3	2.4	2.2
5. Watching ads with pornographic content	71.0	69.1	17.7	15.7	4.8	6.1	3.2	5.7	0	2.2	3.2	1.3
6. Browsing websites with pornographic content	67.7	58.7	13.7	15.7	8.9	13.9	4.0	6.1	2.4	3.9	3.2	1.7

Note. R = Religious; NR = Non-religious.

In Table 4b, the data revealed a consistent trend across all activities, indicating that religious individuals tended to report a higher percentage of "Never" intentionally engaging in online pornography-related activities overall. Religious individuals reported lower frequencies of intentionally perusing sensual narratives, with 53.2% indicating never being exposed, in contrast to non-religious individuals, with 47.0%. Similarly, religious individuals again exhibited lower exposure rates of intentionally observing explicit images, with 57.3% indicating never being exposed. On the other hand, non-religious individuals reported higher frequencies, with 47.4%. Both religious and non-religious groups displayed a relatively similar pattern in intentionally watching pornographic videos (Religious: 41.1%; Non-religious: 43.9%). A notable contrast emerged in engaging in sexually explicit conversations, with a substantial majority of non-religious individuals (83.0%) intentionally participating, compared to religious individuals at 77.4%. Regarding intentionally watching ads with pornographic content, 71.0% of religious individuals reported never being exposed, while 69.1% of non-religious individuals reported the same. In the case of intentionally browsing websites with pornographic content, religious individuals reported lower exposure rates, with 67.7% indicating never being exposed. In contrast, non-religious individuals reported higher frequencies, with 58.7% never being exposed to such content. This observation aligned with H8. Since it suggested that attitudes could serve as predictors of behavior, it could be argued that the disapproval of pornography, which was often more prevalent among religious individuals, might lead to a tendency to refrain from actively seeking out pornographic content (Mesch, 2008).

Based on the information provided, non-religious individuals exhibited a contrasting trend. They intended to engage in these activities more frequently compared to religious individuals. However, it was crucial to notice that the percentage of religious individuals exposed to explicit content in two activities, namely watching pornographic videos (including cartoon videos) and engaging in sexually explicit conversations (sex chat), was higher compared to their non-religious counterparts. Besides, derived from the data presented in Table 4b, it was evident that religious individuals consistently constituted a higher percentage than their non-religious counterparts when intentionally exposing themselves to explicit content on a daily basis across all categories. Religious individuals reported higher frequencies of intentionally perusing sensual narratives (comprising comics), with 4.8% engaging daily. In contrast, non-religious individuals demonstrated a slightly lower occurrence at 3.0% on a daily basis. Similarly, religious individuals again exhibited higher daily exposure rates of both intentionally observing explicit images (Religious: 4.8%; Non-religious: 3.0%) and intentionally watching pornographic videos (Religious: 4.8%; Non-religious: 3.5%). A notable contrast emerged in engaging in sexually explicit conversations (sex chat), with 2.4% of religious individuals participating daily compared to 2.2% of non-religious individuals. Regarding intentionally watching ads with pornographic content, 3.2% of religious individuals reported daily exposure, while non-religious individuals only reported 1.3%. In the case of intentionally browsing websites with pornographic content, 3.2% of religious individuals reported daily exposure, whereas 1.7% of non-religious individuals reported daily exposure. These findings implied that while religiosity generally acted as a protective factor against online pornography engagement, individual variations within the religious cohort could not be ignored.

To conclude, this analysis provided strong support for hypothesis H6, indicating that religious beliefs acted as a protective factor against intentional exposure to sexual content online. H7, which suggested the opposite, was not supported by the data.

DISCUSSION

Table 7. Discussion

Hypotheses	Results
H1: The male gender increases the likelihood of unintended exposure to sexual content online.	Accept
H2: The male gender decreases the likelihood of unintended exposure to sexual content online.	Reject
H3: The male gender increases the likelihood of intended exposure to sexual content online.	Accept
H4: The male gender decreases the likelihood of intended exposure to sexual content online.	Reject
H5: People who have religious beliefs increase the likelihood of unintended exposure to sexual content online.	Reject
H6: People who have religious beliefs decrease the likelihood of unintended exposure to sexual content online.	Accept
H7: People who have religious beliefs increase the likelihood of intended exposure to sexual content online	Reject
H8: People who have religious beliefs decrease the likelihood of intended exposure to sexual content online.	Accept

The results of the study provided significant insights into the correlation between gender, religion, and the likelihood of unintentional or intentional exposure to online sexual content in the Vietnamese context. Based on two main theories, Social Bond Theory and Gender Schema Theory, we discuss 8 hypotheses previously set out.

First, as Hypothesis 1 predicted, the male gender was shown to elevate the probability of both unintentional and deliberate encounters with sexual content on the internet. The data assessed in Tables 3a and 3b provide robust evidence in favour of H1 and H3. It can be observed that the overall incidence of males encountering sexual content online was significantly higher than that of females. Particularly in the daily exposure column for males, encompassing both intentional and unintentional exposure, the frequency overwhelmingly surpassed that of females, with the most substantial difference reaching up to 7.8%. As for H2 and H4, both were refuted as the research outcomes indicate that the male gender did not diminish the likelihood of either accidental or intentional exposure to online sexual content.

Several factors contribute to this divergence. First, in most Asian cultures like Vietnam, which are typically characterized by discretion and reserve,, there is a divergence in the permissions, expectations, or even encouragement for males and females to adopt distinct attitudes toward sex, which can be attributed to social learning (Quackenbush et al., 1995). Moreover, in today's digital world, unintentional exposure to a certain type of content can result from algorithms and content identification systems. These algorithms are designed to categorise and suggest content based on search history, online habits, and individual preferences. Thus, an individual may come across content without actively searching for or following a specific topic, but rather due to the filtering and recommendation mechanisms of the algorithm, which underscores the necessity of conducting more in-depth studies on the subject.Furthermore, the analyses provided by the research team in Tables 4a and 4b also support both H6 and H8. This may suggest that religious beliefs have the potential to reduce students' exposure to explicit online content, both intentional and unintentional encounters.

A noteworthy observation is that, although individuals with religious beliefs decrease their likelihood of inadvertently encountering explicit content online, the disparity in the data is not significant when compared to those without any religious affiliation. This can be attributed to the enduring presence of Lingaism, which has embedded itself deeply in the collective consciousness of the Vietnamese over an extended period (Tran, 1999). In addition, today's youth have extensive access to comprehensive sexual health services, inclusive environments for diverse youth, and open conversations with supportive guidance across various social settings—among peers, within educational institutions, at home, and within their communities - which helps them to be more open-minded and liberal. As a result, lead to the fact that religious teachings no longer have a great influence on young people's exposure to sex-related topics (Narushima et al., 2020; Ngo, 2021). Additionally, the proportion of people without religion is also higher than that of those with religious beliefs. Therefore, people who are not bound by religion will be more likely to be intentionally exposed to pornographic content online. When they share, like, or comment on a post with explicit content, it can be an external factor that increases the likelihood of religious people being accidentally exposed to sexually explicit content because those posts will likely appear on their feeds if they have connections to people who are not religious.

The lack of support for Hypothesis 5 and 7 indicates that religion does not increase the likelihood of unintentional or intentional exposure to online sexual content, which aligns with findings from other studies (see Mesch, 2008; Hardy et al., 2013).

In summary, our research has provided insights into the correlation between gender, religion, and the likelihood of passive or active exposure to online sexual content. However, social theories combined with gender hypotheses cannot fully explain this relationship. Further research is needed to better understand the causes of exposure to online sexual content within different target groups.

LIMITATION

Identifying and acknowledging these limitations plays a crucial role in ensuring the scientific and ethical integrity of the research. In this research paper, we identify limitations encompassing the sample and time-related factors. Firstly, regarding the sample, the study's relatively small sample size is a key limitation, preventing a comprehensive representation of the diversity and variations in exposure to online sexual content among Vietnamese university students, specifically those at the selected university in Ho Chi Minh City. Employing a larger sample would yield more dependable and inclusive results. Additionally, self-report bias is an issue, as data collection heavily relies on students' self-reported opinions, which may introduce biases or rely on individuals' memories of specific experiences. To enhance data accuracy and comprehensiveness, it is recommended to incorporate multiple research methods for data verification and supplementation. Secondly, the study is limited by time constraints and participants' academic schedules, potentially hindering the collection of data over an extended period and resulting in data instability and an incomplete depiction of changes over time.

FUTURE STUDY

In future studies, we will conduct a pilot test to refine and validate our research approach, addressing several key limitations. This pilot test aims to ensure the clarity and effectiveness of survey questions, evaluate the study's focus and data collection time, identify and mitigate biases, and refine our research methodologies. It will involve a select group of students and serve as the foundation for subsequent larger-scale studies on online sexual content within the Vietnamese university student community.

CONTRIBUTION

Our findings suggest that it can assist in the development of more effective gender education programs. Our study also can provide policymakers in Vietnam with insights into the extent of exposure to sexual content among college-age students, enabling them to promote a safer online environment for Vietnamese youth. Moreover, this study lays the groundwork for prospective research endeavors in Vietnam exploring the influence of sexual content on digital media concerning the youth in the area.

CONCLUSION

In summary, this research aims to understand how gender differences and religious beliefs influence exposure to explicit content on social media among the selected students. These factors may increase students' active search for such content or decrease their intentional exposure to explicit content. From the analysis of the collected data, it can be observed that gender has the potential to increase the probability of both intended and unintended exposure to sexual content online, while religious beliefs might decrease the probability. These conclusions indicate the prevalence and forms of exposure to sexual content among the selected students, which may play a role in shaping gender education initiatives or enhancing the establishment of a more secure online environment.

REFERENCES

Ashata, Godwin & Extension, Kiu Publication. (2024). Digital Dynamics: Investigating the Impact of Social Media on Sexual Behavior. IDOSR JOURNAL OF COMMUNICATION AND ENGLISH, 9, 1-6, .DOI: 10.59298/IDOSR/JCE/92.16.202412

Ballester-Arnal, R., García-Barba, M., Castro-Calvo, J., Giménez-García, C., & Gil-Llario, M. D. (2023). Pornography Consumption in People of Different Age Groups: An Analysis Based on Gender, Contents, and Consequences. *Sexuality Research & Social Policy*, *20*(2), 766–779. DOI: 10.1007/s13178-022-00720-z

Bem, S. (1981). Gender Schema Theory: A Cognitive Account of Sex Typing. *Psychological Review*, *88*(4), 354–364. DOI: 10.1037/0033-295X.88.4.354

Campbell, L. F., & Stewart, A. E. (1992). Effects of Group Membership on Perception of Risk for Aids. *Psychological Reports*, *70*(3), 1075–1092. DOI: 10.2466/pr0.1992.70.3c.1075 PMID: 1496075

Chen, A., Leung, M., Chen, C., & Yang, S. C. (2013). Exposure to Internet Pornography Among Taiwanese Adolescents. *Social Behavior and Personality*, *41*(1), 157–164. DOI: 10.2224/sbp.2013.41.1.157

Cochran, J. K., & Beeghley, L. (1991, March). The Influence of Religion on Attitudes toward Nonmarital Sexuality: A Preliminary Assessment of Reference Group Theory. *Journal for the Scientific Study of Religion*, *30*(1), 45–62. DOI: 10.2307/1387148

Cohan, M. (2009). Forbidden Fruit: Sex & Religion in the Lives of American Teenagers. *Contemporary Sociology*, *38*(1), 31–32. DOI: 10.1177/009430610903800115

Coie, J. D., Watt, N. F., West, S. G., Hawkins, J. D., Asarnow, J. R., Markman, H. J., Ramey, S. L., Shure, M. B., & Long, B. (1993). The science of prevention: A conceptual framework and some directions for a national research program. *The American Psychologist*, *48*(10), 1013–1022. https://psycnet.apa.org/doiLanding?doi=10.1037%2F0003-066X.48.10.1013. DOI: 10.1037/0003-066X.48.10.1013 PMID: 8256874

C ng hòa xã h i ch nghĩa Vi t Nam - Ban Tôn Giáo Chính Ph . (2022). Tôn giáo và chính sách tôn giáo Vi t Nam. Th Gi i Publishers.

Cooper, A., Galbreath, N., & Becker, M. A. (2004). Sex on the internet: Furthering our understanding of men with online sexual problems. *Psychology of Addictive Behaviors*, *18*(3), 223–230. DOI: 10.1037/0893-164X.18.3.223 PMID: 15482077

Costello, B. J., & Laub, J. H. (2020, January). Social Control Theory: The Legacy of Travis Hirschi's Causes of Delinquency. *Annual Review of Criminology*, *3*(1), 21–41. DOI: 10.1146/annurev-criminol-011419-041527

Cretacci, M. (2003). Religion and Social Control: An Application of a Modified Social Bond on Violence. *Criminal Justice Review*, *28*(2), 254–277. DOI: 10.1177/073401680302800204

Do, L. H. (2016, May 31). nh hư ng c a tôn giáo đ n tư duy c a ngư i Vi t v m i quan h con ngư i và t nhiên. T p chí Lý lu n chính tr . Retrieved December 13, 2023, from https://lyluanchinhtri.vn/home/index.php/dien-dan/item/1493-anh-huong-cua-ton-giao-den-tu-duy-cua-nguoi-viet-ve-moi-quan-he-con-nguoi-va-tu-nhien.html

Ezzell, M. B., Johnson, J. A., Bridges, A. J., & Sun, C. F. (2020). I (Dis)Like it Like That: Gender, Pornography, and Liking Sex. *Journal of Sex & Marital Therapy*, *46*(5), 460–473. DOI: 10.1080/0092623X.2020.1758860 PMID: 32342728

Fisher, W. A., & Barak, A. (2001). Internet pornography: A social psychological perspective on Internet sexuality. *Journal of Sex Research*, *38*(4), 312–323. DOI: 10.1080/00224490109552102

Goldstein, A. C. (2018). More than an "Unhappy Object": The Ethical, Relational and Pedagogical Possibilities of Talking with Young People about Pornography [Doctoral dissertation].

Golemeeva, E. I. (2020) SEXUAL EXPLORATION IN THE 'DIGITAL AGE': HOW THE INTERNET INFORMS THE SEXUALITY OF YOUNG PEOPLE IN CONTEMPORARY BRITAIN. Doctoral thesis, University of Huddersfield.

Haggstrom-Nordin, E., Sandberg, J., Hanson, U., & Tyden, T. (2006). 'It's everywhere!' Young Swedish people's thoughts and reflections about pornography. *Scandinavian Journal of Caring Sciences*, *20*(4), 386–393. DOI: 10.1111/j.1471-6712.2006.00417.x PMID: 17116147

Hardy, S., Steelman, M., Coyne, S., & Ridge, R. (2013). Adolescent religiousness as a protective factor against pornography use. *Journal of Applied Developmental Psychology*, *34*(3), 131–139. DOI: 10.1016/j.appdev.2012.12.002

Hirschi, T. (1969). *Causes of delinquency*. University of California Press.

Hornor, G. (2020). Child and Adolescent Pornography Exposure. *Journal of Pediatric Health Care*, *34*(2), 191–199. DOI: 10.1016/j.pedhc.2019.10.001 PMID: 32063261

Lewis, L., Somers, J. M., Guy, R., Watchirs-Smith, L., & Skinner, S. R. (2018). 'I see it everywhere': Young Australians unintended exposure to sexual content online. *Sexual Health, 15*(4), 335–341. DOI: 10.1071/SH17132 PMID: 29925462

Liben, L. S., & Signorella, M. L. (1980, March). Gender-Related Schemata and Constructive Memory in Children. *Child Development, 51*(1), 11–18. DOI: 10.2307/1129584

Lim, M. S. C., Carrotte, E. R., & Hellard, M. E. (2015). The impact of pornography on gender-based violence, sexual health and well-being: What do we know? *Journal of Epidemiology and Community Health, 70*(1), 3–5. DOI: 10.1136/jech-2015-205453 PMID: 26022057

Ma, C., Shek, D., & Lai, C. (2017). Individual differences in intentional and unintentional exposure to online pornography among Hong Kong Chinese adolescents. *International Journal on Disability and Human Development : IJDHD, 16*(4), 417–423. DOI: 10.1515/ijdhd-2017-7010

Macleod, P. (2021). Influences on ethical decision-making among porn consumers: The role of stigma. *Journal of Consumer Culture, 21*(2), 381–404. DOI: 10.1177/1469540520970247

Markus, H., Crane, M., Bernstein, S., & Siladi, M. (1982). Self-Schemas and Gender. Journal of Personality and Social Psychology, 42(1), 38-50. https://0022-3514/82/4201-0038$00.75

Martin, C. L., & Halverson, C.Jr. (1981, December). A Schematic Processing Model of Sex Typing and Stereotyping in Children. *Child Development, 52*(4), 1119–1134. DOI: 10.2307/1129498

Mehta, M. D. (2004, July). Pornography in Usenet: A Study of 9,800 Randomly Selected Images. *Cyberpsychology & Behavior, 4*(6), 695–703. DOI: 10.1089/109493101753376641 PMID: 11800177

Mesch, G. (2008, August). Social bonds and Internet pornographic exposure among adolescents. *Journal of Adolescence, 32*(3), 601–618. DOI: 10.1016/j.adolescence.2008.06.004 PMID: 18694593

Narushima, M., Wong, J. P.-H., Li, A. T.-W., Bhagat, D., Bisignano, A., Fung, K. P.-L., & Poon, M. K.-L. (2020). Youth perspectives on sexual health education: Voices from the YEP study in Toronto. *The Canadian Journal of Human Sexuality, 29*(1), 32–44. DOI: 10.3138/cjhs.2019-0049

Nelson, L., Padilla-Walker, L., & Carroll, J. (2010). "I Believe It Is Wrong But I Still Do It": A Comparison of Religious Young Men Who Do Versus Do Not Use Pornography. *Psychology of Religion and Spirituality, 2*(3), 136–147. DOI: 10.1037/a0019127

Ngo, D. (2021, October 14). Ph i chăng gi i tr đang th ơ v i tôn giáo, ch y theo các giá tr hi n đ i? Báo thanh tra. https://thanhtra.com.vn/xa-hoi/doi-song/phai-chang-gioi-tre-dang-tho-o-voi-ton-giao-chay-theo-cac-gia-tri-hien-dai-189296.html

Peter, J., & Valkenburg, P. (2006, April). Adolescents' Exposure to Sexually Explicit Material on the Internet. *Communication Research, 33*(2), 178–204. DOI: 10.1177/0093650205285369

Rodrigues, D., Lopes, D., Dawson, K., Visser, R., & Štulhofer, A. (2021). With or Without You: Associations Between Frequency of Internet Pornography Use and Sexual Relationship Outcomes for (Non)Consensual (Non)Monogamous Individuals. *Archives of Sexual Behavior, 50*(4), 1491–1504. DOI: 10.1007/s10508-020-01782-z PMID: 32696155

Solano, I., Eaton, N. R., & O'Leary, K. D. (2018). Pornography Consumption, Modality and Function in a Large Internet Sample. *Journal of Sex Research, 57*(1), 92–103. DOI: 10.1080/00224499.2018.1532488 PMID: 30358432

Starr, C. R., & Ferguson, G. M. (2012). Sexy Dolls, Sexy Grade-Schoolers? Media & Maternal Influences on Young Girls' Self-Sexualization. *Sex Roles, 67*(7-8), 463–476. DOI: 10.1007/s11199-012-0183-x

Tan, S.-A., Goh, Y. S., Mohd Zaharim, N., Gan, S. W., Yap, C. C., Nainee, S., & Lee, L. K. (2022). Problematic Internet Pornography Use and Psychological Distress among Emerging Adults in Malaysia: Gender as a Moderator. *International Journal of Environmental Research and Public Health, 19*(6), 3682. DOI: 10.3390/ijerph19063682 PMID: 35329369

Tran, N. T. (1999). Cơ s văn hóa Vi t Nam. Giáo d c.

Wysocki, D. K. (1998). Let Your Fingers Do the Talking: Sex on an Adult Chat-line. *Sexualities, 1*(4), 425–452. DOI: 10.1177/136346098001004003

Youn, G. (2006). Subjective Sexual Arousal in Response to Erotica: Effects of Gender, Guided Fantasy, Erotic Stimulus, and Duration of Exposure. *Archives of Sexual Behavior, 35*(1), 87–97. DOI: 10.1007/s10508-006-8997-z PMID: 16502156

Chapter 7

Integrating TAM and UGT to Explore Motivations of Using Social Media for Watching Sport Contents Among a Private University's Students in HCM City

Le Thi My Danh
FPT University, Vietnam

Do Thi My Linh
FPT University, Vietnam

Huynh Ngoc Minh Thu
https://orcid.org/0009-0005-2123-6869
FPT University, Vietnam

Pham Huu Xuan Nhi
https://orcid.org/0009-0009-6533-8460
FPT University, Vietnam

Nguyen Le Bao Ngoc
FPT University, Vietnam

Tran Duy Hung
FPT University, Vietnam

ABSTRACT

This study examines the factors influencing private university students' consumption of sports content on social media. As digital sports media rapidly expands, we integrate the Technology Acceptance Model (TAM) and Uses and Gratifications Theory (UGT) to form a comprehensive framework. TAM assesses how perceived ease of use and usefulness shape engagement, while UGT explains how cognitive, social, and emotional needs drive content consumption. Key motivations include

DOI: 10.4018/979-8-3373-0603-2.ch007

information seeking, social interaction, and emotional gratification. Data is collected and analyzed using SPSS. The study fills a gap in Vietnamese sports media research and offers insights for improving digital engagement strategies among youth.

INTRODUCTION

The global landscape of sports media is characterized by its dynamic and continually evolving nature. Social media is defined as "a group of internet-based applications that build on the ideological and technological foundations of Web 2.0, and that allow the creation and exchange of user-generated content" (Kaplan AM et al., 2010). SM is extremely valuable for marketing and their value is increasing rapidly. On one hand, SM can provide information on what customers prefer and their characteristics (demographic and psychographic), information that is critical for developing a marketing strategy. The history of sports in the media is a captivating subject and has evolved significantly throughout time. The advent of modern mass media, including radio, television, and the internet, has been instrumental in the worldwide dissemination and commercialization of sports.

The evolution of sports media has been marked by significant milestones, beginning with the introduction of radio in the early 20th century. In 1921, KDKA in Pittsburgh made history by broadcasting the first live radio coverage of a sports event, granting fans the ability to listen to live commentary. Television emerged as a game-changer, with the inaugural televised sports event in 1939 featuring a college baseball game between Columbia and Princeton. This marked the start of a surge in televised sports popularity, with substantial events like the Olympics, World Cup,... becoming annual television spectacles, captivating millions of viewers. The 1970s witnessed the ascendancy of satellite and cable television, leading to a proliferation of sports channels and enabling the global broadcast of sports events. This era also saw the establishment of dedicated sports networks like ESPN, laying the foundation for round-the-clock sports coverage.

The advent of the internet in the 1990s marked a new era for sports media. Digital technology and the integration of social media further revolutionized sports coverage, allowing fans to engage with sports content through various online platforms. The proliferation of smartphones and mobile devices has made sports content even more accessible in recent years. This shift granted viewers greater control over their sports consumption, as they were able to personalize their viewing experiences.

Sports mass media play a crucial role in promoting physical activity and influencing social dynamics, reaching a wide demographic. A significant increase has been observed in the number of hours dedicated to sports broadcasts in the United States. In 2010, sports broadcasts amounted to approximately 84,000 hours. This figure demonstrably increased to 134,000 hours by 2018. Furthermore, sports broadcasts consistently hold a dominant position in viewership. Data from Nielsen (2018a) indicates that, in 2017, 86 of the 100 most-watched programs in the United States were sports-related. The prevalence of sports broadcasting extends beyond television. The existence of 600 radio stations in the United States dedicated exclusively to sports broadcasts further underscore the national interest in this domain (Wann & James, 2019).

Commentators' subjective opinions directly impact spectators' behavior, shaping their sentiments towards specific teams based on the euphoria experienced before victories and defeats (Kennard et al. (2018), Ličen (2008)). This underscores the media's sway over societal behavior and character, especially among the more impressionable younger audience. Furthermore, studies suggest that sports fans prioritize live broadcasts over recorded content. This preference may be linked to the belief that their live viewership somehow influences the game's outcome (Tamir, 2019). This emphasis on real-time viewing aligns with the strength of traditional television, which excels at delivering live broadcasts. An intriguing case study of emotional shifts among spectators occurred during the FIFA Confederation Cup in 2013 qualifier games featuring the National Football Team of Japan. Using a unified variance analysis and Tukey's method, it was determined that the Italy game evoked higher levels of positive emotions like pride, joy, and delight in contrast to the other two matches ($p < .001$). Additionally, variations in negative emotions like anxiety and outrage were observed, highlighting that a team's win or loss does not singularly dictate spectator emotions; substantial disparities emerged despite Japan losing all three games (Oshimi, Harada, & Fukuhara, 2014).

The impact of experiencing positive content from both media and sports on our overall well-being is a subject of debate. Some argue that while it may offer a temporary mood boost, it might not have a lasting effect on our long-term happiness. Factors like the content itself, our connection to it, and our surrounding environment play a role. Additionally, the question of whether the combination of positive media and sports leads to even greater happiness is not conclusively settled; some studies suggest a connection, but not all are in agreement. It appears to hinge on the significance of the content to us and its alignment with our interests. Quantifying the extent of this happiness boost is challenging, as happiness is a complex, subjective emotion. Ultimately, more research is needed to comprehensively understand how positive media and sports contribute to our overall happiness. While there is some evidence of their potential synergistic effects on our mood, there is still much to uncover in this area.

Recent research has significantly advanced our comprehension of these phenomena. Günther et al. (2021) underscore the efficacy of social media interventions in promoting physical activity (PA) and enhancing overall health outcomes.

González-Valero et al. (2023) assert that media depictions of physical activity and health exert substantive influences on individual behaviours and well-being. Moreover, their findings indicate that the portrayal of athletes and sporting events can stimulate community engagement, foster social cohesion, and shape individual attitudes towards physical activity.

Social media platforms have become fundamental tools for engaging sports fans, providing a straightforward means to communicate ideas visually, thereby minimizing potential misunderstandings while offering significant time-saving advantages and conveying messages more efficiently and effectively than alternative media channels (Hussain et al., 2022). Athletes, teams, and leagues have embraced platforms such as Twitter, Facebook, Instagram, and YouTube to directly connect with fans, share behind-the-scenes content, and provide live updates. Currently, research articles on sports media are widely popular around the world. However, in Vietnam, research on this topic is rarely exploited and there are not many research articles on the topic of sports media. Therefore, our research will be one of the pioneering articles exploring sports media in Vietnam and mainly about the sport aspect. The research will clarify the motivations that make students in Vietnam watch sports media and whether the positive effects of sport and the positive effects of media combined create greater positivity. Or can it create happiness for those who approach it?

In this study, the Technology Acceptance Model (TAM) and Use and Gratification (UGT) are chosen to be used in this research due to the relevance level of these theories to the topic. They can be applied well to explore What are the motivations that influence private University students in using social media for consuming sports content, as explored through these 2 theories/models.

The research on sports media in Vietnam is going to teach us a lot of new things. Firstly, it will help us understand why students at FPT University in Vietnam like to watch sports on social media. This is important because it will help people who make sports content know what kind of things students enjoy. Secondly, the research will show that two theories, TAM and UGT, are really good at explaining why people use technology and why they like certain types of content. This is like saying that these theories really work. It's important because it helps us understand why people do the things they do when it comes to sports and technology.

This research holds significant value for various groups. FPT University stands to benefit by leveraging these findings to enhance the overall student experience. By backing projects and activities aligned with student interests, particularly in sports, the university can foster a more engaging and enriching environment. Additionally, individuals involved in producing and sharing sports content can utilize this research to tailor their material to resonate with FPT University students. This, in turn, leads to a broader audience appreciating their creations. The importance of this study lies in its foundational contribution to comprehending the student population at

FPT University, as well as in affirming the applicability of technology and content theories to the realm of sports. Ultimately, it strives to enhance the well-being and satisfaction of students by championing their passions and promoting their overall health. Until now, there are not so many research articles that analyse this field in Vietnam. It is considered an obstacle; however, it is also good news in some way, which can give great value.

LITERATURE REVIEW

We created a suitable research framework and produced specific hypotheses based on the fundamental components of TAM (Davis, 1989) and UGT (Katz, 1974).

The Technology Acceptance Model (TAM)

Davis Fred raised this model in the 1980s. He said this model explained user acceptance of technology by considering 2 key factors: perceived usefulness (PU) and perceived ease of use (PEOU). Many researchers such as Niehaves and Plattfaut, 2014; Munoz-Leiva et al., 2017 Nagy, 2018;... had pointed out the relationship between these 2 factors. A technology seems to be not useful if it is complex and difficult to use.

H1: Individuals' perceived ease of use social media technology will positively influence their perceived usefulness of social media.

Perceived Usefulness (PU) mentions the person's belief about how using a particular technology will increase their job performance, even make their life easier. It is influenced by factors such as the functionality, effectiveness, and efficiency of the technology in fulfilling the user's needs or goals.

H2: Individuals' perceived usefulness of social media technology will positively and significantly influence their intentions of using social media to see sport-related content

Perceived Ease of Use (PEOU) refers to the human's belief about the ease or difficulty when using the technology. It included factors such as the user interface, simplicity, and clarity of the technology. A higher perceived ease of use leads to a higher likelihood of technology adoption.

H3: Individuals' perception of the ease of use of social media technology will positively and significantly influence their intentions of using social media to see contents regarding to sports.

The model presents a valuable framework for comprehending the factors that impact user acceptance and adoption of technology. By considering these key factors, organizations and designers can better understand and address user concerns, ultimately increasing the likelihood of successful technology adoption.

This model can be applied well to the research. According to the first factor - PU, technology helps things get done easily. Thus, using technology to watch sports could solve the problems about time, and geography,...of the spectators who don't have time to go to the stadium and watch the match lively or foreigners who want to watch the match of their favourite team but live too far away.

The second factor, PEOU, shows that a simple interface of the technology could increase the percentage of people adopting the technology. According to Hilvert-Bruce et al., 2018 and Needleman, 2015, in recent years, a substantial increase in the popularity of live streaming has appeared, which is a novel form of media service. This surge is primarily driven by the emergence of diverse online platforms such as YouTube live and Twitch. Live streaming has now become the best way to watch a football match, basketball match,...or any sports activity because of the user-friendly interface (Tyreal Yizhou Qian, 2022). Spectators can also interact and connect with many other viewers and express their emotions and reactions to the match. People can also give virtual gifts and other interactional extensions during the stream. This gives them a similar experience to those who are spectating at the stadium and more convenient. According to Lara Stiris (2022), Amazon's Twitch attracted sports organizations to stand out as some of the premier platforms for streaming video games globally, receiving over one million daily views. All these show that sports and technology now have a good relationship with each other.

The Uses and Gratifications Theory (UGT)

The Uses and Gratifications Theory aims to elucidate the rationale behind individuals' selection of specific media forms, the inherent needs compelling such choices, and the gratifications ultimately obtained through their consumption. (Katz and Blumler, 1974). UGT is regarded as a theory that focuses on the user's needs and motivations (West & Turner, 2010). UGT has been applied across diverse media and contexts, addressing users' social, psychological, and spiritual needs via technology (Dhir et al., 2016). Yuemin Han et al. in 2023 utilized UGT to investigate the motivation of Chinese university students in utilizing social media for news consumption.

Blumler and Katz's Uses and Gratification theory articulates that media consumption is intentional, aimed at achieving particular objectives. It posits that audiences actively choose media forms that align with their specific communicative requirements, suggesting a competitive landscape where media outlets strive to meet these diverse needs through varied offerings. This competition is intensified by the presence of both modern and traditional media forms. The theory underscores that audiences are conscious and deliberate in their media engagement, driven by personal motivations and needs, thereby applying individual value judgments to the content they consume.

According to Faiswal Kasirye (2022), the theory operates on two primary assumptions regarding media. Firstly, it posits that audiences actively select content for consumption. Next, it assumes that media users possess a heightened awareness of their reasons for choosing specific media. The theory also acknowledges that individuals wield significant influence in determining their media preferences and the impact that media exerts on them. (Faiswal Kasirye, 2022). Watching sports on media can offer an engaging experience, potentially satisfying various senses individually or collectively (e.g., providing respite from work, cheering for a favourite team/athlete, social interaction). Consequently, this activity on social media holds the potential for fulfilling psychological needs and promoting well-being. However, no study has yet examined the extent of such fulfilment and its benefits, necessitating empirical investigation. Additionally, discerning factors like sports enthusiasm and media environment would enhance understanding of need fulfilment while watching sports on social media.

Integration, social interaction, and a desire for social welfare are core motivators for internet usage (Hennig-Thurau et al., 2004). So, in the case of exploring the motivation for watching sports content on social media, we mention some specific variables:

Cognitive need: social media serves as a conduit for users to access information about transactions, news, shopping, and daily activities, among other closely intertwined aspects of their lives (Whiting & Williams, 2013). The degree to which users' cognitive needs are gratified through social media exhibits a positive correlation with their attitudes and intentions in utilizing these platforms (Camilleri & Falzon, 2020; Chung & Austria, 2010).

Recent research corroborates these claims. Yu Tian et al. (2023) identified a significant positive relationship between media use and sports participation behaviour, encompassing both physical participation and consumption behaviour. This effect is largely due to the media's ability to shape perspectives on sports (Puertas-Molero et al., 2019), offering a didactic narrative that underscores the importance of sports (Marín et al., 2008). Sports are viewed not only as a consumer product but also as an industry that attracts fans, spectators, and participants, becoming a significant consumption factor when produced for mass audiences (Yu Tian et al., 2023). Given that sports fans engage with multiple media platforms, organizations should employ a comprehensive social media strategy to enhance brand perception and, consequently, influence sports consumption behaviour (Eagleman, 2013). Thus, the following hypothesis can be proposed:

H4. Individuals' cognitive needs will positively and significantly influence their intentions to use social media for watching sport-related content.

Social need: personal needs, encompassing integration needs, social interaction needs, and a desire for social welfare (Hennig-Thurau et al., 2004), are regarded as the crucial motivation for users to engage with the internet. In watching sports, there are some specific available needs which can be mentioned as social interaction, connectivity, personal identity and expression. Wang Zhigang et al. (2022) explore how social needs influence meaningful sports consumption, highlighting that consumers seek not only hedonic value but also a greater purpose and meaning through sports, with team affiliation and self-esteem playing significant mediating roles. Thus, the following hypothesis can be proposed:

H5. Individuals' social needs will positively and significantly influence their intentions to use social media for consuming sports content.

Affected need: users seek emotional satisfaction through online streaming technology, finding joy, relieving pressure, and relaxing in their leisure time (Camilleri & Falzon, 2020). This also aids in fulfilling their entertainment needs. Camilleri and Falzon (2020) found that, in line with the UGT, people's drive to utilize online streaming technologies for specific purposes positively and significantly influences their intention to use these technologies. In our study, we assume that our respondents, like those in Camilleri and Falzon's research:

i. were experienced with the use of smartphones and/or tablets (this assisted them in making "decisions driven by motivation");

ii. were using social media to watch sports.

Therefore, the following hypothesis can be suggested that

H6. Affective needs have a positive impact on the intention to use social media for sport-related content.

After discussing based on the frameworks, we conclude that this research will test 5 variables. Among them, the variables of perceived ease of use and versatility will contribute to examining the application of the TAM theory to elucidate the motivations for viewing sport content on social media. UGT will be validated through Cognitive needs, Social needs, and Affected needs. Additionally, there is also the motivation to seek exercise inspiration in practice from sport content on social media platforms.

Figure 1. The conceptual model & hypotheses formulation

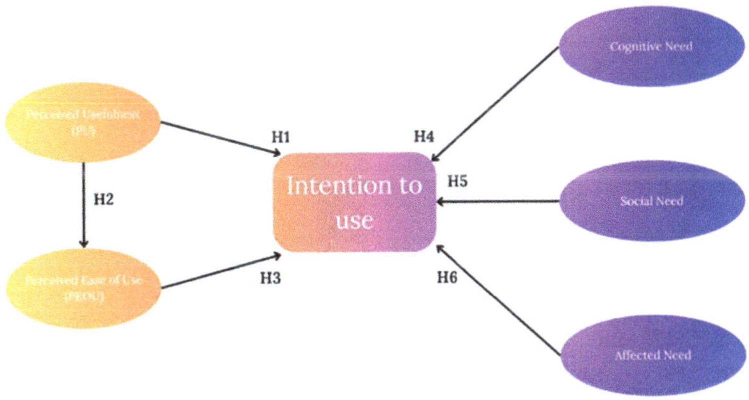

Source: Han et al. (2023)

METHODOLOGY

Research Design

Data collection involves three key components: sampling methods, research sample selection, and use of research tools and measurement items necessary to conduct a questionnaire survey. This research will use Google Forms for data collection, offering an efficient platform for online surveys. It aims to explore students' motivations for using social media for sports viewing and understand their post-match emotional experiences. The questionnaire will cover various aspects of motivation and emotional engagement.

In order to lay the theoretical groundwork for the study, an examination of pertinent academic sources on sports media will be examined. These sources will be accessed through platforms such as Google Scholar and other reputable academic research websites. Through the review of research papers, articles, and journal publications, the study will strive to attain a comprehensive comprehension of the existing body of knowledge in this domain. Essential sources for establishing the research framework will include the User & Gratifications Theory, Technology Acceptance Theory, and prior investigations on the engagement of sports media and social media.

The target participants will be private University students in Vietnam. By selecting university students, who are at the age of 18 to 25 as the participants, the study aims to gain insights into the motivations of the younger population who actively use social media and have an interest in sports. The size of the participant sample will be determined based on the principles of statistical sampling, ensuring sufficient representation to draw meaningful conclusions.

Research Instrument

To assess people's perception of how easy it is to use and how useful social platforms are, we employed scales derived from Davis's seminal work (1989) on the Technology Acceptance Model. Within each of these two constructs, there were three items utilized. The items comprising the constructs 'Cognitive needs', 'Emotional needs', and 'Social needs' were drawn from Hennig-Thurau et al.,'s study in 2004. Each of these constructs encompassed three items, demonstrating a certain level of reliability for applications on mobile platforms and within the domain of social media (Hennig-Thurau et al., 2004). It is noteworthy to mention that the category pertaining to "Finding motivation for Physical Activity" is a theoretical construct that remains untested in the present study, existing solely in a hypothetical framework. Furthermore, the items related to 'Intention to Use' were sourced from both the UGT scale developed by Venkatesh et al. (2000) and the TAM scale by Davis (1989). For the entirety of the study, each item across all variables was assessed employing A 5-grade Likert scale, extending from 1 (strongly disagree) to 5 (strongly agree).

Measures

The questionnaires will likely include these sections:

Demographics: Collecting age, gender, academic major, university, and social media usage frequency for context and potential variations in motivations and experiences.

Motivations for social media sports watching: Using likert scale or agree/disagree options based on User & Gratifications Theory and Technology Acceptance Theory.

Social Media Usage for Sports: exploring participants' preferences and habits in consuming sports content on social media.

Emotional experiences: gaining insights into participants' post-sports-watching emotions through selection from a predefined list and an open-ended question for more detailed responses.

Quantitative analysis will be applied to process survey data, identifying common patterns and trends. This analysis will deepen our understanding of Vietnamese university students' motivations for using social media for sports consumption and contribute to existing research in this area.

Sampling Design

This research employed a random sampling approach and used a structured questionnaire as the data collection tool to evaluate research variables, including college students' motivation and intention to use social media for accessing sport-related content. It is advisable to have sample sizes of 100 or more to ensure robust and reliable results (Hair, Anderson et al., 1995). We gathered 102 questionnaires from the participants. Following data screening, one invalid questionnaire was excluded, resulting in a final count of 101 questionnaires. This sample size of 101 is considered adequate for testing the model fit and research hypothesis.

DATA ANALYSIS

Table 1. The measuring items

Perceived Ease of Use	
PEoU1	**I find it convenient to watch sports on social media platforms.**
PEoU2	Accessing sports news or content in various formats (pictures, texts, videos) is easy on social media
PEoU3	Watching sports content on social media is simple, whether on a phone, tablet, etc.
Perceived Usefulness	
PU1	Social media allows me to access sports content more quickly than traditional methods.
PU2	The technology of social media enhances my experience of consuming sports-related content.
PU3	Given a reliable Wi-Fi or Internet connection, I can access to sports-related content on social media from any location.
Cognitive Need	
CN1	Social media helps me gain a deeper understanding of various aspects of sports.
CN2	Searching for new sport contents, I use social media
CN3	Searching for useful sport contents, I use social media
Social Need	
SN1	Watching sport contents on social media has made me feel more connected to people
SN2	Utilizing social media to watch sports-related information enables me to communicate with and receive feedback from others.
SN3	My capacity to communicate with others has improved as a result of using social media when approaching to sport

continued on following page

Table 1. Continued

Perceived Ease of Use	
PEoU1	**I find it convenient to watch sports on social media platforms.**
Affective Need	
AN1	Engaging in discussions about sports on social media is something I greatly enjoy.
AN2	The visual aspects of sports-related posts on social media, such as layout and illustrations, are appealing.
AN3	Using social media to watch sports related content makes me feel satisfied.
Intention to use	
ITU1	Using social media to read sports content is my future plan
ITU2	It is predicted that I will use social media a lot to read sports content
ITU3	Using social media to read sports content will always be my favorite thing to do
ITU4	I strongly recommend others to use social media for accessing sports-related content.

For data analysis, the research will use SPSS in addition to Google Forms. SPSS is a popular statistical software program that allows researchers to examine data using various approaches such as descriptive statistics, inferential statistics, and correlation analysis. The collected survey data will be inputted into SPSS for comprehensive analysis, enabling the identification of patterns, relationships, and significant findings related to the motivations of Vietnamese university students in using social media for sports watching. The study utilized SPSS 25.0 and AMOS 26.0 for analyzing questionnaire data, involving tasks such as describing the sample, conducting confirmatory factor analysis (CFA), and executing path analysis. Additionally, SPSS and AMOS were employed to assess the reliability and accuracy of the measurement model. The research also applied structural equation modeling to investigate the hypotheses.

Table 2. Reliability analysis results

Construct	Items	Mean Scores	Std. Deviations	Cronbach's Alpha
Perceived Ease of Use	PEoU1	4.3762	.75962	0.816
	PEoU2	4.4950	.67266	
	PEoU3	4.6436	.60966	
Perceived Usefulness	PU1	4.2574	.86780	0.759
	PU2	4.3465	.78020	
	PU3	4.4752	.75623	

continued on following page

Table 2. Continued

Construct	Items	Mean Scores	Std. Deviations	Cronbach's Alpha
Cognitive Need	CN1	4.0594	.83453	0.820
	CN2	3.9010	.96442	
	CN3	3.8317	.98050	
Social Need	SN1	3.8713	.95565	0.805
	SN2	3.9505	.87608	
	SN3	3.3465	1.17844	
Affective Need	AN1	3.3663	1.19769	0.851
	AN2	3.6931	.97717	
	AN3	3.6337	1.04616	
Intention To Use	ITU1	3.5050	1.18848	0.908
	ITU2	3.3861	1.22450	
	ITU3	3.1287	1.30126	
	ITU4	3.5842	1.04180	

Data Analysis Results

The provided data represents the results of a survey conducted at FPT University Ho Chi Minh Campus in Vietnam, involving 101 participants. The survey was focused on " Kh o sát nh ng đ ng l c s d ng m ng xã h i đ xem n i dung th thao c a sinh viên đ i h c FPT TP.HCM"

Perceived ease of use which individuals perceive they can employ social media technology will have an essential and beneficial influence on perception of the practicality of social media.

The statements PEoU1, PEoU2, and PEoU3 received high ratings, indicating a favorable view of social media's convenience for accessing sport-related content. Cronbach's Alpha for this construct was 0.816, indicating strong internal consistency. This value signifies a relatively elevated degree of internal coherence among the survey items pertaining to the concept of Perceived Ease of Use. A higher Cronbach's Alpha value, closer to 1, suggests that the survey items consistently measure the same underlying concept. In this instance, the results suggest that the survey items gauging the ease of using social media to access sports-related content are reliable and consistently measure the same concept.

Perceived usefulness which individuals' perceived utility of social media technology will favorably and considerably affect their intents to consume sports news on social media.

Examining the individual Perceived Usefulness (PU) statements. PU1, PU2, and PU3 highlighting the perceived benefits of using social media for sports content. The assessment of internal consistency or trustworthiness of these survey items, measured by Cronbach's Alpha at 0.759, offers a moderate degree of internal consistency observed within the items associated with Perceived Usefulness.

Cognitive need which individuals' cognitive requirements will have a favorable and considerable effect on their intents to consume sports-related information on social media.

According to survey results, social media evidently serves as a crucial tool for acquiring knowledge and content related to sports. CN1, CN2, and CN3 suggest that social media aids in acquiring sports knowledge and seeking new content. Furthermore, the survey's internal consistency, determined by Cronbach's Alpha at 0.820, demonstrates a reliable assessment of cognitive needs related to sports through these statements.

Social need factor which measures participants' perceptions regarding the impact of social media on their sense of connection and communication with others in relation to sports.

The "Social Need" factor includes SN1, SN2, SN3 sub-variables. These suggest that social media enhances connection and communication about sports. The score indicates that participants feel their ability to communicate with others regarding sports has improved because of social media. Cronbach's Alpha coefficient, at 0.805, illustrates a great degree of internal coherence between the items.

Affective need factor which measures participants' perceptions regarding the aesthetic aspects of sport-related content on social media.

AN1, AN2, and AN3 indicate enjoyment and satisfaction with sports content aesthetics on social media. In terms of internal consistency, Cronbach's Alpha coefficient for this factor is 0.851, indicating a strong level of consistency among the measured items.

Intention to use factor measures participants' intentions and predictions regarding their future use of social media to read sports content.

Looking at the result of the "Intention to use" variable and its 4 sub-variable such as ITU1, ITU2, ITU3, ITU4. These indicate moderate to high intention to use and recommend social media for sports content. Cronbach's Alpha coefficient shows the number 0.908, designating a strong level of internal consistency among the items.

The Confirmatory Factor Analysis

Structural Equation Modeling (SEM) is a robust multivariate analytical approach progressively employed in academic research to examine and evaluate multivariate causal relationships (Fan, Y., et al., 2016). In conducting confirmatory factor analysis, AMOS will be employed. Convergent validity can be affirmed through the evaluation of factor loadings, Average Variance Extracted (AVE), and Composite Reliability (CR), following the recommendations of Hair (2010). It's important to mention that Hair et al. (2009, p. 619) indicated that CR values exceeding 0.7 suggest strong reliability. Furthermore, to ensure an acceptable level of convergent validity, the AVE should not be less than 0.5, highlighting that, according to Fornell and Larcker (1981, p. 46), the latent construct elucidates a minimum of 50% of the indicator variance. In this study, CR values ranged from 0.666 to 0.913, while AVE ranged from 0.401 to 0.780, in line with the aforementioned guidelines.

Table 3. Confirmatory factor analysis

	Factor	Items	CR	AVE
1	Perceived ease of use	PEoU1	0,819	0,602
		PEoU2		
		PEoU3		
2	Perceived usefulness	PU1	0,770	0,528
		PU2		
		PU3		
3	Cognitive need	CN1	0,666	0,401
		CN2		
		CN3		
4	Social need	SN1	0,774	0,535
		SN2		
		SN3		
5	Affective need	AN1	0,809	0,586
		AN2		
		AN3		
6	Intention to use	ITU1	0,913	0,780
		ITU2		
		ITU3		

Hypotheses Testing Results

Table 4. Model Fit Indicator

Common Indicator	χ2	df	p	χ2/df	RMSEA	GFI	CFI	TLI
Judgment Standards	-	-	>0.05	≤ 2	≤ 0.08	≥ 0.9	≥ 0.9	≥ 0.9
Value				1.831	0.091	0.795	0.910	0.893

Table 4 indicates: χ2/df=1.831, RMSEA=0.091, GFI=0.795, CFI=0.910, TLI=0.893. A point to note is that the GFI value was lower than the judgement criteria due to the quantity of sample was not large enough. The results indicated that the final model achieved a satisfactory level of fit, and all fitting indicators are within the specified range as per recommendations.. This suggests that the structural model effectively captured and represented the data. (Hair et al., 2006)

Table 5. Hypotheses testing results

Hypothesis	Path	Unstd. Estimate	S.E.	C.R.	p-value	Std. Estimate	Decision
H1: PEOU → PU	Perceived Ease of Use → Perceived Usefulness	0.65	0.13	5.00	***	0.63	Supported
H2: PU → INT	Perceived Usefulness → Intention to Use	0.54	0.15	3.60	***	0.55	Supported
H3: PEOU → INT	Perceived Ease of Use → Intention to Use	0.47	0.18	2.61	0.009	0.48	Supported
H4: CN → INT	Cognitive Needs → Intention to Use	0.58	0.17	3.41	***	0.51	Supported
H5: SN → INT	Social Needs → Intention to Use	0.43	0.19	2.26	0.024	0.44	Supported
H6: AN → INT	Affective Needs → Intention to Use	0.39	0.16	2.44	0.015	0.40	Supported

Referring to Table 5, the hypotheses testing results reveal significant insights into the factors influencing the intention to use social media for watching sport-related content. Specifically, the standardized path coefficient for Perceived Ease of Use (PEOU) influencing Perceived Usefulness (PU) is 0.63 with a critical ratio (C.R.) of 5.00 and p-value < 0.001, indicating a strong positive effect, thus supporting H1. Similarly, Perceived Usefulness (PU) significantly impacts Intention to Use (INT) with a standardized estimate of 0.55, C.R. = 3.60, and p-value < 0.001, supporting H2.

Moreover, PEOU also positively influences INT with a standardized estimate of 0.48, C.R. = 2.61, and p-value = 0.009, thus supporting H3. The Cognitive Need

(CN) has a substantial positive effect on INT, evidenced by a standardized estimate of 0.51, C.R. = 3.41, and p-value < 0.001, supporting H4. Social Need (SN) and Affective Need (AN) also positively affect INT with standardized estimates of 0.44 and 0.40, critical ratios of 2.26 and 2.44, and p-values of 0.024 and 0.015 respectively, thereby supporting H5 and H6.

In summary, the data analysis demonstrates that all proposed factors significantly contribute to the intention to use social media for sports content consumption. These findings underscore the importance of perceived ease of use, perceived usefulness, and various user needs in shaping user intentions in the digital sports content domain.

Figure 2. Structural equation modelling results

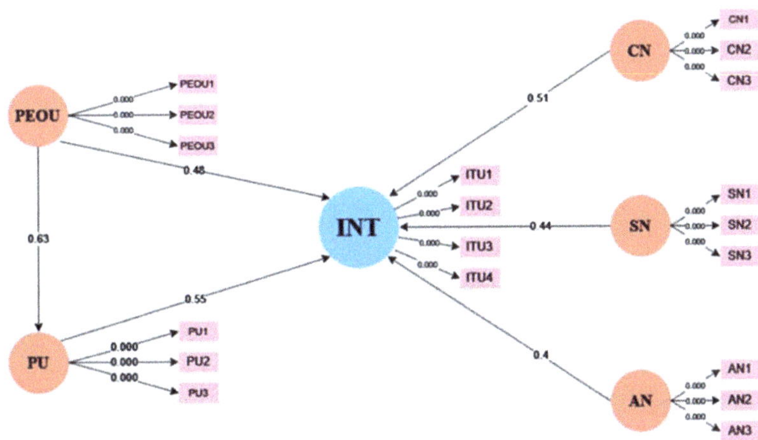

DISCUSSION

This study investigates the motivations behind university students' use of social media for accessing sports-related content, focusing on a sample from FPT University Ho Chi Minh Campus in Vietnam. The findings highlight several key motivations, including perceived ease of use, perceived usefulness, cognitive needs, social needs, and affective needs. These motivations significantly influence students' intentions to use social media for sports content consumption.

Perceived Ease of Use: The results show that students find social media platforms easy to use for accessing sports content. The high ratings for statements such as PEoU1, PEoU2, and PEoU3 indicate that students view social media as convenient and adaptable for consuming sports-related content. This aligns with the Technology

Acceptance Model (TAM), which emphasizes the importance of perceived ease of use in technology adoption (Davis, 1989).

Perceived Usefulness: The findings also reveal that students perceive social media as a valuable tool for accessing sports content. The positive ratings for PU1, PU2, and PU3 suggest that social media enhances the sports-watching experience by providing quick access to content and enriching the overall experience. This supports the TAM's assertion that perceived usefulness influences users' intentions to adopt technology (Davis, 1989).

Cognitive Needs: The study demonstrates that social media serves as an essential tool for acquiring sports knowledge. Statements CN1, CN2, and CN3 received favorable ratings, indicating that students use social media to seek new sports-related content and useful information. This finding aligns with the Uses and Gratifications Theory (UGT), which posits that individuals use media to fulfill their cognitive needs (Hennig-Thurau et al., 2004).

Social Needs: The research highlights the role of social media in fulfilling students' social needs related to sports. The positive ratings for SN1, SN2, and SN3 suggest that social media facilitates communication, feedback, and a sense of connection with others. This finding is consistent with UGT, which emphasizes the importance of social interaction in media usage (Hennig-Thurau et al., 2004).

Affective Needs: The study also reveals that social media fulfills students' affective needs by providing an enjoyable and satisfying experience when consuming sports-related content. The favorable ratings for AN1, AN2, and AN3 indicate that students appreciate the aesthetic aspects of sport-related posts and feel satisfied using social media for sports content. This finding supports UGT's assertion that individuals use media to fulfill their affective needs (Hennig-Thurau et al., 2004).

The findings have practical implications for social media platforms and sports organizations. To enhance user engagement and satisfaction, these entities should focus on improving the ease of use, perceived usefulness, and the ability to fulfill cognitive, social, and affective needs. By doing so, they can better cater to the motivations of university students and other users who consume sports-related content on social media.

Overall, this study contributes to the understanding of university students' motivations for using social media for sports content consumption. The findings highlight the importance of perceived ease of use, perceived usefulness, cognitive needs, social needs, and affective needs in influencing students' intentions to use social media for accessing sports-related content. These insights provide valuable implications for social media platforms and sports organizations aiming to enhance user engagement and satisfaction.

CONCLUSION

The Technology Acceptance Model (TAM) and the Uses and Gratification Theory (UGT) are used in this study to investigate why scholars at FPT University in Ho Chi Minh City view sports content on social media. The findings show that researchers' assessments of the ease of utilizing media technology, its utility, and their contentment with the cognitive, social, and affective rudiments of using social media have a significant influence on their use of sports content. This new collaboration between TAM and UGT offers a fresh perspective on the motivational rudiments that support FPT University scholars' use of social media for sports content. Only UGT continues to impact drug users' proclivity to access sports material on social media, while TAM does not. As a result, the relationship between perceived utility (PU) and perceived ease of use (PEOU), which asserts that "individuals' perceived ease of use of social media technology will appreciatively and considerably impact their perceived utility of social media," isn't completely established. This may be because of the small sample size of only 101 respondents, which may not effectively represent neutrality and variety. This research has the potential to benefit FPT University scholars by encouraging healthy habits. Furthermore, content creators and marketers working in student-led sports systems can use this perception to tailor their content and marketing techniques to the target audience's expectations and preferences, resulting in more successful engagement. Despite the study's sample size limitations, the findings contribute to our knowledge and implementation of TAM and UGT propositions, as well as practical advice for social media platforms. A future study could expand on these findings by investigating other elements that influence social network druggies' interaction with sports content, providing a more comprehensive and in-depth perspective for theoretical inquiry and practical application.

LIMITATIONS AND FUTURE RESEARCH DIRECTIONS

Sports media research articles are currently quite popular all around the world. However, sport media research is infrequently employed in Vietnam, and there are few study studies on the subject. As a result, our research will be among the first to explore sport media in Vietnam, with an emphasis on the sporting side. The future research on this topic in Vietnam constitutes a big milestone, but it is fraught with constraints and potential stumbling blocks. The scarcity of local references and data on this topic is a severe constraint. Furthermore, our data collection efforts will be restricted to FPT University Ho Chi Minh, with a focus on its student body. The potential limitation of these findings is that they may have limited generalizability.

We want to address these constraints in a variety of ways. To begin, we would like to broaden our scope by exploring global research on this topic in the hopes of finding parallels or insights relevant to the Vietnamese context. This necessitates a thorough examination of the processes and data gathering strategies employed in comparable research around the world. Furthermore, we are always looking for contacts with students from different universities and colleges in order to expand our sample pool and improve the perspectives represented. We seek to increase the objectivity and robustness of the data we collect by engaging with the true target audience.

REFERENCES

Camilleri, M. A., & Falzon, L. (2020). Understanding motivations to use online streaming services: Integrating the technology acceptance model (TAM) and the uses and gratifications theory (UGT). *Spanish Journal of Marketing ESIC, 24*(2), 267–289. DOI: 10.1108/SJME-12-2019-0105

Chung, C., & Austria, D. (2010). Social media gratification and attitude toward social media marketing messages: A study of the effect of social media marketing messages on online shopping value. Proceedings of the Northeast Business & Economics Association, 581–586.

Davis, F. D. (1989). Perceived usefulness, perceived ease of use, and user acceptance of information technology. *Management Information Systems Quarterly, 13*(3), 319–340. DOI: 10.2307/249008

Dhir, A., Chen, S., & Nieminen, M. (2016). The effects of demographics, technology accessibility, and unwillingness to communicate in predicting internet gratifications and heavy internet use among adolescents. *Social Science Computer Review, 34*(3), 278–297. DOI: 10.1177/0894439315582854

Eagleman, A. N. (2013). Acceptance, motivations, and usage of social media as a marketing communications tool amongst employees of sport national governing bodies. *Sport Management Review, 16*(4), 488–497. DOI: 10.1016/j.smr.2013.03.004

Fan, Y., Chen, J., Shirkey, G., John, R., Wu, S. R., Park, H., & Shao, C. (2016). Applications of structural equation modeling (SEM) in ecological studies: An updated review. *Ecological Processes, 5*(19), 19. Advance online publication. DOI: 10.1186/s13717-016-0063-3

Fornell, C., & Larcker, D. F. (1981). Evaluating Structural Equation Models with Unobservable Variables and Measurement Error. *JMR, Journal of Marketing Research, 18*(1), 39–50. DOI: 10.1177/002224378101800104

González-Valero, G., Melguizo-Ibáñez, E., Ortega-Caballero, M., Marfil-Carmona, R., Zurita-Ortega, F., & Puertas-Molero, P. (2023). Mass media pressure on psychological and healthy well-being: An explanatory model as a function of physical activity. *Journal of Public Health (Berlin), 31*(10), 1663–1671. DOI: 10.1007/s10389-022-01733-z

Günther, L., Schleberger, S., & Pischke, C. R. (2021). Effectiveness of social media-based interventions for the promotion of physical activity: Scoping review. *International Journal of Environmental Research and Public Health, 18*(24), 13018. DOI: 10.3390/ijerph182413018 PMID: 34948628

Hair, J., Black, W., Babin, B., Anderson, R., & Tatham, R. (2006). *Multivariate Data Analysis* (6th ed.). Pearson Education.

Hair, J. F. (2010). *Multivariate Data Analysis* (7th ed.). Pearson Education Limited.

Hair, J. F., Anderson, R. E., Tatham, R. L., & Black, W. C. (1995). *Multivariate data analysis*. Prentice-Hall.

Hair, J. F., Black, W. C., Babin, B. J., & Anderson, R. E. (2009). *Multivariate Data Analysis* (7th ed.).

Han, Y., Mahamed, M. B., Abdullah, Z., & Abas, W. A. B. W. (2023). Integrating TAM and UGT to Explore Motivations of using Social Media for News Reading among Chinese College Students. *International Journal of Academic Research in Business & Social Sciences.*

Hennig-Thurau, T., Gwinner, K. P., Walsh, G., & Gremler, D. D. (2004). Electronic word-of- mouth via consumer-opinion platforms: What motivates consumers to articulate themselves on the internet? *Journal of Interactive Marketing*, *18*(1), 38–52. DOI: 10.1002/dir.10073

Hilvert-Bruce, Z., Neill, J. T., Sjöblom, M., & Hamari, J. (2018). Social motivations of live-streaming viewer engagement on Twitch. *Computers in Human Behavior*, *84*, 58–67. DOI: 10.1016/j.chb.2018.02.013

Hussain, G., Naz, T., Shahzad, N., & Bajwa, M. J. (2022). *Social media marketing in sports and using social media platforms for sports fan engagement*. Ghulam Hussain's Lab., DOI: 10.47750/cibg.2021.27.06.117

Kaplan, A. M., & Haenlein, M. (2010). Users of the world, unite! the challenges and opportunities of social media. *Business Horizons*, *53*(1), 59–68. DOI: 10.1016/j.bushor.2009.09.003

Kasirye, F. (2022). The Importance of Needs in Uses and Gratification Theory. DOI: 10.31124/advance.14681667.v2

Katz, E., Blumler, J. G., & Gurevitch, M. (1974). Uses and gratifications research. *Public Opinion Quarterly*, *37*(4), 509. DOI: 10.1086/268109

KDKA. Retrieved July 24, 2024, from https://www.britannica.com/topic/KDKA

Kennard, C.. (2018). The impact of sports commentary on viewer emotions and team loyalty. *Journal of Sports Media*, *17*(3), 129–142.

Ličen, S., & Doupona Topič, M. (2008). The imbalance of commentators' discourse during a televised basketball match. University of Ljubljana, Faculty of Sport. Original scientific paper. UDC 796.072.3:796.323.2.

Marín-Montín, J. (2008). Educate in sport through TV: Teaching sport with TV. *Comunicar, 16*(31), 227–233. DOI: 10.3916/c31-2008-03-044

Muñoz-Leiva, F., Climent-Climent, S., & Liébana-Cabanillas, F. (2017). Determinants of intention to use the mobile banking apps: An extension of the classic TAM model. *Spanish Journal of Marketing - ESIC, 21*(1), 25–38. DOI: 10.1016/j.sjme.2016.12.001

Nagy, J. (2018). *Evaluation of online video usage and learning satisfaction: An extension of the Technology Acceptance Model. The International Review of Research in Open and Distributed Learning, 19 (1).* Athabasca University Press., DOI: 10.19173/irrodl.v19i1.2886

Needleman, S. E. (2015, January 29). Twitch's viewers reach 100 million a month. The Wall Street Journal. http://blogs.wsj.com/digits/2015/01/29/twitchs-viewers-reach-100-million-a-month/

Niehaves, B., & Plattfaut, R. (2014). Internet adoption by the elderly: Employing IS technology acceptance theories for understanding the age-related digital divide. *European Journal of Information Systems, 23*(6), 708–726. DOI: 10.1057/ejis.2013.19

Nielsen. (2018, February). 2017 year in sports media. Nielsen. https://www.nielsen.com/insights/2018/2017-year-in-sports-media/#

Oshimi, D. (2015) Emotions of Sport Spectators, ResearchGate. Available at: https://www.researchgate.net/publication/283770561_Emotions_of_Sport_Spectators

Oshimi, D., Harada, M., & Fukuhara, T. (2014). Spectators' emotionsduring live sporting events: Analysis of spectators after the loss of thesupported team at the 2013 FIFA confederations cup. *FootballScience, 11*, 48–58.

Puertas-Molero, P., Marfil-Carmona, R., & Zurita-Ortega, F. (2019). Impact of sports mass media on the behavior and health of society: A systematic review. *International Journal of Environmental Research and Public Health, 16*(3), 486. DOI: 10.3390/ijerph16030486 PMID: 30744007

Qian, T. Y. (2022). Watching sports on Twitch? A study of factors influencing continuance intentions to watch Thursday Night Football co-streaming. *Sport Management Review, 25*(1), 59–80. DOI: 10.1080/14413523.2021.1930700

Quan-Haase, A., & Young, A. L. (2010). Uses and gratifications of social media: A comparison of Facebook and instant messaging. *Bulletin of Science, Technology & Society*, *30*(5), 350–361. DOI: 10.1177/0270467610380009

Stiris, L. (2022, June 24). How Twitch built the global live streaming network that powers Amazon IVS. Amazon Interactive Video Service.

Tamir, D. (2019). The psychology of live sports broadcasts: The impact of live viewing on fan engagement. *Journal of Sport Psychology*, *45*(4), 567–584.

This Day in Tech History. (2023). First Sports TV Broadcast. Retrieved from thisdayintechhistory.com Columbia University. (2019). Columbia Celebrates 80th anniversary of first live televised sporting event in the United States.

Tian, Y., Yang, P., & Zhang, D. (2023). The relationship between media use and sports participation behavior: A meta-analysis. *Digital Health*, *9*, 20552076231185476. Advance online publication. DOI: 10.1177/20552076231185476 PMID: 37434724

Tucker, B. (2022, September 14). History of cable. SeatUp. https://seatup.com/blog/history-of-cable/

Venkatesh, V. (2000). Determinants of perceived ease of use: Integrating control, intrinsic motivation, and emotion into the technology acceptance model. *Information Systems Research*, *11*(4), 342–365. DOI: 10.1287/isre.11.4.342.11872

Wang, Z., Guo, K., Wang, C., Duan, H., Zhang, L., & Zhao, X. (2022). How can social needs impact on meaningful sports consumption? *Frontiers in Psychology*, *13*, 1043080. Advance online publication. DOI: 10.3389/fpsyg.2022.1043080 PMID: 36405184

Wann, D. L., & James, J. D. (2019). Sports broadcasting and fan engagement: The role of media in shaping sports consumption. *International Journal of Sport Communication*, *12*(1), 55–73.

West, R. L., Turner, L. H., & Zhao, G. (2010). *Introducing communication theory: Analysis and application* (Vol. 2). McGraw-Hill.

Whiting, A., & Williams, D. (2013). Why people use social media: A uses and gratifications approach. *Qualitative Market Research*, *16*(4), 362–369. DOI: 10.1108/QMR-06-2013-0041

Chapter 8
Nurturing Future-Ready Talent by Understanding the Role of Talents' Sustainable and Professional Digital Persona on Hiring Decisions

Nur Atikah A. Rahman
https://orcid.org/0000-0001-5544-5769
Universiti Sains Malaysia, Malaysia

Sharifah Nadiah Syed Mukhiar
https://orcid.org/0000-0002-4458-9334
Universiti Sains Malaysia, Malaysia

Rani Ann Balaraman
Universiti Sains Malaysia, Malaysia

ABSTRACT

Social media has become an essential source for hiring professionals to screen and cybervet potential employees. However, talents in Malaysia are unaware of this practice and how negative content can impact their career prospects. This study focuses on leveraging talent's identity to create sustainable and professional digital persona. It aims to investigate the reasons why sustainable and professional digital

DOI: 10.4018/979-8-3373-0603-2.ch008

persona of job seekers impacts the decision-making process of recruiters when selecting candidates. Through qualitative interviews, this study found significant impact of a job candidate's digital persona on recruiters' selection decisions, emphasising the importance of character assessment, communication skills, cultural fit evaluation, consistency, and the use of LinkedIn as the primary platform for professional networking. Understanding on the need of sustainable and professional digital persona in job hunting can further contribute towards the improvement of digital recruitment process for productive employment and sustainable economic growth in Malaysia, in line with SDG8.

INTRODUCTION

In recent years, like many other countries across the world, Malaysia has joined the global effort towards achieving 17 Sustainable Development Goals (SDGs) in its nation-building plan for a sustainable tomorrow. With a target to meet all goals by 2030, Malaysia seeks to eradicate poverty, inequality, environmental protection, and overall well-being for its citizens (WHO, 2024). However, based on the report of Malaysia's Eleventh Plan, the country's labour market faces challenges that may hinder the achievement of productive employment (SDG8). Notably, issues surrounding decent work and economic growth still persist within the country's labour market.

In spite of enhancements in minimum wages and increased employee compensation (CE), the nation continues to experience significant job losses and reduced incomes (Moreira, 2022). According to Trading Economics (2021), during the COVID-19 pandemic, the unemployment rate in Malaysia increased to 4.8% in December 2020. Most people became jobless due to closure of businesses and Movement Control Order (MCO) that was enforced by the government. At that time, 83.4% of the unemployed population were actively seeking for jobs, whereas the rest were inactive.

As Malaysia transitions from pandemic to endemic phases, economic recovery has begun. Businesses resumed operations with the lifting of MCOs and online businesses flourished. The positive momentum of national economic situation and global economic expansion showed an ascending trend in the country's labour market. By January 2024, Malaysia's unemployment rate had dropped to 3.3%, or approximately 567,300 people (Department of Statistics Malaysia, 2024). Although the rate has decreased, the number of unemployed individuals remains significant, highlighting the need for a more robust employment ecosystem.

Coherent with the Twelfth Malaysia Plan tabled on 27 September 2021 and Malaysia MADANI, presented by the 10th Prime Minister in 2023 as part of the national recovery strategy for sustainable and inclusive growth, addressing unemployment challenges is essential to produce future-ready talents. The Twelfth Malaysia Plan

(2021-2025) aims for long-term economic growth (RMK12, 2022) and reflects the government's commitment to create inclusive and sustainable society. Malaysia MADANI emphasises on innovation, respect, care and compassion, where inclusion and equality are the main focus for a more just society. Berg (2015) explained that in establishing a more just society, government should support the creation of valuable careers, good working salaries and conducive working environment as solutions for those that are still unemployed.

To address unemployment issues, Malaysia must prioritise developing future-ready talents through Chapter 10 outlined in the Twelfth Plan – leveraging new technologies (RMK12, 2022). Leveraging emerging technologies like social media for talent acquisition is crucial in today's digital landscape, where recruiters rely on online platforms to assess job candidates' suitability and credibility (The Economic Times, 2023; Walrave et al., 2022). The traditional ways of job seeking and recruitment such as printed resumes and interviews have been largely supplanted by social media, which has become a critical tool for recruiters (Minor-Cooley & Parks-Yancy, 2020). Social media platforms allow users to create and share content (text, audios, videos, pictures, and live stream videos) about themselves. These platforms include social networking sites (SNS) (i.e. Facebook, Instagram, LinkedIn), content communities (i.e. Youtube), blogs and microblogging (i.e. Twitter, Blogspot), and more. Therefore, it is imperative to understand the current recruitment process and help talents provide the right information for better employability ecosystem.

Unfortunately, many young talents are unaware of how cybervetting is used by recruiters to evaluate job candidates based on their digital presence. Arvind and Arpita (2020) shared that recruiters assess job candidates' verbal, non-verbal, and visual information on social media (Harrison & Budworth, 2015). During the initial selections before the interview, hiring professionals seek to understand various aspects of job candidates through the publicly available online information (Walrave et al., 2022). This process helps to validate talents' qualifications and view their professional and personal self-presentation (CareerBuilder, 2018). Moreover, cybervetting is not only prevalent in the United States of America, but is also crucial in countries like Australia, India, Indonesia, Japan, Malaysia and the Philippines (Abate et al., 2015). Nevertheless, many young talents remain oblivious that their daily posts on social media (SNS, blogs, content communities and more) may not portray sustainable digital persona that is professional and positive for better career opportunities. Thus, talents need to play a more active role in their personal brand, particularly in developing sustainable communication that reveals professional digital persona.

CYBERVETTING

Cybervetting is the practice of hiring professionals in evaluating job candidates based on their online presence and social media content to identify suitable employees (Gruzd et al., 2020). This practice is to dig deeper into a candidate's identity and lifestyle, blurring the lines between professional and personal information (McCabe, 2017). In the United States of America, 98% of companies use candidates' social media profiles in the hiring process as cited in Baykal, 2020), with LinkedIn being the most common supplementary recruitment tool (98%), followed by Facebook, Instagram, Twitter, and others. Tarpey (2018) reports 70% of employers use social media to further investigate applicants, and 43% of these employers recruit talents whose social media presence aligns positively with the company's goals.

Malaysian hiring professionals also examine job seekers' digital footprints to verify their identity and suitability for roles (Tengku Siti Meriam et al., 2019). However, Malaysian young users do not realise how their negative social media posts can affect their future career prospects (Tengku Siti Meriam et al., 2019). In digital realm, social media posts leave digital footprints that are publicly accessible and can be scrutinised.

DIGITAL FOOTPRINT ON SOCIAL MEDIA

While social media content posted by job candidates may not always reflect their true character, this information can still influence hiring professionals, potentially leading to negative perceptions and biases (Baykal, 2020). Specifically, employers can uncover extensive details about talents' identity, backgrounds and behaviours from their digital footprint on social media and the Internet, including aspects like appearance, demographics, interests, beliefs, disabilities, and conduct.

Digital footprint comprises data that individuals generate while engaging online, encompassing both active and passive components. Passive digital footprints consist of data inadvertently shared through interactions on websites with tracking mechanisms such as cookies and search engine algorithms (Tengku Siti Meriam et al., 2019). In contrast, active digital footprints involve information intentionally provided on online platforms and social media, such as posts, location tags, and multimedia uploads (i.e. pictures, audio, reels, video, and more). Both types of information, are readily accessible online and can be challenging to erase.

Negative content, such as inappropriate behaviour and appearance on social media can tarnish an individual's reputation and affect their career opportunities (Johnson, 2017). Minor-Cooley and Parks-Yancy (2020) indicated that if an employer perceived a talent's digital persona is negative, this can result in being overlooked from hiring selection. Similarly, Vara (2010) and Johnson (2017) indicated that employers value talents with positive and professional online presence, which can be associated to further trust in talents' abilities. Thus, it is essential for individuals to be mindful of their online activities and strive to maintain a sustainable communication and professional digital persona to safeguard their career opportunities.

SUSTAINABLE COMMUNICATION

Communication, as a fundamental aspect of human interaction, permeates various aspects of life, from personal exchanges to professional engagements. In this process, both sender and receiver actively engage, with the sender constantly, gauging understanding through feedback from the recipients (Genç, 2017).

Sustainability has emerged as a crucial corporate strategy, emphasising responsible stewardship of financial, human, and natural resources to meet present needs without compromising future generations (Ragauskas et al., 2006). Scholars highlight sustainability as a multifaceted concept capable of fostering connections with society, expanding customer bases, reducing operational costs, and benefiting communities at large (Doorley & Garcia, 2007; Ioakimidis, 2007; von Kutzschenbach & Brønn, 2006). Sustainable communication, therefore, involves the exchange of information, ideas, and messages in a manner that minimises adverse environmental, social, and economic impacts while maximising positive outcomes. It necessitates mindful consideration of communication practices on sustainability goals.

In simpler terms, sustainable communication involves communicating in socially responsible and environmentally conscious way, that avoids any negative impacts on society, the economy or the world. More importantly, in the context of job seeking, sustainable communication aims to ensure that interactions and messaging on social media promotes long-term well-being and employability.

SUSTAINABLE AND PROFESSIONAL DIGITAL PERSONA

Individuals need to be strategic in shaping their identity or persona on social media. A significant 37% of employers consider candidate's social media personal brand when differentiating between competitive applicants (Driver, 2018). Personal branding involves strategies used by celebrities, business owners, and politicians to develop a unique persona and image to market themselves (Peters, 2016). It helps to establish an emotional connection between individual and audience (Springer, 2020). Moreover, personal branding allows talents to showcase their competitive advantages and prominent persona to self-present towards society and employers

(Jacobson, 2020), by highlighting one's value, skills, experience, personality, and capabilities for job hunting.

However, research on personal branding in recruitment and social media, especially in Malaysia, remains scarce. Existing studies have predominantly examined on Western perspectives such as cybervetting in social media in recruitment (Walrave et al., 2022); impact of social media content on job seeking and effect of personal branding on job seeking (Minor-Cooley & Parks-Yancy, 2020; Perez & Gringarten, 2020; Nugraha et al., 2020). Other studies have examined presentation of self and hiring recommendations (Johannes & Hung-Yue, 2015); social media as recruitment tool (Baykal, 2020), and using social media in hiring decisions (Arvind & Arpitha, 2020; Scolere, Prunchniewska & Duffy, 2018; Johnson, 2017; El Ouirdi et al., 2016; Dijck, 2013).

Research has also explored how personal branding affects millennials' career success in Indonesia (Melissa et al., 2020). However, limited research has explored on the role of personal branding in Malaysia, including its impact on facing cybervetting in recruitment (Nur Atikah et al., 2022), and the power of self-branding in social media towards job opportunities in Malaysia (Nur Atikah, 2021). Other studies include the awareness of digital footprint management in the new media amongst youth (Tengku Siti Meriam et al., 2019), using social networking sites (SNS) for job searches and online recruitment through social media (Din et al., 2015). There is also scarcity of studies on social media personal branding in nurturing future-ready talent for better employability and labour market equity. Henceforth, to bridge this knowledge gap on realigning labour market equity, it is crucial to understand the fundamentals of personal branding on social media to cultivate digitally savvy individuals who can evolve into future-ready talents.

In Keller's (1993) brand equity model, a strong brand should progress through the phases of salience, performance, imagery, judgments, feelings, and resonance. This model helps shape the audience's (recruiter or employer) perceptions and emotions towards a personal brand. To cultivate a positive, credible and impactful personal brand, individuals on social media should differentiate and position themselves by navigating each stage of the pyramid. In the context of the job market, this model can help for individuals to strategically convey their prominent advantages and desirable identity to employers.

In the first phase, salience focuses on building awareness by establishing an individual's unique brand identity. Kapferer (2012) defined brand identity as setting individuals apart from their competitors and peers. At this stage, individuals can introduce themselves, emphasising on who they are and how they can contribute to a prospective employer. Particularly, users should ensure that their personal brand is aligned with the organisation's objectives, to make it enticing and memorable to hiring professionals.

Moving on to the second phase, social media users should imbue their content to showcase their performance and image. In this process, the content should appeal to both rational and emotional aspects to demonstrate what they can offer to their prospective employers. The rational aspect focuses on how well does the individual perform and how they can meet the recruitment's needs. While emotional aspect influences how they are perceived as – positive or negative. At this stage, users need to carefully craft the right message and content to ensure their brand resonates with the target audience (employers).

Next, the third phase is on judgement and feelings. This phase involves employers forming opinions based on what they observe on social media content. The process encompasses both rational judgements and emotional reactions. This is where employers respond to the candidate's identity and reputation. Thus, personalising content to make it relatable to the audience or employers is the key to foster favourable connection with the personal brand.

Lastly, the resonance phase. In this final stage, individuals or candidates establish positive relationship with their audience or potential employers. Brand resonance occurs when employers perceive the candidate's personal brand on social media is in sync with the organisation's objectives and brand image. To effectively implement strategic personal branding, individuals should consistently share their narrative across various platforms like Facebook, Instagram, YouTube and Twitter. Consequently, professional storytelling along with sustainable communication are important to ensure that their digital persona is perceived to be positive and professional.

Therefore, it can be concluded that there is a lack of attention given to personal branding through social media for job seeking opportunities. The existing theoretical concepts related to personal branding in social media usage lack addressing their role in nurturing future-ready talents in recruitment selections. Thus, this chapter aims to look into the underlying reasons of why sustainable and professional digital persona of talents drives favourable recruitment selection.

METHODOLOGY

This chapter is an exploratory research that utilised a qualitative research approach through in-depth interviews. According to Harding (2019, p. 44), interviews offer "the opportunity to listen and understand the perspectives or experiences of an individual for an extended period of time and ask probing questions to explore ideas further". In-depth interviews were conducted to obtain the viewpoints and experiences of hiring professionals in diverse industries across Malaysia. This qualitative study was aimed to explore why sustainable and professional digital persona is vital for favourable recruitment selection.

In-depth interviews were conducted using non-probability sampling, specifically purposive sampling (Campbell et al., 2020). A semi-structured interview protocol was developed to guide the interviews towards achieving the research objectives. This protocol outlined the main topics the research aimed to address and was open-ended and flexible to elicit insights and experiences from the informants (King, Horrocks & Brooks, 2019).

Furthermore, purposive sampling was used to select hiring professionals in Malaysia from diverse fields that meet the criteria of this research, such as:

1. Informants are responsible for the recruitment of employees in their organisation.
2. Informants have decision-making authority in the employment process.
3. Informants use social media platforms as part of their hiring process.

A total of 12 informants, consisting of managers and executives from various companies, were recruited to represent hiring professionals. The number of informants was based on the richness and saturation of the data (Baker & Edwards, 2012).

DEMOGRAPHIC PROFILE ON RESPONDENTS

The respondents were categorised as R1, referring to Respondent 1, up to R12, referring to Respondent 12. The data regarding the respondents is as follows.

Table 1. Demographic Data of Respondents

Respondent	Position	Work Experience (Year)	Company
Respondent 1	Global Documentation Manager	8	Technical Publication
Respondent 2	Campus Hiring Lead	2.5	Information Technology
Respondent 3	Talent Acquisition Leader	17	T/IT services
Respondent 4	Senior Engineering Manager	10	R&D Semiconductor
Respondent 5	Talent Acquisition Head	21	Information Technology and Computing
Respondent 6	Asst Director Admin ex HR Asst Manager	21	Education

continued on following page

Table 1. Continued

Respondent	Position	Work Experience (Year)	Company
Respondent 7	Business Analysis	2.5	IT and Engineering Services
Respondent 8	Client Partner	8	IT and Engineering service
Respondent 9	Client Partner	12	Software
Respondent 10	Senior Executive, PR & Events	2	Consulting & Events
Respondent 11	Managing Director	3	Advertising
Respondent 12	Director/Founder	3	Video Production House

FINDINGS

A sustainable and professional digital persona of job candidates positively influences recruiters' selection decisions for several reasons. By examining their online presence, recruiters can gain insights into the candidate's values, beliefs, and personality traits. This information is crucial for understanding how the candidate may fit within the company's culture and interact with colleagues and clients. For instance, posts and comments that reflect empathy, integrity, and a positive outlook can signal a candidate who is likely to contribute positively to the workplace environment.

Respondents 1, 6, 7, 8, 9, 10, and 11 emphasised the importance of character when evaluating a candidate's professional digital persona. Observing how a candidate interacts on social media allows recruiters to gauge their attitude and energy levels. Positive interactions, such as encouraging comments and constructive feedback, suggest that the candidate possesses a positive attitude and is likely to bring positive energy to the workplace. This is essential for maintaining a motivated and collaborative work environment.

According to R1,

"I examine the professional digital persona of job candidates to understand their character. A candidate's personality is crucial because they will act as ambassadors who represent the company's reputation" (Interview with R1, May 17, 2024).

Meanwhile, Respondents 2 and 12 focused on the communication skills of potential candidates. According to them, a candidate's ability to communicate effectively online is a critical factor in the hiring decision. Clear, concise, and thoughtful communication displayed on digital platforms suggests that the candidate can articulate ideas well and engage constructively in professional settings.

R12 explained,

"I review job applicants' social media profiles to assess their communication skills, which are essential in my field as it involves frequent interaction with the media" (Interview with R12, May 17, 2024).

Recruiters also use a candidate's online behaviour to assess their potential cultural fit within the organisation. A digital persona that aligns with the company's values and ethos indicates that the candidate is likely to adapt well to the organisational culture. The way a candidate behaves towards others on social media can provide insights into their interpersonal skills and respect for others. Recruiters look for evidence of courteous and respectful interactions, as these behaviours are indicative of a candidate who can foster healthy and productive relationships at work.

According to R4,

"It is very important to observe if the candidate has a positive attitude or not based on their posts because negative or confrontational behaviour can raise red flags about the candidate's ability to work well with others" (Interview with R4, May 17, 2024).

A candidate's digital persona also helps justify their public appearance and reputation. Consistency between a candidate's online presence and their professional image can enhance their credibility. Recruiters look for coherence between what candidates claim in their resumes and how they present themselves online. This consistency reassures recruiters that the candidate is authentic and trustworthy. Recruiters use digital personas to identify any red flags that might indicate potential issues with the candidate.

R9 stated,

"Negative behaviours, such as discriminatory remarks or inappropriate content, can significantly impact the decision to hire. By thoroughly evaluating a candidate's online activities, recruiters can avoid hiring individuals who may bring undesirable traits into the workplace" (Interview with R9, May 18, 2024).

When asked about the most commonly used social media platform by hiring managers, all respondents identified LinkedIn as the primary choice. They highlighted that LinkedIn is the most professional networking platform, offering numerous courses and having a significant impact. With over 700 million users worldwide, LinkedIn provides companies access to a vast and diverse database.

R5 explained,

"Companies can review candidates' work experience, skills, achievements, recommendations, and the content they share, offering a more comprehensive view of the candidates" (Interview with R5, May 6, 2024).

According to R3,

"LinkedIn is the most professional networking platform that companies can use to find potential candidates" (Interview with R3, May 6, 2024).

MAKING INFERENCES AND PERCEPTIONS ABOUT CANDIDATES

The digital persona of a job candidate plays a significant role in shaping recruiters' perceptions and making inferences about their suitability for a position. This theme explores how online behaviour and content can influence recruiters' views and the potential discrepancies between a candidate's digital presence and real-life behaviour. R3 emphasised the importance of clarity in understanding a candidate's online persona. Recruiters rely on the information shared on social media to gauge the candidate's professionalism, interests, and overall fit for the company.

According to him,

"Clear and consistent online behaviour can reinforce a positive perception, while discrepancies or negative content can raise concerns" (Interview with R3, May 6, 2024).

R12 highlighted how a candidate's social media posts can shape their perception of the candidate's personality and lifestyle. For example, posts that showcase a candidate's interests, hobbies, and lifestyle choices can provide a more rounded view of who they are outside of their professional life. This additional layer of understanding can be crucial for determining cultural fit within the organisation. R12 also shared an experience that underscores the potential pitfalls of relying solely on a digital persona. In this case, a candidate presented a very professional image online and during the interview process.

"However, after being hired, the candidate revealed a different personality on social media, using the 'close friends' feature on Instagram to rant and display unprofessional behaviour. This stark contrast between the candidate's digital persona and their real-life actions highlighted the risk that a polished online presence might sometimes be just a mask to secure a job" (Interview with R12, May 17, 2024).

ASSESSING THE SUITABILITY OF CANDIDATES FOR THE COMPANY OR ROLE

Evaluating a candidate's suitability for a company or specific role involves a thorough assessment of their digital persona to ensure it aligns with their professional capabilities and the company's values. Respondents provided varied approaches to this evaluation process, highlighting the importance of both social media behaviour and technical qualifications.

Some companies take a stringent approach, rejecting candidates outright if their social media posts contain negative comments that conflict with the company's beliefs. This immediate rejection underscores the importance of alignment between a candidate's online behaviour and the company's ethos. R6 shared their perspective on this approach,

"We may hire candidates even if they have a somewhat negative social media record, giving them an opportunity to demonstrate their potential. However, if we find that the candidate continues to exhibit negative behaviour on social media, we will review their candidacy during the probation period and terminate their service if necessary" (Interview with R6, May 13, 2024).

This stance illustrates a balance between giving candidates a chance to prove themselves and maintaining strict standards for social media conduct. It acknowledges that while initial impressions based on social media are important, ongoing behaviour is a crucial determinant of a candidate's suitability.

Another approach involves directly addressing discrepancies between a candidate's digital persona and their professional qualifications. Companies might ask candidates to justify the information they share on social media. If the explanation is unsatisfactory or reveals any misconduct, the candidate is rejected. This method emphasises transparency and accountability, ensuring that candidates are given a fair chance to explain themselves while maintaining the integrity of the hiring process. Additionally, technical qualifications remain paramount in the hiring decision.

R7 said,

"If a candidate's qualifications do not match the requirements of the position, they are informed upfront. This practice ensures that both the company and the candidate do not waste time pursuing a misaligned opportunity" (Interview with R7, May 13, 2024).

Moreover, assessing a candidate's authenticity through their social media presence is crucial. Companies seek to verify that the qualifications and persona presented online genuinely reflect the candidate's capabilities and behaviour. This verification helps in gauging whether the candidate is a true fit for the role and the organisational culture.

DRAWBACKS OF RELYING ON DIGITAL PERSONAS IN HIRING DECISIONS

Evaluating candidates based on their digital personas presents several significant drawbacks, potentially impacting the hiring process and outcomes. One major concern is the potential to overlook exceptional candidates who may not have a strong or active online presence.

As R1 highlighted,

"Sometimes, a candidate might not seem suitable through their digital persona, but they actually have extraordinary potential that we are unaware of. So, evaluating through social media has its drawbacks" (Interview with R1, May 17, 2024).

R4 highlighted that crucial aspects like technical skills and interpersonal abilities are often best assessed through direct interactions rather than online profiles. Digital personas tend to provide a limited view, focusing more on surface-level information rather than in-depth evaluations of a candidate's competencies. R7 warned about the discrepancy between digital personas and real-life capabilities, leading to unmet expectations. Many candidates curate their online presence to present an idealised version of themselves, which may not accurately reflect their true abilities or personality.

Relying on digital personas can introduce biases and lead to misconceptions. R2 pointed out that digital evaluations can create biases based on superficial factors such as appearance, social connections, and online activity levels. R5 accentuated that these biases often stem from misinterpretations of online content, potentially leading to wrong judgments about a candidate's suitability. R9 and R12 both noted the misleading nature of digital personas, with R9 mentioning,

"Viewing a digital persona can be misleading if it presents the wrong image of the person" (Interview with R9, May 18, 2024).

R2 raised ethical concerns regarding the extent to which employers should evaluate candidates based on their online activity. The balance between thorough vetting and respecting candidates' privacy and personal boundaries is delicate and requires careful consideration. Over-reliance on digital personas may lead to invasive scrutiny of candidates' private lives, which can be ethically questionable and potentially illegal in certain jurisdictions.

The prevalence of fake resumes and exaggerated skills on digital platforms is a significant issue. R9, R10, and R11 discussed how candidates often embellish their achievements and capabilities online. R11 stated,

"In the digital world, everything appears perfect, but only when we meet face-to-face do we learn the truth. This can lead to hiring decisions based on inflated or false information, which ultimately harms the organisation" (Interview with R11, May 18, 2024).

Not all candidates are active on social media or share much information online, which can limit the effectiveness of digital evaluations. R6 pointed out that some highly qualified candidates might prefer to keep a low online profile, resulting in their exclusion from consideration if digital personas are heavily weighted in the hiring process. Despite these drawbacks, some respondents, like R3, believe there are no significant drawbacks if the digital persona complements the role. However, this perspective underscores the importance of using digital personas as a supplementary tool rather than a primary method of evaluation.

DISCUSSION AND CONCLUSION

The findings of this chapter underscore the significant impact that a talent's digital persona has on recruitment decisions in Malaysia. A sustainable and professional digital persona can enhance a talent's employability by demonstrating positive attributes, effective communication skills, and alignment with company values. Conversely, negative online behaviours and inconsistent digital footprints can lead to unfavourable perceptions and potential rejection.

Recruiters place substantial importance on a candidate's character and communication skills as revealed through their online presence. Positive interactions and clear, professional communication on social media are crucial indicators of a talent's suitability and potential fit within a company's culture. Previous studies indicated that communication skills ranked among the most important characteristics considered by hiring managers in Hong Kong (Moy, 2006) and India (Vijayakumar, 2017). The assessment of a candidate's online behaviour is instrumental in determining cultural fit with the company's values. Recruiters look for alignment between the candidate's values, attitudes, and the company's ethos. Positive and respectful online interactions suggest good interpersonal skills and a propensity to contribute positively to the workplace environment. This finding is aligned with a study by Alston (2019) which found that character traits were consistently ranked higher than academic traits during hiring process of hiring entry level pharmacists.

Consistency between a talent's online persona and their professional qualifications enhances credibility. Recruiters use digital personas to verify the authenticity of the information presented in resumes and during interviews. Discrepancies or negative behaviours online can raise red flags and affect hiring decisions (Johnson, 2017). However, while digital personas provide valuable insights, over-reliance on them can introduce biases and lead to misconceptions. Exceptional talents without a strong online presence might be overlooked, and superficial evaluations based on digital footprints might miss critical skills and qualities best assessed through direct interactions.

The extent of evaluating talents based on their online activity also raises ethical concerns. Balancing thorough vetting with respecting candidates' privacy is essential to avoid invasive scrutiny that could be ethically questionable or illegal. Therefore, it is imperative to educate young talents about the significance of maintaining a positive and professional digital persona (Kleppinger & Cain, 2015). Awareness programs on the impact of social media activities on employability should be integrated into career counselling and educational curricula. Talents should be encouraged to strategically curate their online presence, ensuring that it aligns with their professional goals and the expectations of potential employers. This includes engaging in professional networking, sharing relevant content, and avoiding negative or controversial posts.

Moreover, recruiters should adopt a balanced approach that combines digital persona assessments with traditional evaluation methods such as interviews and skill tests. This ensures a comprehensive understanding of the candidate's capabilities and suitability. Additionally, companies should develop clear policies and guidelines on the ethical use of social media in recruitment, as suggested by Hazelton and Terhorst (2015) and Kluemper (2013). This includes defining the boundaries of digital persona evaluations and ensuring transparency and fairness in the hiring process.

Henceforth, based on the insights from the findings, the influence of talent's sustainable and professional digital persona on recruitment selections align with Malaysia's Twelfth Plan, Malaysia MADANI and SDG8 by emphasising the importance of nurturing future-ready talent and enhancing the employability ecosystem. The focus on character assessment, communication skills and cultural fit evaluation through professional digital personas resonates with the Twelfth Plan's goal of developing skilled and adaptable human capital to drive economic growth and innovation (RMK12, 2022). Moreover, Malaysia MADANI's objectives of fostering a cohesive society is supported by the emphasis on respectful interactions and positive attitudes in the workplace. Additionally, by promoting transparency, fairness, and accountability in recruitment processes, it is in line with SDG's aim of promoting sustained, inclusive and sustainable economic growth, full and productive employment and decent work for all (WHO, 2024), creating a more robust and equitable employability in Malaysia.

Future research could explore on the impact of digital personas across different industries and cultural contexts to provide a more comprehensive understanding of their role in the global job market. Longitudinal studies could also examine how digital personas evolve over time and their long-term impact on career trajectories and employment outcomes. Furthermore, investigating on the role of emerging technologies and AI in digital persona assessments could provide insights into the future of recruitment practices and the ethical considerations they entail.

In conclusion, while digital personas play a crucial role in modern recruitment processes, it is essential to approach their evaluation with a balanced and ethical perspective, ensuring that they complement rather than replace traditional assessment methods. This study highlights the need for strategic personal branding and sustainable communication practices to enhance employability and foster a more equitable labour market. By understanding and leveraging the power of digital personas, talents and recruiters alike can contribute to a more efficient and fair hiring process.

REFERENCES

Abate, D. A., Goodman, M. E., Gorman, M. J., & Goury, R. (2015). *A global guide to background checks in Asia*. The Mayer Brown Practices.

Alston, G. L., Marsh, W., Castleberry, A. N., Kelley, K. A., & Boyce, E. G. (2019). Pharmacists opinions of the value of specific applicant attributes in hiring decisions for entry-level pharmacists. *Research in Social & Administrative Pharmacy, 15*(5), 536–545. DOI: 10.1016/j.sapharm.2018.07.004 PMID: 30006061

Baker, S. E., & Edwards, R. (2012). How many qualitative interviews is enough? Expert voices and early career reflections on sampling and cases in qualitative research. National Centre for Research Methods. https://eprints.ncrm.ac.uk/2273/4/how_many_interviews.pdf

Baykal, E. (2020). Digital era and new methods for employee recruitment. In *Handbook of Research on Strategic Fit and Design in Business Ecosystems* (pp. 412–430). IGI Global. DOI: 10.4018/978-1-7998-1125-1.ch018

Berg, J. (2015). Labour market institutions: the building blocks of just societies. In *Labour Markets, Institutions and Inequality* (pp. 1–36). Edward Elgar Publishing. DOI: 10.4337/9781784712105.00007

Campbell, S., Greenwood, M., Prior, S., Shearer, T., Walkem, K., Young, S., Bywaters, D., & Walker, K. (2020). Purposive sampling: Complex or simple? Research case examples. *Journal of Research in Nursing : JRN, 25*(8), 652–661. DOI: 10.1177/1744987120927206 PMID: 34394687

Dijck, J. V. (2013). 'You have one identity': Performing the self on Facebook and LinkedIn. *Media Culture & Society, 35*(2), 99–215.

Din, S. Z. M., Anuar, R. H. M., Omar, N., Omar, H., & Dahlan, J. M. (2015). Discovering the use of online recruitment via social media of student internship. *Procedia Economics and Finance, 31*, 856–860. DOI: 10.1016/S2212-5671(15)01181-8

Doorley, J., & Garcia, H. F. (2007). *Reputation management. The Key to Successful Public Relations and Corporate Communications*. Routledge.

Driver, S. (2018). Keep it clean: Social media screenings gain in popularity. Accessed from https://www.businessnewsdaily.com/2377-social-media-hiring.html (Accessed on 8 September 2020).

El Ouirdi, M., Pais, I., Seger, J., & El Ouirdi, A. (2016). The relationship between recruiter characteristics and applicant assessment on social media. *Computers in Human Behavior*, *62*, 415–422. DOI: 10.1016/j.chb.2016.04.012

Genç, R. (2017). The importance of communication in sustainability & sustainable strategies. *Procedia Manufacturing*, *8*, 511–516. DOI: 10.1016/j.promfg.2017.02.065

Gruzd, A., Jacobson, J., & Dubois, E. (2020, April-June). Cybervetting and the public life of social media data. *Social Media + Society*, *6*(2), 1–13. DOI: 10.1177/2056305120915618

Harding, J. (2019). *Qualitative Data Analysis: From Start to Finish* (2nd ed.). SAGE Publication.

Harrison, J. A., & Budworth, M. H. (2015). Unintended consequences of a digital presence. *Career Development International*, *20*(4), 294–314. DOI: 10.1108/CDI-06-2014-0080

Hazelton, A. S. & Terhorst, A. (2015) Legal and Ethical Considerations for Social Media Hiring Practices in the Workplace, *The Hilltop Review, 7*(2).

Ioakimidis, M. (2007). Green sport: A game everyone wins. *The Sport Journal*, *10*(2).

Jacobson, J. (2020). You are a brand: Social media managers' personal branding and "the future audience". *Journal of Product and Brand Management*, *29*(6), 715–727. DOI: 10.1108/JPBM-03-2019-2299

Johannes, K. C., & Hung-Yue, S. (2015). Self-presentation and hiring recommendations in online communities: Lessons from LinkedIn. *Computers in Human Behavior*, *48*, 516–524. DOI: 10.1016/j.chb.2015.02.017

Johnson, K. M. (2017). The importance of personal branding in social media: Educating students to create and manage their personal brand. *International Journal of Education and Social Science*, *4*(1), 21–27.

Kapferer, J. N. (2012). *The New Strategic Brand Management* (5th ed.). Kogan Page.

Keller, K. L. (1993). Conceptualizing, measuring and managing customer-based brand equity. *Journal of Marketing*, *57*(1), 1–22. DOI: 10.1177/002224299305700101

King, N., Horrocks, C., & Brooks, J. (2019). *Interviews in Qualitative Research* (2nd ed.). SAGE. DOI: 10.4135/9781036234881

Kleppinger, C. A., & Cain, J. (2015). Personal digital branding as a professional asset in the digital age. *American Journal of Pharmaceutical Education*, *79*(6), 1–4. DOI: 10.5688/ajpe79679 PMID: 26430266

Kluemper, D. H. (2013), Social Network Screening: Pitfalls, Possibilities, and Parallels in Employment Selection, *Social Media in Human Resources Management, Vol.* 12), pp. 1-21.

McCabe, M. B. (2017). Social media marketing strategies for career advancement: An analysis of LinkedIn. *Journal of Business and Behavioural Sciences*, *29*(1), 85–99.

Minor-Cooley, D., & Parks-Yancy, R. (2020). The power of the brand: Personal branding and its effect on job seeking attributes. *Journal of Internet Commerce*, *19*(3), 241–261. DOI: 10.1080/15332861.2020.1777028

Moy, J. W. (2006). Are employers assessing the right traits in hiring? Evidence from Hong Kong companies. *International Journal of Human Resource Management*, *17*(4), 734–754. DOI: 10.1080/09585190600581717

Nur Atikah, A. R. (2021). Rant today and regret it forever! The power of self-branding in social media towards job employments in Malaysia. In Mohamad Saifudin, M.S., Nur Atikah, A. R., & Didik, H. S. (2021). *How trends shape the media landscape: Malaysia and Indonesia* (pp. 17-24). Penerbit Universiti Pendidikan Sultan Idris.

Nur Atikah, , A. RShuhaida, , M. NRani, , A. BSuriati, , SSharifah Nadiah, , S. M. (2022). The role of personal branding for professional digital footprint: Facing employer's cybervetting in recruitment. *International Journal of Early Childhood Special Education, 14*(3), 6404-6412.

Perez, C., & Gringarten, H. (2020, Fall). Personal branding: An essential choise in the Covid-19 era? *Journal of Multidisciplinary Research*, *12*(2), 83–92.

Peters, T. (2016, May 18). The Brand Called You. https://www.fastcompany.com/28905/brand-called-you

Ragauskas, A. J., Williams, C. K., Davison, B. H., Britovsek, G., Cairney, J., Eckert, C. A., & Mielenz, J. R. (2006). The path forward for biofuels and biomaterials. *Science*, *311*(5760), 484–489. DOI: 10.1126/science.1114736 PMID: 16439654

RMK12. (2022). Tweltfh Plan. https://rmke12.epu.gov.my/en/documents/twelfth-plan (Accessed on 21 September 2022).

Scolere, L., Pruchniewska, U., & Duffy, B. E. (2018). Constructing the platform-specific self brand: The labor of social media promotion. *Social Media + Society*, *4*(3), 1–11. DOI: 10.1177/2056305118784768

Springer, K. (2020). *I am my brand: How to build your brand without apology*. Bloomsbury Publishing Plc.

Tarpey, M. (Careerbuilder.com) (August 9, 2018). Not getting job offers? Your social media could be the reason. Accessed from https://www.careerbuilder.com/advice/not-getting-job-offers-your-social-media-could-be-the-reason (Accessed on 10 February 2020).

Tengku Siti Meriam, T. W., Hazura, M., Siti Fadzilah, M. N., Zurina, M., & Intan Yusrina, Z. (2019). Awareness of digital footprint management in the new media amongst youth. *Jurnal Komunikasi, 35*(3), 407–421.

The Economic Times. (2023). What is Labour Market. Accessed from https://economictimes.indiatimes.com/definition/labour-market (Accessed on 28 February 2023).

Trading Economics. (2021). Malaysa Unemployment Rate. https://tradingeconomics.com/malaysia/unemployment-rate (Accessed on 9 February 2021).

Vijayakumar, M. (2017). Skill sets depicted by fresh graduates in campus hiring process. *International Journal of Innovative Science and Research Technology, 2*(7), 64–72.

von Kutzschenbach, M., & Brønn, C. (2006). Communicating sustainable development initiatives: Applying co-orientation to forest management certification. *Journal of Communication Management (London), 10*(3), 304–322. DOI: 10.1108/13632540610681185

Walrave, M., Ouytsel, J. V., Diederen, K., & Ponnet, K. (2022). Checked and approved? Human resources managers' uses of social media for cybervetting. *Journal of Cybersecurity and Privacy, 2022*(2), 402–417. DOI: 10.3390/jcp2020021

WHO. (2024). Sustainable development goals. https://www.who.int/europe/about-us/our-work/sustainable-development-goals#:~:text=The%20Sustainable%20Development%20Goals%20(SDGs,no%20one%20is%20left%20behind (Accessed on 3 May 2024).

Chapter 9
Poverty Eradication via Sustainable Human Development:
A Human Security Approach

Jipson Joseph
https://orcid.org/0009-0005-1795-5051
Christ University, India

Achyutananda Mishra
https://orcid.org/0000-0002-4113-0974
Christ University, India

ABSTRACT

Poverty has been one of the major human insecurities throughout history. It became more evident in the aftermath of the Industrial Revolution. Though economic growth was suggested as an effective mechanism for poverty eradication, it severely increased inequality together with poverty. Realizing the importance of poverty eradication for human well-being, the United Nations initiated many policies and programs including Millennium Development Goals (MDGs) and Sustainable Development Goals (SDGs). Based on the framework of MDGs, the SDGs was moving towards the achievement of 'no poverty' by 2030. But the Covid-19 pandemic slowed this pace, demanding more earnest effort from the international community. This chapter, in this perspective, using critical analytical method examines the possibility of human security approach's sustainable human development model for the realization of SDG1. The chapter advances human security's all-inclusive and comprehensive human-centered sustainable development model as an effective mechanism for poverty eradication in the entire globe.

DOI: 10.4018/979-8-3373-0603-2.ch009

1 INTRODUCTION

Poverty has been one of the major threats and insecurities faced by humanity (UNDP, 2022). It has received wider attention since the Second World War, but with little success. It has been a contested factor among the developed and developing countries, although both UN Charter and Universal Declaration of Human Rights (UDHR) affirmed the importance of poverty eradication. A concerted global effort for poverty eradication gained momentum in 1990s with various initiatives like the World Bank's World Development Report and the Organization for Economic Co-operation and Development's (OECD) cooperative plan for halving extreme poverty by 2015 (OECD, 1996). Thereafter, the United Nations (UN) has given primary attention for poverty eradication in its Millennium Development Goals (MDGs) in 2000 and Sustainable Development Goals (SDGs) in 2015. The UN's 2030 Agenda of sustainable future will be realizable only in the context of poverty eradication (Nzasabayezu et al., 2024).

Poverty is predominantly measured in relation to income and basic minimum standard of life (Munoz-Boudet et al., 2018). But with the initiatives of United Nations Development Program (UNDP) and Oxford Poverty and Human Development Initiative (OPHI), a sincere attention is given to the multidimensionality of poverty (Alkire & Santos, 2014). Besides, scholars like Amartya Sen (2000) and Marta Nussbaum (2006) strongly argue that poverty results from the lack of capabilities and positive freedoms. It shows that poverty is a major human concern due to its nature of adverse deprivation of many essential features for a secure human life (UNDP, 1994).

From the last quarter of the 20th century, many researchers and international organizations called for economic growth as a suitable method for alleviation of poverty and elimination of inequality (Son & Kakwani, 2004; Sasmal et al., 2024). Policies like liberalization and open economy with the support of Bretton Woods Institutions redesigned the world's economic landscape (Wacziarg & Welch, 2008). Opening of the domestic market for international trade and business and foreign investments enlarged the horizon of economic growth leading to many developmental projects and employment opportunities for many in the developing world (Saurav et al., 2020; Emako et al., 2022).

Towards the end of the 20th century, the UNDP proposed the idea of human security intending to secure human life with freedom from want, freedom from fear, and freedom from indignity. Poor people face challenges and severe discrimination in the context of basic wants, security, and dignity. Although the question, "are people experiencing poverty perceived as less than human?" (Belle & Bullock, 2023, p. 39), is not a serious concern for the rich, many poor people feel that they are thoroughly marginalized without any respect towards their human nature. In such a scenario, the UNDP's human security paradigm has high relevance. It is an all-inclusive concept; without excluding anyone it covers all vital dimensions of human life. It strongly argues for empowering the universality of life claims for a meaningful and sustainable development of human race (UNDP, 1994).

The UNDP suggested sustainable human development, a human-centered developmental model, for economic growth, environmental protection, and poverty eradication (Anand & Sen, 1994). This unique model echoes human security paradigm. The globe requires economic development without shelving environmental needs. However, both economic (prosperity) and environmental (planet) aspirations should revolve around people (Čábelková et al., 2023). That is, the benefits of sustainable development should be equitably distributed for the benefit of whole humanity (sustainable human development).

Regardless of all these attempts, poverty still remains a distant dream, which is evident from the reports of the World Bank, the UNDP, and the World Inequality Lab. According to World Bank (2024), 8.5% of global population experience extreme poverty. According to OPHI & UNDP (2024), almost 1.1 billion out of 6.3 billion people belonging to 112 countries are experiencing poverty. The World Inequality Report (2022) states that the top 1% own 38% of global increment in wealth, whereas the bottom 50% has only 2% emphasizing the huge gap between the rich and the poor. All these current data show that instead of poverty eradication, economic growth led to disproportionate concentration of income and wealth into the hands of a few causing unparalleled increase in poverty and inequality.

In this perspective, this chapter analyses the current scenario of global poverty, examines various poverty eradication methods, and explores the feasibility of human security approach for sustainable human development in eradicating poverty and achieving ecofriendly human development.

2 MEANINGS, SCOPE, AND NATURE OF POVERTY

Globalization, liberalization, and open market economic system have widened the scope of international trade and economic interactions increasing the possibilities of employment, income, and wealth (Wacziarg & Welch, 2008). The 1994 Marrakesh agreement and the creation of World Trade Organization (WTO) widened the scope of economic growth (Fukuda-Parr, 2003). But still, poverty remains as a critical issue (Waziri et al., 2020). Although poverty is associated with deficiency, there is no agreement among researchers on the nature of these deficiencies (Wratten, 1995; Rosida, 2018). Joe Feagin (1975) identified three reasons for poverty such as individualistic, which emphasizes the poor people's personal characteristics like laziness, lack of thrift, and lack of motivation; structural, which focuses on the role of social and economic factors such as low wages, discrimination, and the failure of society to provide well-resourced schools; and fatalistic, emphasizing causes like luck and illness that are beyond one's control. Based on these reasons, there also emerged theories of poverty like behavioral, structural, and fatalistic (Law & Shek, 2014).

Poverty is understood as a deprivation, which is associated with the areas of income (Ravallion et al., 1991), nutrition (Allen, 2017), basic needs (ILO, 1976), and multidimensionality (Alkire & Foster, 2011). With the efforts of UNDP & OPHI, the present globe focuses more on the multidimensionality of poverty. It necessitates to evaluate poverty through various lenses (Chirwa & Odhiambo, 2016). Poverty is thus not merely seen as lack of income and wealth, but as a severe deprivation in any of the areas including clean drinking water, food, decent education, quality employment, dresses, housing, safe environment, and meaningful participation of political and community life (Sen, 2000; Farias & Hoffman, 2018). Such a wider perspective for understanding poverty is required as the globe witnesses a huge gap between the rich and the poor.

2.1 Absolute and Relative Poverty

Poverty is primarily understood as absolute and relative. Absolute poverty is the extreme deprivation of income, required for the realization of basic needs (Ravallion et al., 1991, p. 346). Absolute poverty depends on absolute measures that calls for human subsistence, whereas relative poverty emphasizes relative measures for social inclusion (Decerf, 2022). Relative poverty is the deprivation of people in the context of the society they live in. "People with incomes that are less than half of the median income are said to live in relative poverty" (Belle & Bullock, 2023, p. 77). Absolute poverty fixes a threshold common to all the societies like DAD method for capturing the basic needs satisfaction; whereas, relative poverty varies according to the nature of the standard of living of a particular society.

2.2 Chronic and Transient Poverty

Chronic poverty is an individual's permanent and long-standing deprivation. Transient poverty is temporary in nature and it mainly happens due to some natural disasters, business losses, issues with employment, or economic depression. Individuals, in the case of transient poverty, will enter into poverty due to a specific reason and leave from it very soon (Sugiharti et al., 2023). Instances of chronic poverty are more in developing countries. While in the developed countries chronic poverty happens rarely, but there are instances of transient poverty.

2.3 Geographical and Individual Poverty

Geography is a vital concern in the discussions of poverty (Jalan & Ravallion, 2002). There is a close link between the terrain of a region and the magnitude of poverty. The land, soil, water, and air qualities of a particular region affects its inhabitants' quality of life either positively or negatively. Poverty is highly concentrated in hot and landlocked countries. The interaction between people, social formation, and political economy of a particular region also has major impact on the nature of poverty. Besides, the preference of policy makers for some regions over others causes uneven patterns of economic growth and poverty concentration (Mishra, 2011). Individual poverty refers to the condition and incapacity of a person not to satisfy the basic needs and services that are required for one's well-being (Caplan et al., 2017).

2.4 Rural and Urban Poverty

Rural and urban poverty refer to the concentration of poor people in the geographical locators of a society. Urbanization became a common phenomenon in the aftermath of Industrial Revolution. Concentration of industrial units and other employment opportunities invited many people from rural areas to urban towns and cities (Rosida, 2018). However, the cost of living in urban areas is higher than the rural areas. Even then, urban poverty is lower than the rural poverty. 80% of the poor in most of the countries are still residing in rural areas, if the official urban definition is used (Nakamura et al., 2024). The Multidimensional Poverty Index (MPI) states that 83.7% of poor people live in rural areas. That is, compared to 6.6% of urban poor people, 28% global rural population are poor (OPHI & UNDP, 2024).

2.5 Measuring Poverty

Measuring of people in poverty is essential for devising various policies and programs for its eradication. In the present times, there are two internationally acclaimed methods of measuring poverty: income-based (World Bank) and multidimensional (UNDP). This section analyzes the latest reports of these two agencies for an exact understanding of the present status of poverty.

2.5.1 World Bank

From the last decade of 20th century, the World Bank started serious reflections on global poverty issues (World Bank, 1990). It prioritized developing countries as most of them were experiencing severe poverty. Ravallion et al. (1991) provided a theoretical foundation for the measurement of poverty line using the DAD method. The World Bank updates the poverty line on a timely basis. It began with $1/day in 1990, then updated it to $1.08/day in 1993, $1/25/day in 2009, $1.90/day in 2015, and $2.15/day in 2022. The 2022 poverty line measurement was based on the Purchasing Power Parity (PPP) of 2017. The World Bank also stated that the $2.15/day is for lower-income countries, whereas for middle-income countries it will be $3.65/day and for upper-income countries, $6.85/day (Jolliffe et al., 2022). Measurement of absolute poverty (at present $2.15/day) is primarily based on the national poverty lines of low-income countries, tallying the expenditure for 2200 calories of food/day and a small non-food expenditure (Wollburg et al., 2023). According to the World Bank (2014), poverty has three vital features like lack of income and wealth, voicelessness and powerlessness, and vulnerability. It also proposes three basis measures to confront the above-mentioned core areas of poverty such as expanding the opportunities for having more income and wealth, promoting empowerment so that they can substantially express their voice, and enhancing security. The understanding of poverty, as provided by this global institution, includes a variety of things like deprivation of well-being, low income, incapacity for a dignified living with access to basic needs and services, lack of education and health care, shortage of clean water and sanitation, challenges to physical security, and incapacities for the betterment of one's life (World Bank, 1992).

According to the World Bank, there is significant decrease in global poverty from 38% (1990) to 8.1% (2020) of global population (World Bank, 2022). However, after the Covid-19 pandemic, the reduction has slowed down and it became a standstill. The latest report states that almost 8.5% (692 million) of global population are experiencing extreme poverty as per $2.15/day mark. If the $3.65/day mark is used, almost 1.7 billion people are below the poverty line. If the poverty line is increased to $6.85/day, then almost 44% of world population experience poverty (World Bank, 2024). This data affirms that almost half of the global population experience poverty even in the 21st century.

2.5.2 Multidimensional Poverty Index

The UNDP perceived poverty as a multidimensional issue rather than adopting the World Bank's income parameter. It revolves around the idea that one's experience of poverty is different from the other. The reasons that lead one person to poverty also will be different from the other. The UNDP in association with the OPHI published poverty reports from 2010 onwards in view of its multidimensionality under the title Multidimensional Poverty Index (MPI). The MPI calculates poverty on the basis of three dimensions: health, education, and standard of living. The three dimensions are measured with respect to ten indicators. Health and education have two indicators each, whereas standard of living has six indicators (OPHI & UNDP, 2023). As per the latest MPI, 1.1 billion out of 6.3 billion people of 112 countries are in poverty. These 112 countries consist of 21 lower-income countries, 87 middle-income countries, and 4 higher-income countries. This report also notes that almost 83.2% of the global poor people are residing in Sub-Saharan Africa and South Asia (OPHI & UNDP, 2024).

2.6 Nature of Poverty

According to a latest report, except the non-poor countries all others require huge economic growth for reducing extreme poverty to 3% by 2030. The report claims that only the North American countries have so far achieved this target (Wollburg et al., 2023). This implies the global nature of poverty. Data from various international agencies and researchers on poverty affirm that in the present times, not only developing countries but developed countries also experience poverty. The World Bank has specified an international line for the calculation of absolute poverty. Whereas, each country has its own specific parameters for measuring relative poverty (Hulme, 2015). Fang (2021) states that the relative poverty line will be higher in the wealthier countries. It results in an increasing number of people in relative poverty in those countries. Increasing nature of global poverty also affirms lack of good governance at both national and international levels (Hanlon & Christie, 2016). However, there is a sharp criticism against the use of the term 'global poverty' as it is all the more an issue of the developing world and such a usage will divert the attention (Cimadamore & Lange, 2015). But Fang (2021) argues that this usage is beneficial as it will uphold the global moral obligation for poverty eradication. Furthermore, global poverty also echoes to the fact that the experiences of poor people are the same, irrespective of national, regional, or community differences (Narayan, 2000).

3 POVERTY ERADICATION: AN INEVITABLE REQUIREMENT

In the aftermath of Second World War, the globe sincerely addressed the issue of poverty. It started with Franklin D. Roosevelt's speech on four freedoms. The UDHR, thereafter, affirmed people's social security needs and freedom from want in its Article 25. In this background, the UN and other international agencies called for economic growth in order to alleviate poverty and hunger (Fang, 2021). However, poverty eradication became international community's top-most policy agenda only in the 21st century. The UN started this endeavor with the proclamation of 1997-2006 as the decade for poverty eradication. It declared another decade (2008-2017) and yet another decade (2018-2027) with the same objective realizing its significance for human well-being. The present decade focuses on ensuring a world without poverty. The UN's MDGs and SDGs and the World Bank initiatives also prioritize poverty eradication (World Bank Group, 2014; Wollburg et al., 2023). The UNDP further expanded this framework. An effective strategy for poverty eradication is to change people's economic landscape (Nzasabayezu et al., 2024). But it should not be restricted to income alone, other areas are also crucial. Creation of more employment opportunities is seen as a significant tool for poverty alleviation (Korosteleva & Stępień-Baig, 2020). Rasing minimum wage, increasing family income, assisting poor families in moving to neighborhoods with less poverty are also considered as effective measures (Belle & Bullock, 2023). Progress should be assessed not merely from the macroeconomic level evaluating the country's GDP but it should also be valued based on the well-being and progress of individuals at microeconomic level (Hanlon & Christie, 2016). It should be gauged on the basis of Asset-Based Community Development (ABCD) as it helps beneficiaries to be economically more resilient in terms of land, water, food, income, livestock, and physical capital (Raniga, 2018). That is, ABCD model echoes an inclusive developmental scheme that can support people to come out of poverty. However, for the realization of this objective an effective and efficient coordination of international institutions, national governments, policy-makers, NGOs, public and private enterprises, activists, and researchers is required.

3.1 MDG1: A Critique

The UN adopted the MDGs for establishing peace, prosperity, and justice in the world. The primarily objective of its adoption was to eradicate extreme poverty together with hunger as more than a billion of global population experience the dehumanizing conditions of extreme poverty. The UN thus echoed its vision to focus on a developmental environment that can eliminate poverty. The member-States affirmed that they can achieve this target with an efficient governance both at national and international levels. Obviously, the declaration of MDG1 was an unprecedented global effort to reduce poverty. Besides, before the official declaration, the global community sincerely listened to the concerns of the poor countries during the international conferences, affluent countries and international organizations were given specific roles, and the eight goals were designed in such a way to ensure the achievement of MDG1 (Brinkerhoff et al., 2007).

However, its objective of poverty eradication is diluted with the statement, "to halve, by the year 2015, the proportion of the World's poor people whose income is less than one dollar a day and the proportion of people who suffer from hunger and, by the same date, to halve the proportion of people who are unable to reach or to afford safe drinking water" (UN, 2000, no.19). Both eradicating and halving of poverty are different. Surprisingly, the MDGs which was declared in the year 2000 tried to reduce extreme poverty from 1990 onwards (UN, n.d.). How can a policy start working from ten years before its declaration? It shows that the MDG1's achievement of halving extreme poverty in the developing world is mainly due to the economic growth happened in China and India even before the inception of MDGs (UN, 2015a). China's advancement in poverty alleviation before 2000 was the great source of this success (Fang, 2021). That is why, researchers like Pogge (2010) strongly criticize the success saga of MDG1. Various studies also affirm that the achievement of MDGs has been very slow in fragile and conflict affected countries (UNTFHS, 2016).

3.2 Sustainable Development

Sustainable development was an inspirational idea of the UN to ensure economic growth without damaging the environment. Advocates of environmental protection argued that human existence has meaning only when there is a safe environment and the exploiting tendencies of humans towards the nature should be controlled (Shelton, 2012). Whereas, the proponents of individual freedom claim that individual choice for development is an essential prerequisite for human well-being (Boyle, 2007). It should not be controlled for environment protection as unnecessary regulations will curtail economic growth of the less advanced economies (Hashmi & Alam, 2019). Sustainable development was evolved in this context that tried to bridge both developmental and ecofriendly aspirations for the societal well-being (WCED, 1987).

Although sustainable development is a catchphrase from the last quarter of the 20th century, its exact meaning and implications remain unclear for many, and sometimes has the risk of becoming a cliché (Mensah, 2019). Sustainable development is a combination of sustainability and development, and has a plethora of definitions. But the most cited and accepted definition is given by the Brundtland Commission. According to which, it stands for "development that meets the needs of the present without compromising the ability of future generations to meet their own needs" (WCED, 1987). It revolves around the idea that the satisfaction of present generation's demands should not deprive the demands of future generation (Premadasa et al., 2023). Accordingly, it concentrated on the responsible use of natural resources without harming the coming generations' environmental requirements (Chen et al., 2022). After the 1992 Rio de Janeiro Earth Summit, the international community advanced the Agenda 21 by which it integrated economic, social, and environmental concerns into the same framework. Sustainable development thus has three vital dimensions: economic, social, and environmental, known as the triple bottom line that stands for prosperity, people, and planet (Giliberto & Labadi,

2022). The Brundtland report did not propose sustainable development with the characteristic features that are applicable to all the countries. It is not a one-size-fit model, perfectly suitable for all countries, but an international policy design from which the States should incorporate the design appropriate for its own local needs (Nzasabayezu et al., 2024).

Sustainable development is an attempt to balance between the society, economy, and environment (UNDESA, 2018). This model focuses on improving the society's living standards without jeopardizing the ecological health (Mensah, 2019). It proposes how the society should interact with the environment for ensuring economic growth. Though the objective is economic growth, the core element of this model is the interaction between the society and environment. That is, the society needs to use natural resources for development in such a way that they should be allowed to exist for the future generations as well (Mohieldin, 2017). The rationale behind this concept is the realization that the population is rapidly increasing day-by-day, whereas the resources are not. Together with the increasing population, human needs and developmental aspirations also grow, but not the regenerating capacity of the natural resources. Hence, sustainable development in its core emphasizes environmental protection.

The following points of this section explain and examine the general nature of SDGs and the specific role of SDG1 based on this theoretical framework of sustainable development.

3.2.1 SDGs

Sustainable Development Goals are objectives to achieve sustainable development in the economy, society, and environment. In 2015, the UN envisioned a sustainable global agenda for 2030 with 17 SDGs and 169 targets. The objective was to develop them on the basis of MDGs and to achieve the results which the MDGs could not. The 17 SDGs are indivisible in nature and aim at balancing the three dimensions of sustainable development in order to ensure that no one is left behind (UN, 2015b). The framework of SDGs is a program of action for protecting the environment, advancing economic growth, eradicating poverty, and ensuring human welfare and societal well-being (Taylor, 2016). It revolves around five Ps like people, planet, prosperity, peace, and partnership for making the right choice to improve life without harming the environment and peaceful coexistence (Hylton, 2019). All the 17 SDGs, in one way or other, focuses on improving the living standards of people by developing the economy and reducing human-induced harms to the environment. Compared to MDG's eight goals, SDGs proposed 17 goals covering a wide range of areas. These 17 goals are interconnected and interdependent, complementing each other.

3.2.2 SDG1

The priority of SDGs as enshrined in SDG1 is "to end poverty in all its forms everywhere." Poverty eradication is prioritized as the poor people are the most vulnerable section of the society, who can easily become victims of other harms and insecurities. Compared to MDG1, which focused on halving poverty in the developing countries, SDG1 focuses on eradicating poverty in the whole world. Though some people saw this goal as utopic, its realization was within the reach of the global community (Küfeoğlu, 2022). But Jolliffe et al. (2015) argued that any setback in economic growth of the countries with majority of poor people like India, China, and Bangladesh can affect the global poverty eradication agenda. This was proven right with the setback of Covid-19 pandemic as the economic growth of the whole world stood still slowing down the pace of poverty eradications programs. Accordingly, the current data projects that poverty eradication will be unrealistic and almost 6.1% of world population will remain in extreme poverty in 2030. However, if international institutions, national governments, PPPs, and other actors unanimously work with extra developmental projects and reformed policies, this projected rate can be again decreased (Küfeoğlu, 2022). That is, SDG 17 (partnerships for the goals) should become the energizer for the realization of SDG1.

4 POVERTY AND ECONOMIC INEQUALITY

Economic growth is considered as a substantial means for poverty eradication. The UK based Overseas Development Institute projected that the economic growth can reduce extreme poverty from 8% to 5% by 2030. But its projection was based on USD 1.25/day calculus (Shepherd et al., 2013). However, the World Bank has a target of reaching 3% by 2030. But there should a sixfold expansion of the economy for achieving this objective (Wollburg et al., 2023). Economic growth, in this context, is important but insufficient for poverty eradication (ILO, 2016), and considered as a "defining challenge of our time" (Obama, 2013). Besides, economic growth is primarily advantageous to the rich than the poor, leading to increasing inequality. Economic inequality is twofold: income inequality and wealth inequality. "Income is defined as money received, including wages, interest from bank accounts, investment profits, and rental payments from property ownership" and wealth "refers to the total economic value of everything a person owns, minus any debts such as student loans, credit card debt, medical debt, or mortgages" (Belle & Bullock, 2023, p. 5). Income and wealth are different. Compared to income inequality, wealth inequality is very high in the present scenario. Income inequality is measured by Gini coefficient, using 0-1 scale, according to which when everybody has the same income, it shows 0, and when one person has all the income, it shows 1 (Dabla-Norris et al., 2015). Both income and wealth inequalities adversely affect human well-being and societal welfare by delimiting the poor people's access to education, healthcare, and other basic infrastructure, reducing their productivity, and hampering the poverty reduction policies (Ravallion, 2004; Stiglitz, 2012).

Inequality is understood primarily in the context of relative poverty. It is mainly due to the uneven distribution of resources, opportunities, and benefits among the people. Inequality is largely evaluated on the basis of outcome (income) and opportunities. Both of them are firmly interlinked. Income includes not only the monetary outcome from employment but from savings, government support, and the like. Opportunities include the possibilities for education, healthcare, employment, political participation, and community life. That is, basically inequality is associated with social exclusion. Besides, it takes different forms like inequality between persons, regions, communities, and nations. Though inequality can express itself in different ways, economic inequality is the most expressed pattern, which can also cause other inequalities (Yang, 2017).

4.1 World Inequality Report: A Critical Analysis

Inequality in its different forms is increasing in the world. Growing inequalities between people, communities, and nations are a serious concern for the globe. The World Inequality Lab (WIL), established in the Paris School of Economics, focuses on studying the various dimensions of global inequality. It maintains the World Inequality Database (WID) with the contributions of more than 200 researchers. It critically analyzes various themes like income, wealth, gender, political, environmental, and social inequalities. In 2013, the first dataset was included in the WID. Thereafter, it continuously updates with the data of global inequalities. In 2018, based on the findings of the WID, the first World Inequality Report exposing the global inequalities on income and wealth was published (Alvaredo et al., 2018). Thereafter, in 2022, the second World Inequality Report was published on the basis of the recent available data (Chancel et al., 2022).

The World Inequality Report of 2022 states that the richest 10% owns 52% of global income, whereas the poorest 50% gets just 8.5%. Besides, the top 10% of world population owns 76%, whereas the bottom 50% owns just 2% of global wealth. The top 10% also constitute the middle-class people of the rich countries and their wealth is not growing as per the world average. The growth concentrates on the richest 1% of global population. During 1995-2021, the top 1% owned 38% of global increment in wealth, whereas the bottom 50% received only 2%. The report explains the data in eight zones: Europe, East Asia, North America, Russia & Central Asia, South & South-East Asia, Latin America, Sub-Saharan Africa, and MENA. In all zones except Europe, the top 10% leads the income share table. In Europe, the middle 40% leads the table. But coming to wealth share, the top 10% has significant lead in all the zones. The report states that inequality is less in Europe and it is very high in MENA countries. Though the percentage of both income and wealth inequalities vary in these eight zones, it significantly exists in all of them affirming that inequality is a global issue just as global poverty (Chancel et al., 2022).

4.2 Concentration of Economic Benefits

The World Inequality Report's above-mentioned data explicitly notes the unimaginable concentration of the benefits of economic growth and technological advancement in the hands of a few in the form of income and wealth. An average individual from the richest 10% of world population gets USD 122,100/year, whereas an individual from the poorest 50% earns just USD 3920/year. If we examine the data of wealth, then an individual from the top category owns PPP USD 771,300, while the bottom category person owns just USD 4,100. The concentration of global wealth in the hands of a very few is explicit from the fact that 11% of global wealth is owned by 0.01% of world population. That is, just 520,000 adults own 11% of global increment in wealth (Chancel et al., 2022). When both income and wealth concentrate into the hands of few individuals, it increases disparity in the society and leads more people into poverty-trap. The World Inequality Report also noted that during the last few decades the national GDP increased due to economic growth but not the public income. The income was concentrated into the hands of few private industrialists and businessmen. This creates issues with social security schemes. Lack of distributive justice is a vital issue in addressing and reducing poverty and inequality.

4.3 Unparalleled Gap between the Rich and the Poor

Wollburg et al. (2023) states that the national poverty line, which is the basis for the calculation of global poverty line, gets updated every now and then. This implies that there will not be a time to eliminate poverty, especially relative poverty, according to the national standards. They argue that even the wealthiest countries have poverty on account of their national poverty definitions. But there is no rationale in arguing that the poverty line should be static. It should change with time and overall economic growth. The DAD method cannot be applied today for simply claiming that the globe has succeeded in poverty eradication. Although technological and economic growth was expected to reduce poverty, it only increased the gap between the rich and poor through its unequal distribution patterns (Küfeoğlu, 2022). The World Inequality Report, which we analyzed above, clearly exposed the enormous gap with regard to income and wealth in the present world (Chancel et al., 2022). Increase in poverty and economic inequality adversely affect poor people's dignified life (UN, 2015b). It necessitates that together with economic growth, there should be effective mechanism to distribute its benefits to all people without increasing the gap between the rich and poor. Besides the distribution of the benefits of economic growth, care also should be given to empowering other areas of human life. Sen (2000) states that while other States in India tried to alleviate poverty and inequality through economic growth, the State of Kerala emphasized on basic education, healthcare, and meaningful land distribution schemes for addressing the issues of poverty and inequality. That is, income alone cannot be considered as the sole problem for the increasing inequality and poverty. Other areas or capabilities also require crucial attention.

5 SUSTAINABLE HUMAN DEVELOPMENT: A HUMAN SECURITY PERSPECTIVE

Sustainable human development has relevance in the context of conflict between environmental protection (sustainability) and human freedom for developmental policies (Čábelková et al., 2023). It stands for people-centered developmental choices without harming the environment. Existing policy frameworks have proved futile in preventing inequality and eradicating poverty which hinder the achievement of sustainable human development. Although, the last decade has seen significant progress in poverty alleviation, yet, there are millions of people in extreme poverty and inequality, especially in the developing countries (Korosteleva & Stępień-Baig, 2020). This is very evident through the latest reports of the World Bank, UNDP, and World Inequality Lab. It shows that the increasing poverty-rate is still a major concern of humanity (Nzasabayezu et al., 2024). The human security framework advanced by the UNDP has potentials to address such a scenario.

The developmental aspirations in the post-Second World War period were mostly focused on economic growth, calculated on the basis of GNP per capita, without even considering the equitable distribution of its benefits. They did not consider development in terms of human growth by equating quality of life with health, education, and gender and racial justice, but preferred it merely in terms of increasing the GDP and GNP per capita. Such a prejudiced approach only widened the societal inequalities (Nussbaum, 2006). It is in this complex scenario, the UNDP (1990) called for focusing on people. The objective of development should be to ensure a long, healthy, and creative life for people. Additionally, if the definition of WCED (1987) on sustainable development is analyzed, the call for environment protection is also people-centered. Sustainability in environment is viewed as the preservation of environment not only for present generation but also for the coming generations, that is, primarily for humans. Accordingly, both environment protection and economic development are human-centered in theory, leading to sustainable human development.

From 1990 onwards, the UNDP emphasized human development, publishing Human Development Index (HDI), known as Human Development Report (HDR). The 1994 HDR introduced the human security paradigm and clubbed both human-centered development and sustainable development models to form sustainable human development for promoting people-centered developmental and environmental concerns. Sustainable human development revolves around the idea that "people should be the center of development" (UNDP, 1994). Accordingly, it is closely associated with and echoes human security approach.

5.1 Human Security: Meaning and Scope

The Helsinki Accords of 1975 can be considered as the forerunner of human security paradigm. The Clinton administration used the term in many of its foreign policy speeches in 1993 and 1994 (Rothschild, 1995). Then in 1994, the UNDP used this term in its present meaning. The UNDP introduced it to address the 'downside risks' that affect everyone's life. Human security is "safety from such chronic threats as hunger, disease and repression," and "protection from sudden and hurtful disruptions in the patterns of daily life" (UNDP, 1994, p. 23). Human security is defined as "a human- or people-centered and multi-sectoral approach to security, which entails the protection of people from critical and pervasive threats and situations, and the empowerment of people to enhance their potential, through concerted efforts to develop norms, processes and institutions that systematically address insecurities" (Nasu, 2013, pp. 97-98). Human security is comprehensive and addresses several neglected issues like poverty. It focuses on various insecurities that people face in their daily life like the failure to satisfy basic social and economic needs, failure of communities and nations to provide protection to people, and failure to solve conflicts among groups. To confront these insecurities, it aims at providing a substantial policy agenda (Fukuda-Parr, 2003). The UN, on 10 September 2012, with the General Assembly Resolution 66/290 adopted the human security paradigm for identifying and confronting various challenges in relation to people's survival, livelihood, and dignity (UNTFHS, 2016).

Human security, unlike national security, is a non-traditional liberal idea of security concerned with human survival, progress, identity, and governance. It specifically focuses on individuals, humankind, human rights, rule of law and development addressing countless human vulnerabilities in the areas of fear, want, and indignity (Liotta & Bilgin, 2014). Emma Rothschild (1995) states that human security has brought up four changes into the concept of security. *Firstly*, it brought down the security concerns from the State to the individual; *secondly*, it bought up the security responsibility to the international system; *thirdly*, it broadened the security interests from the military to other areas such as environment, society, and economy; and *finally*, without limiting to one particular direction, it diffused in all directions that include local governments, international agreements, NGOs, public opinion, and financial markets as sources of responsibility. Human security is an inclusive concept consisting of seven categories such as economic, food, health, environmental, personal, community, and political securities (UNDP, 1994). The UNTFHS (2016) explains the root causes for these insecurities like persistent poverty, unemployment, lack of access to credit and other economic opportunities for economic insecurity; hunger, famine, and sudden rise in food prices for food insecurity; epidemics, malnutrition, poor sanitation, lack of access to basic healthcare for health insecurity; environmental degradation, natural disasters, and resource depletion for environmental insecurity; all forms of physical violences, human trafficking, and child labor for personal insecurity; crime, terrorism, and any forms of internal tensions for community insecurity; and political repression, lack of rule of law, and human rights violations for political insecurity. A close analysis of all these causes affirms that they either directly or indirectly link with or lead to poverty. For instance, the war of Russia-Ukraine or Israel-Palestine, North Korean human rights violations or Hezbollah attacks, whatever be the reason, lead millions of people into poverty irrespective of rich or poor, but will be more severely affecting the already poor sections of the population.

5.2 Human Security and Economic Growth

Human security approach advances human development model for ensuring economic growth. Human development is "the process to expand people's choices to lead lives they value" (UNDP, 1994). Accordingly, human development is not a synonym for economic growth but a wider and comprehensive term that includes economic growth as well. Human development emphasizes on empowering people's capacities to expand their valuable choices like satisfaction of basic needs, quality environment, decent income, appropriate education and healthcare, and meaningful participation in community life. These choices can vary depending on the requirement of a person. For instance, on 30 November 2024 Delhi's Air Quality Index showed 516 and Times of India reports it, extremely hazardous. Environmental security is a basic and valuable choice of people for meaningful life. Even if, the people in Delhi are having high income or wealth, how can they securely live in this extremely hazardous environment. That is, economic growth or environmental protection is only one side of human security approach. It focuses on securing all essential aspects of human life. Besides, to ensure human security through economic growth, care should be given to proper redistributive policies. During the first years of third millennium, the economic growth of Latin American countries resulted in poverty alleviation and inequality reduction due to their sincere commitment to redistributive policies (Banerjee & Duflo, 2022).

5.3 Human Security and Poverty

Susan E. Rice (2010) argues that poverty is a threat to US national security as it can increase transnational terrorist activities and crimes. She claims that poverty may harm the State's capacity to prevent the spread of diseases and environmental degradation. Such claims to connect poverty with national security are dangerous. Poor people are not threats to the rich and poor countries are not "plagues" to the developed countries. Dehumanizing and marginalizing the poor has done enough damage to universal brotherhood. The present globe requires to consider all people with the same respect, regardless of their economic status. Human security emphasizes the dignity and well-being of people rather than focusing on national borders (Fukuda-Parr, 2003). Human security approach, as designed by the 1994 HDR, had two core elements: freedom from want and freedom from fear. Freedom from want perspective focused on ensuring people's daily life from the insecurities with regard to their basic needs and wants. Japan was the prime advocate of this approach. Whereas, freedom from fear perspective emphasized securing the lives of people from external threats and internal conflicts. It even suggested for responsible interference into the matters of other States, if they create insecurities to people. Canada was the main proponent of this approach. Later on, freedom from indignity was also added to this framework. Dignified life is a basic aspiration of every human being. All these three insecurities merge in the issue of poverty as it can be caused by either downside risks or external shocks affecting primarily their dignified life. Human security concentrates on the individual's security, and not of a State. Poverty becomes a human security issue as it is a situation faced by the individual (King & Murray, 2001-2002). People in extreme poverty face not a single issue, but multitude of threats from various corners.

Human security's poverty eradication agenda focuses on people-centered, context-specific, comprehensive, and prevention-oriented protection and empowerment of all (Commission on Human Security, 2003). These four characteristics affirm the uniqueness of human security paradigm. It does not focus on the State but the unique needs of people. It takes into account the situations that threaten their survival, livelihood, and dignity. Since the threats are interconnected, human security paradigm affirms a comprehensive approach to ensure people's freedom from want, fear, and indignity. Besides, the issue of poverty, for instance, is addressed not from the income-perspective alone, but from its multidimensionality addressing the totality of conditions. Context-specific is a vital prerequisite for ensuring human well-being as the needs of people will be different in each context. The prevention-oriented measures and policies can mitigate the impact of current threats as well as devise various methods to prevent future challenges. Protection and empowerment are complementary in human security. They are like two wings of the welfare government. People require protection from external threats and internal challenges, which will be possible only through effective empowerment mechanisms (UNTFHS, 2016).

5.4 Sustainable Human Development Model

Sustainable human development is an offshoot of the sustainable development principle, which emphasizes the people-centered dimension. It has evolved from the UN's historic decision to adopt all-inclusive and people-centered universal goals for 2030 that emphasized the dignity of human person (UN, 2015b). As a developmental model, it took shape in UNDP's 1994 HDR, which defines sustainable human development as "that not only generates economic growth but distributes its benefits equitably; that regenerates the environment rather than destroying it; that empowers people rather than marginalizing them. It is a development that gives priority to the poor, enlarging their choices and opportunities and providing for their participation that affects their lives" (UNDP 1994, iii). According to this definition, sustainable human development includes economic growth with equitable distribution of its benefits, preservation and regeneration of the environment, empowerment of people, and prioritization of the poor with enlarged choices, opportunities, and participation. This model thus affirms that "human interests take precedence over everything else" (Sultanovich, 2023, 164).

Sustainable human development is a developmental paradigm that lasts forever. Sustainable human development bridges both environmental sustainability and human development underscoring the value of human-centered approach towards development and environmental protection (R & D, 2023). Poverty is both developmental and environmental issue. Lack of human-centered development and improper distribution of economic benefits affect the lives of millions of people forcing them to remain in poverty. Economic growth is unfortunately equated with the increase in GNP and GDP, which does not specifically attend to the concerns of the poor. This shift from mere economic growth to human-centered development can ensure security to all people, realization of SDG1&2, and promote the growth of any country. The State's growth should happen through human security perspective emphasizing the significance of human concerns without prioritizing the demands of the rich. Besides, as explained above, poverty is more persistent in rural areas where people are more reliant on natural resources. Environmental sustainability is an indispensable need of the time. But it should club with the concerns of people. Human-centered development, as it also includes sustainability, does not negate environmental concerns, but reshapes it in such a way to advantage and benefit human needs. Furthermore, sustainable human development model emphasizes on development, equitable distribution, and environmental sustainability for all human beings irrespective of regional, national, economic, and gender differences. It is an all-inclusive approach of development. Accordingly, it can more meaningfully ensure both poverty eradication and hunger elimination agenda of the UN (SDGs1&2).

Sustainable human development model stands for prioritizing the needs of all people regardless of economic status or any other parameters. Universality of life claims (UNDP, 1994) is the rationale for this model. Accordingly, with respect to SDG17, there should be effective coordination and collaboration for reaching out to the poor sections of the global society through various empowerment mechanisms and policies. As analyzed above, majority of poor people are living in the rural areas. It necessitates that the upliftment of rural population should be prioritized in national policies and international support system agenda. High-quality educational institutions, healthcare support systems, employment opportunities, transportation and communication facilities, and government subsidies to farmers and small-scale industrialists should be provided in view of people-centered poverty eradication programs. In the present global society, the poor people should be given reservation in educational institutions and employment opportunities (a good example can be seen in India, where economically weaker section is given 10% reservation in educational institutions and government jobs) for uplifting them. Besides, the States should prioritize equitable distribution of the benefits of economic growth, so that they can control the unparalleled concentration of income and wealth into the hands of a few and ensure people-centered growth. Besides, there needs to have effective mechanism to coordinate the Corporate Social Responsibility (CSR) funding for the benefit of the marginalized sections of the society. Though CSR functions as per legal mandate, many of the MNCs and TNCs have their own proxy trusts that channelize these funds for many other purposes. The State governments should ensure that these funds are primarily spent on empowering people and eradicating poverty. Empowering the poor people with satisfaction of basic needs, quality education, and substantial jobs is the only means for complete eradication of poverty and that can be meaningfully done by employing the sustainable human development model's people-centered approach.

6 CONCLUSION

The nature and extend of poverty in the present times affirm that it is not merely an issue of the developing world, but a global issue. The UN's prestigious SDGs prioritize poverty eradication, and many programs and policies were designed to realize this objective. The UNDP, in line with other international agencies, advance various strategies for the UN's 2030 Agenda of sustainable future. The core element of this endeavor is its human security paradigm, which stands for people-centered model of sustainable development. This model is a gradual development of sustainable development pattern, which clubbed both environmental sustainability and development. This approach provides a new perception to sustainable development emphasizing people-centeredness. It deems that sustainable human development model can more meaningfully contribute to the realization of SDGs.

The UN's poverty eradication agenda as prioritized by the SDGs (SDG1) was moving in a significant pace. But the Covid-19 pandemic and its impact on the economy slowed the pace and thus the objective of complete eradication of poverty may not be achieved as per the latest data of World Bank and the UN. However, if a sincere collaborative effort is undertaken by the international agencies and national governments with the support of all relevant actors, the pace can be increased particularly focusing on human security's people-centered perspective. Poverty eradication will be possible only through a comprehensive and all-inclusive vision of development and that is the core feature of sustainable human development model. Since this model focuses on the welfare of all people regardless of any differentiating parameters, it calls for empowering the weaker sections of the society like the poor people for making them equal with others. This model does not sideline anyone but incorporates them into the mainstream of the society through various supporting and empowering schemes.

REFERENCES

Alkire, S., & Foster, J. (2011). Counting and Multidimensional Poverty Measurement. *Journal of Public Economics, 95*(7/8), 476–487. DOI: 10.1016/j.jpubeco.2010.11.006

Alkire, S., & Sanots, M. E. (2014). Measuring Acute Poverty in the Developing World: Robustness and Scope of the Multidimensional Poverty Index. *World Development, 59*, 251–274. DOI: 10.1016/j.worlddev.2014.01.026

Allen, R. C. (2017). Absolute Poverty: When Necessity Displaces Desire. *The American Economic Review, 107*(12), 3690–3721. DOI: 10.1257/aer.20161080

Alvaredo, F., Chancel, L., Piketty, T., Saez, E., & Zucman, G. (2018). *World Inequality Report*. WIL. DOI: 10.4159/9780674984769

Anand, S., & Sen, A. (1994). *Sustainable Human Development: Concepts and Priorities*. UNDP Human Development Report Office.

Banerjee, A., & Duflo, E. (2022). Foreword. In Chancel, L. (Eds.), *World Inequality Report* (p. 4). WIL.

Belle, D., & Bullock, H. E. (2023). *The Psychology of Poverty, Wealth, and Economic Inequality*. Cambridge University Press.

Boyle, A. (2007). Human Rights or Environmental Rights? A Reassessment. *Fordham Environmental Law Review, 18*(3), 471–511.

Brinkerhoff, J., Smith, S., & Teegen, H. (Eds.). (2007). *NGOs and Millennium Development Goals: Citizen Action to Reduce Poverty*. Springer. DOI: 10.1057/9780230604933

Čábelková, I., Smutka, L., Mareš, D., Ortikov, A., & Kontsevaya, S. (2023). Environmental Protection or Economic Growth? The Effects of Preferences for Individual Freedoms. *Frontiers in Environmental Science, 11*, 1129236. DOI: 10.3389/fenvs.2023.1129236

Caplan, M. A., Purser, G., & Kindle, P. A. (2017). Personal Accounts of Poverty: A Thematic Analysis of Social Media. *Journal of Evidence-Informed Social Work, 14*(6), 433–456. DOI: 10.1080/23761407.2017.1380547 PMID: 29140758

Chancel, L., Piketty, T., Saez, E., & Zucman, G. (2022). *World Inequality Report*. WIL.

Chen, S., Chen, D., Tan, Z., Chen, M., & Han, J. (2022). Knowledge Mapping of Planetary Boundaries based on Bibliometrics Analysis. *Environmental Science and Pollution Research International, 29*(45), 67728–67750. DOI: 10.1007/s11356-022-22292-6 PMID: 35945326

Chirwa, T. G., & Odhiambo, N. M. (2016). Macroeconomic Determinants of Economic Growth: A Review of International Literature. *South East European Journal of Economics and Business, 11*(2), 33–47. DOI: 10.1515/jeb-2016-0009

Cimadamore, A. D., & Lange, L. (2015). The Global Poverty Consensus Report. https://perma.cc/MDN5-6LTW

Commission on Human Security. (2003). *Human Security Now*. UNDP.

Dabla-Norris, E., Kochhar, K., Suphaphiphat, N., Ricka, F., & Tsounta, E. (2015). *Causes and Consequences of Income Inequality: A Global Perspective*. IMF.

Decerf, B. (2022). *Absolute and Relative Poverty Measurement: A Survey* (PRWP 10008). World Bank.

Emako, E., Nuru, S., & Menza, M. (2022). The Effect of Foreign Direct Investment on Economic Growth in Developing Countries. *Transnational Corporations Review, 14*(4), 382–401. DOI: 10.1080/19186444.2022.2146967

Fang, V. (2021). *From Charity to Justice: How NGOs can Revolutionize Our Response to Extreme Poverty*. Palgrave Macmillan. DOI: 10.1007/978-981-16-1433-0

Farias, R. A. S., & Hoffmann, V. E. (2018). Analysis of Scientific Production on Interorganizational Network Study Field. *Innovation & Management Review, 15*(1), 92–115. DOI: 10.1108/INMR-02-2018-006

Feagin, J. R. (1975). *Subordinating the Poor: Welfare and American Beliefs*. A Spectrum Book.

Fukuda-Parr, S. (2003). New Threats to Human Security in the Era of Globalization. *Journal of Human Development, 4*(2), 167–179. DOI: 10.1080/1464988032000087523

Giliberto, F., & Labadi, S. (2022). Harnessing Cultural Heritage for Sustainable Development: An Analysis of Three Internationally Funded Projects in MENA Countries. *International Journal of Heritage Studies, 28*(2), 133–146. DOI: 10.1080/13527258.2021.1950026

Hanlon, R. J., & Christie, K. (2016). *Freedom from Fear, Freedom from Want: An Introduction to Human Security*. University of Toronto Press. DOI: 10.3138/9781442609594

Hashmi, R., & Alam, K. (2019). Dynamic Relationship among Environmental Regulation, Innovation, CO_2 Emissions, Population, and Economic Growth in OECD Countries: A Panel Investigation. *Journal of Cleaner Production, 231*, 1100–1109. DOI: 10.1016/j.jclepro.2019.05.325

Hulme, D. (2015). *Global Poverty: Global Governance and Poor People in the Post-2015 Era*. Routledge. DOI: 10.4324/9781315738932

Hylton, K. N. (2019). When Should We Prefer Tort Law to Environmental Regulation? *Washburn Law Journal, 41*, 515–534.

ILO. (2016). *World Employment and Social Outlook: Transforming Jobs to End Poverty*. ILO.

ILO (International Labor Organization). (1976). *Employment Growth and Basic Needs: A One World Problem*. ILO.

Jalan, J., & Ravallion, M. (2002). Geography Poverty Traps? A Micro Model of Consumption Growth in Rural China. *Journal of Applied Econometrics, 17*(4), 329–346. DOI: 10.1002/jae.645

Jolliffe, D., & Lanjouw, P. (Eds.). (2015). *A Measured Approach to Ending Poverty and Boosting Shared Prosperity: Concepts, Data, and the Twin Goals*. World Bank Group.

Jolliffe, D., Mahler, D. G., Lakner, C., Atamanov, A., & Tetteh-Bah, S. K. (2022). *Assessing the Impact of the 2017 PPPs on the International Poverty Line and Global Poverty*. World Bank., PRWP 9941. DOI: 10.1596/1813-9450-9941

King, G., & Murray, C. (2001-2002). Rethinking Human Security. *Political Science Quarterly, 116*(4), 585–610. DOI: 10.2307/798222

Korosteleva, J., & Stępień-Baig, P. (2020). Climbing the Poverty Ladder: The Role of Entrepreneurship and Gender in Alleviating Poverty in Transition Economies. *Entrepreneurship and Regional Development, 32*(1/2), 197–220. DOI: 10.1080/08985626.2019.1640482

Küfeoğlu, S. (2022). *Emerging Technologies: Value Creation for Sustainable Development*. Springer. DOI: 10.1007/978-3-031-07127-0

Law, B., & Shek, D. T. L. (2014). Beliefs about Poverty. In Michalos, A. C. (Ed.), *Encyclopedia of Quality of Life and Well-Being Research* (pp. 353–359). Springer. DOI: 10.1007/978-94-007-0753-5_166

Liotta, H., & Bilgin, A. (2014). Why Human Security? The Case for Resilience in an Urban Century. In Martin, M., & Owen, T. (Eds.), *Routledge Handbook of Human Security* (pp. 109–122). Routledge.

Mensah, J. (2019). Sustainable Development: Meaning, History, Principles, Pillars, and Implications for Human Action: Literature Review. *Cogent Social Sciences*, *5*(1), 1653531. DOI: 10.1080/23311886.2019.1653531

Mishra, A. (2011). Geography, Poverty, and Development: An Interdisciplinary Debate. *Sociedade & Natureza*, *23*(2), 227–236. DOI: 10.1590/S1982-45132011000200006

Mohieldin, M. (2017). *The Sustainable Development Goals and Private Sector Opportunities*. World Bank Group.

Munoz-Boudet, A. M. M., Buitrago, P.…Suarez-Becerra, P. (2018). Gender Differences in Poverty and Household Composition through Life-Cycle. World Bank (WPS8360).

Nakamura, S., Roberts, M., & Stewart, B. (2024). Has Extreme Poverty been Urbanized? World Bank Blogs. https://blogs.worldbank.org/en/developmenttalk/has-extreme-poverty-been-urbanized

Narayan, D. (2000). Poverty is Powerlessness and Voicelessness. *Finance & Development*, •••, 18–21.

Nasu, H. (2013). The Place of Human Security in Collective Security. *Journal of Conflict and Security Law*, *18*(1), 95–129. DOI: 10.1093/jcsl/krs026

Nussbaum, M. (2006). Poverty and Human Functioning: Capabilities as Fundamental Entitlements. In Grusky, D. B., & Kanbur, R. (Eds.), *Poverty and Inequality* (pp. 47–75). Stanford University Press. DOI: 10.1515/9780804767590-004

Nzasabayezu, O., Jaya Prakash, S. K., & Rama Prasad, M. V. (2024). A Study of Poverty Alleviation Strategies for Sustainable Development: A Scientometric Analysis. *Heliyon*, *10*, e33469. DOI: 10.1016/j.heliyon.2024.e33469 PMID: 39040409

OECD. (1996). *Shaping the 21st Century: The Contribution of Development Co-operation*. OECD.

OPHI & UNDP. (2023). *Global Multidimensional Poverty Index: Unstacking Global Poverty*. Oxford University Press.

OPHI & UNDP. (2024). *Global Multidimensional Poverty Index: Poverty Amid Conflict*. Oxford University Press.

Pogge, T. W. (2010). Politics as Usual: What Lies behind the Pro-Poor Rhetoric. *Polity*.

Premadasa, M., Siyambalapitiya, J., Jayawardhana, K., & Fernando, I. (2023). Conceptualizing the Role of Social Entrepreneurial Orientation in the Triple Bottom Line in the Social Enterprise Context: Developing Country Perspective. *Sustainability (Basel), 15*(11), 8709. DOI: 10.3390/su15118759

Raniga, T. (2018). Poverty Alleviation, Social Protection Policy and Sustainability of Economic Development Cooperatives: Voices of Women Residing in Bhambayi Kwazalu-Natal, South Africa. *Social Work, 54*(4), 395–406.

Ravallion, M. (2004). *Pro-Poor Growth: A Primer* (PRWP 3242). World Bank.

Ravallion, M., Datt, G., & van de Walle, D. (1991). Quantifying Absolute Poverty in the Developing World. *Review of Income and Wealth, 37*(4), 345–361. DOI: 10.1111/j.1475-4991.1991.tb00378.x

Rice, S. E. (2010). The National Security Implications of Global Poverty. In S. E. Rice, C. Graff, & C. Pascual, *Confronting Poverty: Weak States and U.S. National Security* (pp. 1-22). Brookings.

Rosida, L. (2018). Rural and Urban Poverty in Developing Countries. *Media Bina Ilmiah, 13*(1), 835–843. DOI: 10.33758/mbi.v13i1.144

Rothschild, E. (1995). What is Security? The Quest for a World Order. *Daedalus, 124*(3), 53–98.

Sasmal, R., Das, P., & Sasmal, J. (2024). Public Policy, Economic Growth and Poverty Alleviation: A Study in the Indian States. *Athens Journal of Business & Economics, 10*(3), 159–182. DOI: 10.30958/ajbe.10-3-1

Saurav, A., Liu, Y., & Sinha, A. (2020). *Foreign Direct Investment and Employment Outcomes in Developing Countries*. The World Bank Group.

Sen, A. (2000). *Development as Freedom*. Oxford University Press.

Shelton, D. (2012). Resolving Conflicts between Human Rights and Environmental Protection: Is there a Hierarchy? In de Wet, E., & Widmar, J. (Eds.), *Hierarchy in International Law: The Place of Human Rights* (pp. 181–194). Oxford University Press. DOI: 10.1093/acprof:oso/9780199647071.003.0008

Shepherd, A., Mitchell, T., & Muir-Wood, R. (2013). *The Geography of Poverty, Disasters and Climate Extremes in 2030*. ODI.

Son, H. H., & Kakwani, N. (2004). Economic Growth and Poverty Reduction: Initial Conditions Matter. *International Poverty Centre Working Paper 2*. https://ipcig.org/pub/IPCWorkingPaper2.pdf

Stiglitz, J. (2012). *The Price of Inequality: How Today's Divided Society Endangers Our Future*. W. W. Norton.

Sugiharti, L., Esquivias, M. A., Shaari, M. S., Jayanti, A. D., & Ridzuan, A. R. (2023). Indonesia's Poverty Puzzle: Chronic vs. Transient Poverty Dynamics. *Cogent Economics & Finance, 11*(2), 2267927. DOI: 10.1080/23322039.2023.2267927

Sultanovich, M. D. (2023). The Main Directions of Poverty Reduction in our Country. *Galaxy International Interdisciplinary Research Journal, 11*(2), 164–171.

Taylor, S. J. (2016). *A Review of Sustainable Development Principles: Centre for Environmental Studies*. University of Pretoria.

The Times of India. (Nov. 30, 2024). Delhi Air Quality Index Today. https://timesofindia.indiatimes.com/weather/delhi-aqi-level-air-quality-index-today/3291

UN. (2000). Resolution Adopted by the General Assembly. *55/2 United Nations Millennium Declaration*. UN.

UN. (2015a). *The Millennium Development Goals Report*. UN.

UN. (2015b). *Transforming Our World: The 2030 Agenda for Sustainable Development*. UN.

UN. (n.d.). Goal 1: Eradicate Extreme Poverty & Hunger. https://www.un.org/millenniumgoals/poverty.shtml

UNDESA. (2018). *The Sustainable Development Goals Report 2017*. UNDESA.

UNDP. (1994). *Human Development Report*. UNDP.

UNDP. (2022). *New Threats to Human Security in the Anthropocene: Demanding Greater Solidarity*. UNDP.

UNTFHS (United Nations Trust Fund for Human Security). (2016). *Human Security Handbook*. UNTFHS.

Wacziarg, R., & Welch, K. H. (2008). Trade Liberalization and Growth: New Evidence. *The World Bank Economic Review*, *22*(2), 187–231. DOI: 10.1093/wber/lhn007

Waziri, M., Ibrahim, A. B., & Zainal, M. Z. (2020). Investigating the Empirical Relationship between Government Interventions Programs and Poverty Alleviation: A Case of Nigeria. *Journal of Economic and Administrative Sciences*, *36*(4), 323–338. DOI: 10.1108/JEAS-06-2019-0060

WCED (World Commission on Environment and Development). (1987). *Our Common Future.*

Wollburg, P., Hallegatte, S., & Mahler, D. G. (2023). *The Climate Implications of Ending Global Poverty*. World Bank Group., PRWP 10318. DOI: 10.1596/1813-9450-10318

World Bank. (1990). *World Development Report: Poverty*. https://documents1.worldbank.org/curated/en/424631468163162670/pdf/PUB85070REPLACEMENT0WDR01990.pdf

World Bank. (1992). *World Development Report*. https://digitallibrary.un.org/record/1305153?ln=en&v=pdf

World Bank. (2014). *The World Bank Group Goals: End Extreme Poverty and Promote Shared Prosperity*. https://hdl.handle.net/10986/20138

World Bank. (2022). *Poverty and Shared Prosperity Report.*

World Bank. (2024). *Poverty, Prosperity, and Planet Report: Pathways out of the Polycrisis.*

Wratten, E. (1995). Conceptualizing Urban Poverty. *Environment and Urbanization*, *7*(1), 11–38. DOI: 10.1177/095624789500700118

Yang, L. (2017). The Relationship between Poverty and Inequality: Concepts and Measurement. *LSE*. https://sticerd.lse.ac.uk/dps/case/cp/casepaper205.pdf

Chapter 10
Smart Technology and Indian Journalism:
Progress, Problems, and Prospects

Nihaz Anvar
Lovely Professional University, India

Neha Sah
https://orcid.org/0000-0002-8926-4533
Lovely Professional University, India

ABSTRACT

Historically, the term "smart" was mostly used to describe human intelligence and wit, but in the last twenty years, it has also come to describe advanced technologies. Smart engineering, including artificial intelligence (AI), the Internet of Things, and cloud computing, provide widespread data availability, connectivity, and information aggregation. These advancements have significantly impacted journalism globally, including in India, where the media sector is valued at over a trillion Indian rupees. The shift from print to digital news has transformed how news is accessed, produced, and consumed. AI-driven tools now automate content creation, distribution, and audience interaction, introducing new practices like data journalism and drone journalism. This study examines the current use of smart technology in Indian journalism, its benefits, and the challenges to full integration. By analyzing these aspects, the paper intends to provide a clear and comprehensive understanding of the disruptive effects of smart technology on Indian journalism and media organizations.

DOI: 10.4018/979-8-3373-0603-2.ch010

1. INTRODUCTION

The term "smart" was typically once used among human communities to describe someone who is intelligent and able to outmatch others using their wit and up-to-date knowledge. In past twenty years, it has also been more popular in context of technology. Smart technologies, an umbrella term, incorporate mixed rising technologies such as the IoT solutions, cloud (virtual) computing, and machine intelligence applications, such as voice commendation tools, chatbots, image recognition, predictive analytics. These technologies can collect data from their environment using embedded sensors and analyse it remotely. Together, they offer three main capabilities: far-flung data availability, networking among objects, people, and organizations, and the ability to aggregate information (Sharma et al., 2023, Micheler et al., 2019). Technology impacts nearly every facet of human society, and data-driven processes largely influence our decisions. Consequently, investing in technology has become essential for the long-term viability of any industry (de-lima-sentos & Matias, 2021). The journalism and news media sector is also getting reshaped with digital innovations globally. In India this industry is valued at over a trillion Indian rupees and continues to grow. India's media landscape includes substantial number of certified newspapers and periodicals, exceeding 900 private television networks, and over 1,000 radio broadcasters in various native dialects such as Hindi and English. Staying updated and informed with news has become a vital component of daily life for the nation's vast population of over 1.4 billion people (Basuroy, 2023). With a modest beginning of print news which dominated the Indian communication and journalism for over a century, the advent of the internet and digital tools have transformed the way news is accessed, produced and consumed. Artificial intelligence, popularly called "AI" has dilated rapidly into almost all segments of the society and steadily gaining popularity in journalism (Noain-Sánchez, 2022). AI-driven tools are now employed to automatize a range of activities, including content creation, distribution, and audience interaction. Their application is also innovative, as seen in emerging media outputs and methods like data driven reporting, immersive and drone journalism, performance analytics, and process automation (de-lima-Santos & Ceron, 2021). These tools enable news organizations to generate more content quickly, distribute it more efficiently, and interact with audiences in innovative ways. A particularly significant use of AI in the news media and broadcast sector is in content creation, where AI-technologies are used to produce news report, social media content, and other forms of informational material (Ashfaq et al., 2023). Undoubtedly, integrating AI offers numerous advantages to mass media and news organizations, while simultaneously introducing modification in three areas at least: the act of journalists in creating content, their substitution in performing specific tasks, and their engagement with the audience. (Gomez-Diago, 2022). India, with its diverse and dynamic media environment, presents a unique context for the study of smart technology in journalism. The country's rapid technological advancements, coupled with its vast and varied population, create both opportunities and challenges for the implementation of smart technologies in the media sector. This study aims to provide a detailed examination of how these technologies are currently being used and their impact on journalism in India.

The primary objectives of this study are to:

1. Compile and analyze current applications of smart technology in journalism, focusing on its present state and developments in India.
2. Examine the improvements and challenges to the full integration of smart technology in journalism.

Approach

The achievement of the aforementioned objectives followed a systematic review and qualitative content analysis method. This involved thoroughly reviewing 40+ scholarly articles, and industry reports to observe and identify recurring themes and insights related to the usage of smart technology in media and journalism.

2. SMART TECHNOLOGY IN JOURNALISM (FIG. 1)

Artificial Intelligence (AI) tools are rapidly entering the press and media, bringing significant changes to the content creation and distribution process (Aissani et al., 2023) as shown in Figure 1. Technology has changed the style of journalism, reporting, research, purchasing, budgets and advertising, giving rise to presentations such as podcasts, checklists, engaging hooks, animated images, AR and VR technologies, visual data representation and user interaction interfaces (Das and Upadhyay, 2024). JournalismAI's latest report, "Generating Change," explores AI integration in newsrooms, surveying 105 media outlets from 46 countries. Findings show 73% of media organizations see generative AI as an opportunity, with 85% having experimented with it for tasks like code writing and image generation. While AI aids in time-consuming tasks, ethical concerns about bias and accuracy persist. Challenges are especially pronounced in the Global South, due to language, infrastructure, and political issues, highlighting the disparity in AI benefits between regions (Beckett, 2023).

This segment further highlights the new platforms driven by AI in the media and journalism sector.

Automated Journalism: Automated news production involves a sophisticated blend of data accessibility, analytical methods, data-driven insights, and smart automation. Typically, automated news production are free from human involvement unless they choose to be in the process. Unlike data journalism and computational journalism, which still rely on human input and are often referred to as "human journalism" or "natural intelligence journalism" due to the essential role of humans in adding values and a human touch to news, AI-driven news automation stands out as it operates independently, without the need for human involvement (Zhang et al., 2023). News automation has not only handled both simple and complex tasks of content writing but also made it difficult for readers to identify the authorship upon review. Its speculated that with further technological development, doubts about the linguistic aspect of automated content will diminish (Henestrosa et al., 2023).

Robot Journalism

Robot journalism refers to automated news and even machine-written news. Robotization in news organizations aims to help journalists report and process less information (Aljazairi & Ekman, 2016). Automated journalism involves the use of technology in part of the media production process, from the news gathering and selection phase to the editorial phase, quality, processing, and distribution levels (Wu et al., 2018). Technological advances, such as machine learning-capable artificial intelligence software and design languages, facilitate social media automation (Montal & Reich, 2016). Reducing personnel means reducing media production costs (Carlson, 2015; Fanta, 2017), which could lead to a wider acceptance by stakeholders of appropriate media, such as the Washington Post, the Associated Press, and the BBC (Danzon - Chambaud & Cornia, 2021), especially news driven by information such as earthquakes, sports, and business (Tandoc et al., 2022). Guardian Australia has published its first machine-powered article detailing annual donations to the country's politicians. Forbes has also begun experimenting with a tool called Bertie, which provides journalists with articles and stories. As AI becomes part of the corporate legacy, media executives say AI poses no threat to human jobs. Instead, the goal is to allow journalists to focus on important tasks (Peiser, 2019).

Mobile Journalism

Mobile News using mobile devices like smartphones and tablets is nothing new in today's newsroom. However, mobile journalism (also known as "mojo") is a social media technology that uses these tools and continues to evolve with the tools' capabilities. (2021). The growth of mojo can be assigned to various component, such as the extensive use of mobile phones, inexpensive data, and the widespread reach of social networking platforms (Ali, 2023).

Algorithmic news

With the growth of personal media platforms, a basic understanding of what algorithms are and what they can do is an important part of reading the news (Head et al., 2020). The emergence of social media and news in the feeds of consumers, especially those under the age of 25, means that algorithmic gate keeping processes are increasingly influencing news consumption patterns (Kalogeropoulos, 2019). Recommendation algorithms can alleviate over crowding of information and assist users in navigating pertinent information amidst the vast array of data resources (Swaraj, 2021). Algorithmic curation can improve the addictive nature of today's media options, where many content compete for users' attention, and make the cost of finding news high again (The Week and the Line, 2020). Users have developed a habit of relying on algorithms to manage their online experiences. This is because their online behavior is constantly being tracked and used by algorithms to predict and organize their next actions. As a result, they often resort to advertising-based methods that run counter to their character and comfort (Schaetz et al., 2023). The technology behind algorithmic journalism is intelligence-driven natural language processing (NLP), which has two subsets that support journalism, natural language understanding (NLU) and structured language (NLG). NLU programming is a programming that helps computers understand human emotions and extract information from natural language. NLG programming generates natural language from given data. In NLG, digital information is converted into a language that employees can easily understand so that it can be read as news in the AI-powered newsroom. This can be used for sports, weather, elections, and business stories (Elanjimattom, 2023).

Web 3.0 Journalism

Semantic web, often called as web 3.0 intents to create a more intelligent web by embedding meaning and context directly into the structure of websites. This will permit devices to comprehend the content on the website and enhance its accessibility and serviceability for users. Block-chain has emerged as a pivotal technology expected to shape the development of Web 3.0 by enabling decentralized systems that empower users to control their data online and in person (Nasar, 2023). In comparison, Web 1.0 was known for its basic one-way interaction, where users would navigate through a somewhat cumbersome and disorganized system with limited access and slow internet speeds.Web 2.0, the current state which has been dominant for around 15 years, is defined by a more interactive relationship between content creators and consumers. For instance, activities like tweeting, blogging, liking, reviewing, and posting all involve active participation in content generation across various platforms. These actions hold intrinsic value and users both consume and produce content. However, Web 3.0 brings about a significant change by focusing on decentralization, interoperability, and user-centered design (Figure 2 illustrates a visual history of the web, from Web 1.0 to Web 3.0).

It moves beyond mere content creation and consumption to include decentralized applications (dApps) and blockchain technology. Unlike Web 2.0 platforms, which are typically centralized and controlled by a few big companies, Web 3.0 seeks to give users the ability to possess their own data and engage with each other directly, without the need for intermediaries. As an illustration, social networks based on block chain technology such as Steemit offer incentives in the form of cryptocurrency to users for producing and evaluating content, fostering a more democratic and transparent content ecosystem. This shift towards decentralization and user empowerment distinguishes Web 3.0 from its predecessors, emphasizing trust, transparency, and privacy in digital interactions **(Chohan, 2022).**

Immersive journalism:

Immersive journalism takes into account a set of advanced engineering like virtual reality (VR) and augmented reality (AR), 360 video, hybrid Reality, and extended reality (ER) centered around the audience to transport them to an elevated level of sensory experience of the news where they are able to virtually feel the misery, risk and pain of a tragedy, hostility, and vulnerability (Greber et al., 2023a). Digital technology in journalism has been praised as an answer to numerous issues that businesses face in the 21st century, including shrinking audiences, decreasing advertising income, and diminished community reliance (Vettehen et al., 2019). VR and 360° videos have changed the way users interact with content by giving them the freedom to choose their own perspective (Kusuma and Dua, 2020). media engagement (Greber et al., 2023b).

Smart textiles in journalism

The cohesion of electronics with traditional textile materials is addressed as e-textiles, also known as smart wearable or interactive clothing (Meena et al., 2023). Smart textiles differ from traditional textiles in terms of perceiving and responding to the environment. These textiles can sense, detect and react to various environmental stimuli covering thermal, kinetic, electrical and magnetic influences. As science and technology advance, along with the digital shift of the global economy, clothing is evolving into a new high-tech product combined with electronic devices. E-textiles are a new technology that transcends traditional business boundaries and requires innovation (Esmar et al., 2020, Younes, 2023).

Wearable devices also affect development elements: smart watches for employees and Google Glass provide support for recording the environment around the clock. A new class of consumer technology has emerged in the last three years: devices such as computerized smart watches and head-mounted displays (HMDs) such as Google Glass. Equipped with numerous sensors, these devices continuously monitor the user's environment and health, creating more specific and precise data. Media companies can measure the heart rate of their customers while they are reading a particular article and then determine the perception of the article (Angler, 2014).

2.1 Early adoption of technology in Indian journalism

The introduction of the printing press to India in the 16th century was a pivotal event that revolutionized the way information was produced and shared. This technological innovation facilitated the mass production of printed materials, drastically altering the landscape of communication. The advent of newspapers, pamphlets, and journals provided new platforms for the dissemination of information and ideas, becoming instrumental in shaping political discourse and public opinion (Dubey, 2023). As the industry of Indian journalism evolved, it embraced various forms of media. Initially, print media played a dominant role, followed by the rise of radio and later, electronic media. Each new medium brought its own unique advantages, broadening the reach and impact of journalistic endeavors. Radio introduced the ability to broadcast news and information to a wider, often less literate audience, while electronic media, including television, offered visual and auditory engagement, further transforming the journalistic landscape (Saragih & Harahap, 2020; Anooja and Sharma, 2021). However, the most significant transformation accompanied by the advent of the cyberspace and digital communication (Figure 3). This new period of digital journalism revolutionized the industry once again, providing unprecedented speed and accessibility in the dissemination of news and information. The digital age has expanded the boundaries of journalism, making it more interactive and immediate than ever before (Farid, 2023).

The swift spread of touchscreen phones and wireless internet in India has strategically positioned digital media as a significant force in the information industry. Better educated, young city dwellers in India increasingly rely on online sources, including social media platforms, for news. The country boasts over 150 million active online news consumers in various Indian languages, with a majority located in rural areas. In a market with a growing appetite for video content, online news is predominantly consumed through videos, contributing to YouTube's success in India (Basuroy, 2023).

2.2 Technology penetration in Indian media and journalism sector

With the changing digital landscape in India, news broadcasts are constantly reaching television screens from DTH to mobile phones, tablets and laptops through channels and programs on YouTube and Facebook. Broadcasters are not only offering live channels on OTT and YouTube, but are now also offering online special programs and exclusive content for digital audiences. According to the FICCI-EY March 2021 Media and Entertainment Report, the number of online media viewers is set to grow to 450 million by 2020. India has the world's second largest digital population of 468 million and the time spent online increased by 32% in 2020. Online news has the widest reach with 454 million mobile and desktop users of news sites, magazines and texts, and 450 million online entertainment users. In addition, online newspaper and newspaper downloads increased by 12% in 2020, leading to a shift in media from newspapers and television to digital platforms (Kapoor and Bhambri, 2022).

Considered by experts as one of the technologies that make journalism more effective, artificial intelligence has entered every department of media companies and brings many changes to the newsroom with different tools. Its possibilities are very different, from explaining a simple news story to discovering new aspects of the business or developing relationships with users through the processing of data paper (Gutiérrez-Caneda et al., 2023). Updates are usually published a few minutes after the event. This performance is achieved thanks to artificial intelligence that analyzes large amounts of data, extracts important information and creates short news stories (Tiwari, 2024).

Only 35% of media access on smartphones and tablets comes from computers. News aggregation systems and applications like NewsPoint (17%), InShorts (19%), Daily Hunt (25%), and Google News (53%), have surfaced as significant sources to get news and are appreciated for their simplicity. Additionally, the total digital business grew by 29% in 2021, while revenue from advertising and revenue also grew by 29%. In addition to YouTube and WhatsApp, Facebook is used by 43% of people, Instagram by 32%, Twitter by 22%, and Telegram by 21%. In general, 60% of individuals share news through social media, messaging, or email (Jha, 2022).

The application of AI in journalism in India is still in its infancy but is growing rapidly. Indian journalists frequently use AI tools to analyze and verify information, create articles and content, and personalize content according to the reader's preferences. However, the application of AI to Indian journalism has been relatively simple, focusing on simple tasks such as data analysis and content creation. Indian media organizations are also developing the necessary infrastructure to expand the use of AI. One of the biggest concerns in India is the impact on intellectual property and the integrity of technology, especially issues such as corruption and misinformation (Jain and Sriram, 2023).

Automative Insights—Yahoo's natural language processing expert; this newspaper is not yet launched in India. Leading media organizations such as The Times of India, Hindustan Times, The Hindu, The Telegraph, Indian Express, NDTV, and India Today can work with intelligence to streamline the media process (Biswal and Gouda, 2020). The emergence of AI-based Technologies in the fall of 2022 illustrates areas of tension that scholars are familiar with: first, the difficulties of using AI for teaching in an era of transparency and accountability, which is the opposite of the adoption of AI worldwide (Beckett, 2019); third, the dependence on large technology companies to innovate. Lima-Santos and Ceron (2022, p. 23) cite the findings of Rashidian et al. (2018) as saying, "Most applications that use AI in journalism rely on money from large technology companies, such as Google and Facebook, to develop them." This challenge is embedded in general financial problems that are difficult for journalism (Salgado, 2022).

VR journalism in India is still in its infancy and to realize the full potential of VR and AR technology, content and distribution strategies need to be developed with the target audience in mind. The 'sense of presence' in the virtual world is largely dependent on the availability of VR headsets and the experience of using them. Therefore, it is necessary to provide important information and knowledge to the audience, allowing them to put on the VR headset and immerse themselves in the virtual world. If media outlets using VR/AR technology for storytelling do not deliver meaningful content, the technology will not be able to sustain the audience in the long run (Kusuma and Dua, 2020).

3. CHALLENGES

Unemployment concerns: The question of whether skills will create more jobs or take away existing jobs in the media and social media industry is regularly debated in the public domain. As we see more intelligence used to collect, create, manage and distribute information, this will lead to fears of unemployment among those working in the sector. However, studies and economic forecasts reveal two sides of the story. Estimates suggest that global GDP could grow by more than 14% by 2030 with the use of AI alone. However, some changes may occur as routines are disrupted or changed. Recent estimates suggest that 10–25% of construction jobs could amend or vanish over the up coming ten years as a result of automation. The most vulnerable are regular manual tasks and information responsibilities such as assembly line production, document recording, transportation, and basic identification; repetitive tasks are better done automatically. In fact, jobs partially or fully aided by AI in legal services, banking, pharmaceuticals, and artistic fields will flourish as AI matches or surpasses the unique capabilities of humans (George, 2024; Okechukwu et al., 2023). The combination of intelligence and journalism has raised concerns about job security. There is ongoing debate about whether AI will create new jobs in media and journalism or lead to job losses. The use of diverse skills in collecting, creating, managing, and distributing information will lead to fears of unemployment for professionals in this field. Estimates suggest that global GDP could grow by more than 14% by 2030 due to the adoption of AI, but the transition will be accompanied by some job losses or job displacement (George, 2024; Okechukwu et al., 2023). Studies show that 10–25% of manufacturing jobs, especially routine jobs that use physical and intellectual skills such as data and analysis, will likely be replaced or eliminated by technology in the next decade (Farid, 2023).

Even the smartest jobs in fields such as law, finance, and media are not immune to change as AI capabilities continue to improve (Noain-Sánchez, 2022).

The fake news market: The transmission and reception of content has been revised drastically by smartphones and social media, yet not every content is true or authentic. Disinformation, or misleading information, is being disseminated more frequently as a result of the widespread use of social media and the internet. These digital spaces are easy to reach and spread rapidly. Bias and inconsistencies can enter these systems and lead to false results (Santos, 2023). The digital age, marked by the rise of smart-tech and social media networks, has changed the mode of information consumption. The rapid spread of misinformation has become a major problem, and bias can also be reflected in the intelligence process. Misinformation spreads rapidly on social media and other digital platforms, undermining the credibility of the media. Research shows the difficulty of managing disinformation and the need for better tools to detect and combat disinformation (Santos, 2023). Electronic systems designed to identify and combat fake news must address biases in AI training data that can lead to false conclusions (de-Lima-Santos and Ceron, 2021).

Algorithmic Transparency in Journalism:

Algorithmic transparency remains a critical challenge in journalism. As AI systems are used to curate news content and personalize user experiences, there is growing concern over the opaque nature of these algorithms. This lack of transparency can lead to issues like biased news distribution, reinforcing echo chambers and misinformation. Guaranteeing lucidity and liability in AI-driven decision-making processes is essential to maintaining public trust in journalism (Elanjimattom, 2023). Developing standards for algorithmic transparency, such as making AI models interpretable and providing explanations for automated decisions, could help address these concerns (Schaetz et al., 2023).

Moral Concerns:

Harnessing AI for journalism carry numerous moral concerns. Challenges like data privacy, bias in algorithms, and the potential misuse of AI-generated content are paramount. The ethical concerns of AI tools in journalism also include the risks of surveillance and the unauthorized collection of data. As newsrooms increasingly rely on AI for content generation and curation, they must navigate these ethical challenges to avoid compromising journalistic integrity (Ashfaq, Nabi, & Rohit, 2023). Ethical protocols and frameworks are vital to oversee the AI usage in journalism, emphasizing transparency, objectivity, and accountability (Noain-Sánchez, 2022).

Digital Divide:

Smart technology, while transforming journalism, also contributes to a widening digital disparity. Gaps in obtaining technology and internet services result in unequal participation in sthe digital news ecosystem. This gap is particularly evident in rural and underdeveloped areas, where technological infrastructure is lacking. As journalism increasingly moves online, those without digital access are left behind, leading to information inequity and reduced public engagement (Anooja & Sharma, 2021). Bridging this digital divide requires targeted policies and investments in digital literacy and infrastructure to ensure equitable access to digital journalism (Sharma et al., 2023).

4. PROSPECTS IN SMART TECHNOLOGY AND INDIAN JOURNALISM

The Rise of Independent Journalism:

Smart technologies empower journalists to become more independent by reducing reliance on traditional media organizations. Digital tools and platforms enable independent journalists to produce, distribute, and monetize content directly, allowing for diverse voices and perspectives. This shift supports a more pluralistic media landscape, promoting democratic discourse and transparency (Farid, 2023). Moreover, the rise of independent journalism has the potential to counterbalance media monopolies, offering alternative narratives that challenge mainstream viewpoints (Rodrigues, Baldi, & Gala, 2021).

User-Generated Content:

The advent of smart technologies has given rise to user-generated content (UGC), which plays a significant role in the modern media ecosystem. Social media platforms, blogs, and video-sharing sites allow citizens to report news and share their perspectives, thereby contributing to a more participatory form of journalism (Kapoor & Bhambri, 2022). This trend is reshaping the traditional news model by decentralizing information production and fostering public engagement (Ali, 2023). However, the challenge lies in ensuring the accuracy and credibility of UGC, necessitating new strategies for verification and fact-checking by media organizations (Gutiérrez-Caneda, Vázquez-Herrero, & López-García, 2023).

Promote Public Debate:

AI and smart technologies can promote public debate by providing platforms that facilitate open discussions and engagement with diverse audiences. For instance, AI tools can analyze public sentiment, monitor trends, and identify key issues, helping journalists and media organizations better understand and serve their audiences (Beckett, 2023). By leveraging AI to create interactive and immersive content, such as virtual town halls and debates, newsrooms can enhance audience participation and foster a more informed and engaged public (Greber et al., 2023).

5. CONCLUSION

The domain of journalism is witnessing a deep shift, propelled by the digital revolution, rapid technological evolution, and the growing influence of artificial intelligence. This review article has compiled and analyzed the current applications of smart technology in the journalism industry, focusing on the current status and developments in India. It is clear that the advancement of digital platforms and AI is changing media and providing tools to improve news, distribution and consumption. Digital journalism offers dynamic possibilities, such as rapid information dissemination, new content formats, and personalized news delivery, while challenging traditional media's relevance and credibility. In India, smart technologies have enabled faster information dissemination and more personalized content, thereby reshaping journalistic practices to meet evolving audience expectations. AI is reshaping journalism in multiple ways, from news gathering and production to ethical considerations and credibility. While it brings efficiency and personalization, it also poses risks like misinformation, bias, and diminished human editorial judgment. AI systems are also expensive and time-consuming to use, requiring specialized skills that are often beyond the budget of many media organizations. These issues hinder the mainstream use of smart technology in journalism, especially in resource-limited areas. As the media landscape continues to evolve, Indian journalism must address these challenges through strategic planning, investment in digital skills, and a balanced integration of human skills with technological advancement. Journalism ahead is expected to be defined by an integrated framework, uniting human expertise with AI capabilities to enhance journalistic practices rather than replace them. To thrive in this evolving landscape, media organizations must strike an equilibrium between harnessing AI's benefits and addressing its moral and operational limitations. This requires fostering digital literacy, adaptability, and critical thinking among journalists and media professionals. In conclusion, while the integration of AI and digital technologies in journalism presents unprecedented opportunities for innovation, it also requires vigilance and a commitment to ethical standards. Continuous research and adaptation will be essential to ensure journalism remains a crucial element of democratic societies in an increasingly automated world.

REFERENCES

Aissani, R., Abdalla, R. A. Q., Taha, S., & Al Adwan, M. N. (2023). Artificial Intelligence Tools in Media and Journalism: Roles and Concerns,*International Conference on Multimedia Computing, Networking and Applications (MCNA)*, Valencia, Spain, 2023, pp. 19-26, DOI: 10.1109/MCNA59361.2023.10185738

Ali, M. (2023). Deciphering Mobile Journalism: An All-Inclusive Definition of Mobile Journalism in the Modern Era. *Global Media Journal*, *21*, 1–9. https://www.researchgate.net/publication/377239569_Deciphering_Mobile_Journalism_An_All-Inclusive_Definition_of_Mobile_Journalism_in_the_Modern_Era

Aljazairi, S., & Ekman, M. (2016). Robot Journalism: Threat or an opportunity. M.A. thesis. School of Humanities, Education and Social Sciences, Örebro University. https://www.diva-portal.org/smash/get/diva2:938024/FULLTEXT01.pdf

Angler, M. (2014). Wearable Devices: Revolutionising Mobile Journalism Again. DOI: 10.13140/RG.2.1.2098.9685

. Anooja, A. and Sharma, P. (2021). Digital Media: Rise of Online content to makes a Digital

. Ashfaq, R., Nabi, Z. & Rohit. (2023). Artificial Intelligence and the Indian Media Industry: the Future is now. Journal of Media,Culture and Communication. 14-21. .DOI: 10.55529/jmcc.31.14.21

Beckett, C. (2023). Generating change: How newsrooms are using AI in 2023. JournalismAI, London School of Economics and Political Science (LSE). Supported by the Google News Initiative. https://blog.google/technology/ai/how-ai-is-generating-change-in-newsrooms-worldwide

. Biswal, S. K. & Gouda, N. (2020). Artificial Intelligence in Journalism: A Boon or Bane?. .DOI: 10.1007/978-981-15-0994-0_10

Chohan, U. W. (2022). Web 3.0: The Future Architecture of the Internet? https://papers.ssrn.com/sol3/papers.cfm?abstract_id=4037693

Das, D., & Upadhyay, A. K. (2024). Deconstructing complexities in the adoption of new forms in news media: A systematic literature review. *Cogent Arts & Humanities*, *11*(1), 2303819. Advance online publication. DOI: 10.1080/23311983.2024.2303819

de-Lima-Santos, M.-F., & Ceron, W. (2021). Artificial Intelligence in News Media: Current Perceptions and Future Outlook. *Journalism and Media.*, *3*(1), 13–26. https://www.mdpi.com/2673-5172/3/1/2. DOI: 10.3390/journalmedia3010002 de-Lima-Santos, M.-F., & Mesquita, L. (2021). Data Journalism Beyond Technological Determinism. *Journalism Studies*, *22*(11), 1416–1435. https://www.tandfonline.com/doi/full/10.1080/1461670X.2021.1944279. DOI: 10.1080/1461670X.2021.1944279

Dubey, D. D. (2023). Historical Evolution of Media in India: A Critical Analysis. *Indian Journal of Law and Legal Research*, *5*(4), 1–16. https://hcommons.org/deposits/objects/hc:59722/datastreams/CONTENT/content

Elanjimattom, N. J. (2023). Artificial Intelligence as Journalist and Gatekeeper: Ethics of Automated Journalism and Algorithmic Curation of News in the Indian Context. Digital Journalism in India. https://www.academia.edu/99514264/Artificial_Intelligence_as_Journalist_and_Gatekeeper_Ethics_of_Automated_Journalism_and_Algorithmic_Curation_of_News_in_the_Indian_Context

Farid, S. A. (2023). Changing the Paradigm of Traditional Journalism to Digital Journalism: Impact on Professionalism and Journalism Credibility. *Journal International Dakwah and Communication*, *3*(1), 22–32. DOI: 10.55849/jidc.v3i1.374

George, A. S. (2024). Artificial Intelligence and the Future of Work. *Job Shifting Not Job Loss.*, *02*, 17–37. DOI: 10.5281/zenodo.10936490

Gómez-Diago, G. (2022). Perspectivas para abordar la inteligencia artificial en la enseñanza deperiodismo. Una revisión de experiencias investigadoras y docentes. Revista Latina DeComunicación Social, 80, 29-46. https://www.doi.org/10.4185/RLCS-2022-1542

Greber, H., Aaldering, L., & Lecheler, S. (2023a). The Worthwhileness of Immersive Journalism—Taking on an Audience Perspective. *Journalism Practice*, •••, 1–19. DOI: 10.1080/17512786.2023.2177711

Greber, H., Lecheler, S., Aaldering, L., De Haan, Y., Kruikemeier, S., Goutier, N., & De Bruin, K. (2023b). Feeling the News? The Differential Effects of Immersive Journalism on Emotional Response. *Digital Journalism (Abingdon, England)*, *11*(1), 39–60. DOI: 10.1080/21670811.2022.2155205

. Henestrosa, A. L., Greving, H., Kimmerle, J. (2023). Automated journalism: The effects of AI authorship and evaluative information on the perception of a science journalism article,

. India. International Journal of All Research Education and Scientific Methods, 9(3), 1415-1419.

Jain, N., & Sriram, A. (2023). Artificial intelligence (AI) & Indian journalism: Current trends and challenges. International journal of novel research and development. 8(5), 777-783. https://www.ijnrd.org/papers/IJNRD2305099.pdf

Jha, L. (2022). Over half of Indian users consume news on social media. https://www.livemint.com/industry/media/over-half-of-indian-users-consume-news-on-social-media-11655305366849.html#:~:text=India%20is%20a%20strongly%20mobile,and%20are%20valued%20for%20convenience

Kapoor, A., & Bhambri, A. (2022). Raising the curtain: Media industry and the changing landscape. https://economictimes.indiatimes.com/industry/media/entertainment/media/raising-the-curtain-media-industry-and-the-changing-landscape/articleshow/92499946.cms

Kusuma, K. S., & Dua, M. (2020). Immersive Journalism: Emerging Practices and Challengesin Indian Media. *Journal of Media and Communication*, *4*(2), 25–39. http://jmc.cutn.ac.in/docs/JM&C2020DecemberPaper2_01012021.pdf

Meena, J. S., Choi, S. B., Jung, S. B., & Kim, J. W. (2023). Electronic textiles: New age of wearable technology for healthcare and fitness solutions. *Materials Today. Bio*, *19*, 100565. Advance online publication. DOI: 10.1016/j.mtbio.2023.100565

Micheler, S., Goh, Y. M., & Lohse, N. (2019). Innovation landscape and challenges of smart technologies and systems – a European perspective. Production &amp. *Production & Manufacturing Research*, *7*(1), 503–528. DOI: 10.1080/21693277.2019.1687363

Nasar, M. (2023). Web 3.0: A Review and its Future. *International Journal of Computer Applications*, *185*(10), 41–46. DOI: 10.5120/ijca2023922776

Noain-Sánchez, A. (2022). Addressing the Impact of Artificial Intelligence on Journalism: The perception of experts, journalists and academics. *Communicatio Socialis*, *35*(3), 105–121. DOI: 10.15581/003.35.3.105-121

. Okechukwu, Francis & Areji, Anthony & Ugwu, Anayochukwu. (2023). Beyond the Fear of Artificial Intelligence and Loss of Job: a Case for Productivity and Efficiency. .DOI: 10.32388/3BWNXG

Rodrigues, L. P., Baldi, V., & Gala, A. (2021). MOBILE JOURNALISM: The emergence of a new field of journalism. *Brazilian Journalism Research.*, *17*(2), 1. DOI: 10.25200/BJR.v17n2.2021.1368

Salgado, L. (2022). From the classroom to the newsroom: A critical route to introduce AI in journalism education. Facts & Frictions: Emerging Debates. *Pedagogies and Practices in Contemporary Journalism*, *2*(1), 80–97. DOI: 10.22215/ff/v2.i1.04

Santos, F. C. C. (2023). Artificial Intelligence in Automated Detection of Disinformation: A Thematic Analysis. *Journal of Medicine*, *4*(2), 679–687. DOI: 10.3390/journalmedia4020043

. Saragih, M. & Harahap, Ali. (2020). The Challenges of Print Media Journalism in the Digital Era. Budapest International Research and Critics Institute (BIRCI-Journal): Humanities and Social Sciences. 3. 540-548. .DOI: 10.33258/birci.v3i1.805

Schaetz, N., Gagrčin, E., Toth, R., & Emmer, M. (2023). Algorithm dependency in platformized news use. *New Media & Society*, *0*(0). Advance online publication. DOI: 10.1177/14614448231193093

Sharma, S. K., Janssen, M., Bunker, D., Pery, C. D., Singh, J. B., Dwivedi, Y. K., & Misra, S. K. (2023). Unlocking the Potential of Smart Technologies: Addressing Adoption Challenges. *Information Systems Frontiers*, *25*(4), 1293–1298. DOI: 10.1007/s10796-023-10408-3

Swart, J. (2021). Experiencing Algorithms: How Young People Understand, Feel About, and Engage With Algorithmic News Selection on Social Media. *Social Media + Society*, *7*(2), 20563051211008828. Advance online publication. DOI: 10.1177/20563051211008828

Tandoc, E. C., Wu, S., Tan, J., & Contreras-Yap, S. (2022). What is (automated) news? A content analysis of algorithm-written news articles. Media E Jornalismo, 22(41), 103-120. https://hdl.handle.net/10356/173664

Tiwari, S. (2024).The role of artificial intelligence in automated journalism: transforming newsproduction. International journal of creative research thoughts. 12(5): 799-838. https://ijcrt.org/papers/IJCRT21X0233.pdf

Vettehen, P. H., Wiltink, D., Huiskamp, M., Schaap, G., & Ketelaar, P. (2019). Taking the full view: How viewers respond to 360-degree video news. *Computers in Human Behavior*, *91*, 24–32. DOI: 10.1016/j.chb.2018.09.018

Younes, B. (2022). Smart E-textiles: A review of their aspects and applications. *Journal of Industrial Textiles*. Advance online publication. DOI: 10.1177/15280837231215493

Zhang, W., Pérez Tornero, J. M., & Tian, Q. (2023). Dissecting Automated News Production From a Transdisciplinary Perspective: Methodology, Linguistic Application, and Narrative Genres. *SAGE Open*, *13*(4), 21582440231206372. Advance online publication. DOI: 10.1177/21582440231206372

Chapter 11
Streamlining Vaccination Process Through Innovative Solution:
Bakunako – A Rewards-based Health Record Platform

Leah O. Pelias
https://orcid.org/0000-0002-5279-1268
University of Southeastern Philippines, Philippines

Francis O. Sale
https://orcid.org/0009-0006-7904-3039
University of Southeastern Philippines, Philippines

Carl Christian M. Capon
https://orcid.org/0009-0000-5290-5416
University of Southeastern Philippines, Philippines

ABSTRACT

BakunAko is a platform designed to address the challenges of infant vaccination with scheduling and integrated features. A needs assessment in the methodology provides the parents and guardians a relevant tool to keep updated and responsible for the immunization of the infant. The voucher reward system allows incentivization points to be earned. Automated scheduling, digital immunization records, and SMS reminders are the features to combat stigma on vaccination for infants. The platform incorporates innovative solutions through a unique vaccination timetable, addresses financial barriers, and promotes adherence to local health sector programs. It empowers end-users to ensure seamless immunization through its user-friendly

DOI: 10.4018/979-8-3373-0603-2.ch011

interface and comprehensive features. Aiming to improve immunization rates, protect public health, and offer incentives. Pilot testing was conducted to ensure functional and non-functional attainment of the objectives. The result underpins facilitation of faster and effective prevention of infectious diseases, especially among infants in the underserved community.

INTRODUCTION

The timely administration of vaccines, precisely aligned with recommended schedules, serves as the foundation of global public health efforts. Adherence to these schedules is essential for maximizing protection against preventable infectious diseases that may cause potential long-term health complications. While various timetable scheduling applications already exist within the healthcare sector, there remains a need for solutions catered specifically to the unique requirements of infant vaccination.

Current scenario often lacks the features necessary to fully support the needs of parents, guardians, and healthcare providers in optimizing immunization adherence and streamlining related processes, such as the lack of SMS reminder notifications that serve as timely prompts for parents and guardians, the lack of vaccine information, the traditional way of inputting vaccine schedules, and handwritten health records. And to highlight, the voucher rewards system involves the coordination of medium- or large- scale businesses in the form of a tie-up collaboration. The absence of essential features in existing scheduling applications can lead to serious consequences for infant health. Parents and guardians may miss vaccination appointments, lose track of immunization records, struggle to obtain timely schedules, and, in some cases, become hesitant to vaccinate their infants altogether. This made the researchers eager to address the features lacking in those current applications.

The study benefits the parents and guardians of the infants as well as the healthcare provider, particularly those parents and guardians who want a convenient and efficient vaccine streamlining and an innovative scheduling process for their infants. For healthcare providers, they can effectively manage and organize vaccination schedules for the already-administered infants.

The researchers developed a centralized web-based platform where the parents, guardians of the infants, and healthcare providers can administer an automated timetable scheduler, a digitalized immunization record, detailed vaccine information, scheduled monitoring for vaccine appointments (for healthcare providers), an SMS notification reminder for timely prompts to upcoming vaccinations, and the core feature, which is a voucher rewards system for every vaccination administered. Notable feature includes a feedback message for user satisfaction. BakunAko is also a responsive web-based application for its accessibility, collaboration, and administration. To ensure comprehensive immunization coverage, it is necessary that public and private healthcare facilities establish collaborative partnerships with researchers. This coordination facilitates the effective management of vaccine availability and promotes access to the full range of necessary infant health services.

Furthermore, to solicit support, the proponents used the free tier version of the Twilio SMS API to inform the parents through text messages about the schedule of the subsequent vaccinations for their infants. With Twilio SMS API, for instance, there is convenience in delivering text-based reminders as it enables the delivery of messages in the shortest time possible. It is possible to write different messages for each recipient, ensuring the persons receiving these reminders read the messages and take necessary action. In this sense, through the Twilio SMS API, the proponents can quickly establish an efficient flow of information, which can be crucial to parents and guardians who must have information about their infants' vaccination schedules.

BACKGROUND

Vaccines play a critical role in safeguarding infant health against preventable diseases. Infants are especially vulnerable to dangerous diseases, which is why vaccines are so important. Starting from their birth, recommended vaccines and immunizations provide essential protection against illnesses like measles, polio, and hepatitis B. Following a pediatrician's recommended vaccination schedule is crucial for safeguarding an infant's health. According to an article from the Centers for Disease Control and Prevention (CDC), healthcare providers emphasize the importance of infant vaccination quote: "Immunity is the body's way of preventing disease," but a baby's immune system is not fully developed during birth, making them especially susceptible to infections (Rodrigues & Plotkin, 2020). Vaccines train a baby's immune system to recognize and fight off harmful germs, ultimately protecting them from serious illnesses. For decades, a meticulously designed immunization schedule has offered protection from birth, targeting illnesses that can severely impact young children (Kiszewski et al., 2021).

Timely vaccinations in accordance with prescribed schedules are critical to global public health. These schedules are rigorously developed using research findings to ensure immunizations are given at the appropriate ages for maximum protection against dangerous diseases. According to an article from the World Health Organization's newsroom, most countries have already implemented vaccination and immunization routine programs to improve public health approach (*Why Vaccinate," Centers for Disease Control and Prevention*, 2019), yet millions of children just below 5 years old have died globally from diseases that vaccines could have prevented. Every infant vaccination is timed so it corresponds with a certain biological window during which the child's immune system can react most quickly and effectively to protect the child from the underlying infectious disease (UNICEF Philippines, 2021b).

Following the recommended immunization schedule is necessary for reducing vulnerability to vaccine-preventable illnesses and their spread. For instance, A polio epidemic was declared in the Philippines in September 2019. This outbreak puts Filipino children at risk for paralysis for the rest of their lives and prompts the Philippine Department of Health whether the mass immunization campaign should be vaccinated according to the routine immunization schedule (Restivo et al., 2015).

The historically unprecedented reduction in the occurrence of vaccine-preventable diseases over the past several decades has inadvertently fostered a public perception that these illnesses are less severe and that individuals have a diminished risk of contracting them (Wilson et al., 2020). Parental vaccine hesitancy, fueled by limited knowledge about the critical importance of newborn immunization, poses a significant barrier to protecting infants. The lack of transparency surrounding vaccine safety and efficacy remains a concern (Mantel & Cherian, 2020). The Philippine government faces the challenge of addressing this knowledge gap in underserved communities. This is essential to ensure these vulnerable infants receive the life-saving protection that vaccines provide (Murthy et al., 2024).

Timetable scheduling is a valuable method for effectively organizing and managing daily activities within a designated time frame (Dadari et al., 2021). It involves creating a clear schedule that shows when each task should happen. For healthcare, implementing a robust scheduling system has the potential to improve healthcare service significantly. Such systems can reduce patient wait times, streamline access to medical services, and positively influence the overall efficiency and quality of healthcare operations (Mardi et al., 2022). Implementing a structured timetable can enhance time management and productivity. By thoroughly allocating time for various activities, parents, guardians, and healthcare providers can optimize work-life balance, prioritize essential tasks, and minimize the stress associated with time pressure. Additionally, having a timetable can also help with time wastage. In general, timetable scheduling is a valuable tool that enables individuals to make the most of their time and maximize their daily appointment schedules. To achieve herd immunity and protect public health, widespread vaccine uptake is paramount.

Voucher reward systems have gained attention as a strategy to incentivize vaccination, offering individuals tangible benefits upon receiving a vaccine (Erfani & Bourdeaux, 2021). These systems typically provide rewards ranging from modest discounts and gift cards to more substantial benefits, with the intention of motivating individuals to prioritize immunization. Voucher reward systems hold the potential to improve infant vaccination rates significantly. By offering tangible incentives to parents and guardians, this voucher-reward system can address barriers to vaccination, such as financial constraints or lack of perceived urgency. The rewards can offset costs associated with accessing healthcare services and act as a positive reinforcement for prioritizing timely immunization.

Review of Related Literature

Infant Vaccination

Infants, also known as babies, are the youngest and most vulnerable members of the human population (Altmann et al., 2021). They are typically defined as individuals from birth to one-year-old, characterized by their unique needs and development stages. Infants rely heavily on their caregivers for survival, as they are unable to perform basic tasks independently. Immunization is another critical component of health that assists in raising the health standards of the young generation. The government needs to ensure that infants are protected by getting vaccinated to ensure they do not fall victim to easily preventable diseases. Vaccines are safe and effective interventions to boost the body's immune system (Wierzbicka et al., 2021). Vaccination of infants can be effective if administered during infancy to reduce the possibility of fatal disease outbreaks as well as to minimize the prevalence of infectious diseases in societies. Conditions ranging from measles, poliomyelitis, whooping cough, and influenza can result in complications and severe illness, including hospitalizations and mortality among young children (Murthy et al., 2024).

The vaccination of an infant contributes to the aspect of herd immunity. As the World Health Organization (WHO) states, it happens when a sufficiently high percentage of a particular population is vaccinated against a specific disease, preventing its spread, and protecting individuals who cannot be vaccinated for health reasons or are too young (Mantel & Cherian, 2020). The fact is that vaccinations are beneficial to newborns and young children, which helps to strengthen herd immunity. Infant Vaccinations are planned as a protective measure against certain diseases that may cause complications or be fatal to the child. The DoH also recognizes that infants are more prone to infections since their immune systems are not fully developed. That is why vaccination of infants has been considered one of the most effective strategies in the field of public health to prevent deaths and promote better results for children (Altmann et al., 2021). Vaccination programs play a role in decreasing the overall health costs incurred in managing these diseases. However, it is essential to note that vaccines undergo various testing and monitoring to become safe and effective. Finally, it is necessary to understand that vaccines undergo a strict trial and approval before being released into the market (UNICEF Philippines, 2021b). This process ensures that the vaccines developed are safe and will help them prevent some diseases effectively. However, reaching the target coverage rate of first-dose immunization among infants in Davao City, one of the largest cities in the Philippines, remains challenging, even for the Philippines, with its established EPI and locally intensified improvement projects for the immunization program (Antonelli Incalzi et al., 2021).

Importance of Vaccines to Infants

Vaccines are essential for safeguarding the health and well-being of infants. As newborns and young children have vulnerable immune systems, vaccines help to prevent serious diseases and infections that could lead to lifelong complications or even death. The World Health Organization (WHO) recommends that children receive all early childhood vaccines to achieve and maintain appropriate coverage rates, as vaccination is an essential global public health practice that saves two to three million lives annually(Rodrigues & Plotkin, 2020). Immunizations provide infants with a foundation of protection against various infectious diseases. The recommended immunization schedule is aimed at protecting infants and children at an early age to minimize contracting an illness(Dadari et al., 2021). Thus, parents and healthcare providers can decrease the prevalence of these diseases and provide a safer environment for infants and children by providing necessary vaccinations and schedules. Not only does vaccination help an individual child, but it also reduces disease transmission to the rest of the population (Mantel & Cherian, 2020).

Vaccines and Recommended Schedule for Infants

The study of Ulep and Uy noted that the Philippine Expanded Program on Immunization was established 40 years ago (World Health Organization, 2018). They are promoting early childhood immunization among Filipino children against hazardous diseases. The EPI in the Philippines seeks to make sure that children receive all the recommended preventive vaccines before their first birthday (UNICEF Philippines, 2021a). The immunization schedule is critical in establishing the timeframe for immunization of particular diseases in individuals, especially newborn babies (UNICEF Philippines, 2021b). The vaccines and schedules for infants in the Philippines that are recommended by the World Health Organization (WHO), Philippine Pediatric Society (PPS), and United Nations International Children's Emergency Fund (UNICEF) Philippines are the following (V. G. Ulep, 2021) and (Rodrigues & Plotkin, 2020):

1. Bacillus Calmette–Guérin (BCG)
    a. Protects against: Tuberculosis (TB), a bacterial infection affecting the lungs.
    b. Schedule: Given at birth.

2. Hepatitis B
    a. Protects against: Hepatitis B, a liver infection caused by the hepatitis B virus.
    b. Schedule: Given at birth.
3. Pentavalent Vaccine
    a. Protects against: Diphtheria, Tetanus, Pertussis (Whooping Cough), Hepatitis B, Haemophilus influenzae type b (Hib)
    b. Schedule: Typically given in 3 doses starting at 6 weeks of age.
4. Oral Polio Vaccine (OPV)Protects against: Polio
    a. Schedule: Typically given in 3 doses starting at 6 weeks of age.
5. Inactivated Polio Vaccine (IPV)
    a. Protects against: Polio
    b. Schedule: Given in 1 dose at 18 weeks of age.
6. Pneumococcal Conjugate Vaccine (PCV)
    a. Protects against: Streptococcus pneumoniae bacteria, causing pneumonia, meningitis, and other infections
    b. Schedule: Typically given in 3 doses starting at 6 weeks of age.
7. Measles, Mumps, Rubella (MMR)
    a. Protects against:
        i. Measles, a highly contagious viral disease.
        ii. Mumps, a viral infection causing swelling of the parotid glands.
        iii. Rubella, also known as German measles, a viral infection that can be dangerous for pregnant women.
    b. Schedule: Given in 2 doses at 9 months and 1 year of age.

Timetable Scheduling

The timetable is a plan that provides an orderly arrangement of activities or occurrences expected to occur everywhere at certain times (Restivo et al., 2015). The timetables are often employed in schools, workplaces, other institutions, public transportation systems, and the healthcare sector to assist people in planning their time. In vaccination, a schedule that the WHO, CDC, and PPS have provided has a significant role in giving proper guidelines for the time and effective age of vaccinated individuals, especially infants. Health professionals design these schedules to ensure that infants get their best shot at protection in cases of diseases that could have been prevented. Having a schedule for when children should be vaccinated helps parents protect their children from various diseases and prevents them from getting infected severely (Ann & Baumann, 2023). Using a timetable schedule for infant vaccinations is beneficial for the parents as they can know the right time when each of them is due. Since so many vaccinations need to be given in the first years of a child's life, it cannot be evident for parents to know when which one is due. The timetable schedule also helps one understand which vaccine is suitable for the child and at which age to administer the vaccine. Thus, it is helpful for parents to ensure that their infant is up to date with their vaccinations (Wentzell & Racila, 2021). As Khazanov et al.(2023) highlighted, the advanced notion of using a timetable schedule for infant vaccination is timed. Some vaccines work best if given at a precise age, and any postponement will put the child at risk of catching dangerous illnesses. This way, parents are sure that their infant does not miss any of the vaccines they are supposed to take at any given time of their growth, and this is done by following the doctors' advice and staying organized. When developing a schedule for the timetable, parents and guardians will have to set time for each of the scheduled vaccinations so that no activity or session is missed. It fosters responsibility and allows parents and guardians to keep to schedules effectively.

Voucher Rewards System for Vaccination Incentives

Vaccination is considered one of the most effective methods of preventing the transmission of infectious diseases and enhancing health among the population, as WHO pointed out (Førland & Roxå, 2024). Another crucial factor in public health is the immunization of newborns from deadly diseases. However, many people remain skeptical or reluctant about vaccination and, at times, have difficulty addressing all families and guaranteeing that infants are fully immunized (Alkandi et al., 2023),(Calcaterra et al., 2023). The voucher rewards system for vaccination incentives is a program that offers individuals incentives that can be redeemed for rewards such as vouchers, coupons, or gift cards to encourage individuals, particularly infants, to get vaccinated, especially those who may be hesitant or unsure about the vaccine (Kuznetsova et al., 2021), (Mardi et al., 2022). This system not only motivates parents to prioritize their child's vaccination but also serves as a source of encouragement and recognition for their efforts in protecting their baby's health and the health of others. Moreover, the voucher rewards system can also help overcome financial barriers that may prevent parents from getting their infants vaccinated. Some individuals may be hesitant to get vaccinated due to various reasons, such as fear of side effects, misinformation, or misconceptions. The voucher rewards system serves to overcome vaccine hesitancy and resistance. Also, it will help to improve healthcare provider-parent communication and collaboration. According to (Førland & Roxå, 2024), there is compelling evidence indicating that incentive reward programs for vaccination can significantly boost vaccine uptake and engaging parents in the vaccination process and rewarding them for their efforts, healthcare providers can build trust and strengthen the provider-parent relationship. Similarly, the analysis of (Calcaterra et al., 2023) showed that raising vaccination rates is associated with cash incentives and the Vax-a-Million lottery. Since there will be an incentive to get vaccinated, parents and guardians might ensure that their infants get vaccinated against infectious diseases. Parents and guardians are more likely to spend more on taking their infants for vaccination than other expenses when they are offered incentives. This will help to ensure that all infants receive all the mandatory vaccinations on time to avoid outbreaks of diseases and to encourage the hesitant individuals to accept to be vaccinated.

As such, parents and guardians are encouraged to vaccinate their infants to avoid the spread of these diseases within society. In the end, such incentives help not only raise the vaccination rate and reach herd immunity but also contribute to enhancing the state of health of the population.

Integrated SMS Notification in Healthcare

According to the study of Akhu-Zaheya(2018), an integrated Short Message Services (SMS) notification is a great communication tool that combines text messaging with many systems and applications [30]. This feature makes it easy for different platforms to interconnect in a manner that enhances the flow of communication. Considering the modern tendencies in communication, people need to be informed and connected, and SMS notification is an effective method to provide the necessary information, urgent information, or simple reminders. Some benefits of using the technology include real-time communication, higher reach and interactivity, timely and relevant messaging, appointment notifications/reminders, transactional messages, urgent and vital messages, two-factor authentication, and marketing and advertising (Tull et al., 2019).

Communications through integrated Short Message Services (SMS) notifications is a tool that has proven to help improve the portions of Stakeholders' outcomes, especially in healthcare-related service delivery such as vaccination. As Tull et al. (2019) have also pointed out, the use of SMS reminders, if optimized for time delivery, has thus notably contributed to enhancing compliance with recommended immunization schedules among patients by ensuring the timely administration of the vaccines. Integrated SMS notifications can transform how patients are informed about their scheduled healthcare check-ups, including vaccination, and the immediate method of delivering the reminder will be effective in reaching out to the patient. In other words, through SMS reminders, healthcare providers can encourage and compel patients to attend the visits required to complete the details of the necessary vaccinations, thus enhancing overall vaccination compliance. In the studies of (Alkandi et al., 2023), (Førland & Roxå, 2024), highlighted potential regarding the usage across the different spectrums of HLSS about SMS reminders. They pointed out that SMS reminders are very effective when used as both an appointment. Furthermore, the research has shown enhancement on appointment attendance rates (Akhu-Zaheya, 2018). Messaging has been mainly used to remind patients to adhere to some practices in the medical field and show up for more clinic appointments(Tull et al., 2019). In essence, SMS notifications are a viable means of communication in the healthcare sector.

The system's features of the BakunAko web-based system include the generation of SMS notifications to the parents or guardian's module to inform and notify the date and time of the vaccination appointment. The SMS notification feature is intended as a tool to help parents and guardians be aware or reminded of the vaccination schedule for their infant, which is essential in preventing the spread of diseases and promoting the baby's health. As such, the parents and guardians can monitor their baby's vaccination schedule and not miss any of them.

Challenges in Infant Vaccination Programs

Vaccination of infants should be a requirement for every country as the prevention and cure for fatal diseases should start from a tender age. Infant vaccinations have remained a central component of every public health strategy for decades due to their successes in essentially decreasing the rate of Vaccine-Preventable Diseases (VPDs) along with saving countless lives (Fernández-Basanta et al., 2021). But, despite these outstanding achievements of human society, achieving the best immunization coverage remains subject to numerous global and local challenges. These challenges include parents' beliefs about vaccines, perceived barriers to accessing healthcare, and lost chances of vaccination. Further, the mortality rate of infants below the age of five years is still comparatively high in some countries (Wentzell & Racila, 2021). The annual report published by the World Health Organization (WHO) on immunization coverage estimated that in 2022, 14.3 million infants did not receive their first dose of the DTP vaccine, which shows their poor access to immunization and other health services. Furthermore, only 110 million infants globally were administered three doses of diphtheria–tetanus–pertussis (DTP3), indicating the global inequalities in vaccination services, whereby low-income countries are most affected(Ann & Baumann, 2023). Hence, immunization is still acknowledged as one of the most important and influential public health intervention programs for minimizing children's exposure to VPDs.

Like other studies in different parts of the country, there are limitations regarding immunization and other health services in Davao City (World Health Organization, 2018). The WHO report also highlighted that many infants in the Philippines, including those in Davao City, had not received the first dose of the DTP vaccine. Thus, the region needs to ensure adequate access to vaccination services (Haeder, 2021).

MAIN FOCUS OF THE CHAPTER

Issues, Controversies, Problems

Despite the availability of various solutions, the persistence of traditional or handwritten reminders for infant immunization tracking highlights the coexistence of low-tech and modern approaches within the healthcare field. According to a study conducted by (V. G. Ulep, 2021), most users keep track of their children's vaccinations in a notebook or diary. Surprisingly, many of these users do not have any reminders for upcoming vaccines ("State Clinics Barely Fill Healthcare Void in the Philippines," 2022). During an interview with a barangay healthcare worker in Barangay Indangan, Davao City, the authors learned that the City Health Office (CHO) currently utilizes printed cardboards issued by the Philippine Department of Health (DoH) as manual reminders for subsequent infant vaccination schedules. A significant barrier to healthcare access in the Philippines is the limited availability of accessible healthcare facilities.

According to the Department of Health (DoH), half of the Filipino population lacks access to a primary care facility within a 30-minute travel radius. For instance, A case wherein a parent or guardian living in a remote community faces significant challenges if they lose the cardboard vaccination record provided by the health clinic. Without a copy of this document and facing difficulties accessing healthcare, keeping track of an infant's immunization schedule, and ensuring timely protection against preventable diseases becomes extremely difficult, which impacts the infant's well-being. Another possible scenario is that there are instances where a parent or guardian inadvertently misses a scheduled vaccination can have far-reaching consequences for an infant's health. Failure to adhere to recommended immunization leaves the infant vulnerable to preventable diseases that may carry the potential for long-term health complications or even disabilities. These potential adverse outcomes emphasize the critical importance of timely vaccination and the profound impact it has on a child's future well-being.

This leads to the authors to study and develop a vaccination health record platform for infants with a voucher rewards system. A platform that would simplifies the process of scheduling infant vaccinations and facilitates the utilization of its integrated features. A system that provides parents and guardians with intuitive tools to manage their infant's immunization as well as incentivize infant vaccination with a reward system in the form of voucher rewards.

The system would be able to:

1. Provide automated timetable scheduling for dynamic access to vaccination scheduling of infants;

2. Provide easy access to information about vaccines for infants;
3. Provide voucher rewards for every vaccine administered to infants;
4. Provide monitoring and tracking of scheduled vaccines for infants; and
5. Provide SMS notification reminders to serve as timely prompts for parents and guardians.

SOLUTIONS AND RECOMMENDATIONS

The study BakunAko aims to address the need for an efficient and convenient vaccination scheduling system. BakunAko's core feature is a voucher reward system incentivizing every vaccine being administered to the infant, BakunAko will collaborate with businesses allowing a tie-up collaboration. Bakunako provides a convenient and efficient process for the parents and guardians as well as the healthcare providers in charge of administering the vaccines recommended for the infants, promoting timely immunization, and reducing logistical burdens. The authors' aim is to provide parents and guardians a tool and benefits of digitized health records in the form of Vaccination Health Records (VHR), including timely reminders, optimizing adherence to recommended vaccinations.

The platform implements a user verification process to ensure the accuracy and consistency of infant health data. This necessary step involves parents and guardians providing detailed information, aligning it with records held by healthcare providers since birth. This measure safeguards data integrity, which is crucial for the reliable use of the Vaccination Health Record (EHR) feature present in the system. Another feature of the BakunAko system is a timetable scheduling system designed to easily streamline the administration of infant vaccination. Leading towards a simple process and vaccinations are given in a timely manner. Lastly, BakunAko does have SMS notification reminders to serve as timely prompts for parents and guardians, enhancing adherence to recommended vaccination schedules. Minimizing missed schedules and optimizing timely immunization, contribute to improved protection against preventable childhood diseases.

The authors used the input-process-output (IPO) framework model. As shown below:

Figure 1. Conceptual Framework of Project

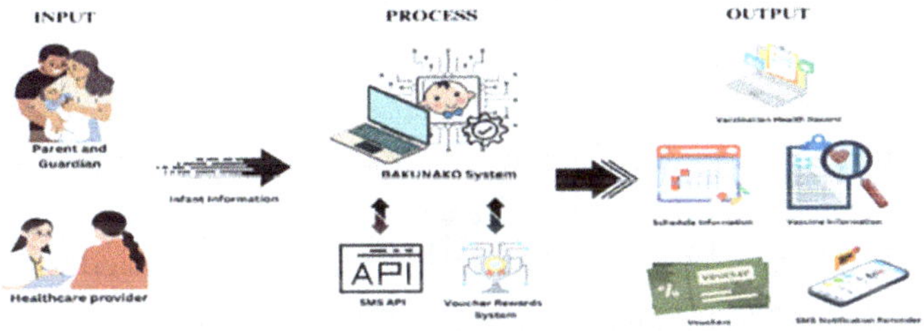

The IPO approach endures that BakunAko is developed to fulfill the needs of parent and guardian users. The information about the infant is one of the necessary inputs that can be identified using the IPO model.

The input includes the parent, guardian, and healthcare provider who sends the information about the infant to the system. The procedures (process) can then be specified, such as organizing the immunization schedules, checking the infant's details for his/her immunization, integrating the SMS API, and the voucher rewards system (in the form of a claimable voucher). The outputs include a vaccination health record, confirmed schedule information, updated vaccination schedule availability, the SMS notification reminder feature, and the rewards voucher.

Software Methodology

The authors have utilized Rapid Application Development (RAD). As the development tool for building the BakunAko system. The RAD model (Sagala, 2021), is a software development process that uses rapid prototyping to generate functional system models. This early engagement enables the user to interact with the system during its early development stages and provide valuable feedback.

Figure 2. Rapid Application Development Framework

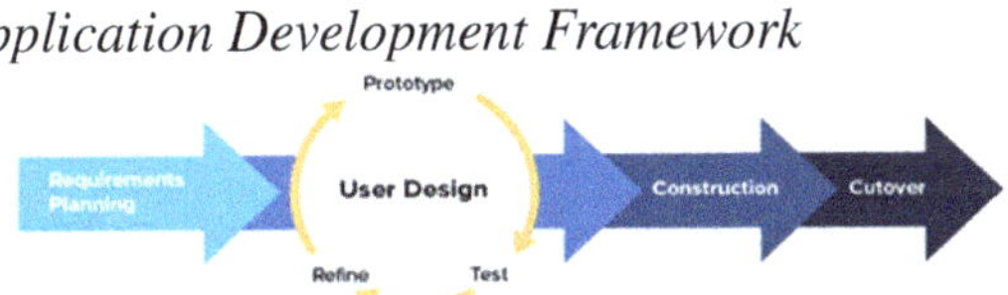

To further ensure that the final product meets users' desires and expectations, rapid prototyping and regular user input are both highly beneficial. The RAD development process follows a structured sequence, starting with Requirements Planning, User Design, Construction, and cutover.

Requirements Planning

The requirements' planning stage was the first stage prior to proceeding to the prototyping stage and after approval of the project proposal. The first phase of the RAD methodology is crucial for laying the foundation of the "BakunAko" project. The authors first identified all the information and requirements by finding the problem they wanted to resolve and the reason why they wanted to solve it. The study is about developing a vaccination health record platform for infants with voucher rewards system, where users are incentivized through vouchers after their infants are vaccinated in every administered vaccine. The authors have finalized all the requirements and information for the project to move on in the following phase.

Needs Assessment on Barangay Clinic Visit

During a site visit to the local Barangay healthcare clinic in Barangay Indangan, Davao City.

Figure 3. Barangay Hall Building Façade of BHW

The dedication of the barangay health workers to administering infant vaccinations was evident, as shown below:

Figure 4. Image captured inside the workplace

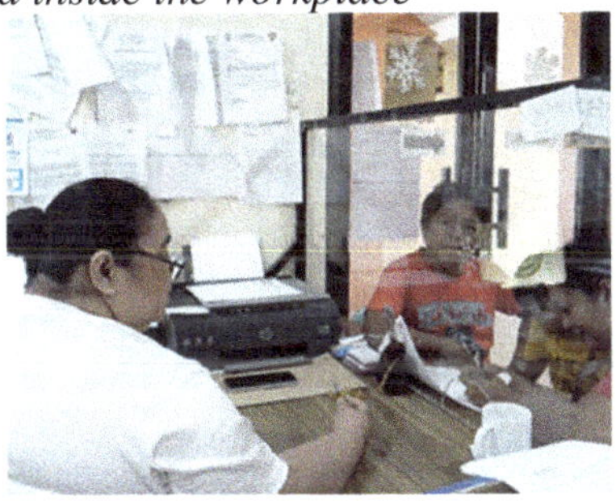

The process commenced with BHWs carefully completing paper forms, meticulously recording each infant's personal information and vaccination history. Following this, brief health assessments were conducted to determine each infant's suitability for vaccination. However, due to restricted access to the actual vaccination room, direct observation of the actual vaccination administration was not possible. While the vaccination procedure could not be directly observed, the visit highlighted potential areas for making the existing process more efficient. The reliance on paper-based documentation and manual processes may introduce inefficiencies and potential for errors in data management. These findings punctuate a clear need for a digital solution such as BakunAko to streamline infant vaccination records, bolster data accuracy, and foster transparency among all involved in the community.

Group Discussion with Identified Healthcare Provider

The authors discussed various topics and activities to collect the necessary data. These activities include:

Research on Local Vaccination Process

During the same site visit to the local barangay healthcare clinic in Barangay Indangan, Davao City, the authors inquired about the vaccination process with the barangay healthcare worker who was administering vaccines to the parent seen the image below. The BHW explained the general procedures and recommended dosages, although some details were difficult to discern due to the BHW's manner of speaking. More, the authors did not feel comfortable asking the barangay health worker too many questions about the vaccination process the processor was not the attending physician or nurse. However, the BHW provided the authors with a cardboard card from the Philippine Department of Health's (DOH) "Todo Ligtas" program

Figure 5. The Philippines DOH "Todo Ligtas Program"

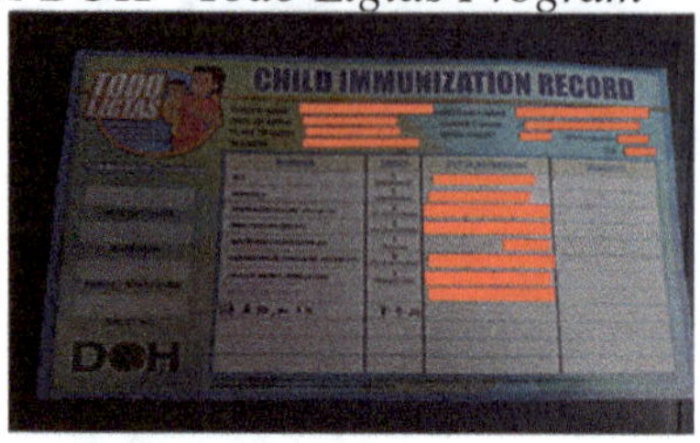

Figure 6. Another View "Todo Ligtas Program"

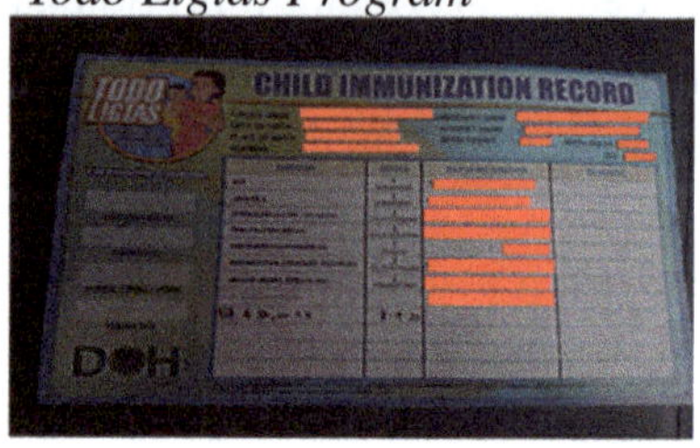

Serves as a guide for parents and guardians regarding their infant's future vaccination schedule and return visits to the clinic.

Research on Vaccine Information

Given the brief clinic visit and the researchers' limited medical knowledge, there were gaps regarding specific vaccines and their dosages for infants. This unfamiliarity with the complexities of infant immunization schedules prompted a need for additional research.

To ensure accurate information on BakunAko's "Infant Description and Information Page," extensive research was conducted using online resources. This included reading reputable medical websites, guidelines from official health organizations, and relevant studies to gather details on vaccine types, dosages, and administration timelines.

This research proved essential in developing the content of the information page, guaranteeing that parents and guardians that should use BakunAko have access to reliable and accurate information about recommended infant vaccination schedules and the specific vaccines their infants need at each stage of development.

Functional Requirements

Table 1. Functional Requirements of BakunAko

Requirement Code	Functional Requirements
F1	User Registration and login: Users (parents/guardians) can register for accounts and log in securely.
F2	Infant profile registration: Parents/guardians can create profiles for their infants, including basic information (name, date of birth, etc.).
F3	Automated timetable scheduler that displays recommended infant vaccination schedules as well as recommended doses based on infant's birthdate.
F4	Allow users to view upcoming and past vaccination appointments.
F5	Enables healthcare providers to update vaccination records (done, pending, and missed) after administering doses.
F6	Allows parents/guardians to download and view vaccination records electronically (via portable document format 'PDF').
F7	Offers an information catalog of vaccine information, including: • Description of each vaccine and its purpose • Importance and benefits of vaccination
F8	Implement an SMS notification system to send timely reminders to parents/guardians regarding upcoming vaccination appointments.
F9	Voucher Reward System: • Integrate a voucher reward system that generates claimable vouchers for parents/guardians after each completed infant vaccination • Define partnerships with businesses to offer relevant rewards through the voucher system. (Applicable to System Administrator only)
F10	Feedback message feature will be implemented to gather user thoughts and queries on the system's functionality and user experience.

Non-Functional Requirements

Table 2. Non-Functional Requirements of BakunAko

Requirement Code	Non - Functional Requirements
NF1	Interface must be designed for accessibility, allowing parents, guardians, and healthcare providers of all skill level to use it with ease. This involves clear navigation, simple language, and an intuitive workflow.
NF2	Should respond quickly to user actions, with minimal language loading times for pages and functionalities.
NF3	SMS reminders for upcoming vaccinations must be sent and received promptly to ensure timely notifications for parents and guardians.
NF4	Data encryption: All sensitive user information, such as infant health records and login credentials, must be encrypted at rest and in transit to protect against unauthorized access.
NF5	High uptime: The platform should be available with minimal downtime, ensuring users can access vaccination information, schedule appointments, and utilize other features whenever needed.

Table 3. Software Used and Specification

Software	**Specifications**
IDE	VSCode
Server	XAMPP
Database	MySQL/phpmyadmin
Programming Language	PHP/JavaScript
Web Development Content	HTML/CSS

Project Timeline

The project timeline where the proponents incorporated the RAD Methodology. There are four phases which are requirements planning, user design, construction, and testing. To enhance clarity, the proponents have included the manuscript's timeline as well. The RAD methodology and its four phases (requirements planning, user design, construction, and testing). Below is the further information.The snippets above demonstrate a structured and iterative approach to the project. This emphasis on rapid prototyping and user feedback allows continuous improvement and ensures the final product aligns with user needs. Additionally, incorporating the manuscript's timeline within the image provides valuable insight into the project's overall progress, facilitating communication and identifying potential areas for optimization.

Hardware Requirements

The authors utilized desktops, laptops, and mobile phones with the necessary coding and development to create the BakunAko system. It is recommended to use a computer with at least an Intel Core i5 processor, 8GB of RAM, Windows 10 OS or macOS, a display of 15.6 inches or larger with at least a Full HD resolution monitor, and access to the internet for efficient and effective website development. Adhering to these standards establishes a strong foundation for developing and programming functional systems.

Software Requirements

In this section, the authors discussed the following technologies and resources used for the development of the capstone project and its software requirements.

Web Browser:

- Any web browsers
  - o Server:
- Web server
- PHP
- MySQL
  - o Client:
- Responsive web design compatible with various screen sizes and resolutions
- HTML, CSS, and JavaScript

Table 3. Software used and its specifications

Shown in Table 3 is the software used and its specifications. Web development involves a combination of tools: VSCode for editing code, XAMPP for local server setup, MySQL/phpMyAdmin for database management, PHP/JavaScript for server-side and client-side logic, and HTML/CSS for defining website structure and visual presentation.

User Design

In the second phase of RAD methodology, the proponents focused on building the BakunAko system. The primary goal was to create an intuitive and user-friendly interface that allows for various adjustments and enhancements. Additionally, this phase includes designing the overall system architecture to ensure it is robust and efficient, supporting the intended functionality of the system.

UI/UX Design

The UX design serves as the entry point for both new and returning users. The landing page prominently displays the system's logo, establishing brand recognition. It also offers clear navigation options for getting a schedule, login as healthcare provider or login as parent and register.

The login page for parents and guardians. It serves as the initial point of access, wherein users, specifically parents and guardians, are prompted to input their credentials, including both a username and password, to gain entry to the system.

In the register page, where users, specifically parents and guardians, input their credentials to create an account. The form prompts users to provide their first name, middle name, last name, email address, phone number, username, and password, as well as confirm the password. Also, in the infant vaccination page, where users view their baby's basic details, including the full name, date of birth, and sex. In addition to viewing existing entries, users can add a new baby by clicking the "Add a Baby" button.

On the other hand, infant profiling page, where users input the credentials of their baby. The form prompts users to provide their infant's first name, middle name, last name, date of birth, place of birth, sex, and address. As well as the father and mother's first name, middle name, and last name. Users can view and verify the credentials they entered data and information. Additionally, the vaccination schedule for their infant is displayed in a clear and easy-to-read timetable format. Users also have the option to download the vaccination information record about their infant as a PDF file for reference.

Lastly, in the vaccine description and information page, where users can easily access and read the description and information about each vaccine for infants. The recommended vaccine schedules page, where users can view an illustration of the recommended vaccine schedule for their infant from well-known healthcare organizations.

The submit feedback page, where users, specifically the parent and guardian, can submit their feedback about the system in the form of a message. And the claim rewards page shows voucher rewards for each vaccine, where users can claim a maximum of one voucher for each vaccine administered to their infant. My voucher page presents my vouchers with the voucher code that is claimed in the claim rewards page.

In addition, in the user information page, where parents and guardians can edit their credentials. Also, they can change their password. While in the login page for healthcare providers. It serves as the initial point of access, wherein the healthcare providers are prompted to input their credentials, including a username and password, to gain entry to the system. And in the vaccine infants page, where the healthcare provider views a list of infants that need to be vaccinated today and manages the infant's vaccination.

The submit feedback page, where a healthcare provider can submit their feedback about the system in the form of a message. The user information page, where healthcare providers can edit their credentials. Also, they can change their password.

In the login page for Admin. It serves as the initial point of access, wherein the admin is prompted to input their credentials, including a username and password, to gain entry to the system. The dashboard page, which displays the number of males, females, and total number of infants within the system. Additionally, it displays all the infants in the system, allowing the administrator to monitor and track each infant's vaccination schedule easily. For the feedbacks page, where the administrator sees and reviews the feedback provided by parents, guardians, and healthcare providers. And in the create an account for healthcare provider page, where the administrator inputs the healthcare provider's credentials to create an account. The form prompts the administrator to provide the healthcare provider's first name, middle name, last name, email address, phone number, username, and password, as well as confirm the password. After inputting the credentials, the data which is the list of all healthcare providers.

Also, in the manage voucher page, where the administrator manages to distribute the vouchers. The form prompts the admin to select a partner, provide the name of the item, the quantity of vouchers, and the allocation of vouchers to the vaccine. As well as the password to confirm the identity of the admin. After distributing the vouchers is the list of all vouchers.

Use Case Diagram

The authors utilized a use case diagram, to clearly outline and illustrate the relationships and functionality of the website. This diagram provided a comprehensive overview of how the website is utilized, making it easier to understand its behavior from the perspective of its users. By highlighting the key functions and interactions between parents, healthcare providers, and the administrator, the use case diagram proves as a valuable tool for understanding and effectively describing the system's operation.

The diagram depicts three actors (parents, healthcare provider, and administrator) as stick objects positioned outside of a rectangular box. Within the box, oval shapes represent the various actions that the system can perform to accomplish specific tasks. The lines connecting the actors to the use cases indicate their interactions and relationships within the system.

Construction

During the construction phase of the Rapid Application Development (RAD) methodology, a significant amount of time is dedicated to coding the BakunAko website. To ensure the quality of the system, continuous development cycles are put into place, and comprehensive testing is carried out to identify and correct any bugs or errors. All system functions are closely aligned with the identified problems and objectives. Furthermore, the developers conduct system testing to ensure that the website is user-friendly and effectively meets its users' needs. This phase ensures a smooth user experience and the system's overall success.

Testing

The website functionalities were verified in the testing phase. Functionalities were assessed to ensure that it is aligned with the identified requirements. The website was tested to confirm the automated timetable scheduler and voucher rewards works as expected, with the website generating a PDF for the infant immunization record and claimable rewards for incentivizing the user, specifically for the parents and guardians.

Cutover

Cutover is the final phase of the RAD cycle. In this phase, the proponents conduct pilot testing, functional requirements testing, and non-functional testing to ensure the successful implementation of the system. Once thorough testing has been completed and positive feedback has been received, the final system is ready to launch. The goal is to provide the best possible experience to the end users with a system that is both well-functioning and well-designed. Additionally, the proponents are open to receiving user feedback or suggestions to continue improving the system.

Pilot Testing

To assess the system's performance and functionality, a pilot test was initiated during the first week of May. The participation of three individuals: a barangay health worker named Melanie from Barangay Indangan, a parent named Jeah, who is a friend of one of BakunAko's authors, and a fellow colleague named Ronmar Sabado pursuing a Bachelor of Science in Information Technology, majoring in Business Technology Management. This diverse group provided valuable feedback from different perspectives to refine and enhance the features and usability of the BakunAko platform.

Based on the results of the Pilot Testing. the overall determination is as follows:

1. PASSED: Requirements have been met satisfactorily.
2. N/A: Not applicable to this specific case or situation.

The proponents' pilot tests are as follows:

Tester 1: Melanie as Healthcare Provider User

The pilot testing conducted on BakunAko system was successful. Based on feedback from the three pilot testers, all assigned scenarios and features were functional, and the author identified areas for improvement and bug fixes. These results affirm that the platform's design aligns well with the needs of the users. BakunAko is now ready to launch.

Attainment of the Project Objectives

Objective 1: Provide automated timetable scheduling for dynamic access to vaccination information for infants

Figure 7. Landing Page of the Platform

Figure 8. Time Schedule For the Vaccination of Infants

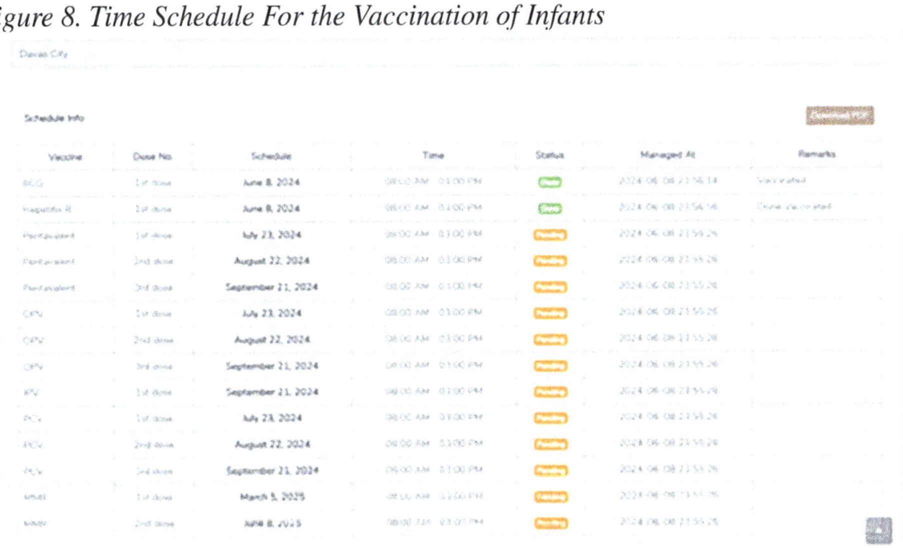

The images above show timetable schedule feature in BakunAko, which provides parents and guardians with a clear, downloadable overview of their infant's vaccination schedule, including specific vaccines, doses, times, and dates. This automated feature enhances convenience and promotes timely vaccination adherence.

BakunAko includes a downloadable PDF feature for infant immunization records, ensuring accessibility in areas with limited internet connectivity and maintaining data integrity.

Objective 2: Provide easy access to information about vaccines for infants

Figure 9. Infant Immunization Record Downloaded

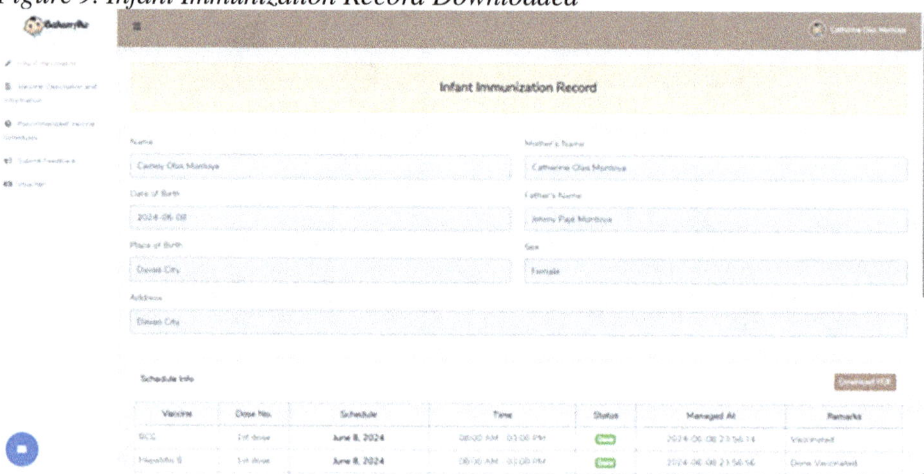

Figure 10. Infant Immunization Record

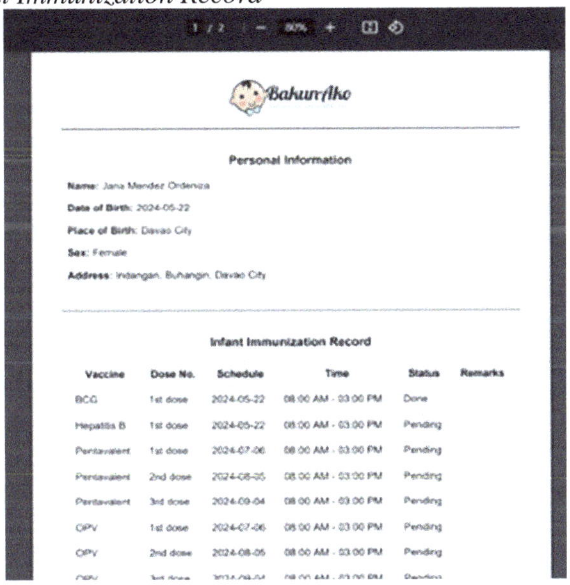

Figure 11. Vaccine Description

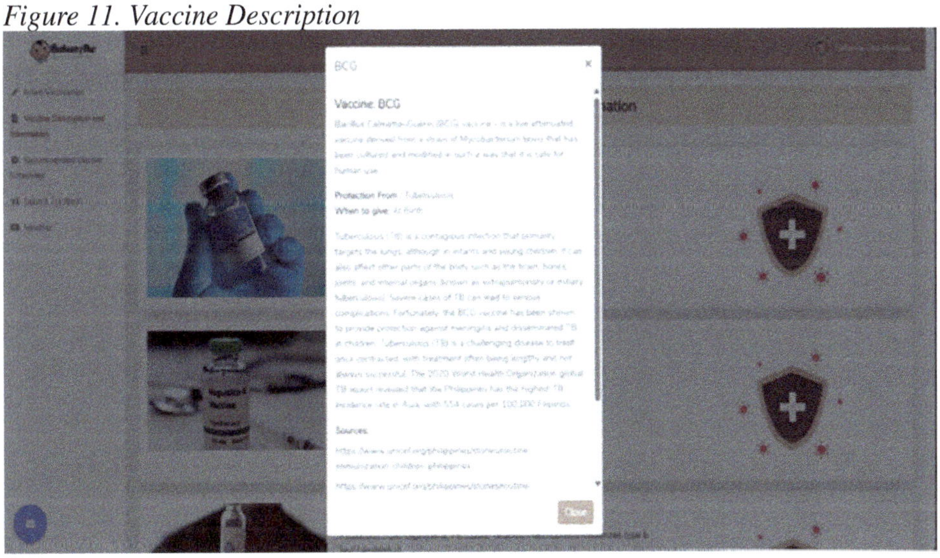

The vaccine description and information feature as seen above, allows provision of access to parents and guardians with easy access to information about vaccines for their infants.

Objective 3: Provide voucher rewards for every vaccine administered to infants

Figure 12. Voucher Reward System Dashboard

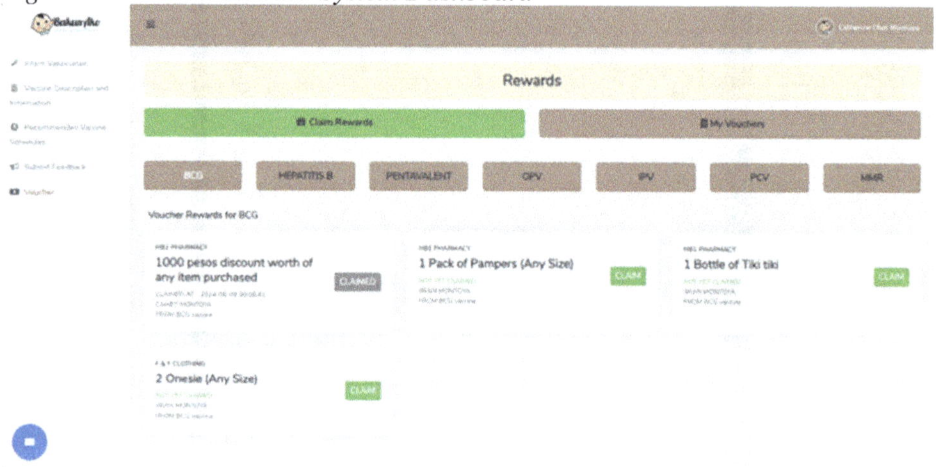

The image above shows an easy way for parents and guardians to view and claim rewards for each vaccination their infants received.

This interface features two clickable options:

- "Claim Rewards": In the dashboard it displays a list of voucher items that the user will claim, providing a record of the rewards earned through infant vaccinations.

Figure 13. Claim Voucher Overview

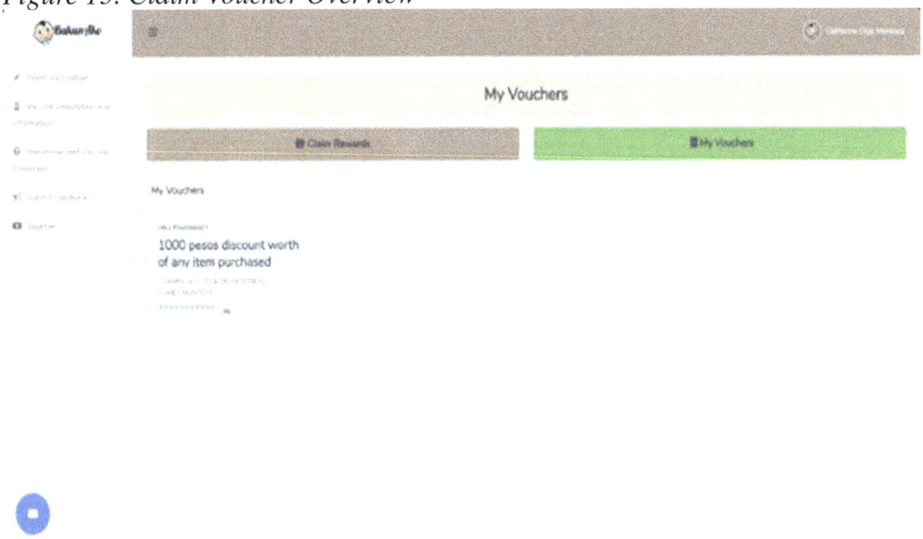

- "My Vouchers": displays a list of available vouchers that are already claimed with the voucher code and ready for use. Users can browse these vouchers, often linked to specific business partnerships

To enhance the appeal of the voucher reward system, strategic partnerships have been established (only in a simulative scenario) with various medium and large-scale businesses. Collaborations like these should enable BakunAko to offer a wide range of rewards tailored to parents and guardians, which will encourage infant vaccination and contribute to the platform's overall success.

Figure 14. Adding User Admins – as Investor

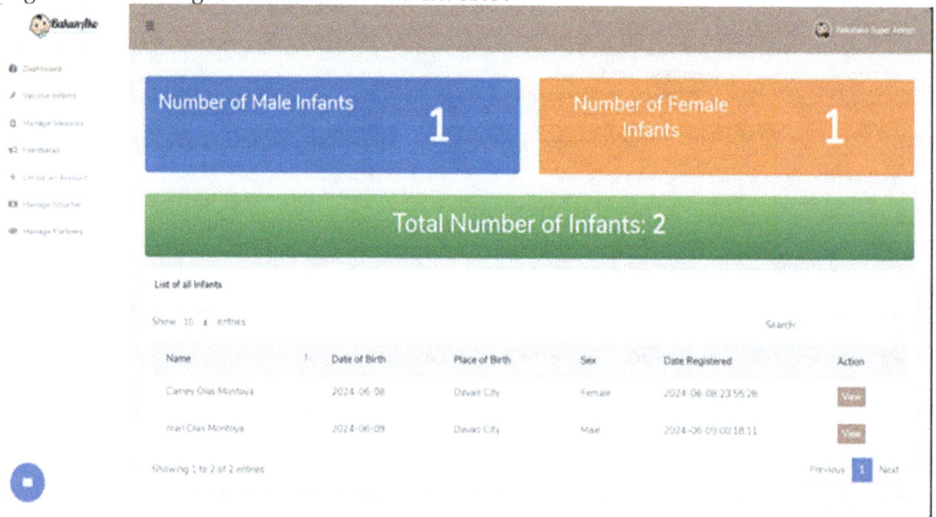

Objective 4: Provide monitoring and tracking of scheduled vaccines for infants

A specialized component was integrated to enhance adherence to infant vaccination schedules

Figure 15. Phone Number Registration Snippets

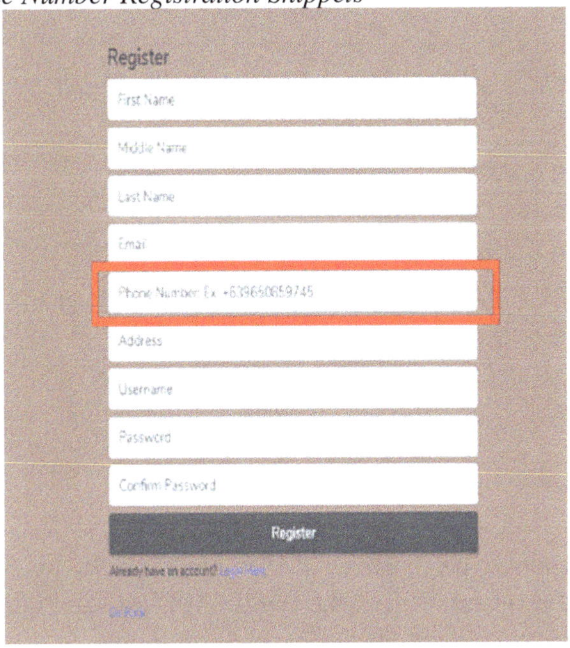

This feature empowers the administrator with improved monitoring and tracking capabilities, ensuring timely and comprehensive immunization and adherence to recommended timelines.

Objective 5: Provide SMS notification reminders to serve as timely prompts for parents and guardians

An SMS notification feature was integrated into BakunAko to enhance communication and ensure timely vaccination. Parents input and verify their mobile number.

Figure 16. Upcoming Vaccination Schedule

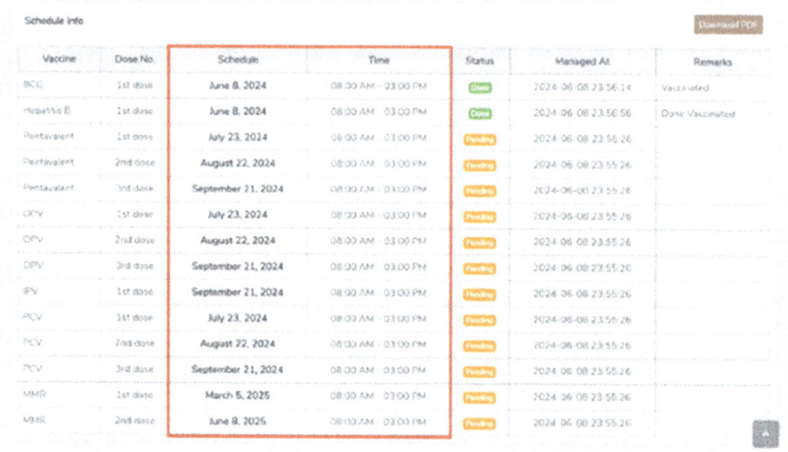

Schedule Info

Download PDF

Vaccine	Dose No.	Schedule	Time	Status	Managed At	Remarks
BCG	1st dose	June 8, 2024	08:00 AM - 03:00 PM	Done	2024-06-08 23:56:14	Vaccinated
Hepatitis B	1st dose	June 8, 2024	08:00 AM - 03:00 PM	Done	2024-06-08 23:50:56	Done Vaccinated
Pentavalent	1st dose	July 23, 2024	08:00 AM - 03:00 PM	Pending	2024-06-08 23:55:26	
Pentavalent	2nd dose	August 22, 2024	08:00 AM - 03:00 PM	Pending	2024-06-08 23:55:26	
Pentavalent	3rd dose	September 21, 2024	08:00 AM - 03:00 PM	Pending	2024-06-08 23:55:26	
OPV	1st dose	July 23, 2024	08:00 AM - 03:00 PM	Pending	2024-06-08 23:55:26	
OPV	2nd dose	August 22, 2024	08:00 AM - 03:00 PM	Pending	2024-06-08 23:55:26	
OPV	3rd dose	September 21, 2024	08:00 AM - 03:00 PM	Pending	2024-06-08 23:55:26	
IPV	1st dose	September 21, 2024	08:00 AM - 03:00 PM	Pending	2024-06-08 23:55:26	
PCV	1st dose	July 23, 2024	08:00 AM - 03:00 PM	Pending	2024-06-08 23:55:26	
PCV	2nd dose	August 22, 2024	08:00 AM - 03:00 PM	Pending	2024-06-08 23:55:26	
PCV	3rd dose	September 21, 2024	08:00 AM - 03:00 PM	Pending	2024-06-08 23:55:26	
MMR	1st dose	March 5, 2025	08:00 AM - 03:00 PM	Pending	2024-06-08 23:55:26	
MMR	2nd dose	June 8, 2025	08:00 AM - 03:00 PM	Pending	2024-06-08 23:55:26	

The system generates personalized SMS reminders based on the infant's vaccination schedule. This feature utilizes the Twilio SMS API's free tier, a cost-effective solution chosen for the project due to financial constraints.

FUTURE RESEARCH DIRECTIONS

Infant vaccination is a cornerstone of public health, protecting vulnerable young lives from preventable diseases. However, challenges like vaccine hesitancy, limited healthcare access, and outdated record-keeping methods hinder progress and lead to stigma among patients and the community. BakunAko, a proposed web-based platform, aims to revolutionize and innovate infant vaccination management in the Philippines. BakunAko addresses these challenges by offering a comprehensive solution and as a tool for breaking barriers of stigma in vaccination. It provides automated timetable scheduling, ensuring parents and guardians have easy access to accurate and up-to-date vaccination information. The platform also includes a digital immunization record, replacing traditional handwritten methods, and sends SMS reminders for upcoming schedules. A unique feature of BakunAko is its voucher reward system, which incentivizes vaccination through partnerships with businesses.

To ensure the accuracy and relevance of the information provided, the authors conducted a thorough review of related literature and systems. This included examining existing vaccination scheduling apps, understanding the importance of infant vaccination, and exploring the potential of voucher reward systems. The research also highlighted the challenges in infant vaccination programs, such as parental concerns and limited healthcare access.

The development of BakunAko followed a Rapid Application Development (RAD) methodology, emphasizing user involvement and iterative prototyping. The design focused on creating a user-friendly interface with clear navigation and accessibility for both parents/guardians and healthcare providers. The system's architecture ensures robustness and efficiency, supporting its intended functionalities.

The needs assessment involving a visit to a barangay health clinic and discussions with healthcare providers revealed the need for a digital solution like BakunAko. The barangay clinic visit highlighted the reliance on paper-based records and manual processes, which could lead to inefficiencies and errors.

This study developed a centralized vaccination health record platform for infants with a voucher rewards system. The platform offers parents and guardians an automated vaccination timetable schedule generation tool, provides access to vital information about the importance of specific vaccines, provides voucher rewards after the infant has received the vaccine, and implements SMS notifications for timely reminders of upcoming immunization schedules.

The primary beneficiaries of the study are:

1. Parents and Guardians: BakunaAko should offer convenient and user-friendly platform paired with a child-centered aesthetic for parents and guardians to easily schedule vaccination appointments for their infants. With the SMS notification feature, they can receive timely updates and reminders about their upcoming vaccinations.
2. Healthcare Providers: BakunAko should offer valuable advantages for health providers involved in administering vaccinations and immunizations. By utilizing a centralized platform, these workers can effectively manage and organize vaccination schedules. This streamlined approach simplifies the overall vaccination process. As a result, health providers can optimize their time and resources, allowing them to administer vaccinations more efficiently and effectively.
3. Researchers: BakunAko has the potential to revolutionize infant vaccination and immunization nationally, especially in Davao City by streamlining scheduling, boosting immunization rates, and empowering communities through information and SMS reminders. In addition, future researchers can enhance the study's findings to develop similar interventions in regions other than Region 11, potentially establishing a national model for effective infant immunization.
4. Students: By conducting research on BakunAko's successes and challenges, students should gain valuable insights into designing and implementing impactful digital interventions for improving health services outcomes across various environments.

5. Medium and Large Scaled Business: Bakunako collaborates with businesses. Businesses could partner with BAKUNAKO for sponsorship or support initiatives. This aligns with CSR goals, demonstrating community investment and potentially improving business and brand image.

BakunAko represents a significant step forward in addressing the challenges of infant vaccination management. By offering a centralized platform with features like automated scheduling, digital records, vaccine information, SMS reminders, and a unique voucher reward system, BakunAko empowers parents, guardians, and healthcare providers to ensure timely and comprehensive immunization for infants. Its user-friendly child-centered aesthetic interface and accessibility features further enhance its value as a tool for promoting public health and protecting the well-being of the youngest members of society.

These suggestions are intended to assist future researchers who will be undertaking similar studies:

- Future iterations of BakunAko must research alternative SMS API providers and consider upgrading to a premium Twilio tier to acquire seamless functionality across all device platforms.
- Include a centralized allocator for vouchers for all administered vaccines.
- Include educational content, such as news and videos about the importance of vaccines, addressing common concerns and misconceptions.

REFERENCES

Akhu-Zaheya, L. & S. (2018). The effect of short message system (SMS) reminder on adherence to a healthy diet, medication, and cessation of smoking among adult patients with cardiovascular diseases. *International Journal of Medical Informatics*. PMID: 28034414

Alkandi, I. G., Khan, M. A., Fallatah, M., Alabdulhadi, A., Alanizan, S., & Alharbi, J. (2023). The Impact of Incentive and Reward Systems on Employee Performance in the Saudi Primary, Secondary, and Tertiary Industrial Sectors: A Mediating Influence of Employee Job Satisfaction. *Sustainability (Basel)*, *15*(4), 3415. Advance online publication. DOI: 10.3390/su15043415

Altmann, D., Borrow, R., Fooks, T., Ishii, K., Lua, L. H. L., Sadarangani, S. P., Barrett, N., Donau, O., Riems, M. B. G., Aurora, A. D., & Geneva, P. D. (2021). Editorial Board/Aims and Scope. *Vaccine, 39*(17), IFC. DOI: 10.1016/S0264-410X(21)00412-6

Ann, S., & Baumann, O. (2023). Psychological mechanisms and interventions directed at vaccination attitudes. *Frontiers in Sociology*, *8*, 1076015. Advance online publication. DOI: 10.3389/fsoc.2023.1076015 PMID: 36844879

Antonelli Incalzi, R., Trevisan, C., Del Signore, S., Volpato, S., Fumagalli, S., Monzani, F., Bellelli, G., Gareri, P., Mossello, E., Malara, A., Coin, A., Zia, G., & Ranhoff, A. H. (2021). Are vaccines against COVID-19 tailored to the most vulnerable people? *Vaccine*, *39*(17), 2325–2327. DOI: 10.1016/j.vaccine.2021.03.066 PMID: 33810907

Calcaterra, V., Cena, H., Rossi, V., Santero, S., Bianchi, A., & Zuccotti, G. (2023). Ultra-Processed Food, Reward System and Childhood Obesity. *Children (Basel, Switzerland)*, *10*(5), 804. Advance online publication. DOI: 10.3390/children10050804 PMID: 37238352

Dadari, I., Higgins-Steele, A., Sharkey, A., Charlet, D., Shahabuddin, A., Nandy, R., & Jackson, D. (2021). Pro-equity immunization and health systems strengthening strategies in select Gavi-supported countries. *Vaccine*, *39*(17), 2434–2444. DOI: 10.1016/j.vaccine.2021.03.044 PMID: 33781603

Erfani, P., & Bourdeaux, M. (2021). *Can Vaccine Incentive Reward Programs Increase COVID-19 Vaccine Uptake?* Fernández-Basanta, S., Lagoa-Millarengo, M., & Movilla-Fernández, M. J. (2021). Encountering parents who are hesitant or reluctant to vaccinate their children: A meta-ethnography. *International Journal of Environmental Research and Public Health, 18*(14), 7584. Advance online publication. DOI: 10.3390/ijerph18147584

Førland, O., & Roxå, T. (2024). Establishing reward systems for excellence in teaching–the experience of academics pioneering a reward system. *European Journal of Higher Education, 14*(3), 451–469. DOI: 10.1080/21568235.2023.2214713

Haeder, S. F. (2021). Joining the herd? U.S. public opinion and vaccination requirements across educational settings during the COVID-19 pandemic. *Vaccine, 39*(17), 2375–2385. DOI: 10.1016/j.vaccine.2021.03.055 PMID: 33810906

Khazanov, G. K., Stewart, R., Pieri, M. F., Huang, C., Robertson, C. T., Schaefer, K. A., Ko, H., & Fishman, J. (2023). The effectiveness of financial incentives for COVID-19 vaccination: A systematic review. *Preventive Medicine, 172*(May), 107538. DOI: 10.1016/j.ypmed.2023.107538 PMID: 37156430

Kiszewski, A. E., Cleary, E. G., Jackson, M. J., & Ledley, F. D. (2021). NIH funding for vaccine readiness before the COVID-19 pandemic. *Vaccine, 39*(17), 2458–2466. DOI: 10.1016/j.vaccine.2021.03.022 PMID: 33781600

Kuznetsova, L., Cortassa, G., & Trilla, A. (2021). Effectiveness of mandatory and incentive-based routine childhood immunization programs in europe: A systematic review of the literature. *Vaccines, 9*(10), 1–30. DOI: 10.3390/vaccines9101173 PMID: 34696280

Mantel, C., & Cherian, T. (2020). New immunization strategies: Adapting to global challenges. *Bundesgesundheitsblatt, Gesundheitsforschung, Gesundheitsschutz, 63*(1), 25–31. DOI: 10.1007/s00103-019-03066-x PMID: 31802153

Mardi, P., Djalalinia, S., Kargar, R., Jamee, M., Esmaeili Abdar, Z., & Qorbani, M. (2022). Impact of incentives on COVID-19 vaccination; A systematic review. *Frontiers in Medicine, 9*, 810323. Advance online publication. DOI: 10.3389/fmed.2022.810323 PMID: 36160125

Murthy, N., Wodi, A. P., McNally, V. V., Daley, M. F., & Cineas, S. (2024). Advisory Committee on Immunization Practices Recommended Immunization Schedule for Adults Aged 19 Years or Older - United States, 2024. *MMWR. Morbidity and Mortality Weekly Report, 73*(1), 11–15. DOI: 10.15585/mmwr.mm7301a3 PMID: 38206880

Philippines, U. N. I. C. E. F. (2021a). *Routine immunization for children in the Philippines*. UNICEF Philippines. https://www.unicef.org/philippines/stories/routine-immunization-children-philippines

Philippines, U. N. I. C. E. F. (2021b). *Vaccines for children: your questions answered | UNICEF Philippines*. UNICEF Philippines. https://www.unicef.org/philippines/vaccines-children-faqs

Restivo, V., Napoli, G., Marsala, M. G. L., Bonanno, V., Sciuto, V., Amodio, E., Calamusa, G., Vitale, F., & Firenze, A. (2015). Factors associated with poor adherence to MMR vaccination in parents who follow vaccination schedule. *Human Vaccines & Immunotherapeutics*, *11*(1), 140–145. DOI: 10.4161/hv.34416 PMID: 25483527

Rodrigues, C. M. C., & Plotkin, S. A. (2020). Impact of Vaccines; Health, Economic and Social Perspectives. *Frontiers in Microbiology*, *11*(July), 1526. Advance online publication. DOI: 10.3389/fmicb.2020.01526 PMID: 32760367

Sagala, J. R. (2021). Model Rapid Application Development (Rad)Dalam Pengembangan Sistem Informasi Penjadwalanbelajar Mengajar. *Jurnal Mantik Penusa, 2*(1).

State clinics barely fill healthcare void in the Philippines. (2022). *BusinessWorld Online*. https://www.bworldonline.com/top-stories/2022/03/14/435670/state-clinics-barely-fill-healthcare-void-in-the-philippines/

Tull, F., Borg, K., Knott, C., Beasley, M., Halliday, J., Faulkner, N., Sutton, K., & Bragge, P. (2019). Short Message Service Reminders to Parents for Increasing Adolescent Human Papillomavirus Vaccination Rates in a Secondary School Vaccine Program: A Randomized Control Trial. *The Journal of Adolescent Health*, *65*(1), 116–123. DOI: 10.1016/j.jadohealth.2018.12.026 PMID: 30879881

Ulep, V. G. J. U. (2021). An assessment of the expanded program on immunization (EPI) in the Philippines: Challenges and ways forward. *Www.Econstor.Eu*. http://hdl.handle.net/10419/241052

Wentzell, E., & Racila, A. M. (2021). The social experience of participation in a COVID-19 vaccine trial: Subjects' motivations, others' concerns, and insights for vaccine promotion. *Vaccine*, *39*(17), 2445–2451. DOI: 10.1016/j.vaccine.2021.03.036 PMID: 33745730

Why Vaccinate," Centers for Disease Control and Prevention. (2019). Cdc. https://www.cdc.gov/vaccines/parents/why-vaccinate/index.html

Wierzbicka, M., Klussmann, J. P., San Giorgi, M. R., Wuerdemann, N., & Dikkers, F. G. (2021). Oral and laryngeal HPV infection: Incidence, prevalence and risk factors, with special regard to concurrent infection in head, neck and genitals. *Vaccine, 39*(17), 2344–2350. DOI: 10.1016/j.vaccine.2021.03.047 PMID: 33812740

Wilson, R. J. I., Vergélys, C., Ward, J., Peretti-Watel, P., & Verger, P. (2020). Vaccine hesitancy among general practitioners in Southern France and their reluctant trust in the health authorities. *International Journal of Qualitative Studies on Health and Well-being, 15*(1), 1757336. Advance online publication. DOI: 10.1080/17482631.2020.1757336 PMID: 32400299

World Health Organization. (2018). *Polio outbreak in the Philippines*. World Health Organization. https://www.who.int/westernpacific/emergencies/polio-outbreak-in-the-philippines

Chapter 12
The Effect of Human Capital on Economic Growth:
The Case of Türkiye

Burak Çanakci
https://orcid.org/0009-0008-0992-4740
Firat University, Turkey

Izzet Taşar
https://orcid.org/0000-0001-9187-6910
Fırat University, Turkey

ABSTRACT

The concept of human capital emerged with the realization that economic growth cannot be explained solely by changes in physical capital. In this context, human capital is directly related to factors such as education, health to increase the productivity of individuals and their contribution to the economy. Economic growth is defined as the increase in the production of goods and services over time. However, the fact that this increase is sustainable and increases the welfare of the society shows the importance also investments in human capital. TDenison, Mankiw-Romer-Weil, Becker-Schultz and Jorgenson approaches from neo-classical growth models and Barro, Lucas and Charles Jones approaches from endogenous growth models are examined as economic approaches that focus on the effect of human capital on economic growth. In this study, which is specific to Türkiye, the long-term relationship between human capital and economic growth is examined in Türkiye with the GDP and human capital index between the years 2000-2022.

DOI: 10.4018/979-8-3373-0603-2.ch012

INTRODUCTION

Human capital is the stock of knowledge, accumulation and skills possessed by the labor force involved in the production process. These knowledge, skills and abilities can undoubtedly be developed through education. Education is of great importance for both individuals and countries as it increases the potential and productivity of the labor force and ensures the continuity of growth with the increase in human capital qualifications.

In the economic literature, economic growth is defined as the increase in the production of goods and services in a given period, but socially, economic growth is understood as the increase in the standard of living and welfare, and the increase in per capita income. In approaches to economic growth, it is stated that the factors affecting growth are natural resources, labor force, physical capital and technology. When natural resources are constant, economic growth is realized as a result of the increase in other factors. The fact that economic growth realized in the long run cannot be explained only by the increase in physical capital has affected the formation of the concept of human capital. The knowledge, skills and qualifications of human capital are of great importance in the use of physical capital, which is effective in the realization of economic growth. In addition to the fact that economic growth cannot be explained only by the increase in physical capital, the fact that human capital has a very high impact on the use of factors used in the production process has contributed to the important position of human capital in the modern economy and to the analysis of the relationship between growth and human capital.

From the past to the present, the concept of human capital has been defined in many different ways and the impact of human capital on economic growth has been analyzed by different methods and researchers. When the analyses are examined, it is understood that there are many approaches to analyzing human capital and there is no single analysis method. In the early periods when human capital started to be included in the literature, it was characterized as labor force. As the number of studies and researches increased, human capital was characterized as educated labor force, and later, qualitative and quantitative dimensions were taken into consideration when evaluating human capital.

The importance of the relationship between human capital and economic growth, which is the subject of the research, is of great importance for the economic literature. Increasing individual welfare and national enrichment are included in government policies. Growth models in the literature have been tested with the data of many countries and policies have been developed as a result of the findings obtained. When the literature is analyzed, according to the results of the studies, it is seen that the share of human capital on economic growth is significant in some countries, while in some countries, physical capital is more significant. When the literature review is conducted for Türkiye, it is understood that the focus is on neoclassical models and the tests on endogenous growth models are limited. The view that each country has different dynamics is frequently encountered in growth theories. Therefore, the efficiency and validity of policies may differ for each country.

ECONOMIC GROWTH AND HUMAN CAPITAL TERMS

Economic Growth

Although different definitions are encountered in the literature on growth, growth is basically known as the increase in the final goods and services produced in an economy within a certain period.

Economic growth, which is one of the most important economic indicators of nations, can give many ideas about the level of welfare and economic performance. While the priority of developed countries in the growth process is the change in economic growth over the years, the priority of developing and underdeveloped countries is economic development (Birinci, 2015). The numerical increase in gross domestic product indicates growth as well as production potential and the change in total output. The growth process is a long-term process since it is not possible to change the human and physical capital, which is one of the main sources of growth, in the short term. While the growth potential of economies can be measured by looking at their numerical data, changes in productivity can also give an idea about the growth potential.

The concept of growth, which became popular after World War II, soon became one of the most important economic objectives of countries. Although the examination and analysis of numerical data on growth started in the Neo-Classical period, this analysis has lost its popularity due to the short-term nature of the Neo-Classical analysis and the necessity to examine the concept of economic growth in the long run. Increases in production, which is one of the most important elements of the growth concept, naturally lead to an increase in growth at the same time. In addition to the physical capital among the factors of production, the improvement in human capital also leads to significant increases in growth (Kazancıgil, 2019).

In addition to physical capital, which is among the factors of production in the growth process, human capital also contributes positively to growth targets. It is known that qualified human capital contributes significantly to the growth of national economies by affecting the increase in production, which is also included in the definition of the concept of growth, with its direct effect on the use of physical capital. Thus, investments made to increase the quality of human capital, in addition to their contributions to the growth of national economies, help to achieve all economic goals, including competition, faster (Kayacan and Alkan, 2005).

Basic Terms Related to Economic Growth

Gross National Product

GNP, which has an important place in the economic literature, is also one of the most important concepts of economic growth. GNP, which is the sum of the final goods and services produced in an economy during the year at market prices, expresses a gross value. During the production process, the wear and tear on factors of production are not taken into account in the calculation process. The calculation of GNP is based only on the price-based value of goods and services produced. Moreover, calculations can also be made according to the sectors of production activity.

Gross Domestic Product

GDP is the current market value of final goods and services produced in an economy during the year. It is a monetary, i.e. nominal, measure of the value of all final goods and services produced in a country in a year at current market prices. Unlike GNP, GDP does not take into account foreign income and payments. Since there are no major differences between the two concepts in terms of definition and calculation, GDP is used to calculate growth, income and production.

Different methods can be used to calculate GDP. GDP, which can be calculated by production, expenditure and income methods, has to give the same result in all three methods.

Two different values can be obtained as a result of calculations. These values, called nominal and real GDP, reveal major differences in the interpretation of economic growth. Since nominal GDP includes inflation effects in its definition and calculation, real GDP is taken into account when calculating growth. CPI or PPI or GDP deflator is used to arrive at real GDP.

National Income

Another concept used in explaining the concept of growth is national income. In the current period, the income obtained by the factor owners involved in production after subtracting indirect taxes from the gross national product refers to national income. Consumers who purchase a good or service do not purchase the good or service at its actual price, but at the price after taxes are added to it. Since this difference is reflected to the treasury as a revenue item, the calculation of national income is important for the calculation of indirect taxes reflected to the treasury.

Human Capital

Human Capital Concept

Although there is no common social definition of human capital, it can be defined as a concept that expresses the value of individuals' knowledge, skills, abilities, experience and behaviors during the production process. Human capital has a continuously renewable and non-stationary structure.

For many years, capital used in the production process was characterized by physical materials such as machinery and equipment. However, if physical capital is insufficient in the production process, the concept of human capital has been added to this definition and with this concept, countries have included the concept of human capital in the improvement process of economic growth.

Calculation of Human Capital

Although the concept of human capital has been the subject of many scientific studies from past to present, the definition of human capital has been limited to human abilities without elaboration. Human capital can be expressed by considering human beings as capital and assigning material value to human labor power and skills. In the data used for more than a century, it has been emphasized that human capital is related to the investment in oneself. The most important problem in the research of human capital is the insufficiency of the data used in the long term. Due to the use of simple and limited data, it is difficult to reach the right conclusion. This situation has led to the emergence of different research methods. Retrospective method, one of the new research methods, makes retrospective calculations. According to the retrospective method, the costs incurred by the individual during the period of education are calculated. Another method, the prospective method, makes forward-looking calculations. It is calculated using the current value of the income that the individual expects in the future (Kazancigil, 2019).

The definition of human capital conceptually has parallel meanings with the productivity and efficiency of the labor force. The productivity of the labor force depends on the skills of the individual, the education received, the level of satisfaction with the job and social opportunities. Labor productivity should not be evaluated according to demographic data such as marital status, age and gender. When measuring labor productivity, the level of education and achievement, experience in business life, health status of the individual, education level and occupational title of family members are used. However, only the level of education is used when calculating human capital in the studies. Although the definition of human capital is limited in economic terms, economic terms should be used when calculating human capital. In order to calculate human capital in economic terms, a long period of time and intensive data are required. Economists who study human capital in different samples prefer easily accessible data. For this reason, the link between human capital and education level has been strengthened. The stock of human capital is generally represented by the level of education. The factor taken into account in the level of education is the formal education and literacy rate. Another difficulty in calculating human capital is that human capital is dynamic.

In recent studies, some researchers have developed new measures for the calculation of human capital stock. With these measurements, econometric models can be used to determine the relationship between human capital and economic growth. The quantitative nature of the results found in these studies is more prominent. The increase in the number of countries calculated in the models has led to the development of human capital measurement. There are also serious limitations in the data used in econometric studies; while obtaining data on education, the results obtained from the census were used, but it was observed that censuses are not conducted with the same frequency in every country.

William Petty was the first to calculate the measurement of human labor in monetary terms in the literature in 1961. Petty argued that labor should be included in the calculation of national income. For this purpose, he developed a measure for the calculation of human labor and calculated the cost of the human population lost due to epidemics and wars. With this method developed, he stated that the labor force should be qualified as human capital and the benefits of the labor force without a job should be determined (Kazancigil, 2019).

In 1853, with the research conducted by William Farr, the monetary value of labor force was calculated for the first time using the scientific method. In other words, Farr conducted a future-oriented research based on income in this study. According to Farr, after calculating the productivity of individuals, they should be taxed as capital.

In 1867 Heodor Wittstein emphasized that human beings are capital. With his capital method, Wittstein used Engel's model of calculating costs and Farr's income-based calculation. Wittstein wanted to guide the compensation of losses due to the loss of life of individuals and emphasized the definition of human capital. In this synthesized calculation, individuals' lifetime income was considered equal to their expenditures.

In 1922, Dublin calculated the capital value of the people living in America. According to his results, the capital value of Americans is 5 times higher than normal. Although the basis of Dublin's calculation is unknown, it has been widely quoted in studies.

In 1930, 80 years after Farr's prospective study, Afread Lotka and Louis Dublin used a similar method. They made a human capital calculation for the life insurance field in which they worked. They said that their human capital calculation would be useful in determining the economic cost of premature infant mortality and some preventable diseases. By predicting the life expectancy of individuals, they calculated the life insurance premium and the economic costs of the family experiencing loss (Kazancigil, 2019).

The parameters used to measure human capital consist of indices calculated by international organizations that can be used for different purposes. The Human Development Index (HCI) created by the United Nations Development Organization (UNDP) is the most frequently used human capital index. The Human Development Index does not only consider economic development as the rate of economic growth, but also reveals the relationship between development and welfare. The Human Development Report, which started to be published by the United Nations Development Organization in 1990, expresses the criterion of wealth with the peaceful environment, good life and high education level of the individuals who make up that society (UNDP, 2015).

Characteristics of Human Capital

Investments in human capital are effective in the development of a country's economy and income levels of individuals, and play a positive role in the quality of life of individuals compared to physical capital. As a result of investments in human capital, there are changes in the quality and quantity of the workforce. The most important feature of human capital is that it is dynamic and open to development (Daşdemir, 2008). The main feature that distinguishes human capital from physical capital is that it cannot be stocked. Due to this feature, it is inevitable to experience economic losses in cases where human capital cannot be used. The human being, who is the basic element of human capital, chooses the job he/she wants to work and the conditions of the job. In this way, people take an active role in the production phase of human capital. Another important feature of human capital is that individuals' work lives are shaped not according to their productivity but according to their personal preferences (Gökmen and Eser, 2009).

As with physical capital investments, human capital investments are also effective in increasing the productivity of other investments. Human capital investments are semi-public goods and can be shaped according to public or private benefit orientation. Investments such as education, health and healthy nutrition, which have a direct impact on individual productivity, support each other (Daşdemir, 2008).

Factors Affecting Human Capital

In the literature, human capital is generally defined as the value of human qualities and skills. Human capital is structurally affected by factors such as population density, education level and health status (Karagül, 2003).

Education

According to Adam Smith's classical view, education positively affects economic growth as it increases the efficiency and productivity of individuals (Machin, 2008)

Education, which is an important criterion for development, also provides individuals with the opportunity to develop their skills, acquire knowledge and gain social life. Education is an important condition for economic, administrative, political and social development (Kaya, 1977).

Education is at the forefront in the beginning and development of human production. The process that starts in the primary education years for individuals provides development in the elements that form the basis of human capital such as education, training and skills. Education is at the most important point in improving the productivity of individuals (Hall, 1999). In addition to its contribution to the productivity of individuals, education is also effective in economic growth by creating a qualified labor force (Afzal, Rehman, Farooq, & Sarwar, 2011).

In order for human capital to reach the maximum level, the individual's receiving the necessary education ensures the sustainability of economic development. For this reason, education is the first and most important step in building human capital (Gökmen and Eser, 2009)

It is more usual for individuals with education to find a job in a short time, to earn the high income they expect, to be productive for the organization they are in and to contribute to the economic development of the country they live in. As the level of education of individuals increases, the rate of participation in the labor force also increases. This leads to an increase in employment, a decrease in unemployment and a decrease in the rate of social insecurity. The relationship between education and human capital affects the social and psychological dimension in the first step and then shows a development effect on economic development (Özütler, 2009)

As individuals' education increases, their performance in the fields they work in also increases (Kazancıgil, 2019).

Health

Health investments are included in human capital investments. Being healthy does not only mean that an individual is not sick. Mental, intellectual and spiritual health is as important as physical health. One of the most important indicators of human capital in a country is a healthy population. Individuals need to be healthy in order to receive education and participate in the labor force.

Yumuşak (2008) stated that the productivity of an individual who stays away from education and social life due to health reasons decreases and ultimately leads to job loss (Çelik, 2006).

The health of the individual affects his/her productivity through factors such as staying in business life for a long time, working willingly and focused (Çelik, 2006). All investments made for health should be included in human capital investments that increase labor productivity and provide economic benefits. For this reason, health investments improve the mental and physical health of individuals and directly affect economic growth and development as human capital investments (Günsoy, 2005). Education and health opportunities offered to individuals in society directly affect the quality of human capital (Gökçen, 2006)

Population Structure

The qualitative and quantitative characteristics of a country's population determine the economic efficiency of its human capital. Quantitative assessment takes into account the amount, growth, gender and age distribution of the population, while qualitative assessment takes into account the health status and education level of the population. Qualitative assessment of the population is important for human capital. In underdeveloped countries, the quantitative assessment of population is prioritized, while in developed countries, the qualitative assessment of population is prioritized. In countries with a large and young population, human capital is more dense and dynamic. In countries where the elderly population is high and the population growth rate is low, human capital loses its dynamism and needs to be protected. These countries need to invest in increasing human capital (Kazancıgil, 2019).

Brain Drain

"Brain Drain", first used by the British royal family to describe the emigration of scientists and technical personnel from the UK to Canada and the United States between 1950 and 1960 In Turkish, it is referred to in the literature as "Brain Drain". Brain drain refers to the one-way relocation of human capital or qualified labor force. The word "brain" in the concept refers to competencies and similar potentials, while “drain” means outward flow or outflow at a higher level than expected (Davenport, 2004).

Brain drain refers to the migration of the labor force, which is qualified and attracts attention with its knowledge and professionalism, to countries with different geographical, cultural and economic characteristics demanded by the labor force. In another definition, brain drain is the migration of labor force with professional qualifications such as engineers and scientists from underdeveloped countries to developed countries (Kıraçlar, 2005). When a skilled labor force works in a foreign company belonging to a different country in its own country, it is called “hidden brain drain”. In other words, the technical labor force of companies financed and managed by developed countries in less developed countries is called “hidden brain drain”. Individuals engage in brain drain in order to have a healthier life and jobs with better conditions. The factors that cause individuals to decide on brain drain are listed as the lack of economic and political stability of the country, the increase in unemployment rates, the inadequacy of education, and the scarcity of science and technology applications. In short, there should be a development gap between the country that individuals leave and the country they migrate to. Brain drain is called the transfer of human resources from a developing country to a developed country (Aksoy, 2019).

Human Capital Investments

Human capital investment expenditures made to improve social quality should be analyzed in terms of quantity and quality. These investments made by individuals in the process of creating their own human capital directly contribute to economic growth and development. In this sense, human capital investments are analyzed qualitatively and the aspects of labor quality, knowledge and skills are underlined. Expenditures that improve an individual's quality of life cannot be considered as human capital investments if they do not increase the individual's labor productivity. Expenditures on individuals should be included in the concept of human capital if they translate into labor force and turn into economic activity (Gümüş, 2005). Human capital investments have a wide range within the framework of education. In addition to formal trainings, trainings provided from different sources also contribute to the development of capital by leading the individual to develop useful aspects. Training for professional specialization is as important for human capital as public health and formal education. Human capital investment has an impact on all aspects of an individual's life, including school, work, family and social life (OECD, 1998).

The feeling of satisfaction that these expenditures give to families plays an important role in their spending on education for their children. Education expenditures for each child should be evaluated bidirectionally. In this evaluation, the cost and the return of the expenditures are associated. However, the family should be willing to provide education to the child. Families contribute directly and indirectly to human capital by providing education to their children. The human capital investment made by families should not be limited to education. The family's encouragement to education, attitudes and behaviors towards the child, and habits are also examples of human capital investments made within the family. While expenditures on tuition fees, fees and educational equipment purchased for education have a direct impact on human capital, behavioral investments made to improve the quality of life of the child have an indirect impact.

In 1992, Haveman and Wolfe conducted a study for the United States and found that spending on the 0-18 age group accounted for 15% of GDP. The income foregone by mothers due to childcare responsibilities was found to be worth 10% of GDP (OECD, 1998).

The simplest measure that can be used to calculate human capital is to determine the time and money spent on education. In order to build human capital, it is important to calculate how much budget the state allocates to education for companies and families. Alternative education programs other than compulsory education and the income that individuals give up to receive education constitute the basis of the cost of education. With the money and time spent on education, the production of human capital is created (OECD, 1998)

Return on Human Capital Investments

Economics emphasizes the relationship between education and income. Education develops social skills and increases economic potential. Education prepares the economy and society for innovative technology and facilitates adaptation and development. In this way, education affects the level of education in different ways. The returns obtained as a result of education are seen as the rewards of the education process. These rewards can be characterized as social pluses such as social status, high income, harmonious attitudes (Afzal, Rehman, Farooq, & Sarwar, 2011).

Human capital investments make individuals feel powerful in society. The source of this power is their preferences in working life and their social status. The mobility of the individual who feels powerful in the society increases and positively affects his/her economic opportunities. Thus, the power that human investment gives to the individual in society ensures economic growth and keeps the economy dynamic (Nesterova and Sabirianova, 1998).

The difference in the earnings of individuals has been the subject of debate for a long time. The main reason for this difference is the education that individuals receive, but the global technological shift is also an important reason. The difference in earnings arising from education depends on the level and quality of education.

While education is seen as a solution to poverty, income inequality, unemployment and similar social problems, it also forms the basis of economic development. Education, which is considered as a human capital investment, does not only create positive economic results. The social benefits of education as an investment are undeniably high. Improvement in public health, reduction in crime rates, development of environmental awareness, being a conscious parent, social solidarity, being open to political participation and increasing social life constitute the social benefits of education (Barro, 2014).

Importance of Human Capital

Economic growth is the period of change covering modernization, industrialization, growth and development that emerged in England with the industrial revolution (Arslan, 2011). In other words, economic growth is the increase in goods and services produced in a country over time (Ünsal, 2009).

If the definition of economic growth is further elaborated, it can be defined as the increase in goods and services produced in a country within 1 year. In economic terms, it is the increase in real GDP within 1 year (Üzümcü, 2008). The basic meaning of economic growth is to raise living standards in society. It is the increase in per capita income and meeting the increase in demand. During economic growth, production for one good should not be increased while production for another good should not be decreased. Only when all items are increased can the living standards of individuals in society be raised (Kaynak, 2011).

Investments in education, health, etc. to improve human capital affect economic productivity and earnings. When making education investment decisions, the individual, the company and the state consider the positive return of education.

In order to eliminate the development gap between countries, it is important to increase the qualitative and quantitative characteristics of physical and human capital. The subject of physical capital to the economy depends on human resources. Human capital is seen as unqualified labor in agricultural societies, qualified or unqualified labor in industrial societies, and only qualified human capital in today's information society. Qualified human capital in the information society directs economic development, economic growth and social development (Afşar, 2009).

The success of an economy does not only consist of the competencies of individuals in the society that they use in the market for production. The preferences and understandings of individuals on how collective work is done, which economic and social policies are followed, and which policies accelerate or slow down economic development affect the economic situation of the society. Policies preferred by individuals according to their expectations have a direct impact on economic growth (Daşdemir, 2008).

Relationship between Human Capital and Economic Growth

From an economic point of view, the most important element of growth is the redistribution of the productivity and income received as a result of work to households. Continuous and sustainable growth is directly proportional to the increase in labor force quality and productivity. In this respect, investments in human capital are very important in addition to physical investments made for the realization of economic growth (Corrigan, 2017).

Human capital as a general provider of economic growth occupies a large place in the literature. Along with the theoretical studies, the effects of human capital on growth are also tested in empirical applications, and as a result of these studies, human capital has become an important issue in the contemporary economic literature (Leeuwen and Foldvari, 2008). The main problem to be overcome in economic growth is not the creation of wealth, but the creation of the capacity to create wealth. Therefore, this problem is only possible with the development of human capital (Kaynak, 2015).

Human capital realizes economic growth by increasing the efficiency in the use of physical capital in the production process (Çakmak and Gümüş, 2005). With the increase in the level of education, it is possible to access, understand and adapt to technologies that are constantly developing and in a dynamic process more easily (Kaynak, 2015).

According to Schumpeter, a development in education can be expressed as growth. With the development of technology, people with high levels of education can become scientists, inventors or researchers by increasing their knowledge. From another point of view, thanks to education, knowledge is transferred more easily and affects economic growth. Educational institutions play an important role in transferring this knowledge and increasing education levels (Neal, 2005).

Education improves the knowledge and qualifications of human capital. Therefore, it can be said that education constitutes the infrastructure of economic growth. The qualifications, knowledge and productivity of human capital play an important role in the effective use of physical capital in the production process. These elements can only be developed through education (Kaya, 1974).

In countries where the labor force is more intensive than other factors of production, it is very important to spread education to the entire population of the country. With the human factor that develops with education, other factors of production can be used effectively and efficiently. In other words, an improvement in physical capital alone is not sufficient for economic growth unless there is an improvement in human capital (Papi, 1966).

The impact of human capital on economic growth is too great to be ignored. In order to increase this contribution of human capital to growth, education investments should be made correctly. It is important that the curricula used in the education process accurately include the current social and political realities of the countries and include global developments and demands (Woodhall, 1987).

ANALYSIS OF THE ECONOMIC GROWTH-HUMAN CAPITAL RELATIONSHIP IN TÜRKİYE

Factors such as labor force, education, health and demographic structure that are effective in the formation of human capital are analyzed for Türkiye. These factors are evaluated with statistical data and the relationship between human capital and economic growth is analyzed with econometric method for Türkiye.

Population

Population, which means all the people living in a certain geography, is involved in many areas for the development of countries and is therefore of great importance. Population and its current structure also shape the social policies of governments. As can be understood from this point, the data generated by population censuses are very important. The first general census of the Republic of Türkiye was conducted in 1927 and the population of the country was announced as 13,648,270 (Köse, 1927).

The total population between 2000 and 2022 and the distribution of the population by age groups are presented in Table 1. Accordingly, there has been an increase of 22.59% in the country's population between 2000 and 2022. Looking at the table data, it is understood that there is a decrease in the 0-14 age group that cannot be ignored. As a matter of fact, there is a continuous decrease in the 0-14 age group between 2000 and 2019. This decrease raises concerns that the average age of the country's population will increase in the long run. Looking at the data for the 15-64 age group, it is understood that this group constitutes half of Türkiye's population. Since the majority of the population is in this age group and this group is a productive population, it is positive in terms of labor force potential. However, the decrease in the 0-14 age group will not only affect the average age of the country's population in the long run, but will also affect the labor force potential. However, the decrease in the 0-14 age group will not only affect the average age of the country's population in the long run, but will also affect the labor force potential. Looking at the table, the share of the population over the age of 65 in the total population increased from 6.7% in 2000 to 9.98% in 2022. The increase in this ratio is not only related to the aging of the population, but also to the positive developments in the medical sector, the increase in the quality of health services and the awareness of the society, which is thought to increase the human life span.

Table 1. 2000 - 2020 Population and Rate of Change (TÜİK, 2022)

Distribution of population by age groups (%)				
Year	**Total Population (Thousand People)**	**0-14**	**15-64**	**65+**
2000	64.729	29,3	64	6,7
2001	65.603	28,9	64,4	6,7
2002	66.402	28,4	64,9	6,7
2003	67.187	27,9	65,4	6,7
2004	68.010	27,5	65,8	6,7
2005	68.861	27	66,2	6,7
2006	69.730	26,6	66,5	6,8
2007	70.586	26,4	66,5	7,1
2008	71.517	26,3	66,9	6,8
2009	72.561	26	67	7
2010	73.723	25,6	67,2	7,2
2011	74.724	25,3	67,7	7,3
2012	75.627	24,9	67,6	7,5
2013	76.668	24,6	67,7	7,7
2014	77.696	24,3	67,8	8
2015	78.741	24	67,8	8,2
2016	79.815	23,7	68	8,3
2017	80.811	23,6	67,9	8,5
2018	82.003	23,4	67,8	8,8
2019	83.154	15,2	67,3	9,02
2020	83.614	22,8	67,6	9,51
2021	84.909	22,9	67,1	9,82
2022	85.911	22,7	67,2	9,98

Figure 1. 2000 - 2020 Population and Rate of Change (TÜİK, 2022)

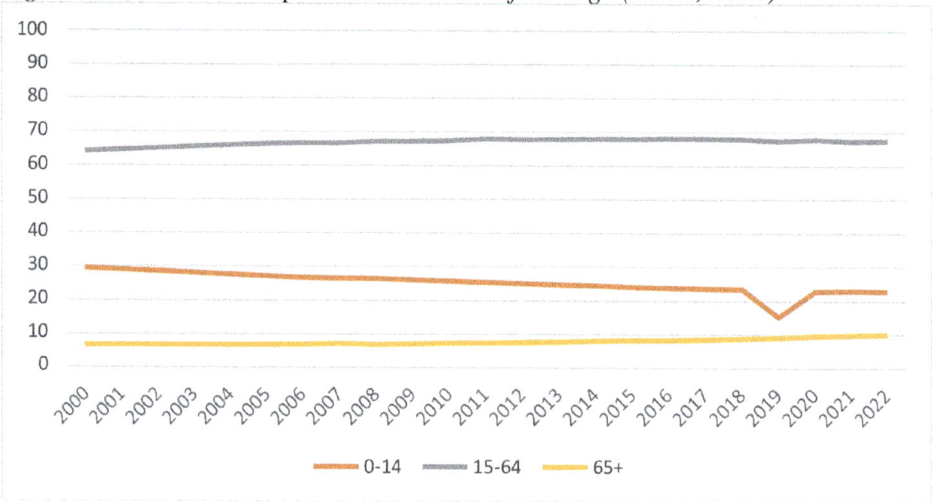

Figure 1 shows the changes in the ratio of the 0-14 age group in the total population more clearly. From 2000 to 2020, the continuous decline in the 0-14 age group reached the lowest level of the last 20 years in 2019. After 2019, although the share of this age group in the total population tended to increase, it tended to decrease again in 2022. The share of the 15-64 age group in the population has been increasing and decreasing over the years, with low rates of increase and decrease. The share of the 65+ age group in the population remained constant until 2005 and increased in all years except 2008.

Labor force

Labor force is the labor supply in a country represented by the number of people. On the other hand, it can also be expressed as the part of the population that is involved in any economic activity. The portion of the total population engaged in economic activity refers to all individuals who are working, looking for work and unemployed. As can be understood from the definition of labor force, the concept does not include those who do not want to work. The labor force participation rate is used to determine the labor force potential and is obtained by dividing the labor force by the non-institutional active population. In other words, this rate shows the rate at which the population with the potential to work is included in the labor supply. Table 2 shows the labor force participation and unemployment rates by education level between 2000 and 2022 in Türkiye (Akça, 2014). When the data in Table 2 are evaluated in general, it is understood that the labor force participation rate has increased in parallel with the increase in the level of education, while the labor force participation of the illiterate population has decreased. Although the labor force participation of individuals with higher education and high school/high school equivalents increased from 2000 to 2022, labor force participation rates decreased in some periods, which cannot be considered significant.

Table 2. Labor force participation and unemployment rates by education level (TÜİK, 2022)

	Labor force participation rate (%) 15+ Age	Unemployment rate (%) 15+ Age	Illiterate	Primary school, primary, secondary and equivalent	General high school, high school equivalent	College or faculty	Total
2000	49,2	6,6	1.813	13.933	3.572	1.837	21.153
2001	49.8	10,6	1.710	13.303	3.678	2.013	20.704
2002	49.5	11,3	1.740	13.626	3.917	2.374	21.658
2003	48.3	10,5	1.424	12.913	4.029	2.445	20.811
2004	46,3	10,8	1.459	13.854	4.156	2.400	21.870
2005	46,4	10,6	1.050	12.095	4.290	2.622	20.057
2006	46,3	10,2	1.029	12.435	4.475	2.755	20.695
2007	46,2	10,3	925	12.225	4.421	2.895	20.466
2008	46,9	11	908	12.395	4.413	3.285	20.999
2009	47,9	14	1.037	12.908	4.393	3.404	21.741
2010	48,8	11,9	1.106	13.559	4.455	3.733	22.854
2011	49,9	9,8	1.207	14.027	4.775	4.257	24.267
2012	50	9,2	1.125	14.502	4.927	4.737	25.291
2013	50,8	9,7	1.045	14.403	5.057	4.938	25.443
2014	50,5	9,9	1.105	15.786	5.792	6.104	28.787
2015	51,3	10,3	1.012	16.114	5.994	6.531	29.651
2016	52	10,9	1.028	16.083	6.277	7.153	30.541
2017	52,8	10,9	1.060	16.558	6.588	7.373	31.579
2018	53,2	11	985	16.267	6.817	7.888	31.957
2019	53	13,7	919	15.852	6.867	8.415	32.053
2020	49,3	13,2	783	14.791	6.763	8.399	30.736
2021	51,4	12	871	15.366	7.967	9.292	33.496
2022	52,6	9,9	867	15.324	8.772	9.698	34.661

Education

With the proclamation of the Republic, radical changes were made in many areas such as social and economy. In the period when even 10% of the population was illiterate, it was understood how important the education level of individuals was in the adoption of these radical changes by the society and more emphasis was placed on the education sector. In this context, in the early periods of the Republic, there was a political education model in which the understanding of republic and democracy was intense (Akyüz, 1982).

With the Republican period, many changes were made in education with the aim of transition to a modern and contemporary education model. In this direction, madrasas were abolished in 1924 with the Tevhid-i Tedrisat law, and all education and training institutions operating within the borders of the country were united and gathered under the roof of the Ministry of Education. A modern education model was established by enacting a law specific to the Ministry of Education. Schools were opened at the primary, secondary, high school, higher education and vocational school levels, and education was made widespread throughout the country. In addition, education at the primary school level was made compulsory. Another important change in the history of Turkish education was the Alphabet Reform in 1928. With this reform, the Latin alphabet was adopted.

It is possible to evaluate the positive improvements realized in the field of education from the past to the present as a result of the radical changes made in the past periods (Akyüz, 1982).

Apart from being one of the fundamental rights and freedoms of individuals, the right to education is of great importance for the exercise of other rights and freedoms. For this reason, the right to education is guaranteed by universal legal regulations as well as national laws. The duration of compulsory education, which countries have secured with laws, refers to the minimum duration of education that individuals should receive. While determining this period, changes in demographic, economic and educational levels are taken into consideration. Since these changes have a dynamic structure, the duration of compulsory education changes from time to time and also varies between countries (Turan, 2016).

Figure 2. Schooling Rate in Education Levels by Years (TÜİK, 2022)

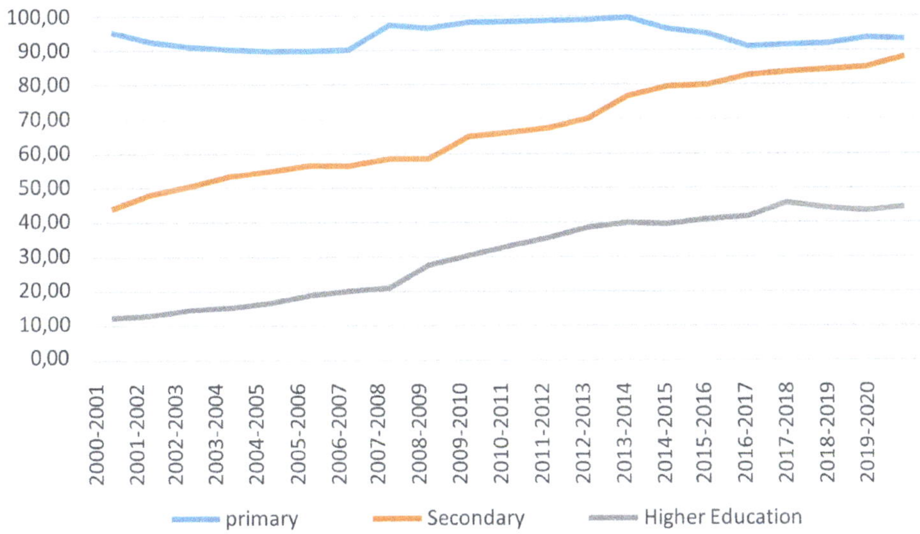

Graph 2 shows the enrollment rates at primary, secondary and higher education levels by years. When the graph is analyzed in general, it is seen that the highest enrollment rate between 2000 and 2021 was at the primary education level. There was a continuous decrease in the enrollment rate at the primary education level between 2000 and the 2006-2007 academic year, reaching the lowest rate in the 21-year period. After this period, there was an increase in the enrollment rate, but the enrollment rate decreased again in the 2013-2014 academic year, and started to increase again in the 2016-2017 academic year. On the other hand, it is observed that the enrollment rate at the secondary education level has continuously increased since 2000, and as of the 2020-2021 academic year, the secondary education enrollment rate has reached the level of the primary education enrollment rate. Especially with the 4+4+4 education model that started to be implemented in Türkiye in 2012, it is noticed that the enrollment rate in secondary education has increased rapidly. With the investments made at the higher education level, curriculum improvements, the increase in the quality of higher education institutions, and the establishment of universities in almost every province, the higher education enrollment rate has also increased significantly between 2000 and 2021.

Health

Before the proclamation of the Republic, the Ministry of Health and Social Welfare was established by law on May 2, 1920. The first Minister of Health appointed on this occasion was Dr. Andan Adıvar. In the first phase, within the framework of health and social assistance, issues such as developing the health sector, preventing the spread of epidemics, increasing the number of personnel in the health sector, reducing infant mortality and increasing the population were emphasized. Thus, thanks to the organization of the health sector at the ministry level, Türkiye became one of the first countries to be organized in this sector (Kazancıgil, 2019).

Between 1929 and 1960, significant efforts were made in areas such as protecting public health, reducing child and infant mortality rates, encouraging childbirth, vaccinating children against epidemics, preventing the spread of epidemics and producing vaccines. In addition, significant investments were made to improve and develop health services, such as increasing the number of health sector personnel, opening hospitals in different provinces, establishing medical faculties and opening colleges to train other auxiliary health personnel.

After 1960, periodic plans were made, and with these plans, efforts were made for the development of the health sector, such as improving health conditions, securing individuals in need of care, and expanding health insurance. Between 1970 and 1980, there was no change in health sector policies and the system continued with its own functioning (Ak, 2002).

Statistics such as crude birth and death rate, infant mortality rate, life expectancy from birth are used to determine the degree of public health. Based on these statistics, comments can be made about the welfare and development levels of countries (Kazancıgil, 2019).

The number of live babies per thousand people in a given region refers to the crude birth rate. The crude birth rate is obtained by dividing the number of live births in a year by the mid-year population and multiplying by one thousand. Since the mid-year population includes male and female individuals who are not of childbearing age, the crude result obtained is not reliable enough (Kazancıgil, 2019). The number of deaths per thousand people in the society refers to the crude mortality rate. According to the definition of crude mortality rate, deaths occurring within a certain region are not differentiated by criteria such as age, sex and cause of death (Kazancıgil, 2019).

Children who die under the age of one are defined as infant deaths. The infant mortality rate shows how many out of a thousand live babies born in a year die under the age of one year. Infant mortality can be caused by many different reasons. Many factors such as problems during pregnancy, lack of nutrition, lack of care and hygiene can cause infant mortality. Preventing or reducing maternal and infant mortality is possible not only through interventions and living conditions during pregnancy, but also through adequate interventions and living conditions in the pre-pregnancy period (Özpınar, 2016). In countries with low infant mortality rates, the likelihood of infant survival and life expectancy also increase. As a result, parents prefer to have fewer children and provide their children with better quality and more opportunities. From another perspective, the decline in infant mortality leads to a parallel decline in the birth rate. Table 3 shows that this is also the case for Türkiye. As the infant mortality rate has decreased over the years, the crude birth rate has also decreased in direct proportion (Mumcu and Çağlar, 2006).

Table 3. Demographic Paces (TÜİK, 2022)

Year	Total fertility	Average birth	Life expectancy at birth	Average mortality	Infant mortality
2000	2,53	21,6	71,0	7,25	31,6
2001	2,38	20,3	71,8	6,89	28,3
2002	2,17	18,6	72,5	6,56	25,4
2003	2,09	17,9	73,2	6,28	22,8
2004	2,11	18,1	73,8	6,05	20,5
2005	2,12	18,2	74,4	5,89	18,4
2006	2,12	18,1	74,9	5,74	16,9
2007	2,16	18,4	75,3	5,62	15,9
2008	2,15	18,2	75,7	5,52	14,9
2009	2,10	17,6	76,1	5,13	13,9
2010	2,08	17,2	76,4	5,01	12,0
2011	2,05	16,9	76,6	5,07	11,6
2012	2,11	17,2	76,8	5,01	11,6
2013	2,10	17,0	78,0	4,90	10,8
2014	2,18	17,5	78,0	5,07	11,1
2015	2,15	17,0	78,0	5,18	10,2
2016	2,10	16,5	78,0	5,32	10,0
2017	2,10	16,4	78,0	5,29	10,1
2018	2,10	16,2	78,2	5,42	10,4
2019	2,10	16,0	78,4	5,45	10,1
2020	2,10	15,8	78,6	5,49	9,9
2021	2,10	15,7	78,8	5,52	9,6
2022	2,10	15,5	79,0	5,55	9,4

When Table 3 is analyzed in general, it is seen that between 2000 and 2022, infant mortality rate in Türkiye decreased from 31.6% to 9.4%, crude mortality rate decreased from 7.25% to 5.55% and crude birth rate decreased from 7.25% to 5.55%.

It is observed that it decreased from 21.6% to 15.5%. On the other hand, life expectancy at birth increased from 71 years in 2000 to 79 years in 2022. In addition to raising awareness of individuals, improving nutritional conditions, paying attention to hygiene and cleanliness issues, sectoral developments such as the development of the health sector and the increase in the use of technology in the health sector have been effective in these developments in demographic rates.

Data Set and Methodology

In the analysis, human capital index representing human capital and GDP data representing economic growth are used. While constructing the human capital index, taking the government expenditures on education sector or the share of education expenditures in GDP as a basis may lead to two different problems. First, the contribution of education expenditures to the productivity of production in the period of the analysis will be realized in the period when the generation for which education expenditures are made joins the labor force. On average, it takes 5 years for this generation to join production productivity (Taşar, 2015). The second problem is that it will not be possible for all individuals whose education level increases as a result of education expenditures to join the labor force. For this reason, in order to provide a more realistic result in the empirical application, the labor force data obtained by TÜİK are grouped according to education levels while constructing the human capital index. In this grouping, data on illiterate, primary, secondary and equivalent, general high school and equivalent, higher education and faculty graduates were used. In this grouping, the number of illiterate labor force is multiplied by 1; the number of primary, secondary and equivalent graduates is multiplied by 2; the number of general high school and equivalent high school graduates is multiplied by 3; and the number of higher education and faculty graduates is multiplied by 4.

Figure 3. Human Capital Index (TÜİK, 2022)

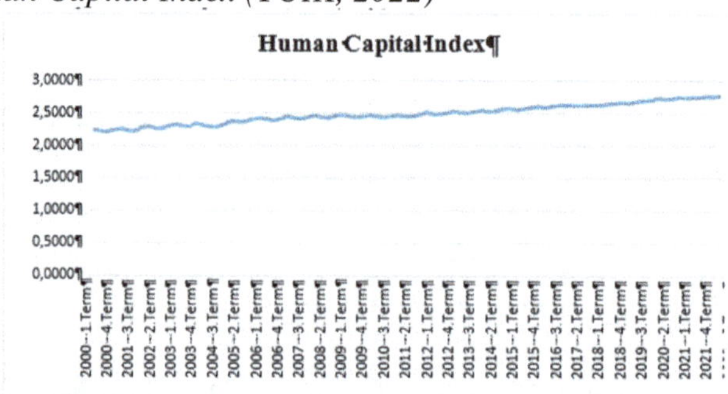

The most noteworthy issue regarding the qualifications of the labor force in the period under review is the fact that while the qualifications of the labor force have generally increased in Türkiye, fluctuations have also been high. In other words, the labor force in the production process in Türkiye is not only composed of university graduates, but also of individuals with low levels of education. Looking at the periods and years in which the index increases, it is understood that the labor force participation of university graduates increased, while the labor force participation of secondary and primary school graduates was higher in other periods.

The distribution of the current labor force by educational level is not surprising for developing Türkiye. Because, when the labor force structure is analyzed, the largest area is filled by individuals with primary school education. In the first quarter of 2000, the share of primary school graduates in the labor force was 50%. In the 22-year period from 2000 to 2022, employment increased from 19,856 to 34,661. The level of output per capita is used to test this increase in employment. All data used in the Lucas (1988) model test are obtained from the Turkish Statistical Institute. The author constructed the labor force index (HCI) using all quarterly data between the first quarter of 2000 and the third quarter of 2022. Again, the natural logarithm of the output per labor force (GDP/L) and labor force index (HCI) variables between the periods of analysis were taken.

Empirical Results

As a variable set, real gross domestic product is used to represent growth and the human capital index, which is formed by the education level of the labor force, is used to represent human capital. The natural logarithm of both variables is taken. All data used in the analysis are obtained from the Turkish Statistical Institute. Descriptive statistics, correlations, Augmented Dickey-Fuller (1981, ADF) and Phillips-Perron (1988, PP) unit root tests and Hatemi J-Roca (2014) Asymmetric, Breitung and Candelon (2006) Frequency Domain and Balcılar et al. (2010) Boostrap Sliding Windows causality tests are performed respectively.

Table 4. Descriptive Statistics of Variables

	LNGDPL	**LNHCI**
Mean	6.987599	0.915950
Median	7.027331	0.911388
Maximum	7.165068	1.021976
Minimum	6.581284	0.802020
Std. Dev.	0.140184	0.061232
Skewness	-1.175688	-0.067854
Kurtosis	3.533195	2.080388

continued on following page

Table 4. Continued

	LNGDPL	LNHCI
Jarque-Bera	21.79976	3.240384
Probability	0.000018***	0.197861

Notes: ***, ** and * denote stationarity of the series at 1%, 5% and 10% levels of significance, respectively.

The statistics show that the period when the average income per labor force was maximum was the 4th quarter of 2007, while the period when the average income per labor force was minimum was the 2nd quarter of 2001. It is not surprising that the period of minimum average income per labor force was 2001. As a matter of fact, the negative effects of the economic crisis that started in Türkiye in February 2001 are reflected in the statistics. Considering the skewness coefficient indicating the asymmetry in the probability distribution of both variables, the distribution of both variables is skewed to the left. The distribution of the real income per labor force variable is steep and the distribution of the human capital index is flattened. According to the JB test, the real income per labor force variable is not normally distributed. The human capital index, on the other hand, is normally distributed.

Table 5. Correlations between Variables

	LNGDPL	LNHCI
LNGDPL	1	-
LNHCI	0.663	1

Correlation provides the opportunity to comment on the strength of the relationship between variables. If the correlation coefficient, which takes a value between -1 and +1, is greater than 0.5, it means that there is a strong relationship between the variables. There is a positive and relatively strong correlation between real income per labor force and human capital index. This shows that a negligence in human capital development will also create a difference in real income per labor force.

Linear unit root tests ignoring structural breaks developed by Dickey-Fuller (1981, ADF) and Phillips-Perron (1988, PP) will be conducted.

Table 6. ADF (1981) and PP (1988) Unit Root Test Results

	Variables	ADF	PP		ADF	PP
Stable Level	**lnGDPL**	-2.265 (4) [0.185]	-2.682 (28) [0.081]*	First Differences	-3.660 (3) [0.00]***	-13.434 (16) [0.00]***
	lnHCI	-0.395 (8) [0.904]	-0.113 (17) [0.943]		-3.136 (7) [0.027]**	-13.425 (17) [0.00]***
Stable+Trend	**lnGDPL**	-2.137 (4) [0.517]	-2.948 (49) [0.152]		-3.760 (3) [0.023]**	-14.735 (16) [0.00]***
	lnHCI	-2.407 (8) [0.372]	-4.816 (6) [0.00]***		-3.117 (7) [0.109]	-13.344 (17) [0.00]***

Notes: ***.** and * denote stationarity of the series at 1%, 5% and 10% levels of significance, respectively. Values in parentheses indicate the optimal lag length according to the Schawarz information criterion. Values in square brackets indicate probability values for the ADF test: Mac Kinnon (1996) critical values at constant 1%. 3.485. -2.885. -2.579 for 5% and 10% values respectively and for constant + trend for 1%. -3.483. -2.884. -2.579 for 5% and 10% probability values for the PP test: Mac Kinnon (1996) critical values for constant 1%. 3.485. -2.885. -2.579 for 5% and 10% values, and 1% for constant + trend. -4.033. -3.446 and -3.148 for 5% and 10% probability values respectively.

In order for the results of the analysis to be meaningful as a result of the empirical application, the data of both variables must be stationary. For this reason, unit root tests are performed on the variables in order to continue the analysis part of the study with different tests.

According to the PP (1988) unit root test, output per labor force is stationary at 10% significance level in the model with constant at the level value. Moreover, according to the PP (1988) unit root test, the human capital index is stationary at the 1% level of significance in the model with constant and trend.

According to the ADF (1981) unit root test, the human capital index is significant at the 1% level of significance in the model with constant and trend. When the first difference of both variables is taken, it is seen that they are free from the effects of economic crises. In the vector autoregression model, the optimal lag length is taken as three.

Table 7. Hatemi J-Roca (2014)Asymmetric Causality Test Results

Nedenselliğin Yönü	**MWALD**	**%1 Bootstrap**	**%5 Bootstrap**	**%10 Bootstrap**
$(lnGDPL)^{+} \neq> (HCI)^{+}$	21.080 (0.00)***	10.761***	6.934**	5.255*
$(lnGDPL)^{+} \neq> (HCI)^{-}$	6.882 (0.076)*	16.138	10.499	8.228
$(lnGDPL)^{-} \neq> (HCI)^{-}$	4.804 (0.091)*	10.972	7.011	5.256
$(lnGDPL)^{-} \neq> (HCI)^{+}$	9.180 (0.027)*	13.174	8.544**	6.931*
$(HCI^{+} \neq> (lnGDPL)^{+}$	7.355 (0.025)**	9.933	6.453**	5.154*

continued on following page

Table 7. Continued

Nedenselliğin Yönü	MWALD	%1 Bootstrap	%5 Bootstrap	%10 Bootstrap
$(HCI)^{+} \neq> (lnGDPL)^{-}$	30.357 (0.00)***	11.960***	8.658**	7.075*
$(HCI)^{-} \neq> (lnGDPL)^{-}$	3.858 (0.145)	12.205	7.616	5.324
$(HCI)^{-} \neq> (lnGDPL)^{+}$	8.235 (0.041)**	14.263	9.939	7.808*

Note: The notation ≠> indicates the null hypothesis of no causality. Values in parentheses indicate asymptotic probability values. ***.** and * values indicate causality between variables at 1%, 5% and 10% levels of significance, respectively. Bootstrap number is 10,000.

There is asymptotic and bootstrap causality from the positive component (increase) of output per labor force to the positive component (increase) of human capital index at the 1% level of significance.

There is asymptotic causality from the positive component (increase) of output per labor force to the negative component (decrease) of the human capital index at the 10% significance level.

There is asymptotic causality from the negative component (decrease) of output per labor force to the negative component (decrease) of human capital index at 10% level of significance.

There is asymptotic causality from the negative component (decrease) of output per labor force to the positive component (increase) of the human capital index at the 10% significance level asymptotically and at the 5% significance level as bootstrap.

There is asymptotic and bootstrap causality from the positive component (increase) of the human capital index to the positive component (increase) of output per labor force at the 5% level of significance. There is asymptotic and bootstrap causality from the positive component (increase) of the human capital index to the negative component (decrease) of output per labor force at the 1% level of significance.

There is no causality from the negative component (decrease) of human capital index to the negative component (decrease) of output per labor force.

There is causality from the negative component (decrease) of the human capital index to the positive component (increase) of output per labor force asymptotically at the 5% significance level and bootstrap at the 10% significance level.

The most important hypothesis in the Lucas (1988) model is that an increase in labor force qualifications will lead to an increase in total output. Therefore, an increase in the human capital index is expected to increase the output per labor force. The analysis conducted with the Hatemi J-Roca (2014) asymmetric causality test reveals that the hypothesis in the Lucas (1988) model is also valid for Türkiye. As a result of the analysis, it is understood that positive shocks in the human capital index cause output per labor force to be positively affected. However, the same is not true for the causality relationship between positive shocks in output per labor force and human capital index. Özsoy (2009) investigated the relationship between GDP and the number of students at different levels of education in Türkiye using impulse response analysis. As a result of the results of the impulse response analysis, which is similar to Hatemi J-Roca (2014) asymmetric causality test, it was found that education, especially vocational and technical education, is important in explaining growth.

The relationship between human capital and economic growth has been tested many times. As a matter of fact, Cui (2008) tested whether there is a relationship between the developments in education and health expenditures, which represent the increase in the quality of human capital, and economic growth with the data of 118 countries. As a result of the test, it was found that the increase in expenditures on education and health also had positive effects on economic growth.

Table 8. Breitung and Candelon (2006) Causality Test Results in the Frequency Domain

Uzun dönem			Orta Dönem		Kısa Dönem	
ω_i	**0.01**	**0.05**	**1.00**	**1.50**	**2.0**	**2.50**
lnGDPL ≠> HCI	2.660*	2.649*	0.798	1.798	0.516	2.768*
HCI ≠> lnGDPL	1.203	1.183	2.256	5.347***	1.163	1.255

Note: With (2.T-2p) degrees of freedom, the F table value is 4.870, 3.106 and 2.367 for approximately 1%, 5% and 10% significance levels, respectively. For each frequency domain (ωi) between 0 and π.ω ∈ (0,π).

Examining the causality in periods explains some points that are not noticed in other tests and gives an idea about the lag of the relationship between the variables. This test increases the importance of the test as it allows us to understand whether the relationship between the two variables is permanent or temporary and in which periods the causality relationship is significant. The results of this test for the period under review are in line with the results of other tests.

As a result of the analysis, there is causality from output per labor force to human capital index in the short and long run at 10% significance level. There is causality from the human capital index to output per labor force only in the medium run at the 1% significance level. In other words, as in Lucas (1988)'s theory, it can be interpreted that as countries become richer, the quality of labor force also increases. According to the results of this analysis for Türkiye, it is understood that improvements in the duration and quality of education will be reflected in the economy as real output in the medium term.

Terzi and Telatar (2010) analyzed economic growth by using population and education variables. As a result of the analysis, it is concluded that economic growth positively affects the number of individuals graduating from higher education. The results of the Breitung and Candelon (2006) Causality Test in the Frequency Domain, which shows that economic growth leads to an increase in labor force quality in the short and long run, support Terzi and Telatar (2010).

Lebe and Yaylalı (2011) conducted a causality analysis using data between 1938 and 2007. As a result of the analysis, they concluded that there is a bidirectional causality relationship between growth and education.

Figure 4. Balcılar et al. (2010) Sliding Windows Causality Test Results

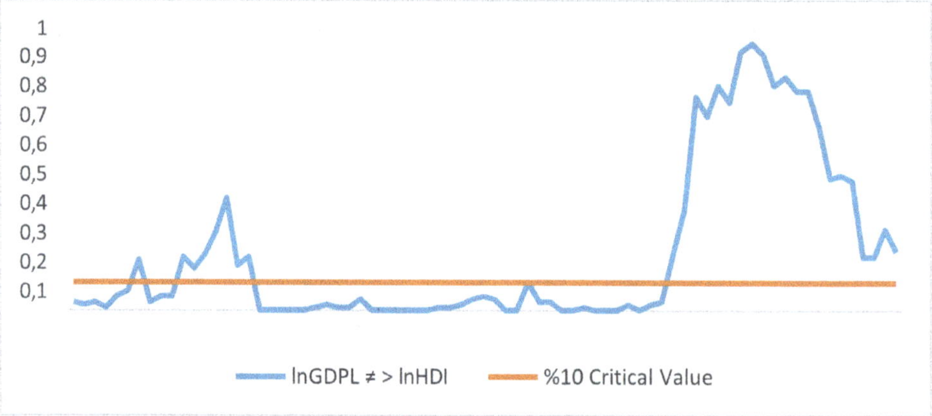

There is causality from output per labor force to human capital index between 2003:Q4-2005:Q1, 2005:Q3-2006:Q1, 2008:Q1-2013:Q4, 2014:Q2-2017:Q2.

Figure 5. Balcılar et al. (2010) Sliding Windows Causality Test Results

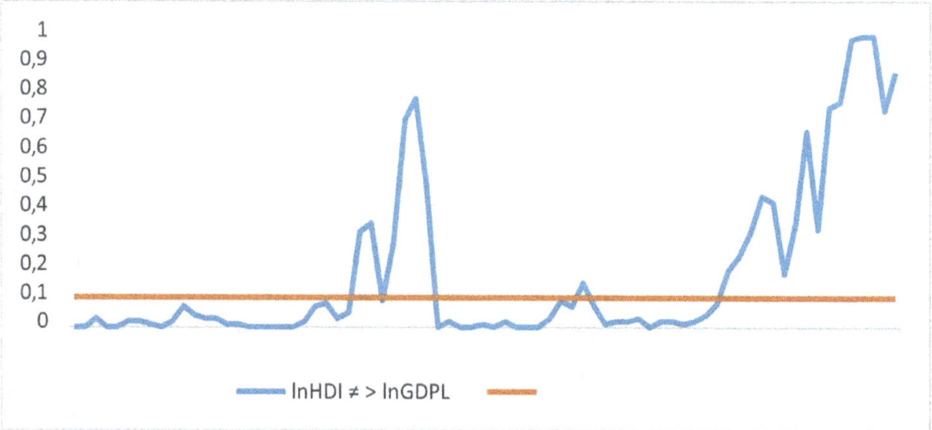

There is causality from human capital index to output per labor force between 2003:Q4 - 2010:Q1 and between 2012:Q1-2018:Q2 except 2015:Q2.

The Bootstrap Rolling Window Causality causality test developed by Balcılar et al. (2010) can be used to analyze the causality relationship for each period. Probability values above the 10% significance level indicate that there is no causality between the two variables in the relevant periods, while probability values below the 10% significance level indicate that there is a causality relationship between the two variables in the relevant period.

As a result of the analysis, a causality relationship was found both from output per labor force to human capital and from human capital to labor force. According to the causality results from output per labor force to human capital index, it is understood that the labor force spends some of its income on individual development as a result of economic recovery. For the periods when there is no causality relationship, it would not be correct to interpret that the labor force does not allocate time and resources for individual development. A close analysis of the 2018:Q2-2021:Q4 periods, where there is no causality relationship between the variables in Graph 4, reveals the repercussions of the currency crisis in Türkiye, which started in 2018 and still continues to have an impact.

According to the causality results from the human capital index to output per labor force, it is observed that the development in human capital also contributes to economic growth. The relationship between the two variables is in line with the expected results and the theories in the literature. Graph 5, which shows the causality relationship, shows that there is no causality between human capital development and output per labor force between 2009 and 2012.

Between 2010 and 2012, the absence of a causality relationship between both variables can be associated with the economic crisis that started in the US in 2008 and affected the whole world. As a matter of fact, Cemil Ertuğrul, Evren İpek and Olcay Çolak (2010), in their study on the effects of the 2008 economic crisis on the Turkish economy, state that the production volumes in 2009 were highly affected by the crisis and that the industrial sector contracted by a quarter. Moreover, in the same study, it was stated that this contraction in the industrial sector was higher than the 1994, 1999 and 2001 crises.

CONCLUSION

The central point of macro-level economic policies of developing countries such as Türkiye is economic growth. Having a dynamic structure of economic growth is among the important economic goals and policies in Türkiye as in all countries. A dynamic economic growth is only possible with the full and efficient utilization of factors of production. The labor factor in the production process can have an impact on all other factors. This situation shows that the improvement in the knowledge, skills and qualifications of the labor force will also affect the production process and factors. It is usual for the growth process to reach a steady state as the development in countries progresses. Economic growth theories in the literature have been analyzed theoretically and empirically from past periods to the present. Endogenous growth theories are the latest stream of growth theories in the literature. Although it is of great importance to test economic growth theories for Türkiye, theoretical and empirical studies on the subject are not sufficient.

Education, which is one of the development indicators of human capital, has an important place in keeping up with the requirements of the current period of individual development. With a high level of education, the qualifications and productivity of the individual increase and thus contribute to the national economy. Although many indicators representing human capital are examined in the studies, it is understood that the level of education is the most commonly used indicator representing human capital.

In the analyzed period, it can be said that Lucas (1988) model, which is among the growth theories, is the most appropriate model for Türkiye. Lucas (1988) argued that there is a positive relationship between labor force development and growth, and as a matter of fact, Lucas (1988)'s theory was confirmed in the analysis results of the study. The human capital index, one of the variables, is constructed with the education levels of individuals involved in the production process in the current labor force. While constructing the index, the coefficient of illiterate individuals is set as '1', the coefficient of primary and secondary school graduates as '2', the coefficient of high school graduates as '3' and the coefficient of higher education graduates as '4'. It has been determined that the human capital index has generally been on an upward trend during the period analyzed, and the majority of the individuals in the labor force are higher education graduates. With the structural transformations in the economy over the years, the development of production from agriculture to the industrial sector and from the industrial sector to the service sector causes the employed labor force to consist of qualified individuals.

According to the results of Hatemi J-Roca (2014) Asymmetric Causality test, which is one of the causality tests applied in the analysis, the increase in human capital index positively affects the output per labor force. As a result of this test, it is once again seen that the theory of positive increase in growth with the increase in labor force qualifications advocated by Lucas (1988) is valid for Türkiye. However, according to the results of this test, decreases in the human capital index do not lead to any change in the amount of output per capita. Therefore, it is understood that the labor force structure in the production processes in Türkiye has not yet changed completely over the years. According to the results of Breitung and Candelon (2006)

Frequency Domain Causality Test, which is another causality test and examines the causality relationship between variables in periods, changes in the human capital index affect output per labor force only in the medium term, while a change in output per labor force affects the human capital index in the long and short term. The theory of Lucas (1988), which suggests that countries that become richer will also experience an increase in labor force qualifications, is also confirmed by this test. On the other hand, it has been determined that the development and quality increases in human capital will be reflected in the country's economy in the medium term. According to Balcılar et al. (2010) Bootstrap Rolling Window Causality test, which is the last causality test and examines the causality relationship between variables in short periods, causality is detected both from human capital index to output per labor force and from output per labor force to human capital index. As a result of the test, the periods that are above the predetermined critical value, which means that there is no causality relationship between the variables, are closely analyzed. In this context, it was determined that there was a currency crisis in Türkiye between 2018 and 2021, when there was no causality relationship both from income per labor force to human capital index and from human capital index to output per labor force. With this currency crisis, a contraction occurred in the economic markets and the amount of output in the production process decreased due to the contraction. Therefore, it is concluded that the lack of causality between human capital and output per labor force between 2018 and 2021 is due to the contraction in output rather than the fact that the development of the human capital index does not affect the labor market. Another period in which there is no causality from the human capital index to the output per labor force is the period between 2010 and 2012, which is marked by the effects of the global crisis that started in the US in 2008 and affected especially developing countries.

When the analyses are analyzed in general, it is understood that human capital quality is of great importance for economic growth in Türkiye and Lucas (1988)'s growth model is valid for Türkiye. Increasing the share of education expenditures in the budget, increasing the number of intermediate staff trained through vocational high schools, increasing in-service trainings, and including housewives who are not included in the labor force in the production process will lead to an increase in labor force quality in Türkiye. Based on the results of the analysis, it is believed that these steps that will increase the quality of human capital will also contribute positively to economic growth. It is of great importance to transfer the science produced in universities to real sectors and to encourage cooperation between universities and industry.

When planning education processes, taking into account the requirements of the current era, these plans will benefit the socio-cultural levels of individuals as well as the positive effects they will have on the country's economy. Investments to be made in the education sector within the individual framework will provide more qualified job opportunities and higher incomes with the increase in the qualifications of individuals. With the higher income earned, individual quality of life increases and can make positive contributions to the concepts explaining human capital.

In order to realize a sustainable economic model, the physical and human capital involved in the production process must be brought together in the right way. In this way, it is thought that the amount of production will increase to the optimum level and economic growth will increase. Movements in human capital due to economic and social reasons have both positive and negative consequences for developed and undeveloped countries. Human capital mobility, which can be defined as the migration of skilled labor, benefits the economy of the country of migration through the participation of skilled labor in the production processes of developed countries. In a developing country, however, this situation is reversed. The outflow of skilled labor from a developing country will harm the economy of the developing country in terms of growth and development processes. Since Türkiye is also in the category of developing countries, in order to avoid the described negative situation, increasing the employment of qualified labor force, shortening and facilitating the integration of human capital into the production process in order to prevent the migration of the limited number of qualified human capital in the labor force is of great importance in terms of economic growth.

In order to guide the studies on the relationship between economic growth and human capital, it is necessary to analyze the same models with different period data. It is known that the most important goals and policies of countries are development and growth, and for this reason, it is thought that the contribution of academic studies on the relevant subject is of great importance for countries.

REFERENCES

Afşar, M. (2009). Türkiye'de Eğitim Yatırımları ve Ekonomik Büyüme İlişkisi.

Afzal, M., Rehman, H. U., Farooq, M. S., & Sarwar, K. (2011). Education and economic growth in Pakistan: A cointegration and causality analysis. *International Journal of Educational Research, 50*(5-6), 321–335. DOI: 10.1016/j.ijer.2011.10.004

Akça, F. (2014). *Beşeri sermayenin ekonomik büyümeye etkisi: Türkiye üzerine bir uygulama* (Master's thesis, Sosyal Bilimler Enstitüsü).

Aksoy, M. (2019). *Beşeri Sermaye, Sosyal Sermaye ve Öz Yeterliliğin Restoran Performansına Etkisi* (Master's thesis).

Akyüz, Y. (1982). *Türk eğitim tarihi:(başlangıçtan 1982'ye)* (Vol. 114). Ankara Üniversitesi Eğitim Bilimleri Fakültesi.

Arslan, M. L. (2011). Devletin iktisadi büyümedeki rolü. *Bilgi Ekonomisi ve Yönetimi Dergisi, 6*(2), 160–175.

Arslan, Ü. (2011). Siyasi istikrarsizlik ve ekonomik performans: Türkiye örneği.

Barro, R. J. (2014). [Human Capital and Growth), Beşeri Sermaye ve Büyüme. *Journal of Economics and Political Economy, 1*(2), 351–358.

Birinci, E. (2015). *AR-GE harcamalarının ekonomik büyüme üzerine etkisi: İçsel büyüme modeli zaman serisi analizi* (Master's thesis, Sosyal Bilimler Enstitüsü).

Çakmak, E. ve Gümüş, S. (2005). Türkiye'de beşeri sermaye ve ekonomik büyüme: ekonometrik bir analiz (1960-2002). *Ankara Üniversitesi SBF Dergisi, 60*(01), 59-72.

Çelik, N. (2006). *Küreselleşme sürecinde gelişmekte olan ülkelerde teknolojik gelişme ve devletin rolü: Yeni sanayileşen ülkeler deneyimi ve Türkiye örneği* (Doctoral dissertation, Marmara Universitesi (Turkey)).

Çolak, M. (2010). Eğitim ve beşeri sermayenin kalkınma üzerine etkisi. *Kamu-İş Dergisi, 11*(3), 109–125.

Corrigan, G. (2017). The Inclusive Growth And Development Report 2017. World Economic Forum. Çağlar, A. ve Gülel, F. E. (2017). Eğitimin toplumsal fayda üzerinde etkisi.

Daşdemir, A. (2008). AB Üyesi Ülkelerde Beşeri Sermaye ve Ekonomik Büyüme İlişkisi: Panel Veri Analizi (Doctoral Dissertation). *DEÜ Sosyal Bilimleri Enstitüsü.*

Davenport, S. (2004). Panic and panacea: Brain drain and science and technology human capital policy. *Research Policy*, *33*(4), 617–630. DOI: 10.1016/j.respol.2004.01.006

Ertuğrul, C., & Evren, İ. ve Çolak, O. (2010). Küresel mali krizin Türkiye ekonomisine etkileri. *Journal of Management and Economics Research*, *8*(13), 59–72.

Eser, K. ve Gökmen, Ç. E. (2009). Beşeri sermayenin ekonomik gelişme üzerindeki etkileri: Dünya deneyimi ve Türkiye üzerine gözlemler. *Sosyal ve Beşeri Bilimler Dergisi*, *1*(2), 41–56.

Farr, W. (1853). The income and property tax. *Journal of the Statistical Society of London*, *16*(1), 1–44. DOI: 10.2307/2338101

Gökçen, B. (2006). *Beşeri sermayenin iktisadi gelişmedeki rolü ve önemi: Adana iline ilişkin bir uygulama* (Master's thesis, Sosyal Bilimler Enstitüsü).

Gümüş, S. (2005). *Beşeri Sermaye ve Ekonomik Kalkınma: Türkiye Üzerine Ekonometrik Bir Analiz (1960- 2002),(Atatürk Üniversitesi Doktora Tezi 2005: Erzurum).* İktisadi Araştırmalar Vakfı.

Günsoy, G. (2005). İnsani gelişme kavramı ve sağlıklı yaşam hakkı. *Uluslararası Yönetim İktisat ve İşletme Dergisi*, *1*(2), 35–52.

Hall, R. E., & Jones, C. I. (1999). Why do some countries produce so much more output per worker than others? *The Quarterly Journal of Economics*, *114*(1), 83–116. DOI: 10.1162/003355399555954

Karagül, M. (2003). Beşeri sermayenin ekonomik büyümeyle ilişkisi ve etkin kullanımı. *Akdeniz İİBF Dergisi*, *3*(5), 79–90.

Kaya, Y. K. (1974). *İnsan yetiştirme düzenimiz: politika, eğitim, kalkınma*. Nüve Matbaasi. Kaya, Y. K. (1977). *İnsan yetiştirme düzenimiz*. Hacettepe Üniversitesi..

Kayacan, M., & Alkan, N. (2005). *Turkiye'deki bes ,eri sermayenin ekonomik de geri ve Avrupa Birligi ulkeleri ile kars ,ılas ,tırılması. Ankara*. Yayınları.

Kazancıgil, D. (2019). Beşeri sermaye ekonomik büyüme ilişkisi Türkiye örneği.

Kıraçlar, F. (2005). *Ekonomik büyüme modellerinde beşeri sermaye: içsel büyüme modelinin analizi*. Erciyes Üniversitesi Yayımlanmamış Yüksek Lisans Tezi.

Köse, M. (1927). Nüfus sayımı ve sonuçlarının değerlendirilmesi. *Yayınlanmamış Yüksek Lisans Tezi), Afyonkarahisar Üniversitesi Sosyal Bilimler Enstitüsü.*

Lucas, R. E.Jr. (1988). On the mechanics of economic development. *Journal of Monetary Economics*, *22*(1), 3–42. DOI: 10.1016/0304-3932(88)90168-7

Machin, S. (2008). Big ideas: Rising wage inequality. *CentrePiece, 13*(2), 8–10.

Mumcu, O. ve Çağlar, E. (2006). Türkiye'nin Nüfusu Zenginlik Kaynağı Olabilir mi? *Ekonomi Politikaları Araştırma Enstitüsü Politika Notu, 24*, 2011.

Nesterova, D. V. ve Sabirianova, K. Z. (1998). *Investment in human capital under economic transformation in Russia*. Economic Education and Research Consortium.

Organisation for Economic Co-operation and Development (1998). Human Capital: How What You Know Shapes Your Life.

Organisation for Economic Co-operation and Development. (2001). *The well-being of nations: The role of human and social capital*. OECD publishing.

Özpınar, E. (2016). *Bebek Ölüm Hızı Türkiye Genelinde Azalıyorken Neden Suriyeli Nüfusun Fazla Olduğu Yerlerde Artıyor. Türkiye Ekonomi Politikaları Araştırma Vakfı (TEPAV)*. Değerlendirme Notu.

Özsoy, C. (2009). Türkiye'de eğitim ve iktisadi büyüme arasindaki ilişkinin VAR modeli ile analizi. *Bilgi Ekonomisi ve Yönetimi Dergisi, 4*(1).

Özütler, H. Ş. (2009). *Beşeri sermaye ve bilgi ekonomisinin iktisadi kalkınmadaki önemi: Türkiye üzerine bir uygulama*. İstanbul Üniversitesi Sosyal Bilimler Enstitüsü, İktisat Anabilim Dalı, İktisat Politikası Bilim Dalı, Yüksek Lisans Tezi.

Papi, G. U. (1966). General problems of the economics of education. In *The Economics of Education* (pp. 3–23). Palgrave Macmillan. DOI: 10.1007/978-1-349-08464-7_1

Schultz, T. W. (1961). Investment in human capital. *The American Economic Review, 51*(1), 1–17.

Turan, F. (2016). Türkiye'nin Zorunlu Eğitim Politikaları-Tarihsel Perspektif 1. *Çağdaş Yönetim Bilimleri Dergisi, 3*(1), 1-10.

Ünsal, E. M. (2009). *Makro İktisat, Gözden Geçirilmiş 8*. Baskı, İmaj Yayınevi.

Üzümcü, A. (2008). Türkiye ekonomisinde büyüme ve kalkınma dinamikleri: 1923–2007. *Türkiye'nin Ekonomi-Politiği, 312*(384), 281.

Woodhall, M. (1987). Economics of education: a review: economics of education research and studies. *Economics of Education Research and Studies*.

Yaylali, M. ve Lebe, F. (2011). Beşeri sermaye ile iktisadi büyüme arasındaki ilişkinin ampirik analizi. *Marmara University Journal of the Faculty of Economic & Administrative Sciences, 30*(1).

Chapter 13

The Supply Chain Risk Analysis Using the House of Risk (HOR) Method:

Integration of the Supply-Chain Operation Reference (SCOR) Model and the Fuzzy Logic

Aisyah Larasati
https://orcid.org/0000-0001-7084-8777
Universitas Negeri Malang, Indonesia

Ahmad Danial Ubaidillah
Universitas Negeri Malang, Indonesia

Abdul Muid
Universitas Negeri Malang, Indonesia

Anik Dwiastuti
https://orcid.org/0000-0002-5885-8734
Universitas Negeri Malang, Indonesia

ABSTRACT

The object study is a sugar factory. During the milling period, several obstacles occur, such as delays in raw materials and machine damage. This can be anticipated with mitigation actions, which are the main output of the House of Risk (HOR) and are mapped based on the Supply-Chain Operations Reference (SCOR) model. However, the HOR method has an extensive range in its assessment, so it needs to be integrated with fuzzy logic to provide firm values. This research aims to analyze

DOI: 10.4018/979-8-3373-0603-2.ch013

what risks arise, the risk agents, priority risk agents, and the steps to handle them in sugar production. This research uses the SCOR model and the Fuzzy House of Risk method. The research instruments include interviews, closed questionnaires, and brainstorming with the experts. Based on the interview results, 17 risk events and 19 risk agents were obtained. Based on the nine priority risk agents, several mitigation actions were formulated, such as mentoring sugar cane care for partner farmers, improving farming business management, weather prediction, and analysis of transport routes.

INTRODUCTION

According to data from the Central Statistics Agency in 2019, the need for sugar consumption in Indonesia is 5.1 million tons and will increase in 2020-2021 by 5.25 million tons (Muharja et al., 2022). This large sugar consumption must be balanced with the appropriate production capacity of sugar producing companies in order to meet the existing demand in Indonesia. The object study is a sugar factory with a capacity of up to 6,000 tons of sugar cane per day so it is necessary to carry out supply chain risk management analysis to minimize losses, so research is carried out on risk management analysis as a step to prevent supply chain risks in the object study using the House of Risk (HOR) method based on the Supply-Chain Operations Reference (SCOR) model integrated with Fuzzy Logic.

The House of Risk (HOR) method was chosen because this method focuses on prevention, namely reducing the possibility of risk agents occurring. So, the earliest stage is to identify risk events and risk agents (Magdalena & Vannie, 2019). Apart from that, in the HOR method, there is also a process of assessing the effectiveness between mitigation actions and risk agents so that the results of the research can be more visible, but the data used in House of Risk is data that tends to be subjective. In practice regarding risk management, several researchers use the HOR approach. However, during the process of collecting severity and occurrence data, the severity and occurrence questionnaire collects data using a 1-10 Likert scale, so doubts arise in determining the answer. When compared with other logic systems, fuzzy logic can produce fairer decisions (Puji, 2018).

Another study also proposed the use of fuzzy HOR to enable policy makers to systematically analyze potential risks in manufacturing companies (Rakadhitya & Hartono, 2019). Fuzzy is used so that there is no bias in the values obtained (Wafi, 2017). This research aims to determine risk events, risk agents, and priority risk agents as well as mitigation steps in sugar production in the object study.

THEORETICAL CONCEPTS

Supply Chain Management

(Heizer et al., 2020) stated that the supply chain describes the coordination of all supply chain activities, starting with raw materials and ending with satisfied customers. So, the supply chain includes suppliers, manufacturers and/or service providers, distributors, wholesalers, and/or retailers who deliver products and/or services to end customers. Meanwhile, according to (Russell & Taylor, 2019) the supply chain includes all activities related to the flow and transformation of goods and services from the raw material stage to the end user (customer), as well as those related to the flow of information. The supply chain is also a group of processes that are integrated into sourcing, making, and delivering products.

According to (Muhammad & Sumarauw, 2014), Supply chain is a physical network consisting of various agencies involved from procurement, production, to delivery to customers. Supply Chain Management is a collection of interrelated activities and decisions to connect suppliers, producers, warehouses, transportation services, retailers and customers efficiently. Meanwhile, according to another opinion, supply chain management (SCM) is a network of various institutions (independent/groups) working together to make and deliver a product to customers (farm to the table). In practice, SCM is related to money, information, and the flow of goods. In addition, SCM is also related to retail services and products, transportation, warehousing, production, and planning, as well as management of waste (Jaya et al., 2021). Several parties who play an important role and have interests in the sugar factory supply chain are:

1. Farmer Groups
2. Factories
3. Collectors
4. Retailers
5. Consumers

(Russell & Taylor, 2019) argue that supply chain management is needed to regulate the flow of information through the supply chain to achieve a level of synchronization that will make it more responsive to customer needs while reducing costs. While another opinion according to (Muhammad & Sumarauw, 2014) states that Supply Chain Management is a collection of interrelated activities and decisions to connect suppliers, producers, warehouses, transportation services, retailers and customers efficiently. Generally, supply chain management is a process that involves the management of activities related to the flow of products and services from suppliers to end customers with the target of competitive advantage, optimizing value, and increasing efficiency. Collaboration, integration, and risk management are also vital aspects of risk management. The objectives of supply chain management include (Syamil et al., 2023):

1. Achieving competitive advantage
2. Increasing efficiency
3. Meeting customer needs
4. Optimizing profits
5. Managing risk

Supply Chain Risk Management

Risk is a deviation of the results obtained from those expected. Whatever the definition of risk, it includes at least two important aspects, namely the aspect of probability/possibility and the aspect of loss/impact. However, the most common in society when hearing risk, the orientation of public understanding is always about losses (Arifudin et al., 2020). So that risk management is a culture, process, and structure that is directed at effective management of potential opportunities and detrimental influences. Risk management is one of the important elements in running a company's business because the increasing development of the corporate world and the increasing complexity of company activities result in an increase in the level of risk faced by the company. The main goal of implementing risk management is to protect the company against possible losses.

Supply chain risk management is an effort to process every risk that has the potential to occur in a supply chain activity until a supply chain is obtained that is free from constraints and runs optimally. Supply chain risk management is an urgent discussion and requires more attention, because of the impact of the risks that may occur, and the potential for significant influence on the performance of the parties involved in the supply chain. Supply chain risk management has the nature of supply chain risk, namely focusing on every factor that requires attention because it can have a sustainable influence (Nadhira et al., 2019). Generally, the stages of supply chain risk management consist of:

1. Risk identification. Risk identification is a process of activities to recognize and analyze possible sources of risk.
2. Risk assessment. A risk assessment is to determine the level of severity resulting from each level of risk.
3. Risk evaluation. A risk evaluation is the determination of which risks are acceptable and which risks need to be prioritized for handling.

4. Risk mitigation

The third stage is to provide a response to each risk that will be experienced. Risk identification is recommended as a very important stage in risk management activities. Dominant potential risks are not limited to the organization alone but can also be in members of the supply network and between the supply network and the surrounding environment must also be identified (Ulfah et al., 2016). The focus of supply chain risk management is to understand and try to avoid the negative impacts that can be caused by disasters or business disruptions along the supply chain (Norrman & Jansson, 2004). The goal is to reduce the possibility of unwanted risk events so as to increase resilience, namely the ability to recover from disruptions. In this study, the intended risk management is to analyze the risks in sugar production, where later the risk factors will be identified so that the risk can be controlled before it occurs.

Supply Chain Operation Reference (SCOR)

SCOR combines elements of business process engineering, metrics, benchmarking, best practices, and human skills into one framework. Under SCOR, supply chain management is defined as the integrated process of plan, source, make, deliver, and return from suppliers to customers (Bolstorff & Rosenbaum, 2007). The SCOR (Supply Chain Operation Reference) approach is a model that can be used in SCM performance measurement, meaning that this model can also be used in supply chain risk management. The SCOR model describes the scope and content of the supply chain. The SCOR model is a framework for supply chain operations.

The independent organization Supply Chain Council defines it as a standard model for analyzing, evaluating, and optimizing processes developed along the supply chain. The supply chain requires maintaining an overview, adapting, and making continuous improvements to facilitate the flow of goods from producers to customers and optimize the structure. This model connects business processes, metrics, practices, and technologies into a unified structure to support communication between supply chain partners and improve their effectiveness. In this sense, the SCOR model provides a single framework for connecting business processes, management indicators, best practices, and technologies in a unified structure (APICS, 2015). The SCOR model was developed to describe business activities related to all phases of customer demand satisfaction. It is organized around six key management processes, namely Planning, Source, Make, Delivery, Return, and Support (ASCM, 2021).

SCOR has 4 levels, where the Supply-Chain Council defines levels 1-3 as general basic levels, while level 4 is a specific step for each company.

- Level 1: Macro processes. Organizations develop their strategies to plan, supply, produce, distribute products or perform services. At this level, specific objectives for response times are set.
- Level 2: Category processes. Organizations configure their operational strategies through the sequence of processes and activities they choose for their chains. Like macro processes, they are grouped into operational, support and strategic.
- Level 3: Elemental processes. Describes standard process elements or activities. The previously identified processes are in turn divided into the activities they encompass. Each activity has a definition, metrics that facilitate diagnosis, observing good practices and the necessary software tools. Each activity groups specific tasks that represent the work of each organization, so they cannot be standardized.
- Level 4: Improvement. In the form of handling steps and actions formulated by each company in overcoming the problems that have been identified.

House of Risk (HOR)

HOR is a development of Failure Modes and Effect of Analysis (FMEA) and HOQ (House of Quality) to rank the causes of risk that need to be prioritized for mitigation actions in order to reduce the chances of risk and its agents occurring. The advantage of FMEA is a tool for analyzing and evaluating reliability through error mode checks and is one of several systematic approaches that function in failure analysis (Ulfah et al., 2016). The HOR approach underlies risk management by focusing on mitigating or suppressing the probability of risk agents to occur. Generally, a risk agent can be the cause of several risk events. A risk event can be defined as a specific event that has a negative impact on decisions, plans, companies, or organizations. While the risk agent is a source or cause that can result in a risk event (Hidayatusibyan, 2018). Based on FMEA assessment on the risks applied is the Risk Priority Number (RPN) covering 3 aspects, including the chance of occurrence, severity level, and detection. House of Risk (HOR) has 2 phases, namely HOR Phase 1 as the risk identification stage and HOR Phase 2 as the risk handling stage (Magdalena and Vannie, 2019).

House of Risk Phase 1

HOR phase 1 serves to determine which risk agents are very urgent to immediately take preventive action. The following are the stages of HOR phase 1:

1. Identify supply chain business activities according to the SCOR approach. This classification is useful for seeing where a risk occurs.
2. Identify Risk Events (Ei) that exist in each agency's business activities.
3. Identify the severity or level of severity (Si) of a risk event. This assessment shows how much influence is caused by a risk event. The severity used uses a scale of 1-10 from those with no impact to those with serious impacts.
4. Identification of risk agents (Aj) which are the cause of the emergence of risk events and the risk agent's opportunities for the probability level of the number of occurrences of a risk agent.
5. Identification of the occurrence level (Oj) of the probability of the occurrence of risk events. This research applies an assessment of 1-10.
6. Identification of the relationship between risk events and agents is shown by Rij (0, 1, 3, 9) where 0 means no relationship, 1 is a small relationship, 3 is a moderate relationship, and 9 is a strong relationship.
7. Calculating the Aggregate Risk Potential (ARP) score. The ARP score will later function as a determinant of which risk agent should be prioritized based on the magnitude of the ARP value.
8. Sorts risk agents by ARP value.

House of Risk Phase 2

In the stages of HOR phase 2, several treatments will be selected that are considered effective in reducing the probability of risk agent occurrence. The stages of HOR phase 2 include:

1. Determining the number of risk agents according to the value of ARP in each risk agent.
2. Formulating preventive actions (PA) that are considered capable of reducing or minimizing the probability of risk agent occurrence. A risk agent can be tackled with several PAs and vice versa.
3. Determining the relationship score between each PA and risk agent with a score of 0 (unrelated), 1 (low relationship), 3 (moderate relationship), and 9 (high relationship).
4. Calculating the Total Effectiveness (TEk) score for each PA
5. Assessment of the level of difficulty of implementing PAk with a score of 3: if easy, 4: medium and 5: if difficult
6. Calculating the TEk (Total Effectiveness) and Dk (level of difficulty) values
7. Determining the urgency ranking of each strategy (Rk) which ranks top with the highest ETD score.

Fuzzy Logic

Fuzzy is a theory that has credibility in manipulating/representing uncertain information and data using free statistics. Not only that, fuzzy is systematically designed to represent unclear and uncertain cases and provide various tools related to the ambiguity related to the problem of decision-making (Ariyani, 2018). Fuzzy theory is useful in overcoming uncertain things, this makes fuzzy able to interpret vague or vague data. Fuzzy theory has been applied to various problems that require the ability to manage uncertainty and biased scores in risk management. The membership function value of uncertain data and conditions that require answers that cannot be determined absolutely "yes" or "no" can be assessed by applying fuzzy logic (Roghanian & Mojibian, 2015). Fuzzy has 3 stages, namely:

a. Fuzzification, this stage applies linguistic variables in converting severity and occurrence value factors into fuzzy. With linguistic variables accompanied by definitions, then rank these two aspects on a basic scale, with the intention of obtaining the membership function value of each class.
b. Rule evaluation, contains researcher insights regarding the interaction of causative indicators with risk events and agents in the form of fuzzy "if then" rules. These rules are easier to create in linguistic form than numeric.
c. Defuzzification, is the stage of determining the output in the form of severity and occurrence scores and can later be calculated to provide a priority level of error mode. The defuzzification process uses the centroid method (Ariyani 2018).

RESEARCH METHODS

In this research, data collection was carried out through interviews, questionnaires, and brainstorming. Interviews were conducted to obtain data related to supply chain activities based on the SCOR model in a sugar company. Then, each existing activity will be used as a basis for interviews with expert judgment to identify Risk Events and Risk Agents. Each Risk Event and Risk Agent obtained will be used as the basis for a questionnaire adapted from (Nyoman Pujawan & Geraldin, 2009) to assess the severity and occurrence so that it is known which Risk Agent is the priority after the analysis is carried out. These priority Risk Agents will then become the basis for brainstorming to formulate Preventive Actions. The Preventive Actions obtained will be used as a questionnaire to obtain correlation values between Preventive Actions and priority Risk Agents and the degree of difficulty in implementing Preventive

Actions. Respondents in this research are four experts determined based on representatives from each division in a sugar production company.

Data Sources

Data collection is carried out to obtain the data needed to solve the problems discussed in the study. The data used in this study consists of primary data and secondary data.

1. Primary Data is data that comes directly from objects related to research, either through observation, interviews, questionnaires, or discussions. Primary data is data collected from research objects directly from the main or original source. The primary data in this study are:
    a. Mapping of supply chain activities of the sugar company
    b. Data on risk events and risk agents of supply chain activities of the sugar company
    c. Severity and occurrence values of risk events and risk agents and their correlation values
    d. Correlation values of priority risk agents with mitigation actions
    e. Degree of difficulty values of mitigation actions
2. Secondary data is obtained from a second source, in other words, this data is data that is useful for supporting research and research outputs. This means that this data is obtained from existing sources. Secondary data in this study are:
    a. Products produced by the sugar company
    b. Sugar production process flow of the sugar company

Data Collecting Techniques

In this study, data collection was carried out through interviews, questionnaires, and brainstorming. Interviews were conducted to obtain data related to supply chain activities based on the SCOR model by (ASCM, 2021) at the sugar company then from each existing activity will be used as the basis for interviews to identify Risk Events and Risk Agents, then from each Risk Event and Risk Agent obtained will be used as the basis for a questionnaire adapted from (Puji, 2018) to assess severity and occurrence so that it is known which Risk Agent is a priority after the analysis is carried out. The priority Risk Agent will then be the basis for brainstorming to formulate Preventive Action, from the Preventive Action obtained will be used as a questionnaire to obtain the correlation value between Preventive Action and priority Risk Agent and the value of the degree of difficulty in implementing Preventive Action.

Interview

An interview is an approach in collecting data based on a problem by asking questions to obtain answers to the problem, asking for views on a problem to individuals or agencies related to their views on the problem. In this study, the interview approach was used to obtain data related to the supply chain flow of the sugar company and identification of risk events and risk agents in the supply-production of sugar at the sugar company. In this study, interviews were conducted with expert judges who were representatives of each division, the interview design in Appendices 1 and 2 was made based on the SCOR approach with a scope or dimensions based on (ASCM, 2021) and (Nadhira, Oktiarso, and Harsoyo, 2019).

Questionnaire

A questionnaire is a useful tool in measuring an event or incident that consists of several question points in order to obtain information related to the research being conducted (Amalia and Dianingati, 2022). The questionnaire in this study was used to obtain the severity and occurrence values of risk events and risk agents using a Likert scale of 1-5. The questionnaire was created based on the results of interviews with expert judgment. After knowing what the risk events and risk agents are from each supply chain activity at the sugar company, the data on risk events and risk agents are used as a questionnaire, the design of this questionnaire refers to research conducted by (Puji, 2018). The questionnaire that has been created will then be assessed for severity and occurrence by expert judgment.

Brainstorming

Brainstorming is a method used by a group of people to discuss and aims to collect ideas and concepts spontaneously from all group members. Brainstorming aims to encourage creative thinking to emerge, so that product idea designs can be maximized. The next goal of brainstorming is that this method eliminates mental barriers of group members to the creativity that is expressed and also expands the area of searching for solutions (Ginting and Kokman, 2022). In this study, the brainstorming or brainstorming approach was used to obtain data related to:

a. Correlation value between risk event and risk agent
b. The degree of difficulty of implementing mitigation actions
c. Formulation of mitigation actions or preventive actions
d. Correlation value of preventive action with risk agents

Expert judgment is a resource person in this study which should consist of managers from each division in the sugar company. However, because the research was conducted during the milling season and each manager was unable to attend, the company provided representatives from each section at the sugar company, namely:

1. Secretariat of the Engineering Division
2. Head of the Fabrication Division Sub-Division
3. Head of the Plant Division Sub-Division
4. Staff of the TUK Division

Supply-Chain Operation Reference (SCOR)

The Supply Chain Operation Reference (SCOR) method is an approach method for measuring supply chain performance, in other words, this method is used to carry out supply chain management. The SCOR method is used to facilitate the mapping of supply chain activities to identify Risk Events and Risk Agents through each stage which includes Planning, Procurement, Making, Delivery, and Return. Broadly speaking, SCOR has 4 levels where the Supply-Chain Council sets levels 1-3 as general basic levels while level 4 is a specific step for each company.

In this study, SCOR is used to facilitate the identification of supply chain activities at the sugar company. Based on these needs, the one used in this study is up to SCOR Level 1 with a focus on the macro flow of supply chain activities. In this study, which focuses on the tactical level of the company, SCOR level 1 has been sufficient as a reference for identifying supply chain activities, because at the tactical level of the sugar company, the focal or dominant entity involved is the farmer group as a supplier and the sugar company as an industry that produces sugar, for the sales, purchases, and product returns taken over by the parent company of the sugar company. SCOR Levels 2 and 3 are not used because at this level it is too detailed and generally focuses on Key Performance Indicator (KPI) measurements that are not needed in this study. The questionnaire was made based on the SCOR model.

House of Risk (HOR)

The first phase focuses on identifying risks and priority levels of importance based on the Aggregate Risk Potential (ARP) value after obtaining severity, occurrence, and correlation values from the questionnaire, following equation 1 to determine the ARP for each risk agent (Cahyani et al., 2016):

$$ARPj = Oj \sum i \; SiRij \tag{1}$$

where: Oj: Occurrence level of risk (level 0); Si: Severity level of risk (Level of risk impact); Rij: Correlation (relationship) between risk agent j and risk i.

Severity, occurrence, correlation, and ARP values will be collected.

The second phase of House of Risk focuses on mitigation or handling actions from prioritized risk agents. Prioritized Risk Agents will have their handling strategies formulated. The correlation between each Risk Agent and each mitigation action will be identified with a score of 0 for no correlation, 1 for small correlation, 3 for medium correlation, and 9 for high correlation. Next, the Total Effectiveness value is calculated to determine the level of effectiveness of each mitigation action using Equation 2.

$$TEK = \sum j\ ARPjEjk \qquad (2)$$

Where: Ejk: The relationship between each strategy and each risk agent

After knowing the level of effectiveness of each mitigation action, the Degree of Difficulty (Dk) of implementing the mitigation action is then identified based on the company's ability with a scale of implementation difficulty of 3: low, 4: medium, and 5: high (Cahyani et al., 2016). Calculate the ratio of Total Effectiveness (TEk) and level of difficulty (Dk) using equation 3:

$$ETDk = \frac{\mathrm{TE}k}{\mathrm{D}k} \qquad (3)$$

ETDk: Effectiveness to Difficulty

The final step is to sort the mitigation actions based on the highest ETD value.

Fuzzy Logic

House of Risk has a disadvantage, namely that there is bias or lack of clarity in the data obtained because the data obtained is subjective, especially in assessing severity and occurrence, because parameters that are not clear enough can lead to differences in assessments based on the same views of experts, both on severity and occurrence values. A fuzzy logic approach is needed in this research to confirm the value of this vague membership. Fuzzy logic models intuition or feelings during the fuzzification stage and then incorporates them into fuzzy rules created based on knowledge. Apart from that, the function of fuzzy logic is also to accommodate fundamental human nature, which is difficult to determine with certainty or is uncertain.

RESULTS AND DISCUSSIONS

Identify Supply Chain Activities using the SCOR Model

The identification of supply chain flow is carried out by interviews based on the SCOR approach starting from the Plan stage which consists of mapping activities of people's sugarcane land and private company sugarcane, assessment and production planning; Source which consists of dividing the number of regional supplies per day, making cutting and transport order (SPTA), and shipping sugar cane; Make which consists of grinding, refining, evaporation, crystallization, packaging, and warehouse; Delivery which consists of product auction and product collection by the buyer; Return which consists of returning the product.

In this study, which focuses on the tactical level of the sugar company, the identification of supply chain activities is carried out using SCOR level 1. The supply chain flow of the sugar company begins with the farmer group as a supplier, which then supplies raw sugar cane as the main ingredient for sugar production to the sugar company, then after the finished product will be purchased by collectors and then sold in retail so that it finally reaches consumers. In the supply chain flow, the farmer group and the sugar company play a role as focal elements that play an important role at the company's tactical level so that SCOR level 1 can be used to identify supply chain activities in sugar supply and production at the sugar company.

The supply chain flow of the sugar company begins with the planning stage by mapping the people's sugarcane fields and also the company's private sugarcane so that the area of land is known as the basis for estimating the amount of sugarcane harvest which determines the readiness of raw materials to start the milling period and this is what is used as the basis for the estimation, then the estimation process is carried out to estimate the yield of land expansion as the basis for production planning during the milling period. After the yield is known, production planning is carried out including the length of the milling period and also the daily milling capacity.

The next stage is the source with, the division of the amount of supply for each area per day for sugarcane farmers, namely the scheduling of deliveries and also the amount of deliveries for each area coordinated by the PL from the company, this is intended so that the process of supplying raw materials runs in an orderly manner, making a sugarcane delivery contract agreement with the farmers with SPTA (Cutting and Transport Order) which contains the amount of sugarcane loaded and the delivery date which will later be verified by the raw material receiving officer during loading and unloading after all agreements have been made, the delivery of raw materials is carried out based on the provisions stated in the SPTA.

After that, it enters the making stage, namely sugar production which begins with the milling process to reduce the size of the sugar cane and facilitate the squeezing process to obtain as much sap as possible, followed by purification which aims to separate the impurities in the sugar cane sap, then evaporation is carried out to evaporate the water content of the sap so that thick sap is formed after the thick sap is formed, crystallization is then carried out by cooking the thick sap so that sugar crystals are formed, the finished sugar is then wrapped in the packaging process, and then stored in the warehouse. After the production stage, the next stage is the delivery stage, namely the collection of products by buyers who have previously placed orders to the ordering section at the holding company of the sugar company or buyers who have purchased sugar from the auction system, and returns, namely the return of products by buyers if the product quality is not appropriate.

House of Risk

House of Risk phase 1 is the risk identification stage by identifying risk events and risk agents as well as severity, occurrence, and correlation values to find Aggregate Risk Potential (ARP) values so that a ranking of priority risk agents can be determined from which mitigation actions can then be formulated. The first stage was the identification of risk events and risk agents. The identification was carried out by interviewing expert judgment. A total of 17 Risk Events and 19 Risk Agents were obtained. Then each risk agent is given a code with the letter A which means Risk agent. The occurrence risk error estimation occurs when the calculation of yield at the beginning before the milling season begins does not match the milling season. This occurs due to the amount and quality of sugar cane decreasing during the harvest season so the calculation at the beginning does not match the reality in the field during the milling season.

Inaccurate production planning occurs due to uncertain weather and causes the harvest to not be maximized so that the estimated production capacity planned at the beginning is not implemented optimally, in addition this is also caused by the Human Error factor during the harvest or during production so the target determined at the beginning cannot be realized properly.

The risk of increasing raw material prices is a risk that can be detrimental to the company because it can increase the expenses needed to carry out production. This risk arises due to the transfer of partner farmers to other companies so that farmers who supply the company are reduced and the price of sugar cane will be more expensive if they look for new sugar cane farmers who are not in the partnership. The risk of excess daily raw materials can be detrimental because if the sugar cane raw material is not processed immediately, its quality will decrease and result in the sugar produced not being in accordance with the quality standards set, this risk occurs due to new farmers joining the partnership and a decrease in the price of sugar cane, this generally occurs when other factories have fulfilled their grinding capacity, but this rarely happens. The risk of raw materials not meeting standards occurs when the sugar cane supplied to the company is in poor condition such as lots of soil, gravel, and even burnt. This usually happens to non-partner farmers who find it difficult to supervise farmers in caring for their sugar cane, but it can also happen to partner farmers. The risk of foreign material in raw materials occurs due to miscoordination between employees and suppliers such as gravel, wooden blocks, or even crane chains that enter the mill when transporting sugar cane from the truck to the milling machine.

Steam and vacuum leaks occur in the production process, generally at the cooking station, this occurs because of the age of the machine and old machine parts so that their reliability is reduced. Machine damage is something that happens in sugar factories, this is caused not only by the age of the old machine but also by less-than-optimal machine maintenance before the milling season. The occurrence of delays in the production process is something that can result in losses due to inefficiency, this is caused by the late arrival of daily raw materials which results in the milling capacity not being met or even delaying milling, in addition, this can also be caused by a decrease in machine performance so that it is less able to work optimally or its capacity is reduced.

The occurrence of product quality risks that are not appropriate or not good is caused by a decrease in the quantity and quality of sugar cane so the quality of the product is also not optimal. In addition, the production process is not optimal, especially in the cooking section, namely the temperature or pressure that is not achieved so the production results are not optimal. This can also result in the failure of sugar crystallization as its worst impact and is closely related to a decrease in machine performance. The occurrence of congestion at the sugar channel opening is a risk that can cause inefficiency because this makes sugar unable to be carried to the next process, this is caused by sugar crust which causes congestion at the sugar channel opening which is not optimally cleaned. Damage to product packaging can be a loss for the company because the quality of the product cannot be maintained if the packaging is damaged, this is caused by damage to the packer machine and also human error so that the product is packaged poorly.

The risk of uneven product distribution is a risk that arises due to the increase in products on Java Island, which is generally prioritized by companies in meeting their demand. Delays in product collection by buyers can be detrimental to the company because if the product is stored for too long, its quality will decrease, this is caused by internal problems of buyers who are late in paying off payments. Delays in product collection by buyers occur due to buyers returning damaged products at the same time as taking new products, this makes the prepared transportation load often inadequate.

The Risk Event and Risk Agent obtained will then be used as the basis for designing a questionnaire based on impact and cause indicators which will later be used for Severity and Occurrence assessments as input at the Fuzzy stage. The assessment is carried out by expert judgment with a rating scale of 1-5.

Fuzzy Logic Implementation

Input and Output Fuzzy

The first step required in fuzzy input is to determine the input variables along with the universe of discussion or range of values permitted in the fuzzy input. The input variables in this study use impact indicators for risk events and causal indicators for risk agents. The next step is to determine the fuzzy set and membership value for each input variable. Examples of input variables, conversation universes, fuzzy sets and their membership values are presented in Table 1.

Table 1. Input Variables, Universe of Talks, Fuzzy Input, and Fuzzy Input Membership Function

Input	Semesta Pembicaraan	Nama Himpunan Fuzzy	Nilai Keanggotaan
Yield estimates are inaccurate	[0-5]	No Influence (TP)	[-0.5 0 1 1.5]
		Little Influence (PK)	[1 1.5 2 2.5]
		Medium Influence (PS)	[1.75 2.25 2.75 3.25]
Raw material supply estimates are inaccurate	[0-5]	High Influence (PT)	[2.5 3 3.5 4]
		Very High Influence (PST)	[3.5 4.5 5 6.5]

The output of fuzzy in this research is the severity value of the risk event and the occurrence value of the risk agent which is obtained from the input values of the impact and cause indicators. What needs to be done to get the output is to determine the output variable, conversation universe, fuzzy set, and also membership values for the fuzzy output. The following are examples of output variables, conversation universes, fuzzy sets, and also membership values for the fuzzy severity output shown in Table 2.

Table 2. Output Variables, Universes of Talk, Fuzzy Set, and Fuzzy Severity Output Membership Function

Output	Universes of Talk	Name of Fuzzy Set	Membership Function
A taxation error occurred		No impact (TB)	[-1 0 2 3]
		Small Impact (DK)	[2 3.5 5]
	[0-10]	Medium Impact (DS)	[3.5 5 6.5]
		High Impact (DT)	[5 6.5 8]
		Very High Impact (DST)	[7 9 10 13]

Fuzzy Rules

Based on the input and output variables, they are then made into rules or fuzzy rules. Fuzzy rules are made based on if-then rules. The following is an example of a risk event rule as follows:

1. If (Inaccurate production estimate is TP) and (Inaccurate raw material supply estimate is TP) then (A taxation error occurred is TB)
2. If (Inaccurate production estimate is TP) and (Inaccurate raw material supply estimate is PK) then (A taxation error occurred is TB)
3. If (Inaccurate production estimate is TP) and (Inaccurate raw material supply estimate is PS) then (A taxation error occurred is DK)
4. If (Inaccurate production estimate is TP) and (Inaccurate raw material supply estimate is PT) then (A taxation error occurred is DS)
5. If (Inaccurate production estimate is TP) and (Inaccurate raw material supply estimate is PST) then (A taxation error occurred is DS)
6. If (Inaccurate production estimate is PK) and (Inaccurate raw material supply estimate is TP) then (A taxation error occurred is TB)
7. If (Inaccurate production estimate is PK) and (Inaccurate raw material supply estimate is PK) then (A taxation error occurred is TB)
8. If (Inaccurate production estimate is PK) and (Inaccurate raw material supply estimate is PS) then (A taxation error occurred is DK)
9. If (Inaccurate production estimate is PK) and (Inaccurate raw material supply estimate is PT) then (A taxation error occurred is DS)
10. If (Inaccurate production estimate is PK) and (Inaccurate raw material supply estimate is PST) then (A taxation error occurred is DT)
11. If (Inaccurate production estimate is PS) and (Inaccurate raw material supply estimate is TP) then (A taxation error occurred is TB)

12. If (Inaccurate production estimate is PS) and (Inaccurate raw material supply estimate is PK) then (A taxation error occurred is DK)
13. If (Inaccurate production estimate is PS) and (Inaccurate raw material supply estimate is PS) then (A taxation error occurred is DS)
14. If (Inaccurate production estimate is PS) and (Inaccurate raw material supply estimate is PT) then (A taxation error occurred is DT)
15. If (Inaccurate production estimate is PS) and (Inaccurate raw material supply estimate is PST) then (A taxation error occurred is DT)
16. If (Inaccurate production estimate is PT) and (Inaccurate raw material supply estimate is TP) then (A taxation error occurred is DK)
17. If (Inaccurate production estimate is PT) and (Inaccurate raw material supply estimate is PK) then (A taxation error occurred is DS)
18. If (Inaccurate production estimate is PT) and (Inaccurate raw material supply estimate is PS) then (A taxation error occurred is DT)
19. If (Inaccurate production estimate is PT) and (Inaccurate raw material supply estimate is PT) then (A taxation error occurred is DT)
20. If (Inaccurate production estimate is PT) and (Inaccurate raw material supply estimate is PST) then (A taxation error occurred is DST)
21. If (Inaccurate production estimate is PST) and (Inaccurate raw material supply estimate is TP) then (A taxation error occurred is DS)
22. If (Inaccurate production estimate is PST) and (Inaccurate raw material supply estimate is PK) then (A taxation error occurred is DS)
23. If (Inaccurate production estimate is PST) and (Inaccurate raw material supply estimate is PS) then (A taxation error occurred is DT)
24. If (Inaccurate production estimate is PST) and (Inaccurate raw material supply estimate is PT) then (A taxation error occurred is DT)
25. If (Inaccurate production estimate is PST) and (Inaccurate raw material supply estimate is PST) then (A taxation error occurred is DST)

Correlation Identification among Risk Event and Risk Agent

Correlation assessment is carried out by expert judgment with values of 0 (no correlation), 1 (small correlation), 3 (medium correlation), and 9 (high correlation). The next step is calculating the ARP value, the ARP calculation is the multiplication of the fuzzy occurrence value multiplied by the number of fuzzy severity values multiplied by the correlation value.

Based on the calculation of the ARP value, a ranking of risk agents with the largest ARP value to the smallest is then made. This is done to find out which risk agents should be prioritized. Apart from that, the percentage of each risk agent and also the cumulative percentage are calculated as in Table 3.

Table 3. Risk Event, Risk Agent, ARP, Cumulative Percentage and Risk Agent Ranking

	Risk Event	Risk Agent	Code	ARP	% Cumulative	Rank
E1	Taxation error	The quantity and quality of sugar cane is decreasing	A1	1881,89	15,51%	1
E2	Inaccurate production planning	Unpredictable weather	A2	1795,74	30,31%	2
		Human Error	A4	921,87	57,77%	5
E3	Increase in raw material prices	Transfer of partner farmers to other companies	A3	1382,789	41,71%	3
		Poor road access when harvesting sugar cane	A5	646,588	89,14%	10
E4	Delays in raw materials	The presence of new farmers joining the partnership exceeds planning				14
			A6	176,25	97,56%	
E5	Excess daily raw materials	Decline in sugar cane prices	A7	176,3	96,10%	13
E6	Raw materials do not meet standards	Lack of supervision of suppliers	A9	282,2495	94,65%	12
E7	The presence of foreign material in raw materials	Missing coordination between the employee on duty and the sugar cane supplier	A8	93,347	99,27%	16
E8	Steam and vacuum leaks	The lifespan of the machine or machine parts is old	A10	704,0712	83,81%	9
E9	Machine failure	Maintenance is less than optimal	A11	386,9	92,32%	11
E10	Delay in the production process The quality of the product produced is not appropriate	Daily raw material delays	A12	1027,53	50,18%	4
		Decreased engine performance	A13	709,9	78,00%	8
E11	Failure of crystallization of sugar There is a blockage at the opening of the sugar channel	Failure to achieve temperature or pressure in the production process	A14	863,395	72,15%	7
		The quantity and quality of sugar cane is decreasing	A1			
E12	Damaged product packaging Uneven product distribution	Failure to achieve temperature or pressure in the production process	A14			
		Decreased engine performance	A13			
E13	Delay in picking up the product by the buyer	Sugar crust that causes opening jams	A15	881,1875	65,04%	6
E14	Lack of buyer's load capacity when picking up the product Delay in the production process	The packing machine is having problems	A16	114	98,50%	15
		Human Error	A4			
E15	The quality of the product produced is not appropriate	Increasing demand for products on the island of Java	A17	40,6118	99,60%	17
E16	Failure of crystallization of sugar	Buyer's internal problems	A18	34,5376	99,89%	18
E17	There is a blockage at the opening of the sugar channel	Mistakes in estimates of product loads by buyers	A19	13,95	100,00%	19

This data will then be presented in the form of a Pareto Diagram so that it can be more concise and informative in conveying the existing information. Based on the Pareto rule which states the 80:20 provision, risk agents will be taken who contribute a cumulative percentage up to 80%, so that 9 risk agents are prioritized or the most important of which is (A1) The quantity and quality of sugar cane is decreasing, like most of the problems that arise. Most sugar factories in Indonesia face problems with the quality of sugar cane and also its quantity. Many things can affect the quality and quantity of the sugar cane harvest. One of the impacts of inefficiency in the on-farm and off-farm sectors is the low yield and quality of the sugar cane crop, which greatly influences the average sugar crystals per hectare (Maghfiroh et al., 2017); (A2) uncertain weather, the influence of weather and climate on farming productivity has the largest percentage distribution in the influential to very influential categories. For farmers, climate change is mainly related to irregular rainfall patterns, it seems reasonable because in recent years, during field surveys, farmers recalled poor crop yields due to late, irregular, and insufficient rainfall (Maharani & Hanani, 2023).

(A3) The movement of partner farmers to other companies, sugar companies offering selling prices for sugar cane is one of the factors that influences the satisfaction and loyalty of sugar cane farmers (Saufi, 2019). In buying and selling sugar cane plants, it is the sugar entrepreneur who determines the price of the sugar cane to the sugar cane farmers who want to sell their sugar cane plants (Rozzaq, 2022). Generally, sugar cane farmers will prefer companies that offer higher prices so they switch to other companies; (A12) Daily raw material delays, the sugar company's daily production is carried out on a large scale so it requires large production costs. Delays in the delivery of raw materials can cause milling capacity not to be optimal or can even cause milling to stop and this can cause big losses to the company. Delays in the delivery of raw materials also have the potential to cause the production process to stop in the short term, which could be very detrimental to the company (Romanto & Handoko, 2022).

(A4) Human error, can be defined as an inappropriate human decision or behavior that reduces or has the potential to reduce the effectiveness, safety or performance of a system. Mistakes or errors made by operators and one of the causes of this occurrence are a bad environment, complex tasks, lack of proper procedures, operator indifference and poor operator selection and training (Rohmadhon & Yuamita, 2023); (A15) Sugar crust causing opening jam, on the sugar company, especially at cooking stations, when sugar crystallization occurs, crusts sometimes appear at the openings of the sugar channels. This causes the channels to become obstructed or clogged due to the high Brix content of the sugar. The brix unit is a unit used to indicate the level of sugar dissolved in a solution. The higher the Brix degree, the thicker the liquid sugar (Sjarif et al., 2021); (A14) Failure to achieve temperature or pressure in the production process, in the sugar company, temperature is obtained from the boiler, when the targeted temperature is not reached, it indicates a problem with the boiler (Novi, 2022). Several problems can occur in the factory when the temperature is not reached in the primary heater, such as the lack of temperature from the bleeding steam.

(A13) Decreased engine performance, decreased engine performance still often occurs in sugar company, especially the ripening station which is closely related to chemical processes as well as temperature and pressure. This condition may cause the production process to slow down and cause losses (Pratama, 2022). The problem with many sugar factories is that most of the equipment and production machines are old so the effectiveness has decreased. A decrease in effectiveness can reduce sugar production figures or increase the basic price of sugar from a factory and hamper the process which then impacts availability or reduces demand fulfillment rates; (A10) The lifespan of machines or machine parts is long, sugar factory industrial machines are relics of the colonial era, considered too old (Pratama, 2022). As a solution to this condition, the sugar company always rejuvenates the engine when it is not the milling season so that the existing engine can continue to function with good performance, but engine damage still occurs because all components have their limitations. All components have a life limit, the number of failures that commonly occur follows a bathtub curve. This curve describes the service life of a tool, where the longer it is used, the higher the maintenance costs.

House of Risk Phase 2

House of Risk phase 2 focuses on handling or preventive action (PA) for Risk Agents. The initial stage in HOR phase 2 is to identify preventive actions for priority risk agents obtained from HOR phase 1. The next step is to assess the correlation between preventive actions and priority risk agents and can be continued by calculating the Total Effectiveness value for each strategy. After that, the degree of difficulty of implementing preventive action is measured and then the ratio of Total Effectiveness and level of difficulty of preventive action is calculated. The final step in HOR phase 2 is determining the priority ranking of each mitigation strategy (preventive action).

Identify Preventive Action (PA)

In this phase, preventive action will be formulated with the hope that this mitigation action can prevent the occurrence of risk agents and risk events. Preventive action is formulated by considering input from expert judgment.

Identify the Correlation Value of PA with Risk Agent and Calculate the Value of the Degree of Effectiveness of Preventive Action (TEk)

The correlation assessment is carried out by expert judgment with a value of 0 if there is no relationship, 1 if the relationship is small, 3 if the relationship is medium, and 9 if the relationship is high. This assessment will later be used to calculate the value of the degree of effectiveness of preventive action. Next, the Tech value is calculated. The TEk value of all preventive actions is shown in Table 4.

Table 4. Assess the Level of Effectiveness (TEk) Every Preventive Action

Code	*Preventive Actions*	TEk Value
P1	Mentoring sugarcane care for partner farmers	44017,1
P2	Improved farming business management	48626,36
P3	Providing climate field schools	40329,63
P4	Weather prediction	36181,26
P5	Provide rewards and punishment	9710,801
P6	Transport route analysis and delivery scheduling	25138,93
P7	Conduct regular training	17772,49
P8	Scheduling regular descaling	13354,64
P9	Carrying out Total Productive Maintenance	18881,36
P10	Competitive price offer	24505,52

Identification of Degrees of Difficulty (Dk) and Calculation of values Effectiveness to Difficulty (ETD_k)

The assessment of the degree of difficulty is carried out by expert judgment with a score of 3 if it is easy to apply, a score of 4 if the level of difficulty is medium, and 5 if the level of difficulty is high. After the ETDk value is known and the priority Mitigation Action is known, the ETDk value of all preventive actions and their ranking are shown in Table 5.

Table 5. Score Effectiveness to Difficulty in Every Preventive Actions (ETD_k)

Code	*Preventive Actions*	ETD_k Value
P1	Mentoring sugarcane care for partner farmers	14.672,37
P2	Improved farming business management	12.156,59
P4	Weather prediction	9.045,315
P3	Providing climate field schools	8.065,925
P6	Transport route analysis and delivery scheduling	6.284,731
P10	Competitive price offer	6.126,379

continued on following page

Table 5. Continued

Code	*Preventive Actions*	ETD_k Value
P9	Carrying out Total Productive Maintenance	4.720,34
P7	Conduct regular training	4.443,123
P8	Scheduling regular descaling	3.338,661
P5	Provide rewards and punishment	2.427,7

In terms of mentoring or guiding sugar cane farmers (P1) (Maghfiroh et al., 2017) proposes consolidating sugar cane planting areas while (Irawan et al., 2023) recommends the use of superior sugar cane varieties and optimizing sprouting, guidance can also be given regarding handling pests and weeds during the growing period. sugarcane. This can make it easier for companies to control quality. Farming business management including felling and hauling (P2) is one of the critical points in sugarcane cultivation. As a result of improper felling management, sugar cane that has high yield potential will lose a lot of sugar because it is milled too late (Maghfiroh et al., 2017). In other words, a long sugarcane farming effort for one year of planting will be in vain within 1-2 days due to errors in the cutting and transport process. Based on research (Dyatmiko, 2019), farmers have had an ancient method for predicting the weather using *pranoto mongso*. However, a more precise weather prediction method (P4) is needed, using data from the Meteorology, Climatology and Geophysics Agency (BMKG) or you can also forecast the weather using the Weather Research and Forecasting (WRF) model with an error percentage value below 4%. (Sulistiyono et al., 2023).

Climate field school (P3) is an activity that gives groups the opportunity to learn how to increase productivity by collaborating on agro-climate knowledge and then applying it directly. During climate field school activities, farmers learn about crop management, controlling pests and weeds, observing the environment around the cultivated land, measuring temperatures and analyzing soil conditions (Sari & Yusnita Arvianti, 2018). Transport route analysis (P6) can be carried out using the SATURN application (Simulation and Assignment of Traffic on Urban Road Network, such as research conducted by (Naufal & Triana, 2016). Competitive price offers (P10) need to be made to retain partner farmers apart from the approach mentoring but also paying attention to and adjusting the company's production planning budget. In accordance with research (Rozzaq, 2022) which argues that sugar cane farmers' income is aimed at the welfare of their families and to meet their needs. TPM (P9) is a maintenance program that involves all parties in a companies can work together to eliminate breakdowns, reduce downtime and maximize utility, production activities, and the quality of the production produced (Yudha, 2019).

Based on the research by (Pratama, 2022), it can be seen that there is an influence between training (P7) on the performance of the sugar company employees, in this case regarding the quality, quantity and ability of employees to use working time which has increased. Actions or solutions that must be taken by companies to overcome crusting include scheduling regular cleaning of tools and machines, including scale (P8) (Mahardika, 2023). (P5) Reward is an award to employees for improving performance. So, it can be concluded that rewards are employee performance appreciation given for performing well. Punishment is a step taken to provide education by giving punishments ranging from light to severe. Companies can implement a strategy of giving punishment in stages. By providing punishment, it is hoped that it will increase work morale (Wicaksono et al., 2023).

CONCLUSIONS

Based on the analysis, the study concludes that the SCOR method successfully identifies 17 risk events and 19 risk agents in the company. The results of the House of Risk phase 1 analysis finds out 9 priority risk agents so that 10 risk management steps or preventive actions have been formulated in HOR phase 2. The preventive actions are: mentoring sugar cane care for partner farmers, improving farming business management, weather prediction, providing climate field schools, analyzing transport routes and scheduling deliveries, offering competitive prices, carrying out total productive maintenance, carrying out routine training, scheduling regular descaling, providing rewards and punishment.

REFERENCES

APICS, S. C. C. (2015). Supply Chain Operations Reference Model: SCOR Version 11.0. *Supply Chain Council.*

Arifudin, O., Wahrudin, U., & Rusmana, F. D. (2020). *Manajemen risiko.* Penerbit Widina.

Bolstorff, P., & Rosenbaum, R. G. (2007). *Supply chain excellence: a handbook for dramatic improvement using the SCOR model.* AMACOM/American Management Association.

Cahyani, Z. D., Pribadi, S. R. W., & Baihaqi, I. (2016). Studi Implementasi Model House of Risk (HOR) untuk Mitigasi risiko keterlambatan Material dan komponen Impor pada pembangunan kapal baru. *Jurnal Teknik ITS, 5*(2).

Dyatmiko, W. W. (2019). *Sekolah Lapang Iklim Sebagai Upaya Menginisiasi Keberdayaan Petani Tebu Desa Wonokerto Kecamatan Bantur Kabupaten Malang.* Universitas Brawijaya.

Heizer, J., Render, B., & Munson, C. (2020). *Operations management: Sustainability and supply chain management.* Pearson.

Irawan, K. A., Setyo, B., & Suhaili, S. (2023). Keragaman Morfologi Pertumbuhan 7 Klon dan 2 Varietas Tanaman Tebu (Saccharum officinarum L.) di PT Perkebunan Nusantara X Ploso Klaten-Kediri. *Gema Agro, 28*(1), 42–51. DOI: 10.22225/ga.28.1.6634.42-51

Jaya, R., Yusriana, Y., & Fitria, E. (2021). Review manajemen rantai pasok produk pertanian berkelanjutan: Konseptual, isu terkini, dan penelitian mendatang. *Jurnal Ilmu Pertanian Indonesia, 26*(1), 78–91. DOI: 10.18343/jipi.26.1.78

Magdalena, R., & Vannie, V. (2019). Analisis risiko supply chain dengan model house of risk (HOR) pada PT Tatalogam Lestari. *J@ Ti Undip. Jurnal Teknik Industri, 14*(2), 53–62.

Maghfiroh, I. S., Setyawati, I. K., & Wibowo, R. (2017). Mutu tebu industri gula di Indonesia. *Seminar Nasional Pembangunan Pertanian*, 94–100.

Maharani, I. M., Hanani, N., & Syafrial, S. (2023). Bagaimana Petani Dalam Pengelolaan Risiko? Persepsi Dan Perilaku Petani Tebu Di Jawa Timur. [Journal of Social and Agricultural Economics]. *JSEP, 16*(1), 25–40. DOI: 10.19184/jsep.v16i1.38094

Mahardika, E. W. (2023). *Penerapan Standard Operating Procedure (SOP) Pengemasan dan Penyimpanan Produk Gula Retail pada PT Sinergi Gula Nusantara Unit Pabrik Gula Glenmore.*

Muhammad, M. R., & Sumarauw, J. S. B. (2014). Evaluasi kinerja manajemen rantai pasok pada pemasok daging ayam, Jeky PM. *Jurnal EMBA: Jurnal Riset Ekonomi, Manajemen, Bisnis Dan Akuntansi, 2*(4).

Muharja, M., Darmayanti, R. F., Widjaja, A., Firmansyah, A. A., & Karima, N. (2022). Simulasi Kenaikan Kapasitas Produksi Gula pada Proses Karbonatasi di PT. Industri Gula Glenmore Menggunakan Perangkat Lunak Aspen Plus. [Jurnal Sains Dan Teknologi]. *JST, 11*(1), 125–131.

Nadhira, A. H. K., Oktiarso, T., & Harsoyo, T. D. (2019). Manajemen risiko rantai pasok produk sayuran menggunakan metode supply chain operation reference dan model house of risk. *Kurawal-Jurnal Teknologi. Informasi Dan Industri, 2*(2), 101–117.

Naufal, F., & Triana, S. (2016). Simulasi Pemodelan Transportasi pada Jaringan Jalan Menggunakan Aplikasi SATURN. *RekaRacana: Jurnal Teknil Sipil, 2*(1), 72–82.

Norrman, A., & Jansson, U. (2004). Ericsson's proactive supply chain risk management approach after a serious sub-supplier accident. *International Journal of Physical Distribution & Logistics Management, 34*(5), 434–456. DOI: 10.1108/09600030410545463

Novi, W. R. (2022). *Pengenalan Alat Proses Pengolahan Gula Di PT. Gendhis Multi Manis (GMM)-BULOG.* Politeknik LPP Yogyakarta.

Nyoman Pujawan, I., & Geraldin, L. H. (2009). House of risk: A model for proactive supply chain risk management. *Business Process Management Journal, 15*(6), 953–967. DOI: 10.1108/14637150911003801

Pratama, P. A. S. A. (2022). *Analisis Proses Produksi di Stasiun Gilingan Tebu Menggunakan Metode Overall Equipment Effectiveness (OEE) di PT Industri Gula Glenmore.*

Puji, A. A. (2018). *Analisis Mitigasi Risiko Rantai Pasok dengan Integrasi Fuzzy Logic, House of Risk dan AHP (Studi Kasus pada CV. Multiguna).* Universitas Islam Indonesia.

Rakadhitya, R., Hartono, N., & Laurence, L. (2019). Studi kasus mitigasi risiko rantai pasok dengan integrasi house of risk dan fuzzy logic pada PT X. *Journal of Integrated System, 2*(2), 192–207. DOI: 10.28932/jis.v2i2.1974

Rohmadhon, E., & Yuamita, F. (2023). Analisis Human Error untuk Mengurangi Kecelakaan Kerja pada Stasiun Penggilingan PG. Madukismo Menggunakan Metode SHERPA dan HEART. *Jurnal Cakrawala Ilmiah*, *2*(11), 4129–4140. DOI: 10.53625/jcijurnalcakrawalailmiah.v2i11.6117

Romanto, F., & Handoko, F. (2022). Metode Supply Chain Operation Reference (SCOR) Sebagai Analisis Kinerja Manajemen Rantai Pasok di Pabrik Gula Pandjie. *Jurnal Valtech*, *5*(1), 107–113.

Rozzaq, A. (2022). *Hubungan Patron Klien Petani Tebu dengan Pengusaha Gula Tebu*.

Russell, R. S., & Taylor, B. W. (2019). *Operations and supply chain management*. John Wiley & Sons.

Sari, D., & Yusnita Arvianti, E. (2018). Pembangunan Pertanian (Agriculture Development). *Available at SSRN* 3110561.

Saufi, M. (2019). ANALISA Faktor-Faktor yang Mempengaruhi Kepuasan Petani Tebu sebagai Upaya Menigkatkan Loyalitas terhadap Pabrik Gula Pesantren Baru. *REVITALISASI: Jurnal Ilmu Manajemen*, *6*(3), 19–26.

Sjarif, S. R., Nuryadi, A. M., Sulistiorini, J., & Sukron, A. (2021). Penambahan Glukosa Dan Pengaruh Derajat Brix Untuk Menghambat Proses Kristalisasi Pada Produk Gula Cair Nira Aren. *Jurnal Penelitian Teknologi Industri*, *13*(1), 27–36.

Sulistiyono, W., Zuliandry, M. I. R., & Haryanto, Y. D. (2023). Uji Verifikasi Data Permukaan dan Indeks Udara atas Hasil Model WRF dengan Data Observasi Stasiun Meteorologi Sultan Hasanudin:(Studi Kasus: 6 Desember 2021). *OPTIKA: Jurnal Pendidikan Fisika*, *7*(1), 10–22. DOI: 10.37478/optika.v7i1.2354

Syamil, A., Subawa, S., Budaya, I., Munizu, M., Darmayanti, N. L., Fahmi, M. A., Wanda, S. S., Murwani, I. A., Utami, F. N., & Dulame, I. M. (2023). *Manajemen Rantai Pasok*. PT. Sonpedia Publishing Indonesia.

Ulfah, M., Maarif, M. S., & Sukardi, S. R. (2016). Analisis dan perbaikan manajemen risiko rantai pasok gula rafinasi dengan Pendekatan house of risk. *Jurnal Teknologi Industri Pertanian, 26*(1).

Wafi, N. N. (2017). *Identifikasi Dan Strategi Mitigasi Risiko Rantai Pasok Komoditas Kakao Menggunakan Metode Fuzzy-House Of Risk (Fuzzy-Hor)(Studi Kasus Di PT. Kampung Coklat Blitar)*. Universitas Brawijaya.

Wicaksono, R. S., Pardiman, P., & Rahmawati, R. (2023). Pengaruh Punishment, Reward, dan Motivasi Kerja Terhadap Kinerja Karyawan Pada PT. PG Rajawali 1. *E-JRM: Elektronik Jurnal Riset Manajemen*, *12*(02), 1335–1344.

Yudha, B. S. (2019). *Evaluasi 8 Pilar TPM (Total Productive Maintenance) dan Pengaruhnya Terhadap Kinerja Manufaktur (OEE-Overall Equipment Effectiveness dan Waste)(Studi kasus: PT. XYZ Divisi Biskuit)*. http://unugha.ac.id

ADDITIONAL READING

Chopra, S., & Meindl, P. (2013). *Supply Chain Management: Strategy, Planning, and Operation* (5th ed.). Pearson Prentice Hall.

Heizer, J., Render, B., & Munson, C. (2020). *Operations management: Sustainability and supply chain management*. Pearson.

Roghanian, E., & Mojibian, F. (2015). Using fuzzy FMEA and fuzzy logic in project risk management. [IJMS]. *Iranian Journal of Management Studies*, *8*(3), 373–395.

KEY TERMS AND DEFINITIONS

Fuzzy Rules: rules that resulted from the fuzzification process

Preventive Action: set of actions that are formulated by considering input from expert judges for each risk event

Risk Agent: causes of the emergence of Risk Events.

Risk Event: a condition in which a danger or error may occur.

Compilation of References

Abate, D. A., Goodman, M. E., Gorman, M. J., & Goury, R. (2015). *A global guide to background checks in Asia*. The Mayer Brown Practices.

Adli, A., & Chin, W. L. (2021). Homestay Accommodation in Brunei Darussalam: An exploratory study. *Southeast Asia: A Multidisciplinary Journal, 21*(1), 15-29.

Afşar, M. (2009). Türkiye'de Eğitim Yatırımları ve Ekonomik Büyüme İlişkisi.

Afzal, M., Rehman, H. U., Farooq, M. S., & Sarwar, K. (2011). Education and economic growth in Pakistan: A cointegration and causality analysis. *International Journal of Educational Research, 50*(5-6), 321–335. DOI: 10.1016/j.ijer.2011.10.004

Agnew, J. (2011). Space and place. *Handbook of geographical knowledge, 2011*, 316-331.

Ahmad, A. (2013). The constraints of tourism development for a cultural heritage destination: The case of Kampong Ayer (Water Village) in Brunei Darussalam. *Tourism Management Perspectives, 8*, 106–113. DOI: 10.1016/j.tmp.2013.09.002

Aissani, R., Abdalla, R. A. Q., Taha, S., & Al Adwan, M. N. (2023). Artificial Intelligence Tools in Media and Journalism: Roles and Concerns, *International Conference on Multimedia Computing, Networking and Applications (MCNA)*, Valencia, Spain, 2023, pp. 19-26, DOI: 10.1109/MCNA59361.2023.10185738

Ajzen, I. (1991). The theory of planned behavior. *Organizational Behavior and Human Decision Processes, 50*(2), 179–211.

Ajzen, I., & Fishbein, M. (1980). *Understanding attitudes and predicting social behavior*. Prentice-Hall.

Akça, F. (2014). *Beşeri sermayenin ekonomik büyümeye etkisi: Türkiye üzerine bir uygulama* (Master's thesis, Sosyal Bilimler Enstitüsü).

Akhu-Zaheya, L. & S. (2018). The effect of short message system (SMS) reminder on adherence to a healthy diet, medication, and cessation of smoking among adult patients with cardiovascular diseases. *International Journal of Medical Informatics*. PMID: 28034414

Aksoy, M. (2019). *Beşeri Sermaye, Sosyal Sermaye ve Öz Yeterliliğin Restoran Performansına Etkisi* (Master's thesis).

Akyüz, Y. (1982). *Türk eğitim tarihi:(başlangıçtan 1982'ye)* (Vol. 114). Ankara Üniversitesi Eğitim Bilimleri Fakültesi.

Ali, M. (2023). Deciphering Mobile Journalism: An All-Inclusive Definition of Mobile Journalism in the Modern Era. *Global Media Journal, 21*, 1–9. https://www.researchgate.net/publication/377239569_Deciphering_Mobile_Journalism_An_All-Inclusive_Definition_of_Mobile_Journalism_in_the_Modern_Era

Aljazairi, S., & Ekman, M. (2016). Robot Journalism: Threat or an opportunity. M.A. thesis. School of Humanities, Education and Social Sciences, Örebro University. https://www.diva-portal.org/smash/get/diva2:938024/FULLTEXT01.pdf

Alkandi, I. G., Khan, M. A., Fallatah, M., Alabdulhadi, A., Alanizan, S., & Alharbi, J. (2023). The Impact of Incentive and Reward Systems on Employee Performance in the Saudi Primary, Secondary, and Tertiary Industrial Sectors: A Mediating Influence of Employee Job Satisfaction. *Sustainability (Basel), 15*(4), 3415. Advance online publication. DOI: 10.3390/su15043415

Alkire, S., & Foster, J. (2011). Counting and Multidimensional Poverty Measurement. *Journal of Public Economics, 95*(7/8), 476–487. DOI: 10.1016/j.jpubeco.2010.11.006

Alkire, S., & Sanots, M. E. (2014). Measuring Acute Poverty in the Developing World: Robustness and Scope of the Multidimensional Poverty Index. *World Development, 59*, 251–274. DOI: 10.1016/j.worlddev.2014.01.026

Allen, R. C. (2017). Absolute Poverty: When Necessity Displaces Desire. *The American Economic Review, 107*(12), 3690–3721. DOI: 10.1257/aer.20161080

Alston, G. L., Marsh, W., Castleberry, A. N., Kelley, K. A., & Boyce, E. G. (2019). Pharmacists opinions of the value of specific applicant attributes in hiring decisions for entry-level pharmacists. *Research in Social & Administrative Pharmacy, 15*(5), 536–545. DOI: 10.1016/j.sapharm.2018.07.004 PMID: 30006061

Altmann, D., Borrow, R., Fooks, T., Ishii, K., Lua, L. H. L., Sadarangani, S. P., Barrett, N., Donau, O., Riems, M. B. G., Aurora, A. D., & Geneva, P. D. (2021). Editorial Board/Aims and Scope. *Vaccine, 39*(17), IFC. DOI: 10.1016/S0264-410X(21)00412-6

Alvaredo, F., Chancel, L., Piketty, T., Saez, E., & Zucman, G. (2018). *World Inequality Report*. WIL. DOI: 10.4159/9780674984769

Alves, I. R., Mesquita, E., Caneppele, N. R., & Martins, F. S. (2025). Beyond practicing: understanding the influence of ESG perceptions on employee retention. *Management Research*. Vol. ahead-of-print No. ahead-of-print. https://doi.org/DOI: 10.1108/MRJIAM-06-2024-1562

Anand, S., & Sen, A. (1994). *Sustainable Human Development: Concepts and Priorities*. UNDP Human Development Report Office.

Angler, M. (2014). Wearable Devices: Revolutionising Mobile Journalism Again. DOI: 10.13140/RG.2.1.2098.9685

Ann, S., & Baumann, O. (2023). Psychological mechanisms and interventions directed at vaccination attitudes. *Frontiers in Sociology*, *8*, 1076015. Advance online publication. DOI: 10.3389/fsoc.2023.1076015 PMID: 36844879

Antonelli Incalzi, R., Trevisan, C., Del Signore, S., Volpato, S., Fumagalli, S., Monzani, F., Bellelli, G., Gareri, P., Mossello, E., Malara, A., Coin, A., Zia, G., & Ranhoff, A. H. (2021). Are vaccines against COVID-19 tailored to the most vulnerable people? *Vaccine*, *39*(17), 2325–2327. DOI: 10.1016/j.vaccine.2021.03.066 PMID: 33810907

Anymind Group. (2023). Case study: Marketing strategy in Vietnam. https://anymindgroup.com/vi/news/case-study/3621/

APICS, S. C. C. (2015). Supply Chain Operations Reference Model: SCOR Version 11.0. *Supply Chain Council*.

Appadurai, A. (Ed.). (1988). *The social life of things: Commodities in cultural perspective*. Cambridge University Press.

Arifudin, O., Wahrudin, U., & Rusmana, F. D. (2020). *Manajemen risiko*. Penerbit Widina.

Arslan, Ü. (2011). Siyasi istikrarsizlik ve ekonomik performans: Türkiye örneği.

Arslan, M. L. (2011). Devletin iktisadi büyümedeki rolü. *Bilgi Ekonomisi ve Yönetimi Dergisi*, *6*(2), 160–175.

Ashata, Godwin & Extension, Kiu Publication. (2024). Digital Dynamics: Investigating the Impact of Social Media on Sexual Behavior. IDOSR JOURNAL OF COMMUNICATION AND ENGLISH, 9, 1-6, .DOI: 10.59298/IDOSR/JCE/92.16.202412

Ashby, J. A. (1987). The effects of different types of farmer participation on the management of on-farm trials. *Agricultural Administration and Extension*, *25*(4), 235–252. DOI: 10.1016/0269-7475(87)90079-1

Assembly, U. G. (2007). United Nations declaration on the rights of indigenous peoples. *UN Wash*, *12*, 1–18.

Azalie, I. A., & Yong, G. Y. V. (2022). *Heritage industry as a conservation strategy for Kampong Ayer*. The Brunei Museums Journal.

Baah, C., Opoku-Agyeman, D., Acquah, I. S. K., Agyabeng-Mensah, Y., Afum, E., Faibil, D., & Abdoulaye, F. A. M. (2021). Examining the correlations between stakeholder pressures, green production practices, firm reputation, environmental and financial performance: Evidence from manufacturing SMEs. *Sustainable Production and Consumption*, *27*, 100–114. DOI: 10.1016/j.spc.2020.10.015

Bakar, H. T. B. H. A. (2018). Pembinaan dan Penyediaan Rumah Menaik Taraf Kampong Ayer di Negara Brunei Darussalam. *SOSIOHUMANIKA*, *11*(1), 33–46.

Bakar, H. T. B. H. A. (2018). The Residents of Kampong Ayer, 1906–1940: The Activities of Pengalu, Padian, and Handiwork. *TAWARIKH*, *9*(2), 151–158.

Baker, S. E., & Edwards, R. (2012). How many qualitative interviews is enough? Expert voices and early career reflections on sampling and cases in qualitative research. National Centre for Research Methods. https://eprints.ncrm.ac.uk/2273/4/how_many_interviews.pdf

Bakker, A. B., & Demerouti, E. (2007). The Job Demands-Resources model: State of the art. *Journal of Managerial Psychology*, *22*(3), 309–328. DOI: 10.1108/02683940710733115

Ballester-Arnal, R., García-Barba, M., Castro-Calvo, J., Giménez-García, C., & Gil-Llario, M. D. (2023). Pornography Consumption in People of Different Age Groups: An Analysis Based on Gender, Contents, and Consequences. *Sexuality Research & Social Policy*, *20*(2), 766–779. DOI: 10.1007/s13178-022-00720-z

Bandura, A. (1997). *Self-efficacy: The exercise of control*. W. H. Freeman.

Ba, Q. X., Lu, D. J., Kuo, W. H. J., & Lai, P. H. (2018). Traditional farming and sustainable development of an indigenous community in the mountain area—A case study of Wutai village in Taiwan. *Sustainability (Basel)*, *10*(10), 3370. DOI: 10.3390/su10103370

Barro, R. J. (2014). [Human Capital and Growth), Beşeri Sermaye ve Büyüme. *Journal of Economics and Political Economy*, *1*(2), 351–358.

Bawa, A. S., & Anilakumar, K. R. (2013). Genetically modified foods: Safety, risks and public concerns—a review. *Journal of Food Science and Technology*, *50*(6), 1035–1046. DOI: 10.1007/s13197-012-0899-1 PMID: 24426015

Baykal, E. (2020). Digital era and new methods for employee recruitment. In *Handbook of Research on Strategic Fit and Design in Business Ecosystems* (pp. 412–430). IGI Global. DOI: 10.4018/978-1-7998-1125-1.ch018

Bayong, D., Bawuah, B., & Amoah, E. (2024). Advancing environmental, social, and governance disclosure in emerging economies: Does regulatory environment and ownership structure matter? *SN Business & Economics*, *5*(1), 11. DOI: 10.1007/s43546-024-00766-8

B-Company. (2023). Healthy drinks in Vietnam: Current situation and growth potential. https://b-company.jp/healthy-drinks-in-vietnam-current-situation-and-growth-potential/

Beck, A. T. (1987). *Cognitive therapy of depression*. Guilford Press.

Beckett, C. (2023). Generating change: How newsrooms are using AI in 2023. JournalismAI, London School of Economics and Political Science (LSE). Supported by the Google News Initiative. https://blog.google/technology/ai/how-ai-is-generating-change-in-newsrooms-worldwide

Belle, D., & Bullock, H. E. (2023). *The Psychology of Poverty, Wealth, and Economic Inequality*. Cambridge University Press.

Bellon, M. R., Dulloo, E., Sardos, J., Thormann, I., & Burdon, J. J. (2017). In situ conservation—Harnessing natural and human-derived evolutionary forces to ensure future crop adaptation. *Evolutionary Applications*, *10*(10), 965–977. DOI: 10.1111/eva.12521 PMID: 29151853

Bem, S. (1981). Gender Schema Theory: A Cognitive Account of Sex Typing. *Psychological Review*, *88*(4), 354–364. DOI: 10.1037/0033-295X.88.4.354

Berg, J. (2015). Labour market institutions: the building blocks of just societies. In *Labour Markets, Institutions and Inequality* (pp. 1–36). Edward Elgar Publishing. DOI: 10.4337/9781784712105.00007

Bhattacharya, S. (2014). Bioprospecting, biopiracy and food security in India: The emerging sides of neoliberalism. *International Letters of Social and Humanistic Sciences*, *23*(12), 49–56. DOI: 10.18052/www.scipress.com/ILSHS.23.49

Birinci, E. (2015). *AR-GE harcamalarının ekonomik büyüme üzerine etkisi: İçsel büyüme modeli zaman serisi analizi* (Master's thesis, Sosyal Bilimler Enstitüsü).

Bisht, I. S., Rana, J. C., Yadav, R., & Ahlawat, S. P. (2020). Mainstreaming agricultural biodiversity in traditional production landscapes for sustainable development: The Indian scenario. *Sustainability (Basel), 12*(24), 10690. DOI: 10.3390/su122410690

Bolstorff, P., & Rosenbaum, R. G. (2007). *Supply chain excellence: a handbook for dramatic improvement using the SCOR model.* AMACOM/American Management Association.

Borowiak, C. (2004). Farmers' rights: Intellectual property regimes and the struggle over seeds. *Politics & Society, 32*(4), 511–543. DOI: 10.1177/0032329204269979

Bourdieu, P. (1990). *In other words. (Various Trans.).* Polity Press.

Bourdieu, P. (2000). *Pascalian meditations* (Nice, R., Trans.). Polity Press.

Boyle, A. (2007). Human Rights or Environmental Rights? A Reassessment. *Fordham Environmental Law Review, 18*(3), 471–511.

Braga, C. A. P., & Fink, C. (1998). The relationship between intellectual property rights and foreign direct investment. *Duke J. Comp. & Int'l L., 9*, 163.

Brahmi, P., Saxena, S., & Dhillon, B. S. (2004). The protection of plant varieties and Farmers' Rights Act of India. *Current Science, 86*(3), 392–398.

Breen, D. (2009). *Farmers' Rights as Human Rights.* OHCR.

Bremer, T. S. (2006). Sacred spaces and tourist places. In *Tourism, religion and spiritual journeys* (pp. 25–35). Routledge.

Brinkerhoff, J., Smith, S., & Teegen, H. (Eds.). (2007). *NGOs and Millennium Development Goals: Citizen Action to Reduce Poverty.* Springer. DOI: 10.1057/9780230604933

Brown, J. D., Tai, J. D., & June, T. (2005). Introduction: An Overview of Intellectual Property. *Biopharm International, 2005*(2).

Brush, S. B. (2007). Farmers' rights and protection of traditional agricultural knowledge. *World Development, 35*(9), 1499–1514. DOI: 10.1016/j.worlddev.2006.05.018

Buiatti, M., Christou, P., & Pastore, G. (2013). The application of GMOs in agriculture and in food production for better nutrition: Two different scientific points of view. *Genes & Nutrition, 8*(3), 255–270. DOI: 10.1007/s12263-012-0316-4 PMID: 23076994

Bunkše, E. V. (2012). Sensescapes: Or a Paradigm Shift from Words and Images to All Human Senses in Creating Feelings of Home in Landscapes. *Proceedings of the Latvia University of Agriculture: Landscape Architecture & Art, 1*(1).

Čábelková, I., Smutka, L., Mareš, D., Ortikov, A., & Kontsevaya, S. (2023). Environmental Protection or Economic Growth? The Effects of Preferences for Individual Freedoms. *Frontiers in Environmental Science, 11*, 1129236. DOI: 10.3389/fenvs.2023.1129236

Cabrera Cornide, J. (2016). *The control over seeds: the confrontation between human rights and intellectual property rights* (Doctoral dissertation).

Cahyani, Z. D., Pribadi, S. R. W., & Baihaqi, I. (2016). Studi Implementasi Model House of Risk (HOR) untuk Mitigasi risiko keterlambatan Material dan komponen Impor pada pembangunan kapal baru. *Jurnal Teknik ITS, 5*(2).

Çakmak, E. ve Gümüş, S. (2005). Türkiye'de beşeri sermaye ve ekonomik büyüme: ekonometrik bir analiz (1960-2002). *Ankara Üniversitesi SBF Dergisi, 60*(01), 59-72.

Calcaterra, V., Cena, H., Rossi, V., Santero, S., Bianchi, A., & Zuccotti, G. (2023). Ultra-Processed Food, Reward System and Childhood Obesity. *Children (Basel, Switzerland), 10*(5), 804. Advance online publication. DOI: 10.3390/children10050804 PMID: 37238352

Camilleri, M. A., & Falzon, L. (2020). Understanding motivations to use online streaming services: Integrating the technology acceptance model (TAM) and the uses and gratifications theory (UGT). *Spanish Journal of Marketing - ESIC, 24*(2), 267–289. DOI: 10.1108/SJME-12-2019-0105

Campbell, L. F., & Stewart, A. E. (1992). Effects of Group Membership on Perception of Risk for Aids. *Psychological Reports, 70*(3), 1075–1092. DOI: 10.2466/pr0.1992.70.3c.1075 PMID: 1496075

Campbell, S., Greenwood, M., Prior, S., Shearer, T., Walkem, K., Young, S., Bywaters, D., & Walker, K. (2020). Purposive sampling: Complex or simple? Research case examples. *Journal of Research in Nursing : JRN, 25*(8), 652–661. DOI: 10.1177/1744987120927206 PMID: 34394687

Campi, M., & Nuvolari, A. (2021). Intellectual property rights and agricultural development: Evidence from a worldwide index of IPRs in agriculture (1961-2018). *The Journal of Development Studies, 57*(4), 650–668. DOI: 10.1080/00220388.2020.1817395

Camprag, N. (2017). Museumification of Historical Centres: The Case of Frankfurt Alstadt Reconstruction. In Bellini, N., & Pasquinelli, C. (Eds.), *Tourism in the City: Towards an Integrative Agenda on Urban Tourism* (pp. 165–178). Springer. DOI: 10.1007/978-3-319-26877-4_11

Caplan, M. A., Purser, G., & Kindle, P. A. (2017). Personal Accounts of Poverty: A Thematic Analysis of Social Media. *Journal of Evidence-Informed Social Work, 14*(6), 433–456. DOI: 10.1080/23761407.2017.1380547 PMID: 29140758

Çelik, N. (2006). *Küreselleşme sürecinde gelişmekte olan ülkelerde teknolojik gelişme ve devletin rolü: Yeni sanayileşen ülkeler deneyimi ve Türkiye örneği* (Doctoral dissertation, Marmara Universitesi (Turkey)).

Celsi, R. L., & Olson, J. C. (1988). The role of involvement in attention and comprehension processes. *The Journal of Consumer Research, 15*(2), 210–224. DOI: 10.1086/209158

Chakraborty, S. K. (2021). Genetically Modified Seeds, Intellectual Property and Agriculture: Has India Addressed the Challenges of Commodifying Plant Genetic Resources and Farmers' Right to Access Seed? *CMR University Journal of Contemporary Legal Affairs, 3*, 90.

Chapman, D. S., Uggerslev, K. L., Carroll, S. A., Piasentin, K. A., & Jones, D. A. (2005). Applicant attraction to organizations and job choice: A meta-analytic review of the correlates of recruiting outcomes. *The Journal of Applied Psychology, 90*(5), 928–944. DOI: 10.1037/0021-9010.90.5.928

Charnley, B., & Radick, G. (2013). Intellectual property, plant breeding and the making of Mendelian genetics. *Studies in History and Philosophy of Science, 44*(2), 222–233. DOI: 10.1016/j.shpsa.2012.11.004

Chatterjee, A. B. (2021). Challenges for Cultural Tourism & Sustainability of the World Heritage Site of Angkor, Cambodia. *Journal of Heritage* [JHAM]. *Archaeology & Management, 1*(1), 30.

Chen, A., Leung, M., Chen, C., & Yang, S. C. (2013). Exposure to Internet Pornography Among Taiwanese Adolescents. *Social Behavior and Personality, 41*(1), 157–164. DOI: 10.2224/sbp.2013.41.1.157

Chen, S., Chen, D., Tan, Z., Chen, M., & Han, J. (2022). Knowledge Mapping of Planetary Boundaries based on Bibliometrics Analysis. *Environmental Science and Pollution Research International, 29*(45), 67728–67750. DOI: 10.1007/s11356-022-22292-6 PMID: 35945326

Childress, C., Baumann, S., Rawlings, C. M., & Nault, J. F. (2021). Genres, Objects, and the Contemporary Expression of Higher-Status Tastes. *Sociological Science, 8*, 8. DOI: 10.15195/v8.a12

Chillakuri, B. (2020). Understanding Generation Z expectations for effective onboarding. *Journal of Organizational Change Management, 33*(7), 1277–1296. DOI: 10.1108/JOCM-02-2020-0058

Chin, S. W. L., Hassan, N. H., & Yong, G. Y. (2023). The new ecotourists of the 21st century: Brunei as a case study. *Cogent Social Sciences, 9*(1), 2191444. DOI: 10.1080/23311886.2023.2191444

Chirwa, T. G., & Odhiambo, N. M. (2016). Macroeconomic Determinants of Economic Growth: A Review of International Literature. *South East European Journal of Economics and Business, 11*(2), 33–47. DOI: 10.1515/jeb-2016-0009

Chohan, U. W. (2022). Web 3.0: The Future Architecture of the Internet? https://papers.ssrn.com/sol3/papers.cfm?abstract_id=4037693

Cho, Y., Kim, S., You, J., Moon, H., & Sung, H. (2021). Application of ESG measures for gender diversity and equality at the organizational level in a Korean context. *European Journal of Training and Development, 45*(4/5), 346–365. DOI: 10.1108/EJTD-05-2020-0090

Chu, Y. (2024). The Social Landscape of Kampong Ayer: Marginalization and Modernization in a Traditional Water Village. *Journal of Humanities, Arts and Social Science, 8*(7).

Chung, C., & Austria, D. (2010). Social media gratification and attitude toward social media marketing messages: A study of the effect of social media marketing messages on online shopping value. Proceedings of the Northeast Business & Economics Association, 581–586.

Cimadamore, A. D., & Lange, L. (2015). The Global Poverty Consensus Report. https://perma.cc/MDN5-6LTW

Cimigo. (2022). *Healthy food and beverage needs in Vietnam*. Cimigo.

Claeys, P., & Edelman, M. (2020). The United Nations Declaration on the rights of peasants and other people working in rural areas. *The Journal of Peasant Studies, 47*(1), 1–68. DOI: 10.1080/03066150.2019.1672665

Clancy, M. S., & Moschini, G. (2017). Intellectual property rights and the ascent of proprietary innovation in agriculture. *Annual Review of Resource Economics, 9*(1), 53–74. DOI: 10.1146/annurev-resource-100516-053524

Clements, A. J., & Kamau, C. (2018). Understanding students' motivation towards proactive career behaviours through goal-setting theory and the job demands–resources model. *Studies in Higher Education, 43*(12), 2279–2293. DOI: 10.1080/03075079.2017.1326022

Cochran, J. K., & Beeghley, L. (1991, March). The Influence of Religion on Attitudes toward Nonmarital Sexuality: A Preliminary Assessment of Reference Group Theory. *Journal for the Scientific Study of Religion, 30*(1), 45–62. DOI: 10.2307/1387148

Cohan, M. (2009). Forbidden Fruit: Sex & Religion in the Lives of American Teenagers. *Contemporary Sociology, 38*(1), 31–32. DOI: 10.1177/009430610903800115

Coie, J. D., Watt, N. F., West, S. G., Hawkins, J. D., Asarnow, J. R., Markman, H. J., Ramey, S. L., Shure, M. B., & Long, B. (1993). The science of prevention: A conceptual framework and some directions for a national research program. *The American Psychologist, 48*(10), 1013–1022. https://psycnet.apa.org/doiLanding?doi=10.1037%2F0003-066X.48.10.1013. DOI: 10.1037/0003-066X.48.10.1013 PMID: 8256874

Çolak, M. (2010). Eğitim ve beşeri sermayenin kalkınma üzerine etkisi. *Kamu-İş Dergisi, 11*(3), 109–125.

Coman, I. A., Yuan, S., & Tsai, J. Y. (2022). Toward an audience-centric framework of corporate social advocacy strategy: An exploratory study of young consumers from Generation Z. *Sustainability (Basel), 14*(7), 4099. DOI: 10.3390/su14074099

Commission on Human Security. (2003). *Human Security Now*. UNDP.

C ng hòa xã h i ch nghĩa Vi t Nam - Ban Tôn Giáo Chính Ph . (2022). Tôn giáo và chính sách tôn giáo Vi t Nam. Th Gi i Publishers.

Connelly, B. L., Certo, S. T., Ireland, R. D., & Reutzel, C. R. (2011). Signaling theory: A review and assessment. *Journal of Management, 37*(1), 39–67. DOI: 10.1177/0149206310388419

Cooke, P., & Leydesdorff, L. (2006). Regional development in the knowledge-based economy: The construction of advantage. *The Journal of Technology Transfer, 31*(1), 5–15. DOI: 10.1007/s10961-005-5009-3

Coomes, O. T., McGuire, S. J., Garine, E., Caillon, S., McKey, D., Demeulenaere, E., Jarvis, D., Aistara, G., Barnaud, A., Clouvel, P., Emperaire, L., Louafi, S., Martin, P., Massol, F., Pautasso, M., Violon, C., & Wencélius, J. (2015). Farmer seed networks make a limited contribution to agriculture? Four common misconceptions. *Food Policy, 56*, 41–50. DOI: 10.1016/j.foodpol.2015.07.008

Cooper, A., Galbreath, N., & Becker, M. A. (2004). Sex on the internet: Furthering our understanding of men with online sexual problems. *Psychology of Addictive Behaviors, 18*(3), 223–230. DOI: 10.1037/0893-164X.18.3.223 PMID: 15482077

Correa, C. M. (2001). Traditional knowledge and intellectual property. *Geneva: The Quaker United Nations Office (QUNO), 17.*

Corrigan, G. (2017). The Inclusive Growth And Development Report 2017. World Economic Forum. Çağlar, A. ve Gülel, F. E. (2017). Eğitimin toplumsal fayda üzerinde etkisi.

Costello, B. J., & Laub, J. H. (2020, January). Social Control Theory: The Legacy of Travis Hirschi's Causes of Delinquency. *Annual Review of Criminology, 3*(1), 21–41. DOI: 10.1146/annurev-criminol-011419-041527

Cottier, T., & Panizzon, M. (2004). Legal perspectives on traditional knowledge: The case for intellectual property protection. *Journal of International Economic Law, 7*(2), 371–399. DOI: 10.1093/jiel/7.2.371

Cretacci, M. (2003). Religion and Social Control: An Application of a Modified Social Bond on Violence. *Criminal Justice Review, 28*(2), 254–277. DOI: 10.1177/073401680302800204

Dabla-Norris, E., Kochhar, K., Suphaphiphat, N., Ricka, F., & Tsounta, E. (2015). *Causes and Consequences of Income Inequality: A Global Perspective*. IMF.

Dadari, I., Higgins-Steele, A., Sharkey, A., Charlet, D., Shahabuddin, A., Nandy, R., & Jackson, D. (2021). Pro-equity immunization and health systems strengthening strategies in select Gavi-supported countries. *Vaccine, 39*(17), 2434–2444. DOI: 10.1016/j.vaccine.2021.03.044 PMID: 33781603

Das, D., & Upadhyay, A. K. (2024). Deconstructing complexities in the adoption of new forms in news media: A systematic literature review. *Cogent Arts & Humanities, 11*(1), 2303819. Advance online publication. DOI: 10.1080/23311983.2024.2303819

Daşdemir, A. (2008). AB Üyesi Ülkelerde Beşeri Sermaye ve Ekonomik Büyüme İlişkisi: Panel Veri Analizi (Doctoral Dissertation). *DEÜ Sosyal Bilimleri Enstitüsü.*

Davenport, S. (2004). Panic and panacea: Brain drain and science and technology human capital policy. *Research Policy, 33*(4), 617–630. DOI: 10.1016/j.respol.2004.01.006

Davis, F. D. (1989). Perceived usefulness, perceived ease of use, and user acceptance of information technology. *Management Information Systems Quarterly, 13*(3), 319–340. DOI: 10.2307/249008

De Macedo, J. B., & Chino, T. (2002). *Technology and poverty reduction in Asia and the Pacific*. Development Centre of the Organisation for Economic Co-operation and Development.

Decerf, B. (2022). *Absolute and Relative Poverty Measurement: A Survey* (PRWP 10008). World Bank.

de-Lima-Santos, M.-F., & Ceron, W. (2021). Artificial Intelligence in News Media: Current Perceptions and Future Outlook. *Journalism and Media.*, *3*(1), 13–26. https://www.mdpi.com/2673-5172/3/1/2. DOI: 10.3390/journalmedia3010002

de-Lima-Santos, M.-F., & Mesquita, L. (2021). Data Journalism Beyond Technological Determinism. *Journalism Studies*, *22*(11), 1416–1435. https://www.tandfonline.com/doi/full/10.1080/1461670X.2021.1944279. DOI: 10.1080/1461670X.2021.1944279

Dell Technology. (2018). Gen Z: The future has arrived. Retrieved from https://www.dell.com/en-us/dt/perspectives/gen-z.htm

Dellios, P. (2002). 'Museumification of the Village: Cultural Subversion in the 21st century. *Culture Mandala: The Bulletin of the Centre for East-West Cultural and Economic Studies*, *5*(1), 1–16.

Deloitte. (2024). 2024 Gen Z and Millennial Survey, Living and working with purpose in a transforming world. https://www.deloitte.com/global/en/issues/work/content/genz-millennialsurvey.html

Demerouti, E., Bakker, A. B., Nachreiner, F., & Schaufeli, W. B. (2001). The job demands-resources model of burnout. *The Journal of Applied Psychology*, *86*(3), 499–512. DOI: 10.1037/0021-9010.86.3.499 PMID: 11419809

Dhir, A., Chen, S., & Nieminen, M. (2016). The effects of demographics, technology accessibility, and unwillingness to communicate in predicting internet gratifications and heavy internet use among adolescents. *Social Science Computer Review*, *34*(3), 278–297. DOI: 10.1177/0894439315582854

Dijck, J. V. (2013). 'You have one identity': Performing the self on Facebook and LinkedIn. *Media Culture & Society*, *35*(2), 99–215.

Din, S. Z. M., Anuar, R. H. M., Omar, N., Omar, H., & Dahlan, J. M. (2015). Discovering the use of online recruitment via social media of student internship. *Procedia Economics and Finance*, *31*, 856–860. DOI: 10.1016/S2212-5671(15)01181-8

Djafarova, E., & Foots, S. (2022). Exploring ethical consumption of generation Z: Theory of planned behaviour. *Young Consumers*, *23*(3), 413–431. DOI: 10.1108/YC-10-2021-1405

Do, L. H. (2016, May 31). nh hư ng c a tôn giáo đ n tư duy c a ngư i Vi t v m i quan h con ngư i và t nhiên. T p chí Lý lu n chính tr . Retrieved December 13, 2023, from https://lyluanchinhtri.vn/home/index.php/dien-dan/item/1493-anh-huong-cua-ton-giao-den-tu-duy-cua-nguoi-viet-ve-moi-quan-he-con-nguoi-va-tu-nhien.html

Doorley, J., & Garcia, H. F. (2007). *Reputation management. The Key to Successful Public Relations and Corporate Communications*. Routledge.

Drahos, P. (1999). *The universality of intellectual property rights: origins and development. Intellectual Property and Human Rights*. World Intellectual Property Organization.

Driver, S. (2018). Keep it clean: Social media screenings gain in popularity. Accessed from https://www.businessnewsdaily.com/2377-social-media-hiring.html (Accessed on 8 September 2020).

Dubey, D. D. (2023). Historical Evolution of Media in India: A Critical Analysis. *Indian Journal of Law and Legal Research*, *5*(4), 1–16. https://hcommons.org/deposits/objects/hc:59722/datastreams/CONTENT/content

Dutfield, G. (2011). Food, biological diversity and intellectual property. *Global Economic Issue Publications Intellectual Property, Issue Paper*, (9).

Dyatmiko, W. W. (2019). *Sekolah Lapang Iklim Sebagai Upaya Menginisiasi Keberdayaan Petani Tebu Desa Wonokerto Kecamatan Bantur Kabupaten Malang*. Universitas Brawijaya.

Eagleman, A. N. (2013). Acceptance, motivations, and usage of social media as a marketing communications tool amongst employees of sport national governing bodies. *Sport Management Review*, *16*(4), 488–497. DOI: 10.1016/j.smr.2013.03.004

Eagly, A. H., & Chaiken, S. (1993). *The psychology of attitudes*. Harcourt Brace Jovanovich.

Eccles, R. G., & Klimenko, S. (2019). The investor revolution: Shareholders are getting serious about sustainability. *Harvard Business Review*. https://hbr.org/2019/05/the-investor-revolution

Eccles, R. G., Lee, L.-E., & Stroehle, J. C. (2019). The Social Origins of ESG: An Analysis of Innovest and KLD. *Organization & Environment*, *33*(4), 575–596. DOI: 10.1177/1086026619888994

Edelman (2022). *Edelman Trust Barometer 2022 – Global Report*. https://www.edelman.com/sites/g/files/aatuss191/files/2022-01/2022%20Edelman%20Trust%20Barometer%20FINAL_Jan25.pdf

Eide, A. (1998). *The Human Right to Adequate Food and Freedom from Hunger, In the Right to Food in Theory and Practice*. FAO Publication.

El Ouirdi, M., Pais, I., Seger, J., & El Ouirdi, A. (2016). The relationship between recruiter characteristics and applicant assessment on social media. *Computers in Human Behavior, 62*, 415–422. DOI: 10.1016/j.chb.2016.04.012

Elanjimattom, N. J. (2023). Artificial Intelligence as Journalist and Gatekeeper: Ethics of Automated Journalism and Algorithmic Curation of News in the Indian Context. Digital Journalism in India. https://www.academia.edu/99514264/Artificial_Intelligence_as_Journalist_and_Gatekeeper_Ethics_of_Automated_Journalism_and_Algorithmic_Curation_of_News_in_the_Indian_Context

Ellis, F., & Allison, E. (2004). *Livelihood diversification and natural resource access. Overseas Development Group*. University of East Anglia.

Emako, E., Nuru, S., & Menza, M. (2022). The Effect of Foreign Direct Investment on Economic Growth in Developing Countries. *Transnational Corporations Review, 14*(4), 382–401. DOI: 10.1080/19186444.2022.2146967

Erfani, P., & Bourdeaux, M. (2021). *Can Vaccine Incentive Reward Programs Increase COVID-19 Vaccine Uptake?* Fernández-Basanta, S., Lagoa-Millarengo, M., & Movilla-Fernández, M. J. (2021). Encountering parents who are hesitant or reluctant to vaccinate their children: A meta-ethnography. *International Journal of Environmental Research and Public Health, 18*(14), 7584. Advance online publication. DOI: 10.3390/ijerph18147584

Ertan, T., & Egercioglu, Y. (2016). 'The Impact of UNESCO World Heritage list on Historic Urban City Centers and Its Place in Urban Regeneration: The Case of Melaka, Malaysia and Tire, Turkey. *Procedia: Social and Behavioral Sciences, 216*, 591–602. DOI: 10.1016/j.sbspro.2015.12.031

Ertuğrul, C., & Evren, İ. ve Çolak, O. (2010). Küresel mali krizin Türkiye ekonomisine etkileri. *Journal of Management and Economics Research, 8*(13), 59–72.

Eser, K. ve Gökmen, Ç. E. (2009). Beşeri sermayenin ekonomik gelişme üzerindeki etkileri: Dünya deneyimi ve Türkiye üzerine gözlemler. *Sosyal ve Beşeri Bilimler Dergisi, 1*(2), 41–56.

Ezell, S., & Cory, N. (2019). *The way forward for intellectual property internationally*. Information Technology and Innovation Foundation.

Ezzell, M. B., Johnson, J. A., Bridges, A. J., & Sun, C. F. (2020). I (Dis)Like it Like That: Gender, Pornography, and Liking Sex. *Journal of Sex & Marital Therapy, 46*(5), 460–473. DOI: 10.1080/0092623X.2020.1758860 PMID: 32342728

Fang, V. (2021). *From Charity to Justice: How NGOs can Revolutionize Our Response to Extreme Poverty*. Palgrave Macmillan. DOI: 10.1007/978-981-16-1433-0

Fan, Y., Chen, J., Shirkey, G., John, R., Wu, S. R., Park, H., & Shao, C. (2016). Applications of structural equation modeling (SEM) in ecological studies: An updated review. *Ecological Processes*, *5*(19), 19. Advance online publication. DOI: 10.1186/s13717-016-0063-3

Farias, R. A. S., & Hoffmann, V. E. (2018). Analysis of Scientific Production on Interorganizational Network Study Field. *Innovation & Management Review*, *15*(1), 92–115. DOI: 10.1108/INMR-02-2018-006

Farid, S. A. (2023). Changing the Paradigm of Traditional Journalism to Digital Journalism: Impact on Professionalism and Journalism Credibility. *Journal International Dakwah and Communication*, *3*(1), 22–32. DOI: 10.55849/jidc.v3i1.374

Farr, W. (1853). The income and property tax. *Journal of the Statistical Society of London*, *16*(1), 1–44. DOI: 10.2307/2338101

Feagin, J. R. (1975). *Subordinating the Poor: Welfare and American Beliefs*. A Spectrum Book.

Filatova, E. A. (2021). *Intellectual Property Rights in the Seed Industry: Barriers to Sustainable Agriculture* (Master's thesis, University of Denver).

Fishbein, M., & Ajzen, I. (1975). *Belief, attitude, intention, and behavior: An introduction to theory and research*. Addison-Wesley.

Fisher, W. A., & Barak, A. (2001). Internet pornography: A social psychological perspective on Internet sexuality. *Journal of Sex Research*, *38*(4), 312–323. DOI: 10.1080/00224490109552102

Florida, R. (2003). Cities and the creative class. *City & Community*, *2*(1), 3–19. DOI: 10.1111/1540-6040.00034

Førland, O., & Roxå, T. (2024). Establishing reward systems for excellence in teaching–the experience of academics pioneering a reward system. *European Journal of Higher Education*, *14*(3), 451–469. DOI: 10.1080/21568235.2023.2214713

Fornell, C., & Larcker, D. F. (1981). Evaluating Structural Equation Models with Unobservable Variables and Measurement Error. *JMR, Journal of Marketing Research*, *18*(1), 39–50. DOI: 10.1177/002224378101800104

Fredriksson, M. (2021). Open-source seeds and the revitalization of local knowledge. *Sustainability (Basel)*, *13*(21), 12270. DOI: 10.3390/su132112270

Friso, F., Mendive, F., Soffiato, M., Bombardelli, V., Hesketh, A., Heinrich, M., Menghini, L., & Politi, M. (2020). Implementation of Nagoya Protocol on access and benefit-sharing in Peru: Implications for researchers. *Journal of Ethnopharmacology, 259*, 112885. DOI: 10.1016/j.jep.2020.112885 PMID: 32311487

Fukuda-Parr, S. (2003). New Threats to Human Security in the Era of Globalization. *Journal of Human Development, 4*(2), 167–179. DOI: 10.1080/1464988032000087523

Gabrielova, K., & Buchko, A. A. (2021). Here comes Generation Z: Millennials as managers. *Business Horizons, 64*(4), 489–499. DOI: 10.1016/j.bushor.2021.02.013

Gaikwad, N., Hanson, K., & Tóth, A. (2024). Bridging the gulf: How migration fosters tolerance, cosmopolitanism, and support for globalization. *American Journal of Political Science*.

Gamage, A., Gangahagedara, R., Gamage, J., Jayasinghe, N., Kodikara, N., Suraweera, P., & Merah, O. (2023). Role of organic farming for achieving sustainability in agriculture. *Farming System, 1*(1), 100005. DOI: 10.1016/j.farsys.2023.100005

Gautam, P. L., Singh, A. K., Srivastava, M., & Singh, P. K. (2012). Protection of plant varieties and farmers' rights: A review. *Indian Journal of Plant Genetic Resources, 25*(01), 9–30.

Genç, R. (2017). The importance of communication in sustainability & sustainable strategies. *Procedia Manufacturing, 8*, 511–516. DOI: 10.1016/j.promfg.2017.02.065

George, A. S. (2024). Artificial Intelligence and the Future of Work. *Job Shifting Not Job Loss., 02*, 17–37. DOI: 10.5281/zenodo.10936490

George, D., & Mallery, P. (2003). *SPSS for Windows step by step: A simple guide and reference, 11.0 update* (4th ed.). Allyn & Bacon.

Giliberto, F., & Labadi, S. (2022). Harnessing Cultural Heritage for Sustainable Development: An Analysis of Three Internationally Funded Projects in MENA Countries. *International Journal of Heritage Studies, 28*(2), 133–146. DOI: 10.1080/13527258.2021.1950026

Goh, E., & Okumus, F. (2020). Avoiding the hospitality workforce bubble: Strategies to attract and retain generation Z talent in the hospitality workforce. *Tourism Management Perspectives, 33*, 100603. DOI: 10.1016/j.tmp.2019.100603

Gökçen, B. (2006). *Beşeri sermayenin iktisadi gelişmedeki rolü ve önemi: Adana iline ilişkin bir uygulama* (Master's thesis, Sosyal Bilimler Enstitüsü).

Goldstein, A. C. (2018). More than an "Unhappy Object": The Ethical, Relational and Pedagogical Possibilities of Talking with Young People about Pornography [Doctoral dissertation].

Golemeeva, E. I. (2020) SEXUAL EXPLORATION IN THE 'DIGITAL AGE': HOW THE INTERNET INFORMS THE SEXUALITY OF YOUNG PEOPLE IN CONTEMPORARY BRITAIN. Doctoral thesis, University of Huddersfield.

Gomes, S., Lopes, J. M., & Nogueira, S. (2023). Willingness to pay more for green products: A critical challenge for Gen Z. *Journal of Cleaner Production, 390*, 136092. DOI: 10.1016/j.jclepro.2023.136092

Gómez-Diago, G. (2022). Perspectivas para abordar la inteligencia artificial en la enseñanza deperiodismo. Una revisión de experiencias investigadoras y docentes. Revista Latina DeComunicación Social, 80, 29-46. https://www.doi.org/10.4185/RLCS-2022-1542

González-Valero, G., Melguizo-Ibáñez, E., Ortega-Caballero, M., Marfil-Carmona, R., Zurita-Ortega, F., & Puertas-Molero, P. (2023). Mass media pressure on psychological and healthy well-being: An explanatory model as a function of physical activity. *Journal of Public Health (Berlin), 31*(10), 1663–1671. DOI: 10.1007/s10389-022-01733-z

Gornostaeva, Z. V., & Chernysheva, Y. S. (2023). Improving the quality of corporate governance with reliance on ESG-based HR management. In *Smart Green Innovations in Industry 4.0: New Opportunities for Climate Change Risk Management in the "Decade of Action"* (pp. 247-255). Cham: Springer Nature Switzerland. https://doi.org/DOI: 10.1007/978-3-031-45830-9_28

Greber, H., Aaldering, L., & Lecheler, S. (2023a). The Worthwhileness of Immersive Journalism—Taking on an Audience Perspective. *Journalism Practice*, •••, 1–19. DOI: 10.1080/17512786.2023.2177711

Greber, H., Lecheler, S., Aaldering, L., De Haan, Y., Kruikemeier, S., Goutier, N., & De Bruin, K. (2023b). Feeling the News? The Differential Effects of Immersive Journalism on Emotional Response. *Digital Journalism (Abingdon, England), 11*(1), 39–60. DOI: 10.1080/21670811.2022.2155205

Gruberg, H., Meldrum, G., Padulosi, S., Rojas, W., Pinto, M., & Crane, T. A. (2013). *Towards a better understanding of custodian farmers and their roles: insights from a case study in Cachilaya.*

Grunert, K. G., Harmsen, H., Larsen, H. H., Sørensen, E., & Bisp, S. (1997). New areas in agricultural and food marketing. *Agricultural marketing and consumer behavior in a changing world*, 3-30.

Gruzd, A., Jacobson, J., & Dubois, E. (2020, April-June). Cybervetting and the public life of social media data. *Social Media + Society*, *6*(2), 1–13. DOI: 10.1177/2056305120915618

Gümüş, S. (2005). *Beşeri Sermaye ve Ekonomik Kalkınma: Türkiye Üzerine Ekonometrik Bir Analiz (1960- 2002),(Atatürk Üniversitesi Doktora Tezi 2005: Erzurum)*. İktisadi Araştırmalar Vakfı.

Günsoy, G. (2005). İnsani gelişme kavramı ve sağlıklı yaşam hakkı. *Uluslararası Yönetim İktisat ve İşletme Dergisi*, *1*(2), 35–52.

Günther, L., Schleberger, S., & Pischke, C. R. (2021). Effectiveness of social media-based interventions for the promotion of physical activity: Scoping review. *International Journal of Environmental Research and Public Health*, *18*(24), 13018. DOI: 10.3390/ijerph182413018 PMID: 34948628

Haeder, S. F. (2021). Joining the herd? U.S. public opinion and vaccination requirements across educational settings during the COVID-19 pandemic. *Vaccine*, *39*(17), 2375–2385. DOI: 10.1016/j.vaccine.2021.03.055 PMID: 33810906

Haggstrom-Nordin, E., Sandberg, J., Hanson, U., & Tyden, T. (2006). 'It's everywhere!' Young Swedish people's thoughts and reflections about pornography. *Scandinavian Journal of Caring Sciences*, *20*(4), 386–393. DOI: 10.1111/j.1471-6712.2006.00417.x PMID: 17116147

Hair, J. F., Anderson, R. E., Tatham, R. L., & Black, W. C. (1995). *Multivariate data analysis*. Prentice-Hall.

Hair, J., Black, W., Babin, B., Anderson, R., & Tatham, R. (2006). *Multivariate Data Analysis* (6th ed.). Pearson Education.

Halewood, M., Bedmar Villanueva, A., Rasolojaona, J., Andriamahazo, M., Rakotoniaina, N., Bossou, B., Mikpon, T., Vodouhe, R., Fey, L., Drews, A., Kumar, P. L., Rasoanirina, B., Rasoazafindrabe, T., Aigbe, M., Agbahounzo, B., Otieno, G., Garforth, K., Kiene, T., & Nnadozie, K. (2021). Enhancing farmers' agency in the global crop commons through use of biocultural community protocols. *Agriculture and Human Values*, *38*(2), 579–594. DOI: 10.1007/s10460-020-10164-z

Halewood, M., Chiurugwi, T., Sackville Hamilton, R., Kurtz, B., Marden, E., Welch, E., Michiels, F., Mozafari, J., Sabran, M., Patron, N., Kersey, P., Bastow, R., Dorius, S., Dias, S., McCouch, S., & Powell, W. (2018). Plant genetic resources for food and agriculture: Opportunities and challenges emerging from the science and information technology revolution. *The New Phytologist*, *217*(4), 1407–1419. DOI: 10.1111/nph.14993 PMID: 29359808

Hallett, S., Hoagland, L., & Toner, E. (2016). Urban agriculture: Environmental, economic, and social perspectives. *Horticultural Reviews*, *44*(44), 65–120. DOI: 10.1002/9781119281269.ch2

Hall, R. E., & Jones, C. I. (1999). Why do some countries produce so much more output per worker than others? *The Quarterly Journal of Economics*, *114*(1), 83–116. DOI: 10.1162/003355399555954

Hanlon, R. J., & Christie, K. (2016). *Freedom from Fear, Freedom from Want: An Introduction to Human Security*. University of Toronto Press. DOI: 10.3138/9781442609594

Hannigan, J. (2002). Culture, globalization, and social cohesion: towards a de-territorialized, global fluid models. *Canadian Journal of Communication, 27(2)*, 1-9. Retrieved from http://cjc- online.ca/index.php/journal/article/viewArticle/1301/1333

Han, Y., Mahamed, M. B., Abdullah, Z., & Abas, W. A. B. W. (2023). Integrating TAM and UGT to Explore Motivations of using Social Media for News Reading among Chinese College Students. *International Journal of Academic Research in Business & Social Sciences.*

Harding, J. (2019). *Qualitative Data Analysis: From Start to Finish* (2nd ed.). SAGE Publication.

Hardy, S., Steelman, M., Coyne, S., & Ridge, R. (2013). Adolescent religiousness as a protective factor against pornography use. *Journal of Applied Developmental Psychology*, *34*(3), 131–139. DOI: 10.1016/j.appdev.2012.12.002

Harrison, J. A., & Budworth, M. H. (2015). Unintended consequences of a digital presence. *Career Development International*, *20*(4), 294–314. DOI: 10.1108/CDI-06-2014-0080

Hashmi, R., & Alam, K. (2019). Dynamic Relationship among Environmental Regulation, Innovation, CO_2 Emissions, Population, and Economic Growth in OECD Countries: A Panel Investigation. *Journal of Cleaner Production*, *231*, 1100–1109. DOI: 10.1016/j.jclepro.2019.05.325

Hassan, N. H. & Yong, G. Y. V. (2019). The cultural value of bakuts in Kampong Ayer, Brunei Darussalam. *South East Asia: A Multidisciplinary Journal, 19*, 47–63.

Hassan, N. H., Azalie, I. A., Ibrahim, K., Yong, G., & Maricar, H. H. A. (2011). Cultural Consideration in Vertical Living in Brunei Darussalam. 44th EAROPH Conference 'Managing Urban Growth: Challenges for Small Cities.

Hassan, N. H. (2023). The Sociocultural Significance of Homeownership in Brunei Darussalam. In *Re) presenting Brunei Darussalam: A Sociology of the Everyday* (pp. 185–206). Springer Nature Singapore. DOI: 10.1007/978-981-19-6059-8_11

Hassan, N. H., Rigg, J., Azalie, I. A., Yong, G. Y., Zainuddin, N. H. H., & Shamsul, M. A. S. M. (2022). Making do and staying poor: The poverty context of Urban Brunei. *Geoforum, 136*, 132–141. DOI: 10.1016/j.geoforum.2022.09.012

Hassan, N. H., Rigg, J., Yong, G. Y., Azalie, I. A., Muhammad Shamsul, M. A. S., & Zainuddin, N. H. (2024). Administering and encountering the poor: Poverty from above and below in Brunei Darussalam. *Singapore Journal of Tropical Geography, 45*(2), 311–331. DOI: 10.1111/sjtg.12545

Hazelton, A. S. & Terhorst, A. (2015) Legal and Ethical Considerations for Social Media Hiring Practices in the Workplace, *The Hilltop Review, 7*(2).

Heizer, J., Render, B., & Munson, C. (2020). *Operations management: Sustainability and supply chain management*. Pearson.

Helfer, L. R. (2004). *Intellectual property rights in plant varieties: International legal regimes and policy options for national governments* (No. 31). Food & Agriculture Org.

Hennig-Thurau, T., Gwinner, K. P., Walsh, G., & Gremler, D. D. (2004). Electronic word-of- mouth via consumer-opinion platforms: What motivates consumers to articulate themselves on the internet? *Journal of Interactive Marketing, 18*(1), 38–52. DOI: 10.1002/dir.10073

Hilvert-Bruce, Z., Neill, J. T., Sjöblom, M., & Hamari, J. (2018). Social motivations of live-streaming viewer engagement on Twitch. *Computers in Human Behavior, 84*, 58–67. DOI: 10.1016/j.chb.2018.02.013

Hirschi, T. (1969). *Causes of delinquency*. University of California Press.

Hofstede, G. (1984). Cultural dimensions in management and planning. *Asia Pacific Journal of Management, 1*(1), 81–99. DOI: 10.1007/BF01733682

Holbrook, M. B., & Hirschman, E. C. (1982). The experiential aspects of consumption: Consumer fantasies, feelings, and fun. *The Journal of Consumer Research, 9*(2), 132–140. DOI: 10.1086/208906

Hollenbeck, J. R., & Klein, H. J. (1987). Goal commitment and the goal-setting process: Problems, prospects, and proposals for future research. *Academy of Management Review, 12*(2), 212–220. DOI: 10.5465/amr.1987.4307798

Hornor, G. (2020). Child and Adolescent Pornography Exposure. *Journal of Pediatric Health Care, 34*(2), 191–199. DOI: 10.1016/j.pedhc.2019.10.001 PMID: 32063261

Hubbard, P. (2017). *City*. Routledge. DOI: 10.4324/9781315471259

Hui, L. K., & Har, W. M. (2008). Sanitising and Satanising Malaysia's Cityspaces: Cultural Power from Malay Decolonialism to Islamic Occidentalism and Beyond. *Asian Social Science, 4*(11), 44–52.

Hulme, D. (2015). *Global Poverty: Global Governance and Poor People in the Post-2015 Era*. Routledge. DOI: 10.4324/9781315738932

Hussain, G., Naz, T., Shahzad, N., & Bajwa, M. J. (2022). *Social media marketing in sports and using social media platforms for sports fan engagement*. Ghulam Hussain's Lab., DOI: 10.47750/cibg.2021.27.06.117

Hylton, K. N. (2019). When Should We Prefer Tort Law to Environmental Regulation? *Washburn Law Journal, 41*, 515–534.

ILO (International Labor Organization). (1976). *Employment Growth and Basic Needs: A One World Problem*. ILO.

ILO. (2016). *World Employment and Social Outlook: Transforming Jobs to End Poverty*. ILO.

Ioakimidis, M. (2007). Green sport: A game everyone wins. *The Sport Journal, 10*(2).

Irawan, K. A., Setyo, B., & Suhaili, S. (2023). Keragaman Morfologi Pertumbuhan 7 Klon dan 2 Varietas Tanaman Tebu (Saccharum officinarum L.) di PT Perkebunan Nusantara X Ploso Klaten-Kediri. *Gema Agro, 28*(1), 42–51. DOI: 10.22225/ga.28.1.6634.42-51

Jacobson, J. (2020). You are a brand: Social media managers' personal branding and "the future audience". *Journal of Product and Brand Management, 29*(6), 715–727. DOI: 10.1108/JPBM-03-2019-2299

Jain, N., & Sriram, A. (2023). Artificial intelligence (AI) & Indian journalism: Current trends and challenges. International journal of novel research and development. 8(5), 777-783. https://www.ijnrd.org/papers/IJNRD2305099.pdf

Jalan, J., & Ravallion, M. (2002). Geography Poverty Traps? A Micro Model of Consumption Growth in Rural China. *Journal of Applied Econometrics*, *17*(4), 329–346. DOI: 10.1002/jae.645

James, T. C., & Rajasekharan, S. (2023). Access and Benefit Sharing of Biological Resources and Associated TK: A Multi-tiered Responsibility. In *Biodiversity Conservation Through Access and Benefit Sharing (ABS) Himalayas and Indian Sub-Continent* (pp. 81–102). Springer International Publishing.

Jaya, R., Yusriana, Y., & Fitria, E. (2021). Review manajemen rantai pasok produk pertanian berkelanjutan: Konseptual, isu terkini, dan penelitian mendatang. *Jurnal Ilmu Pertanian Indonesia*, *26*(1), 78–91. DOI: 10.18343/jipi.26.1.78

Jha, L. (2022). Over half of Indian users consume news on social media. https://www.livemint.com/industry/media/over-half-of-indian-users-consume-news-on-social-media-11655305366849.html#:~:text=India%20is%20a%20strongly%20mobile,and%20are%20valued%20for%20convenience

Johannes, K. C., & Hung-Yue, S. (2015). Self-presentation and hiring recommendations in online communities: Lessons from LinkedIn. *Computers in Human Behavior*, *48*, 516–524. DOI: 10.1016/j.chb.2015.02.017

Johnson, K. M. (2017). The importance of personal branding in social media: Educating students to create and manage their personal brand. *International Journal of Education and Social Science*, *4*(1), 21–27.

Johnson, L. C., & Oakley, S. (2013). Place-taking and place-making in waterfront Australia. *Urban Studies (Edinburgh, Scotland)*, *50*(2), 341–355. DOI: 10.1177/0042098012452328

Jolliffe, D., & Lanjouw, P. (Eds.). (2015). *A Measured Approach to Ending Poverty and Boosting Shared Prosperity: Concepts, Data, and the Twin Goals*. World Bank Group.

Jolliffe, D., Mahler, D. G., Lakner, C., Atamanov, A., & Tetteh-Bah, S. K. (2022). *Assessing the Impact of the 2017 PPPs on the International Poverty Line and Global Poverty*. World Bank., PRWP 9941. DOI: 10.1596/1813-9450-9941

Jones, A. (1997). Urban conservation issues in Brunei Darussalam: The case of Brunei's water villages. *Planning Perspectives*, *12*(4), 457–475. DOI: 10.1080/026654397364627

Kamereo. (2022). Coca-Cola's marketing strategy in Vietnam. https://kamereo.vn/blog/en/coca-colas-marketing-strategy/

Kapferer, J. N. (2012). *The New Strategic Brand Management* (5th ed.). Kogan Page.

Kaplan, A. M., & Haenlein, M. (2010). Users of the world, unite! the challenges and opportunities of social media. *Business Horizons, 53*(1), 59–68. DOI: 10.1016/j.bushor.2009.09.003

Kapoor, A., & Bhambri, A. (2022). Raising the curtain: Media industry and the changing landscape. https://economictimes.indiatimes.com/industry/media/entertainment/media/raising-the-curtain-media-industry-and-the-changing-landscape/articleshow/92499946.cms

Karagül, M. (2003). Beşeri sermayenin ekonomik büyümeyle ilişkisi ve etkin kullanımı. *Akdeniz İİBF Dergisi, 3*(5), 79–90.

Kasirye, F. (2022). The Importance of Needs in Uses and Gratification Theory. DOI: 10.31124/advance.14681667.v2

Katz, E., Blumler, J. G., & Gurevitch, M. (1974). Uses and gratifications research. *Public Opinion Quarterly, 37*(4), 509. DOI: 10.1086/268109

Kaya, Y. K. (1974). *İnsan yetiştirme düzenimiz: politika, eğitim, kalkınma*. Nüve Matbaasi. Kaya, Y. K. (1977). *İnsan yetiştirme düzenimiz*. Hacettepe Üniversitesi..

Kayacan, M., & Alkan, N. (2005). *Turkiye'deki bes ,eri sermayenin ekonomik de geri ve Avrupa Birligi ulkeleri ile kars ,ılas ,tırılması. Ankara*. Yayınları.

Kazancıgil, D. (2019). Beşeri sermaye ekonomik büyüme ilişkisi Türkiye örneği.

KDKA. Retrieved July 24, 2024, from https://www.britannica.com/topic/KDKA

Keller, K. L. (1993). Conceptualizing, measuring and managing customer-based brand equity. *Journal of Marketing, 57*(1), 1–22. DOI: 10.1177/002224299305700101

Kennard, C.. (2018). The impact of sports commentary on viewer emotions and team loyalty. *Journal of Sports Media, 17*(3), 129–142.

Kennedy, G., Nantel, G., & Shetty, P. (2004). Globalization of food systems in developing countries: impact on food security and nutrition.

Khazanov, G. K., Stewart, R., Pieri, M. F., Huang, C., Robertson, C. T., Schaefer, K. A., Ko, H., & Fishman, J. (2023). The effectiveness of financial incentives for COVID-19 vaccination: A systematic review. *Preventive Medicine, 172*(May), 107538. DOI: 10.1016/j.ypmed.2023.107538 PMID: 37156430

King, G., & Murray, C. (2001-2002). Rethinking Human Security. *Political Science Quarterly*, *116*(4), 585–610. DOI: 10.2307/798222

King, N., Horrocks, C., & Brooks, J. (2019). *Interviews in Qualitative Research* (2nd ed.). SAGE. DOI: 10.4135/9781036234881

Kinnard, J. N. (2014). *Places in motion: The fluid identities of temples, images, and pilgrims*. Oxford University Press. DOI: 10.1093/acprof:oso/9780199359653.001.0001

Kıraçlar, F. (2005). *Ekonomik büyüme modellerinde beşeri sermaye: içsel büyüme modelinin analizi*. Erciyes Üniversitesi Yayımlanmamış Yüksek Lisans Tezi.

Kirves, K., Kinnunen, U., De Cuyper, N., & Mäkikangas, A. (2014). Trajectories of perceived employability and their associations with well-being at work: A three-wave study. *Journal of Personnel Psychology*, *13*(1), 46–57. DOI: 10.1027/1866-5888/a000103

Kiszewski, A. E., Cleary, E. G., Jackson, M. J., & Ledley, F. D. (2021). NIH funding for vaccine readiness before the COVID-19 pandemic. *Vaccine*, *39*(17), 2458–2466. DOI: 10.1016/j.vaccine.2021.03.022 PMID: 33781600

Kleppinger, C. A., & Cain, J. (2015). Personal digital branding as a professional asset in the digital age. *American Journal of Pharmaceutical Education*, *79*(6), 1–4. DOI: 10.5688/ajpe79679 PMID: 26430266

Kluemper, D. H. (2013), Social Network Screening: Pitfalls, Possibilities, and Parallels in Employment Selection, *Social Media in Human Resources Management, Vol.* 12), pp. 1-21.

Klümper, W., & Qaim, M. (2014). A meta-analysis of the impacts of genetically modified crops. *PLoS One*, *9*(11), e111629. DOI: 10.1371/journal.pone.0111629 PMID: 25365303

Knight, D. M. (2024, January). The death of vernacular cosmopolitanism. [). Routledge.]. *Anthropological Forum*, *34*(1), 135–149. DOI: 10.1080/00664677.2023.2218583

Kompa. (2022). *Social listening report on low-sugar products in Vietnam (2020–2022)*. Kompa AI.

Korosteleva, J., & Stępień-Baig, P. (2020). Climbing the Poverty Ladder: The Role of Entrepreneurship and Gender in Alleviating Poverty in Transition Economies. *Entrepreneurship and Regional Development*, *32*(1/2), 197–220. DOI: 10.1080/08985626.2019.1640482

Köse, M. (1927). Nüfus sayımı ve sonuçlarının değerlendirilmesi. *Yayınlanmamış Yüksek Lisans Tezi), Afyonkarahisar Üniversitesi Sosyal Bilimler Enstitüsü.*

Kruft, D. (2001). Impacts of genetically-modified crops and seeds on farmers. *The Agricultural Law Resource and Reference Center*, 1-11.

Küfeoğlu, S. (2022). *Emerging Technologies: Value Creation for Sustainable Development*. Springer. DOI: 10.1007/978-3-031-07127-0

Kusuma, K. S., & Dua, M. (2020). Immersive Journalism: Emerging Practices and Challengesin Indian Media. *Journal of Media and Communication*, *4*(2), 25–39. http://jmc.cutn.ac.in/docs/JM&C2020DecemberPaper2_01012021.pdf

Kuzior, A., Kettler, K., & Rąb, Ł. (2022). Great resignation—Ethical, cultural, relational, and personal dimensions of generation Y and Z employees' engagement. *Sustainability (Basel)*, *14*(11), 6764. DOI: 10.3390/su14116764

Kuznetsova, L., Cortassa, G., & Trilla, A. (2021). Effectiveness of mandatory and incentive-based routine childhood immunization programs in europe: A systematic review of the literature. *Vaccines*, *9*(10), 1–30. DOI: 10.3390/vaccines9101173 PMID: 34696280

Lambin, E. F., & Meyfroidt, P. (2011). Global land use change, economic globalization, and the looming land scarcity. *Proceedings of the National Academy of Sciences of the United States of America*, *108*(9), 3465–3472. DOI: 10.1073/pnas.1100480108 PMID: 21321211

Law, B., & Shek, D. T. L. (2014). Beliefs about Poverty. In Michalos, A. C. (Ed.), *Encyclopedia of Quality of Life and Well-Being Research* (pp. 353–359). Springer. DOI: 10.1007/978-94-007-0753-5_166

Lawson, C. (2015). Implementing Farmers' Rights: Finding Meaning and Purpose for the International Treaty on Plant Genetic Resources for Food and Agriculture Commitments? *Available at SSRN* 2626668.

Lent, R. W., Brown, S. D., & Hackett, G. (2002). Social cognitive career theory. In Brown, D. (Eds.), *Career choice and development* (4th ed., pp. 255–311). Jossey-Bass.

Leslie, B., Anderson, C., Bickham, C., Horman, J., Overly, A., Gentry, C., Callahan, C., & King, J. (2021). Generation Z perceptions of a positive workplace environment. *Employee Responsibilities and Rights Journal*, *33*(3), 171–187. DOI: 10.1007/s10672-021-09366-2

Lewis, L., Somers, J. M., Guy, R., Watchirs-Smith, L., & Skinner, S. R. (2018). 'I see it everywhere': Young Australians unintended exposure to sexual content online. *Sexual Health*, *15*(4), 335–341. DOI: 10.1071/SH17132 PMID: 29925462

Liben, L. S., & Signorella, M. L. (1980, March). Gender-Related Schemata and Constructive Memory in Children. *Child Development*, *51*(1), 11–18. DOI: 10.2307/1129584

Ličen, S., & Doupona Topič, M. (2008). The imbalance of commentators' discourse during a televised basketball match. University of Ljubljana, Faculty of Sport. Original scientific paper. UDC 796.072.3:796.323.2.

Light, D. (2014). Tourism and toponymy: Commodifying and Consuming Place Names. *Tourism Geographies*, *16*(1), 141–156. DOI: 10.1080/14616688.2013.868031

Lim, M. S. C., Carrotte, E. R., & Hellard, M. E. (2015). The impact of pornography on gender-based violence, sexual health and well-being: What do we know? *Journal of Epidemiology and Community Health*, *70*(1), 3–5. DOI: 10.1136/jech-2015-205453 PMID: 26022057

Liotta, H., & Bilgin, A. (2014). Why Human Security? The Case for Resilience in an Urban Century. In Martin, M., & Owen, T. (Eds.), *Routledge Handbook of Human Security* (pp. 109–122). Routledge.

Locke, E. A., & Latham, G. P. (1990). *A theory of goal setting & task performance*. Prentice Hall.

Locke, E. A., & Latham, G. P. (2002). Building a practically useful theory of goal setting and task motivation: A 35-year odyssey. *The American Psychologist*, *57*(9), 705–717. DOI: 10.1037/0003-066X.57.9.705 PMID: 12237980

Lucas, R. E.Jr. (1988). On the mechanics of economic development. *Journal of Monetary Economics*, *22*(1), 3–42. DOI: 10.1016/0304-3932(88)90168-7

Ma, C., Shek, D., & Lai, C. (2017). Individual differences in intentional and unintentional exposure to online pornography among Hong Kong Chinese adolescents. *International Journal on Disability and Human Development : IJDHD*, *16*(4), 417–423. DOI: 10.1515/ijdhd-2017-7010

Macalik, J., & Sulich, A. (2019, May). External employer branding of sustainable organizations. In *International Scientific Conference Contemporary Issues in Business, Management and Economics Engineering*, 239-250. https://doi.org/DOI: 10.3846/cibmee.2019.054

Machin, S. (2008). Big ideas: Rising wage inequality. *CentrePiece*, *13*(2), 8–10.

Macleod, P. (2021). Influences on ethical decision-making among porn consumers: The role of stigma. *Journal of Consumer Culture*, *21*(2), 381–404. DOI: 10.1177/1469540520970247

Magdalena, R., & Vannie, V. (2019). Analisis risiko supply chain dengan model house of risk (HOR) pada PT Tatalogam Lestari. *J@ Ti Undip. Jurnal Teknik Industri, 14*(2), 53–62.

Maghfiroh, I. S., Setyawati, I. K., & Wibowo, R. (2017). Mutu tebu industri gula di Indonesia. *Seminar Nasional Pembangunan Pertanian*, 94–100.

Mahapatra, G. P., Bhullar, N., & Gupta, P. (2022). Gen Z: An emerging phenomenon. *NHRD Network Journal, 15*(2), 246–256. DOI: 10.1177/26314541221077137

Maharani, I. M., Hanani, N., & Syafrial, S. (2023). Bagaimana Petani Dalam Pengelolaan Risiko? Persepsi Dan Perilaku Petani Tebu Di Jawa Timur. [Journal of Social and Agricultural Economics]. *JSEP, 16*(1), 25–40. DOI: 10.19184/jsep.v16i1.38094

Mahardika, E. W. (2023). *Penerapan Standard Operating Procedure (SOP) Pengemasan dan Penyimpanan Produk Gula Retail pada PT Sinergi Gula Nusantara Unit Pabrik Gula Glenmore.*

Mail, H. A. A. (2018). Yayasan Sultan Haji Hassanal Bolkiah, 1992-2012: Sejarah, Perumahan, dan Melayu Islam Beraja. *INSANCITA, 3*(2).

Mantel, C., & Cherian, T. (2020). New immunization strategies: Adapting to global challenges. *Bundesgesundheitsblatt, Gesundheitsforschung, Gesundheitsschutz, 63*(1), 25–31. DOI: 10.1007/s00103-019-03066-x PMID: 31802153

Mardi, P., Djalalinia, S., Kargar, R., Jamee, M., Esmaeili Abdar, Z., & Qorbani, M. (2022). Impact of incentives on COVID-19 vaccination; A systematic review. *Frontiers in Medicine, 9*, 810323. Advance online publication. DOI: 10.3389/fmed.2022.810323 PMID: 36160125

Marín-Montín, J. (2008). Educate in sport through TV: Teaching sport with TV. *Comunicar, 16*(31), 227–233. DOI: 10.3916/c31-2008-03-044

Market Research Future. (2024). *Sugar-free beverage market research report.* https://www.marketresearchfuture.com/reports/sugar-free-beverage-market-3869

Markus, H., Crane, M., Bernstein, S., & Siladi, M. (1982). Self-Schemas and Gender. Journal of Personality and Social Psychology, 42(1), 38-50. https://0022-3514/82/4201-0038$00.75

Markusen, A. (2007). A consumption base theory of development: An application to the rural cultural economy. *Agricultural and Resource Economics Review, 36*(1), 1–15. DOI: 10.1017/S1068280500009412

Martin, C. L., & Halverson, C.Jr. (1981, December). A Schematic Processing Model of Sex Typing and Stereotyping in Children. *Child Development, 52*(4), 1119–1134. DOI: 10.2307/1129498

Maskus, K. E. (2000). *Intellectual property rights in the global economy*. Peterson Institute.

Massey, D. (1995, April). Places and their pasts. In *History workshop journal* (No. 39, pp. 182-192). Oxford University Press. DOI: 10.1093/hwj/39.1.182

Matthews, D. (2003). *Globalising intellectual property rights: the TRIPS Agreement*. Routledge. DOI: 10.4324/9780203165683

McCabe, M. B. (2017). Social media marketing strategies for career advancement: An analysis of LinkedIn. *Journal of Business and Behavioural Sciences, 29*(1), 85–99.

McGarrigle, D. (1994). Unsettling Brunei. *Australian Plants, 31*(3), 159–164. DOI: 10.1080/07293682.1994.9657627

McGuire, E., Al-Zu'bi, M., Boa-Alvarado, M., Luu, T. T. G., Sylvester, J. M., & Leñero, E. M. V. (2024). Equity principles: Using social theory for more effective social transformation in agricultural research for development. *Agricultural Systems, 218*, 103999. DOI: 10.1016/j.agsy.2024.103999

McKinsey & Company. (2022). The new faces of the Vietnamese consumer. https://www.mckinsey.com/featured-insights/future-of-asia/the-new-faces-of-the-vietnamese-consumer

Meena, J. S., Choi, S. B., Jung, S. B., & Kim, J. W. (2023). Electronic textiles: New age of wearable technology for healthcare and fitness solutions. *Materials Today. Bio, 19*, 100565. Advance online publication. DOI: 10.1016/j.mtbio.2023.100565

Mehta, M. D. (2004, July). Pornography in Usenet: A Study of 9,800 Randomly Selected Images. *Cyberpsychology & Behavior, 4*(6), 695–703. DOI: 10.1089/109493101753376641 PMID: 11800177

Mensah, J. (2019). Sustainable Development: Meaning, History, Principles, Pillars, and Implications for Human Action: Literature Review. *Cogent Social Sciences, 5*(1), 1653531. DOI: 10.1080/23311886.2019.1653531

Merges, R. P. (2011). *Justifying intellectual property*. Harvard University Press. DOI: 10.4159/harvard.9780674061125

Mesch, G. (2008, August). Social bonds and Internet pornographic exposure among adolescents. *Journal of Adolescence, 32*(3), 601–618. DOI: 10.1016/j.adolescence.2008.06.004 PMID: 18694593

Micheler, S., Goh, Y. M., & Lohse, N. (2019). Innovation landscape and challenges of smart technologies and systems – a European perspective. Production &amp. *Production & Manufacturing Research, 7*(1), 503–528. DOI: 10.1080/21693277.2019.1687363

Michelson, H., Gourlay, S., Lybbert, T., & Wollburg, P. (2023). Purchased agricultural input quality and small farms. *Food Policy, 116*, 102424. DOI: 10.1016/j.foodpol.2023.102424

Minor-Cooley, D., & Parks-Yancy, R. (2020). The power of the brand: Personal branding and its effect on job seeking attributes. *Journal of Internet Commerce, 19*(3), 241–261. DOI: 10.1080/15332861.2020.1777028

Mishra, A. (2011). Geography, Poverty, and Development: An Interdisciplinary Debate. *Sociedade & Natureza, 23*(2), 227–236. DOI: 10.1590/S1982-45132011000200006

Mitchell, D. (2002). Cultural landscapes: The dialectical landscape–recent landscape research in human geography. *Progress in Human Geography, 26*(3), 381–389. DOI: 10.1191/0309132502ph376pr

Mohieldin, M. (2017). *The Sustainable Development Goals and Private Sector Opportunities*. World Bank Group.

Moore, A. D. (2008). Personality-based, rule-utilitarian, and lockean justifications of intellectual property. *The handbook of information and computer ethics*, 105.

Moore, G. K., & Tymowski, W. (2005). *Explanatory guide to the international treaty on plant genetic resources for food and agriculture* (No. 57). IUCN.

Moy, J. W. (2006). Are employers assessing the right traits in hiring? Evidence from Hong Kong companies. *International Journal of Human Resource Management, 17*(4), 734–754. DOI: 10.1080/09585190600581717

Muhammad, M. R., & Sumarauw, J. S. B. (2014). Evaluasi kinerja manajemen rantai pasok pada pemasok daging ayam, Jeky PM. *Jurnal EMBA: Jurnal Riset Ekonomi, Manajemen, Bisnis Dan Akuntansi, 2*(4).

Muharja, M., Darmayanti, R. F., Widjaja, A., Firmansyah, A. A., & Karima, N. (2022). Simulasi Kenaikan Kapasitas Produksi Gula pada Proses Karbonatasi di PT. Industri Gula Glenmore Menggunakan Perangkat Lunak Aspen Plus. [Jurnal Sains Dan Teknologi]. *JST, 11*(1), 125–131.

Mumcu, O. ve Çağlar, E. (2006). Türkiye'nin Nüfusu Zenginlik Kaynağı Olabilir mi? *Ekonomi Politikaları Araştırma Enstitüsü Politika Notu, 24*, 2011.

Mundy, P., & Compton, L. (1991). Indigenous communication and indigenous knowledge. *Development Communication Report*, *74*(3), 1–3.

Munoz-Boudet, A. M. M., Buitrago, P.…Suarez-Becerra, P. (2018). Gender Differences in Poverty and Household Composition through Life-Cycle. World Bank (WPS8360).

Muñoz-Leiva, F., Climent-Climent, S., & Liébana-Cabanillas, F. (2017). Determinants of intention to use the mobile banking apps: An extension of the classic TAM model. *Spanish Journal of Marketing - ESIC*, *21*(1), 25–38. DOI: 10.1016/j.sjme.2016.12.001

Murthy, N., Wodi, A. P., McNally, V. V., Daley, M. F., & Cineas, S. (2024). Advisory Committee on Immunization Practices Recommended Immunization Schedule for Adults Aged 19 Years or Older - United States, 2024. *MMWR. Morbidity and Mortality Weekly Report*, *73*(1), 11–15. DOI: 10.15585/mmwr.mm7301a3 PMID: 38206880

Nadhira, A. H. K., Oktiarso, T., & Harsoyo, T. D. (2019). Manajemen risiko rantai pasok produk sayuran menggunakan metode supply chain operation reference dan model house of risk. *Kurawal-Jurnal Teknologi. Informasi Dan Industri*, *2*(2), 101–117.

Nagy, J. (2018). *Evaluation of online video usage and learning satisfaction: An extension of the Technology Acceptance Model. The International Review of Research in Open and Distributed Learning, 19 (1)*. Athabasca University Press., DOI: 10.19173/irrodl.v19i1.2886

Nakamura, S., Roberts, M., & Stewart, B. (2024). Has Extreme Poverty been Urbanized? World Bank Blogs. https://blogs.worldbank.org/en/developmenttalk/has-extreme-poverty-been-urbanized

Narayan, D. (2000). Poverty is Powerlessness and Voicelessness. *Finance & Development*, •••, 18–21.

Narushima, M., Wong, J. P.-H., Li, A. T.-W., Bhagat, D., Bisignano, A., Fung, K. P.-L., & Poon, M. K.-L. (2020). Youth perspectives on sexual health education: Voices from the YEP study in Toronto. *The Canadian Journal of Human Sexuality*, *29*(1), 32–44. DOI: 10.3138/cjhs.2019-0049

Nasar, M. (2023). Web 3.0: A Review and its Future. *International Journal of Computer Applications*, *185*(10), 41–46. DOI: 10.5120/ijca2023922776

Nasu, H. (2013). The Place of Human Security in Collective Security. *Journal of Conflict and Security Law*, *18*(1), 95–129. DOI: 10.1093/jcsl/krs026

Naufal, F., & Triana, S. (2016). Simulasi Pemodelan Transportasi pada Jaringan Jalan Menggunakan Aplikasi SATURN. *RekaRacana: Jurnal Teknil Sipil*, *2*(1), 72–82.

Needleman, S. E. (2015, January 29). Twitch's viewers reach 100 million a month. The Wall Street Journal. http://blogs.wsj.com/digits/2015/01/29/twitchs-viewers-reach-100-million-a-month/

Nelson, L., Padilla-Walker, L., & Carroll, J. (2010). "I Believe It Is Wrong But I Still Do It": A Comparison of Religious Young Men Who Do Versus Do Not Use Pornography. *Psychology of Religion and Spirituality*, *2*(3), 136–147. DOI: 10.1037/a0019127

Nesterova, D. V. ve Sabirianova, K. Z. (1998). *Investment in human capital under economic transformation in Russia*. Economic Education and Research Consortium.

Ngo, D. (2021, October 14). Ph i chăng gi i tr đang th ơ v i tôn giáo, ch y theo các giá tr hi n đ i? Báo thanh tra. https://thanhtra.com.vn/xa-hoi/doi-song/phai-chang-gioi-tre-dang-tho-o-voi-ton-giao-chay-theo-cac-gia-tri-hien-dai-189296.html

Nguyen Ngoc, T., Viet Dung, M., Rowley, C., & Pejić Bach, M. (2022). Generation Z job seekers' expectations and their job pursuit intention: Evidence from transition and emerging economy. *International Journal of Engineering Business Management*, *14*, 1–13. DOI: 10.1177/18479790221112548

Nguyen, T. T. H., & De Steur, H. (2021). Consumer interest in food fortification in Vietnam: The role of perceived necessity and product familiarity. *Sustainability*, *13*(23), 13422. DOI: 10.3390/su132313422

Nguyen, T. T., & Tran, T. K. (2020). Nutritional transition and beverage consumption patterns in Vietnam. *Nutrients*, *12*(11), 3335. DOI: 10.3390/nu12113335 PMID: 33138339

Niehaves, B., & Plattfaut, R. (2014). Internet adoption by the elderly: Employing IS technology acceptance theories for understanding the age-related digital divide. *European Journal of Information Systems*, *23*(6), 708–726. DOI: 10.1057/ejis.2013.19

Nielsen. (2018). Explore Generation Z in Vietnam: Consumer of tomorrow. https://www.nielsen.com/insights/2018/explore-generation-z-in-vietnam-consumer-of-tomorrow/

Nielsen. (2018, February). 2017 year in sports media. Nielsen. https://www.nielsen.com/insights/2018/2017-year-in-sports-media/#

Noain-Sánchez, A. (2022). Addressing the Impact of Artificial Intelligence on Journalism: The perception of experts, journalists and academics. *Communicatio Socialis*, *35*(3), 105–121. DOI: 10.15581/003.35.3.105-121

Norrman, A., & Jansson, U. (2004). Ericsson's proactive supply chain risk management approach after a serious sub-supplier accident. *International Journal of Physical Distribution & Logistics Management*, *34*(5), 434–456. DOI: 10.1108/09600030410545463

Novi, W. R. (2022). *Pengenalan Alat Proses Pengolahan Gula Di PT. Gendhis Multi Manis (GMM)-BULOG*. Politeknik LPP Yogyakarta.

Nugraheni, S. A., Muljaningsih, S., Mahardika, P., & Saputra, A. (2023). Are We Being Rational? Economics Perspectives on Sacred Natural Sites Commodification. *Экономическая социология, 24*(5), 175-192.

Nur Atikah, A. R. (2021). Rant today and regret it forever! The power of self-branding in social media towards job employments in Malaysia. In Mohamad Saifudin, M.S., Nur Atikah, A. R., & Didik, H. S. (2021). *How trends shape the media landscape: Malaysia and Indonesia* (pp. 17-24). Penerbit Universiti Pendidikan Sultan Idris.

Nur Atikah, , A. RShuhaida, , M. NRani, , A. BSuriati, , SSharifah Nadiah, , S. M. (2022). The role of personal branding for professional digital footprint: Facing employer's cybervetting in recruitment. *International Journal of Early Childhood Special Education, 14*(3), 6404-6412.

Nussbaum, M. (2006). Poverty and Human Functioning: Capabilities as Fundamental Entitlements. In Grusky, D. B., & Kanbur, R. (Eds.), *Poverty and Inequality* (pp. 47–75). Stanford University Press. DOI: 10.1515/9780804767590-004

Nyoman Pujawan, I., & Geraldin, L. H. (2009). House of risk: A model for proactive supply chain risk management. *Business Process Management Journal*, *15*(6), 953–967. DOI: 10.1108/14637150911003801

Nzasabayezu, O., Jaya Prakash, S. K., & Rama Prasad, M. V. (2024). A Study of Poverty Alleviation Strategies for Sustainable Development: A Scientometric Analysis. *Heliyon*, *10*, e33469. DOI: 10.1016/j.heliyon.2024.e33469 PMID: 39040409

OECD. (1996). *Shaping the 21st Century: The Contribution of Development Co-operation*. OECD.

OPHI & UNDP. (2023). *Global Multidimensional Poverty Index: Unstacking Global Poverty*. Oxford University Press.

OPHI & UNDP. (2024). *Global Multidimensional Poverty Index: Poverty Amid Conflict*. Oxford University Press.

Organisation for Economic Co-operation and Development (1998). Human Capital: How What You Know Shapes Your Life.

Organisation for Economic Co-operation and Development. (2001). *The well-being of nations: The role of human and social capital*. OECD publishing.

Oshimi, D. (2015) Emotions of Sport Spectators, ResearchGate. Available at: https://www.researchgate.net/publication/283770561_Emotions_of_Sport_Spectators

Oshimi, D., Harada, M., & Fukuhara, T. (2014). Spectators' emotionsduring live sporting events: Analysis of spectators after the loss of thesupported team at the 2013 FIFA confederations cup. *FootballScience, 11*, 48–58.

Özpınar, E. (2016). *Bebek Ölüm Hızı Türkiye Genelinde Azalıyorken Neden Suriyeli Nüfusun Fazla Olduğu Yerlerde Artıyor. Türkiye Ekonomi Politikaları Araştırma Vakfı (TEPAV)*. Değerlendirme Notu.

Özsoy, C. (2009). Türkiye'de eğitim ve iktisadi büyüme arasindaki ilişkinin VAR modeli ile analizi. *Bilgi Ekonomisi ve Yönetimi Dergisi, 4*(1).

Özütler, H. Ş. (2009). *Beşeri sermaye ve bilgi ekonomisinin iktisadi kalkınmadaki önemi: Türkiye üzerine bir uygulama*. İstanbul Üniversitesi Sosyal Bilimler Enstitüsü, İktisat Anabilim Dalı, İktisat Politikası Bilim Dalı, Yüksek Lisans Tezi.

Paasi, A. (2001). Europe as a social process and discourse: Considerations of place, boundaries and identity. *European Urban and Regional Studies, 8*(1), 7–28. DOI: 10.1177/096977640100800102

Pandita, D. (2022). Innovation in talent management practices: Creating an innovative employer branding strategy to attract generation Z. *International Journal of Innovation Science, 14*(3/4), 556–569. DOI: 10.1108/IJIS-10-2020-0217

Papi, G. U. (1966). General problems of the economics of education. In *The Economics of Education* (pp. 3–23). Palgrave Macmillan. DOI: 10.1007/978-1-349-08464-7_1

Parker, S. K., Bindl, U. K., & Strauss, K. (2010). Making things happen: A model of proactive motivation. *Journal of Management, 36*(4), 827–856. DOI: 10.1177/0149206310363732

Pawlak, K., & Kołodziejczak, M. (2020). The role of agriculture in ensuring food security in developing countries: Considerations in the context of the problem of sustainable food production. *Sustainability (Basel), 12*(13), 5488. DOI: 10.3390/su12135488

Perez, C., & Gringarten, H. (2020, Fall). Personal branding: An essential choise in the Covid-19 era? *Journal of Multidisciplinary Research, 12*(2), 83–92.

Peter, J., & Valkenburg, P. (2006, April). Adolescents' Exposure to Sexually Explicit Material on the Internet. *Communication Research, 33*(2), 178–204. DOI: 10.1177/0093650205285369

Peter, K. Y. (2017). The objectives and principles of the TRIPS agreement. In *The Regulation of Services and Intellectual Property* (pp. 255–322). Routledge.

Peters, T. (2016, May 18). The Brand Called You. https://www.fastcompany.com/28905/brand-called-you

Philippines, U. N. I. C. E. F. (2021a). *Routine immunization for children in the Philippines.* UNICEF Philippines. https://www.unicef.org/philippines/stories/routine-immunization-children-philippines

Philippines, U. N. I. C. E. F. (2021b). *Vaccines for children: your questions answered | UNICEF Philippines.* UNICEF Philippines. https://www.unicef.org/philippines/vaccines-children-faqs

Pieterse, J. N. (2009). *Globalization and culture: global melange* (2nd ed.). Rowman and Littlefield Publishers Inc.

Pingali, P. (2007). Agricultural growth and economic development: A view through the globalization lens. *Agricultural Economics, 37*(s1), 1–12. DOI: 10.1111/j.1574-0862.2007.00231.x

Pogge, T. W. (2010). Politics as Usual: What Lies behind the Pro-Poor Rhetoric. *Polity.*

Ponte, S., & Gibbon, P. (2005). Quality standards, conventions and the governance of global value chains. *Economy and Society, 34*(1), 1–31. DOI: 10.1080/0308514042000329315

Popaitoon, P. (2022). Fostering work meaningfulness for sustainable human resources: A study of generation Z. *Sustainability (Basel), 14*(6), 3626. DOI: 10.3390/su14063626

Pratama, P. A. S. A. (2022). *Analisis Proses Produksi di Stasiun Gilingan Tebu Menggunakan Metode Overall Equipment Effectiveness (OEE) di PT Industri Gula Glenmore.*

Premadasa, M., Siyambalapitiya, J., Jayawardhana, K., & Fernando, I. (2023). Conceptualizing the Role of Social Entrepreneurial Orientation in the Triple Bottom Line in the Social Enterprise Context: Developing Country Perspective. *Sustainability (Basel), 15*(11), 8709. DOI: 10.3390/su15118759

Prip, C. (2024). Farmers' Rights in the Plant Treaty: Interrelations and recent interactions with other international regimes and processes. *Development Studies Research, 11*(1), 2357095. DOI: 10.1080/21665095.2024.2357095

Puertas-Molero, P., Marfil-Carmona, R., & Zurita-Ortega, F. (2019). Impact of sports mass media on the behavior and health of society: A systematic review. *International Journal of Environmental Research and Public Health, 16*(3), 486. DOI: 10.3390/ijerph16030486 PMID: 30744007

Puji, A. A. (2018). *Analisis Mitigasi Risiko Rantai Pasok dengan Integrasi Fuzzy Logic, House of Risk dan AHP (Studi Kasus pada CV. Multiguna)*. Universitas Islam Indonesia.

Qian, T. Y. (2022). Watching sports on Twitch? A study of factors influencing continuance intentions to watch Thursday Night Football co-streaming. *Sport Management Review, 25*(1), 59–80. DOI: 10.1080/14413523.2021.1930700

Quan-Haase, A., & Young, A. L. (2010). Uses and gratifications of social media: A comparison of Facebook and instant messaging. *Bulletin of Science, Technology & Society, 30*(5), 350–361. DOI: 10.1177/0270467610380009

Ragauskas, A. J., Williams, C. K., Davison, B. H., Britovsek, G., Cairney, J., Eckert, C. A., & Mielenz, J. R. (2006). The path forward for biofuels and biomaterials. *Science, 311*(5760), 484–489. DOI: 10.1126/science.1114736 PMID: 16439654

Rahmah, M., Barizah, N., & Blay, S. (2020). Ensuring disclosure of origin of genetic resources in patent applications: Indonesia's efforts to combat biopiracy.

Rakadhitya, R., Hartono, N., & Laurence, L. (2019). Studi kasus mitigasi risiko rantai pasok dengan integrasi house of risk dan fuzzy logic pada PT X. *Journal of Integrated System, 2*(2), 192–207. DOI: 10.28932/jis.v2i2.1974

Raniga, T. (2018). Poverty Alleviation, Social Protection Policy and Sustainability of Economic Development Cooperatives: Voices of Women Residing in Bhambayi Kwazalu-Natal, South Africa. *Social Work, 54*(4), 395–406.

Rapaport, P., & Orbell, S. (2000). Augmenting the theory of planned behaviour: Motivation to provide practical assistance and emotional support to parents. *Psychology & Health, 15*(3), 309–324.

Ravallion, M. (2004). *Pro-Poor Growth: A Primer* (PRWP 3242). World Bank.

Ravallion, M., Datt, G., & van de Walle, D. (1991). Quantifying Absolute Poverty in the Developing World. *Review of Income and Wealth, 37*(4), 345–361. DOI: 10.1111/j.1475-4991.1991.tb00378.x

Restivo, V., Napoli, G., Marsala, M. G. L., Bonanno, V., Sciuto, V., Amodio, E., Calamusa, G., Vitale, F., & Firenze, A. (2015). Factors associated with poor adherence to MMR vaccination in parents who follow vaccination schedule. *Human Vaccines & Immunotherapeutics*, *11*(1), 140–145. DOI: 10.4161/hv.34416 PMID: 25483527

Rice, S. E. (2010). The National Security Implications of Global Poverty. In S. E. Rice, C. Graff, & C. Pascual, *Confronting Poverty: Weak States and U.S. National Security* (pp. 1-22). Brookings.

RMK12. (2022). Tweltfh Plan. https://rmke12.epu.gov.my/en/documents/twelfth-plan (Accessed on 21 September 2022).

Robinson, G. M., & Carson, D. A. (2015). The globalisation of agriculture: Introducing the Handbook. In *Handbook on the globalisation of agriculture* (pp. 1–28). Edward Elgar Publishing. DOI: 10.4337/9780857939838.00006

Rodrigues, C. M. C., & Plotkin, S. A. (2020). Impact of Vaccines; Health, Economic and Social Perspectives. *Frontiers in Microbiology*, *11*(July), 1526. Advance online publication. DOI: 10.3389/fmicb.2020.01526 PMID: 32760367

Rodrigues, D., Lopes, D., Dawson, K., Visser, R., & Štulhofer, A. (2021). With or Without You: Associations Between Frequency of Internet Pornography Use and Sexual Relationship Outcomes for (Non)Consensual (Non)Monogamous Individuals. *Archives of Sexual Behavior*, *50*(4), 1491–1504. DOI: 10.1007/s10508-020-01782-z PMID: 32696155

Rodrigues, L. P., Baldi, V., & Gala, A. (2021). MOBILE JOURNALISM: The emergence of a new field of journalism. *Brazilian Journalism Research.*, *17*(2), 1. DOI: 10.25200/BJR.v17n2.2021.1368

Rogers, R. W. (1975). A protection motivation theory of fear appeals and attitude change. *The Journal of Psychology*, *91*(1), 93–114. DOI: 10.1080/00223980.1975.9915803 PMID: 28136248

Rohmadhon, E., & Yuamita, F. (2023). Analisis Human Error untuk Mengurangi Kecelakaan Kerja pada Stasiun Penggilingan PG. Madukismo Menggunakan Metode SHERPA dan HEART. *Jurnal Cakrawala Ilmiah*, *2*(11), 4129–4140. DOI: 10.53625/jcijurnalcakrawalailmiah.v2i11.6117

Rojas-Rivas, E., Espinoza-Ortega, A., Thomé-Ortíz, H., Moctezuma-Pérez, S., & Cuffia, F. (2019). Understanding consumers' perception and consumption motives towards amaranth in Mexico using the Pierre Bourdieu's theoretical concept of Habitus. *Appetite*, *139*, 180–188. DOI: 10.1016/j.appet.2019.04.021 PMID: 31059761

Romanto, F., & Handoko, F. (2022). Metode Supply Chain Operation Reference (SCOR) Sebagai Analisis Kinerja Manajemen Rantai Pasok di Pabrik Gula Pandjie. *Jurnal Valtech*, *5*(1), 107–113.

Rosenberg, M. J. (1979). *Conceiving the self.* Basic Books.

Rosida, L. (2018). Rural and Urban Poverty in Developing Countries. *Media Bina Ilmiah*, *13*(1), 835–843. DOI: 10.33758/mbi.v13i1.144

Rothschild, E. (1995). What is Security? The Quest for a World Order. *Daedalus*, *124*(3), 53–98.

Rowe, S., Brady, C., Sarang, R., Wiipongwii, T., Leu, M., Jennings, L., Peterson, T., Boston, J., Roach, B., Phillips, J., & Conrad, Z. (2024). Improving Indigenous Food Sovereignty through sustainable food production: A narrative review. *Frontiers in Sustainable Food Systems*, *8*, 1341146. DOI: 10.3389/fsufs.2024.1341146

Roy, A., & Chatterjee, B. (2022). Evolution and Application of IPR Laws with Reference to Pepsico vs. Gujarat Farmers Case. *IUP Law Review*, *12*(3).

Rozzaq, A. (2022). *Hubungan Patron Klien Petani Tebu dengan Pengusaha Gula Tebu.*

Ruggles, F., & Silverman, H. (2009). *From tangible to intangible heritage. Intangible heritage embodied, 1-14*. Springer.

Russell, R. S., & Taylor, B. W. (2019). *Operations and supply chain management.* John Wiley & Sons.

Rzemieniak, M., & Wawer, M. (2021). Employer branding in the context of the company's sustainable development strategy from the perspective of gender diversity of generation Z. *Sustainability (Basel)*, *13*(2), 828. DOI: 10.3390/su13020828

Sagala, J. R. (2021). Model Rapid Application Development (Rad)Dalam Pengembangan Sistem Informasi Penjadwalanbelajar Mengajar. *Jurnal Mantik Penusa*, *2*(1).

Sagoff, M. (2001). Biotechnology and agriculture: The common wisdom and its critics. *Indonesian Journal of Global Legal Studies*, *9*, 13.

Sahai, S. (2003). India's plant variety protection and Farmers' Rights Act, 2001. *Current Science*, *84*(3), 407–412.

Salgado, L. (2022). From the classroom to the newsroom: A critical route to introduce AI in journalism education. Facts & Frictions: Emerging Debates. *Pedagogies and Practices in Contemporary Journalism*, *2*(1), 80–97. DOI: 10.22215/ff/v2.i1.04

Santos, F. C. C. (2023). Artificial Intelligence in Automated Detection of Disinformation: A Thematic Analysis. *Journal of Medicine*, *4*(2), 679–687. DOI: 10.3390/journalmedia4020043

Sari, D., & Yusnita Arvianti, E. (2018). Pembangunan Pertanian (Agriculture Development). *Available at SSRN* 3110561.

Sasmal, R., Das, P., & Sasmal, J. (2024). Public Policy, Economic Growth and Poverty Alleviation: A Study in the Indian States. *Athens Journal of Business & Economics*, *10*(3), 159–182. DOI: 10.30958/ajbe.10-3-1

Saufi, M. (2019). ANALISA Faktor-Faktor yang Mempengaruhi Kepuasan Petani Tebu sebagai Upaya Menigkatkan Loyalitas terhadap Pabrik Gula Pesantren Baru. *REVITALISASI: Jurnal Ilmu Manajemen*, *6*(3), 19–26.

Saurav, A., Liu, Y., & Sinha, A. (2020). *Foreign Direct Investment and Employment Outcomes in Developing Countries*. The World Bank Group.

Schaetz, N., Gagrčin, E., Toth, R., & Emmer, M. (2023). Algorithm dependency in platformized news use. *New Media & Society*, *0*(0). Advance online publication. DOI: 10.1177/14614448231193093

Schanbacher, W. D. (2010). *The politics of food: The global conflict between food security and food sovereignty*. Bloomsbury Publishing USA. DOI: 10.5040/9798400698576

Schaufeli, W. B., & Taris, T. W. (2014). A critical review of the job demands-resources model: Implications for improving work and health. In Bauer, G. F., & Hämmig, O. (Eds.), *Bridging occupational, organizational and public health: A transdisciplinary approach* (pp. 43–68). Springer., DOI: 10.1007/978-94-007-5640-3_4

Schroth, H. (2019). Are you ready for Gen Z in the workplace? *California Management Review*, *61*(3), 5–18. DOI: 10.1177/0008125619841006

Schultz, T. W. (1961). Investment in human capital. *The American Economic Review*, *51*(1), 1–17.

Scolere, L., Pruchniewska, U., & Duffy, B. E. (2018). Constructing the platform-specific self-brand: The labor of social media promotion. *Social Media + Society*, *4*(3), 1–11. DOI: 10.1177/2056305118784768

Scoones, I. (2013). Livelihoods perspectives and rural development. In *Critical perspectives in rural development studies* (pp. 159–184). Routledge.

Scott, A. (2004). Cultural products industries and urban economic development. *Urban Economic Review,* 461-490.

Scott, A. (2010). Cultural economy and creative field of the city. *Geografiska Annaler. Series B, Human Geography*, *92*(2), 115–130. DOI: 10.1111/j.1468-0467.2010.00337.x

Secretariat of the Convention on Biological Diversity. (2011). *Nagoya Protocol on access to genetic resources and the fair and equitable sharing of benefits arising from their utilization to the convention on biological diversity: text and annex.* UN.

Sen, A. (2000). *Development as Freedom.* Oxford University Press.

Seshia, S. (2002). Plant variety protection and farmers' rights: Law-making and cultivation of varietal control. *Economic and Political Weekly,* •••, 2741–2747.

Sharma, S. K., Janssen, M., Bunker, D., Pery, C. D., Singh, J. B., Dwivedi, Y. K., & Misra, S. K. (2023). Unlocking the Potential of Smart Technologies: Addressing Adoption Challenges. *Information Systems Frontiers*, *25*(4), 1293–1298. DOI: 10.1007/s10796-023-10408-3

Shelton, D. (2012). Resolving Conflicts between Human Rights and Environmental Protection: Is there a Hierarchy? In de Wet, E., & Widmar, J. (Eds.), *Hierarchy in International Law: The Place of Human Rights* (pp. 181–194). Oxford University Press. DOI: 10.1093/acprof:oso/9780199647071.003.0008

Shepherd, A., Mitchell, T., & Muir-Wood, R. (2013). *The Geography of Poverty, Disasters and Climate Extremes in 2030.* ODI.

Simply Psychology. (2024, February 1). Albert Bandura's social learning theory in psychology. https://www.simplypsychology.org/bandura.html

Singh, K., Abraham, R., Yadav, J., Agrawal, A. K., & Kolar, P. (2023). Linking CSR and organizational performance: The intervening role of sustainability risk management and organizational reputation. *Social Responsibility Journal, 19*(10), 1830–1851. DOI: 10.1108/SRJ-07-2022-0309

Singh, P. (2021). Politics of knowledge in development: Explorations in seed sovereignty. *Studies in Indian Politics*, *9*(1), 105–117. DOI: 10.1177/2321023021999179

Sirgy, M. J. (1982). Self-concept in consumer behavior: A critical review. *The Journal of Consumer Research*, *9*(3), 287–300. DOI: 10.1086/208924

Sjarif, S. R., Nuryadi, A. M., Sulistiorini, J., & Sukron, A. (2021). Penambahan Glukosa Dan Pengaruh Derajat Brix Untuk Menghambat Proses Kristalisasi Pada Produk Gula Cair Nira Aren. *Jurnal Penelitian Teknologi Industri, 13*(1), 27–36.

Skuland, S. E. (2015). Healthy eating and barriers related to social class. The case of vegetable and fish consumption in Norway. *Appetite, 92*, 217–226. DOI: 10.1016/j.appet.2015.05.008 PMID: 25982927

Smith, M. (2023, October 31). 50% of Gen Z wants to ditch corporate jobs and run their own businesses, according to new research. *CNBC*. https://www.cnbc.com/2023/10/31/50percent-of-gen-z-wants-to-ditch-corporate-jobs-run-their-own-business-says-report.html

Solano, I., Eaton, N. R., & O'Leary, K. D. (2018). Pornography Consumption, Modality and Function in a Large Internet Sample. *Journal of Sex Research, 57*(1), 92–103. DOI: 10.1080/00224499.2018.1532488 PMID: 30358432

Son, H. H., & Kakwani, N. (2004). Economic Growth and Poverty Reduction: Initial Conditions Matter. *International Poverty Centre Working Paper 2*. https://ipcig.org/pub/IPCWorkingPaper2.pdf

Springer, K. (2020). *I am my brand: How to build your brand without apology*. Bloomsbury Publishing Plc.

Starr, C. R., & Ferguson, G. M. (2012). Sexy Dolls, Sexy Grade-Schoolers? Media & Maternal Influences on Young Girls' Self-Sexualization. *Sex Roles*, *67*(7-8), 463–476. DOI: 10.1007/s11199-012-0183-x

State clinics barely fill healthcare void in the Philippines. (2022). *BusinessWorld Online*. https://www.bworldonline.com/top-stories/2022/03/14/435670/state-clinics-barely-fill-healthcare-void-in-the-philippines/

Statista. (2024). Non-alcoholic drinks market in Vietnam - statistics & facts. https://www.statista.com/outlook/cmo/non-alcoholic-drinks/soft-drinks/vietnam

Sthapit, B. R., Lamers, H., & Rao, R. (2013). Custodian farmers of agricultural biodiversity: selected profiles from South and South East Asia: proceedings of the workshop on custodian farmers of agricultural biodiversity, 11-12 February 2013, New Delhi, India.

Stiglitz, J. (2012). *The Price of Inequality: How Today's Divided Society Endangers Our Future*. W. W. Norton.

Stiris, L. (2022, June 24). How Twitch built the global live streaming network that powers Amazon IVS. Amazon Interactive Video Service.

Strauss, K., Griffin, M. A., & Parker, S. K. (2012). Future work selves: How salient hoped-for identities motivate proactive career behaviors. *The Journal of Applied Psychology*, *97*(3), 580–598. DOI: 10.1037/a0026423 PMID: 22122111

Stringer, L. C., Fraser, E. D., Harris, D., Lyon, C., Pereira, L., Ward, C. F., & Simelton, E. (2020). Adaptation and development pathways for different types of farmers. *Environmental Science & Policy*, *104*, 174–189. DOI: 10.1016/j.envsci.2019.10.007

Sugiharti, L., Esquivias, M. A., Shaari, M. S., Jayanti, A. D., & Ridzuan, A. R. (2023). Indonesia's Poverty Puzzle: Chronic vs. Transient Poverty Dynamics. *Cogent Economics & Finance*, *11*(2), 2267927. DOI: 10.1080/23322039.2023.2267927

Sulistiyono, W., Zuliandry, M. I. R., & Haryanto, Y. D. (2023). Uji Verifikasi Data Permukaan dan Indeks Udara atas Hasil Model WRF dengan Data Observasi Stasiun Meteorologi Sultan Hasanudin:(Studi Kasus: 6 Desember 2021). *OPTIKA: Jurnal Pendidikan Fisika*, *7*(1), 10–22. DOI: 10.37478/optika.v7i1.2354

Sultanovich, M. D. (2023). The Main Directions of Poverty Reduction in our Country. *Galaxy International Interdisciplinary Research Journal*, *11*(2), 164–171.

Sumita. (2023). Farmers' Rights in the International Treaty on Plant Genetic Resources for Food and Agriculture. *Part 2 Indian J. Integrated Rsch. L.*, *3*, 1.

Swart, J. (2021). Experiencing Algorithms: How Young People Understand, Feel About, and Engage With Algorithmic News Selection on Social Media. *Social Media + Society*, *7*(2), 20563051211008828. Advance online publication. DOI: 10.1177/20563051211008828

Swiderska, K., Reid, H., Song, Y., Li, J., Mutta, D., Ongugo, P., ... & Barriga, S. (2011). The role of traditional knowledge and crop varieties in adaptation to climate change and food security in SW China. *Bolivian Andes and coastal Kenya.*

Syamil, A., Subawa, S., Budaya, I., Munizu, M., Darmayanti, N. L., Fahmi, M. A., Wanda, S. S., Murwani, I. A., Utami, F. N., & Dulame, I. M. (2023). *Manajemen Rantai Pasok*. PT. Sonpedia Publishing Indonesia.

Tajfel, H., Turner, J. C., & Austin, W. G. (1982). Social psychology of intergroup relations. *Annual Review of Psychology*, *33*(1), 1–39. DOI: 10.1146/annurev.ps.33.020182.000245

Tamir, D. (2019). The psychology of live sports broadcasts: The impact of live viewing on fan engagement. *Journal of Sport Psychology*, *45*(4), 567–584.

Tandoc, E. C., Wu, S., Tan, J., & Contreras-Yap, S. (2022). What is (automated) news? A content analysis of algorithm-written news articles. Media E Jornalismo, 22(41), 103-120. https://hdl.handle.net/10356/173664

Tan, S. M., & Yeo, B. J. (2023). Between life, death, and modernity at Bukit Brown Cemetery, Singapore. In *New Perspectives on Urban Deathscapes* (pp. 42–60). Edward Elgar Publishing.

Tan, S.-A., Goh, Y. S., Mohd Zaharim, N., Gan, S. W., Yap, C. C., Nainee, S., & Lee, L. K. (2022). Problematic Internet Pornography Use and Psychological Distress among Emerging Adults in Malaysia: Gender as a Moderator. *International Journal of Environmental Research and Public Health, 19*(6), 3682. DOI: 10.3390/ijerph19063682 PMID: 35329369

Tarpey, M. (Careerbuilder.com) (August 9, 2018). Not getting job offers? Your social media could be the reason. Accessed from https://www.careerbuilder.com/advice/not-getting-job-offers-your-social-media-could-be-the-reason (Accessed on 10 February 2020).

Taylor, S. J. (2016). *A Review of Sustainable Development Principles: Centre for Environmental Studies*. University of Pretoria.

Tengku Siti Meriam, T. W., Hazura, M., Siti Fadzilah, M. N., Zurina, M., & Intan Yusrina, Z. (2019). Awareness of digital footprint management in the new media amongst youth. *Jurnal Komunikasi, 35*(3), 407–421.

The Economic Times. (2023). What is Labour Market. Accessed from https://economictimes.indiatimes.com/definition/labour-market (Accessed on 28 February 2023).

The Times of India. (Nov. 30, 2024). Delhi Air Quality Index Today. https://timesofindia.indiatimes.com/weather/delhi-aqi-level-air-quality-index-today/3291

This Day in Tech History. (2023). First Sports TV Broadcast. Retrieved from thisdayintechhistory.com Columbia University. (2019). Columbia Celebrates 80th anniversary of first live televised sporting event in the United States.

Thompson, F. C. (2009). Nomenclature and classification, principles of. In *Encyclopedia of insects* (pp. 707–714). Academic Press. DOI: 10.1016/B978-0-12-374144-8.00191-0

Thwaites, K., & Simkins, I. (2006). *Experiential landscape: an approach to people, place and space*. Routledge. DOI: 10.4324/9780203462096

Tian, Y., Yang, P., & Zhang, D. (2023). The relationship between media use and sports participation behavior: A meta-analysis. *Digital Health, 9*, 20552076231185476. Advance online publication. DOI: 10.1177/20552076231185476 PMID: 37434724

Tilley, C. (2006). Introduction: Identity, place, landscape and heritage. *Journal of Material Culture, 11*(1-2), 7–32. DOI: 10.1177/1359183506062990

Tims, M., & Bakker, A. B. (2010). Job crafting: Towards a new model of individual job redesign. *SA Journal of Industrial Psychology, 36*(1), 841. Advance online publication. DOI: 10.4102/sajip.v36i2.841

Tiwari, S. (2024).The role of artificial intelligence in automated journalism: transforming newsproduction. International journal of creative research thoughts. 12(5): 799-838. https://ijcrt.org/papers/IJCRT21X0233.pdf

Tomlinson, J. (2003). Globalization and cultural identity. In Held, D., & McGrew, A. (Eds.), *The Global transformation reader: An introduction to the globalization debate* (2nd ed., pp. 268–277). Polity Press.

Touch, V., Tan, D. K., Cook, B. R., & Liu, L. D., Cross, R., Tran, T. A., ... & Cowie, A. (2024). Smallholder farmers' challenges and opportunities: Implications for agricultural production, environment and food security. *Journal of Environmental Management, 370*, 122536.

Trading Economics. (2021). Malaysa Unemployment Rate. https://tradingeconomics.com/malaysia/unemployment-rate (Accessed on 9 February 2021).

Tran, N. T. (1999). Cơ s văn hóa Vi t Nam. Giáo d c.

Trigg, A. B. (2001). Veblen, Bourdieu, and conspicuous consumption. *Journal of Economic Issues, 35*(1), 99–115. DOI: 10.1080/00213624.2001.11506342

Tripathi, S. K. (2003). Intellectual property and genetic resources, Traditional Knowledge and Folklore: International, regional and national perspectives, trends and strategies.

Tuan, Y. F. (1979). Space and place: humanistic perspective. In *Philosophy in geography* (pp. 387–427). Springer Netherlands. DOI: 10.1007/978-94-009-9394-5_19

Tuan, Y. F. (1991). Language and the making of place: A narrative-descriptive approach. *Annals of the Association of American Geographers, 81*(4), 684–696. DOI: 10.1111/j.1467-8306.1991.tb01715.x

Tuan, Y. F. (2017). *A historical geography of China*. Routledge. DOI: 10.4324/9781315083537

Tucker, B. (2022, September 14). History of cable. SeatUp. https://seatup.com/blog/history-of-cable/

Tull, F., Borg, K., Knott, C., Beasley, M., Halliday, J., Faulkner, N., Sutton, K., & Bragge, P. (2019). Short Message Service Reminders to Parents for Increasing Adolescent Human Papillomavirus Vaccination Rates in a Secondary School Vaccine Program: A Randomized Control Trial. *The Journal of Adolescent Health, 65*(1), 116–123. DOI: 10.1016/j.jadohealth.2018.12.026 PMID: 30879881

Turan, F. (2016). Türkiye'nin Zorunlu Eğitim Politikaları-Tarihsel Perspektif 1. *Çağdaş Yönetim Bilimleri Dergisi, 3*(1), 1-10.

Twarog, S., & Kapoor, P. (2004). *Protecting and promoting traditional knowledge: systems, national experiences and international dimensions* (p. 418). UN.

Ulep, V. G. J. U. (2021). An assessment of the expanded program on immunization (EPI) in the Philippines: Challenges and ways forward. *Www.Econstor.Eu.* http://hdl.handle.net/10419/241052

Ulfah, M., Maarif, M. S., & Sukardi, S. R. (2016). Analisis dan perbaikan manajemen risiko rantai pasok gula rafinasi dengan Pendekatan house of risk. *Jurnal Teknologi Industri Pertanian, 26*(1).

UN. (2000). Resolution Adopted by the General Assembly. *55/2 United Nations Millennium Declaration.* UN.

UN. (2015a). *The Millennium Development Goals Report.* UN.

UN. (2015b). *Transforming Our World: The 2030 Agenda for Sustainable Development.* UN.

UN. (n.d.). Goal 1: Eradicate Extreme Poverty & Hunger. https://www.un.org/millenniumgoals/poverty.shtml

UNDESA. (2018). *The Sustainable Development Goals Report 2017.* UNDESA.

UNDP. (1994). *Human Development Report.* UNDP.

UNDP. (2022). *New Threats to Human Security in the Anthropocene: Demanding Greater Solidarity.* UNDP.

United Nations Global Compact. (2021). Principles for Responsible Investment. https://www.unpri.org/download?ac=10948

United Nations Office of the High Commissioner for Human Rights. (1966). Article 15, ICESCR. https://www.ohchr.org/en/instruments-mechanisms/instruments/international-covenant-economic-social-and-cultural-rights

United Nations. (n.d.). Article 27, UDHR. https://www.un.org/en/about-us/universal-declaration-of-human-rights

Ünsal, E. M. (2009). *Makro İktisat, Gözden Geçirilmiş 8*. Baskı, İmaj Yayınevi.

UNTFHS (United Nations Trust Fund for Human Security). (2016). *Human Security Handbook*. UNTFHS.

Urry, J. (1995). *Consuming Places*. Routledge.

Üzümcü, A. (2008). Türkiye ekonomisinde büyüme ve kalkınma dinamikleri: 1923–2007. *Türkiye'nin Ekonomi-Politiği*, *312*(384), 281.

Venkatesh, V. (2000). Determinants of perceived ease of use: Integrating control, intrinsic motivation, and emotion into the technology acceptance model. *Information Systems Research*, *11*(4), 342–365. DOI: 10.1287/isre.11.4.342.11872

Verified Market Research. (2023). *Sugar-free beverages market size, share & trends*. https://www.verifiedmarketresearch.com/product/sugar-free-beverages-market/

Vernooy, R., Adokorach, J., Kimani, D., Marwa, A., Mayoyo, A., & Nyadanu, D. (2023). On the margins: a review of policies and laws in support of farmer-managed seed systems in.

Vettehen, P. H., Wiltink, D., Huiskamp, M., Schaap, G., & Ketelaar, P. (2019). Taking the full view: How viewers respond to 360-degree video news. *Computers in Human Behavior*, *91*, 24–32. DOI: 10.1016/j.chb.2018.09.018

Viana, C. M., Freire, D., Abrantes, P., Rocha, J., & Pereira, P. (2022). Agricultural land systems importance for supporting food security and sustainable development goals: A systematic review. *The Science of the Total Environment*, *806*, 150718. DOI: 10.1016/j.scitotenv.2021.150718 PMID: 34606855

Vietnam Chamber of Commerce and Industry. (2022). Vietnam to act on surge of sugary drinks. https://en.vcci.com.vn/vietnam-to-act-on-surge-of-sugary-drinks

Vietnam News. (2024, March 15). Viet Nam takes move to curb obesity. https://vietnamnews.vn/society/1398219/viet-nam-takes-move-to-curb-obesity.html

Vijayakumar, M. (2017). Skill sets depicted by fresh graduates in campus hiring process. *International Journal of Innovative Science and Research Technology*, *2*(7), 64–72.

von Kutzschenbach, M., & Brønn, C. (2006). Communicating sustainable development initiatives: Applying co-orientation to forest management certification. *Journal of Communication Management (London), 10*(3), 304–322. DOI: 10.1108/13632540610681185

Wacziarg, R., & Welch, K. H. (2008). Trade Liberalization and Growth: New Evidence. *The World Bank Economic Review, 22*(2), 187–231. DOI: 10.1093/wber/lhn007

Wafi, N. N. (2017). *Identifikasi Dan Strategi Mitigasi Risiko Rantai Pasok Komoditas Kakao Menggunakan Metode Fuzzy-House Of Risk (Fuzzy-Hor)(Studi Kasus Di PT. Kampung Coklat Blitar)*. Universitas Brawijaya.

Walrave, M., Ouytsel, J. V., Diederen, K., & Ponnet, K. (2022). Checked and approved? Human resources managers' uses of social media for cybervetting. *Journal of Cybersecurity and Privacy, 2022*(2), 402–417. DOI: 10.3390/jcp2020021

Wang, Z., Guo, K., Wang, C., Duan, H., Zhang, L., & Zhao, X. (2022). How can social needs impact on meaningful sports consumption? *Frontiers in Psychology, 13*, 1043080. Advance online publication. DOI: 10.3389/fpsyg.2022.1043080 PMID: 36405184

Wann, D. L., & James, J. D. (2019). Sports broadcasting and fan engagement: The role of media in shaping sports consumption. *International Journal of Sport Communication, 12*(1), 55–73.

Waples, C. J., & Brachle, B. J. (2020). Recruiting millennials: Exploring the impact of CSR involvement and pay signaling on organizational attractiveness. *Corporate Social Responsibility and Environmental Management, 27*(2), 870–880. DOI: 10.1002/csr.1851

Warner, M., Bourdieu, P., & Nice, R. (1985). Distinction: A Social Critique of the Judgement of Taste. *MLN, 100*(5), 1133. DOI: 10.2307/2905454

Warren, D. M. (1991). *Using indigenous knowledge in agricultural development* (No. 127, p. 46pp).

Watal, J., Taubman, A., & Cottier, T. (2015). The making of the TRIPS agreement: Personal insights from the Uruguay round negotiations.

Waziri, M., Ibrahim, A. B., & Zainal, M. Z. (2020). Investigating the Empirical Relationship between Government Interventions Programs and Poverty Alleviation: A Case of Nigeria. *Journal of Economic and Administrative Sciences, 36*(4), 323–338. DOI: 10.1108/JEAS-06-2019-0060

WCED (World Commission on Environment and Development). (1987). *Our Common Future*.

Wentzell, E., & Racila, A. M. (2021). The social experience of participation in a COVID-19 vaccine trial: Subjects' motivations, others' concerns, and insights for vaccine promotion. *Vaccine*, *39*(17), 2445–2451. DOI: 10.1016/j.vaccine.2021.03.036 PMID: 33745730

West, R. L., Turner, L. H., & Zhao, G. (2010). *Introducing communication theory: Analysis and application* (Vol. 2). McGraw-Hill.

Whiting, A., & Williams, D. (2013). Why people use social media: A uses and gratifications approach. *Qualitative Market Research*, *16*(4), 362–369. DOI: 10.1108/QMR-06-2013-0041

WHO. (2024). Sustainable development goals. https://www.who.int/europe/about-us/our-work/sustainable-development-goals#:~:text=The%20Sustainable%20Development%20Goals%20(SDGs,no%20one%20is%20left%20behind (Accessed on 3 May 2024).

Why Vaccinate," Centers for Disease Control and Prevention. (2019). Cdc. https://www.cdc.gov/vaccines/parents/why-vaccinate/index.html

Wicaksono, R. S., Pardiman, P., & Rahmawati, R. (2023). Pengaruh Punishment, Reward, dan Motivasi Kerja Terhadap Kinerja Karyawan Pada PT. PG Rajawali 1. *E-JRM: Elektronik Jurnal Riset Manajemen*, *12*(02), 1335–1344.

Wierzbicka, M., Klussmann, J. P., San Giorgi, M. R., Wuerdemann, N., & Dikkers, F. G. (2021). Oral and laryngeal HPV infection: Incidence, prevalence and risk factors, with special regard to concurrent infection in head, neck and genitals. *Vaccine*, *39*(17), 2344–2350. DOI: 10.1016/j.vaccine.2021.03.047 PMID: 33812740

Wilson, R. J. I., Vergélys, C., Ward, J., Peretti-Watel, P., & Verger, P. (2020). Vaccine hesitancy among general practitioners in Southern France and their reluctant trust in the health authorities. *International Journal of Qualitative Studies on Health and Well-being*, *15*(1), 1757336. Advance online publication. DOI: 10.1080/17482631.2020.1757336 PMID: 32400299

Witte, K. (1992). Putting the fear back into fear appeals: The extended parallel process model. *Communication Monographs*, *59*(4), 329–349. DOI: 10.1080/03637759209376276

Wollburg, P., Hallegatte, S., & Mahler, D. G. (2023). *The Climate Implications of Ending Global Poverty*. World Bank Group., PRWP 10318. DOI: 10.1596/1813-9450-10318

Woodhall, M. (1987). Economics of education: a review: economics of education research and studies. *Economics of Education Research and Studies.*

Woodhall-Melnik, J., & Matheson, F. I. (2017). More than convenience: The role of habitus in understanding the food choices of fast food workers. *Work, Employment and Society, 31*(5), 800–815. DOI: 10.1177/0950017016648255

World Bank. (1990). *World Development Report: Poverty.* https://documents1.worldbank.org/curated/en/424631468163162670/pdf/PUB85070REPLACEMENT0WDR01990.pdf

World Bank. (1992). *World Development Report.* https://digitallibrary.un.org/record/1305153?ln=en&v=pdf

World Bank. (2014). *The World Bank Group Goals: End Extreme Poverty and Promote Shared Prosperity.* https://hdl.handle.net/10986/20138

World Bank. (2022). *Poverty and Shared Prosperity Report.*

World Bank. (2024). *Poverty, Prosperity, and Planet Report: Pathways out of the Polycrisis.*

World Health Organization. (2015). *Guideline: Sugars intake for adults and children.* https://www.who.int/publications/i/item/9789241549028

World Health Organization. (2016). *Global report on diabetes.* https://www.who.int/publications/i/item/9789241565257

World Health Organization. (2018). *Polio outbreak in the Philippines.* World Health Organization. https://www.who.int/westernpacific/emergencies/polio-outbreak-in-the-philippines

World Health Organization. (2020). *The state of food security and nutrition in the world 2020: transforming food systems for affordable healthy diets* (Vol. 2020). Food & Agriculture Organization.

World Health Organization. (2023, May 15). WHO advises not to use non-sugar sweeteners for weight control in newly released guideline [News release]. https://www.who.int/news/item/15-05-2023-who-advises-not-to-use-non-sugar-sweeteners-for-weight-control-in-newly-released-guideline

Wratten, E. (1995). Conceptualizing Urban Poverty. *Environment and Urbanization, 7*(1), 11–38. DOI: 10.1177/095624789500700118

Wyer, S. (2024). 'Palermo is a mosaic': Cosmopolitan rhetoric in the capital of Sicily. *Modern Italy, 29*(4), 1–20. www.bruneitourism.com. DOI: 10.1017/mit.2024.13

Wynberg, R. (2023). Biopiracy: Crying wolf or a lever for equity and conservation? *Research Policy*, *52*(2), 104674. DOI: 10.1016/j.respol.2022.104674

Wysocki, D. K. (1998). Let Your Fingers Do the Talking: Sex on an Adult Chat-line. *Sexualities*, *1*(4), 425–452. DOI: 10.1177/136346098001004003

Yamane, T. (1973). *Statistics: An introductory analysis* (3rd ed.). Harper & Row.

Yang, L. (2017). The Relationship between Poverty and Inequality: Concepts and Measurement. *LSE*. https://sticerd.lse.ac.uk/dps/case/cp/casepaper205.pdf

Yasin, R., Huseynova, A., & Atif, M. (2023). Green human resource management, a gateway to employer branding: Mediating role of corporate environmental sustainability and corporate social sustainability. *Corporate Social Responsibility and Environmental Management*, *30*(1), 369–383. DOI: 10.1002/csr.2360

Yaylali, M. ve Lebe, F. (2011). Beşeri sermaye ile iktisadi büyüme arasındaki ilişkinin ampirik analizi. *Marmara University Journal of the Faculty of Economic & Administrative Sciences, 30*(1).

Yerkes, R. M., & Dodson, J. D. (1908). The relation of strength of stimulus to rapidity of habit-formation. *The Journal of Comparative Neurology and Psychology*, *18*(5), 459–482. DOI: 10.1002/cne.920180503

Younes, B. (2022). Smart E-textiles: A review of their aspects and applications. *Journal of Industrial Textiles*. Advance online publication. DOI: 10.1177/15280837231215493

Youn, G. (2006). Subjective Sexual Arousal in Response to Erotica: Effects of Gender, Guided Fantasy, Erotic Stimulus, and Duration of Exposure. *Archives of Sexual Behavior*, *35*(1), 87–97. DOI: 10.1007/s10508-006-8997-z PMID: 16502156

Yuan, G. N., Marquez, G. P. B., Deng, H., Iu, A., Fabella, M., Salonga, R. B., Ashardiono, F., & Cartagena, J. A. (2022). A review on urban agriculture: Technology, socio-economy, and policy. *Heliyon*, *8*(11), e11583. DOI: 10.1016/j.heliyon.2022.e11583 PMID: 36406682

Yudha, B. S. (2019). *Evaluasi 8 Pilar TPM (Total Productive Maintenance) dan Pengaruhnya Terhadap Kinerja Manufaktur (OEE-Overall Equipment Effectiveness dan Waste)(Studi kasus: PT. XYZ Divisi Biskuit)*. http://unugha.ac.id

Yu, P. K. (2024). WIPO Negotiations on Intellectual Property, Genetic Resources and Associated Traditional Knowledge. *Akron Law Review*, *57*, 23–71.

Zhang, T., Zhang, J., & Tu, S. (2024). An empirical study on corporate ESG behavior and employee satisfaction: A moderating mediation model. *Behavioral Sciences (Basel, Switzerland)*, *14*(4), 274. DOI: 10.3390/bs14040274

Zhang, W., Pérez Tornero, J. M., & Tian, Q. (2023). Dissecting Automated News Production From a Transdisciplinary Perspective: Methodology, Linguistic Application, and Narrative Genres. *SAGE Open*, *13*(4), 21582440231206372. Advance online publication. DOI: 10.1177/21582440231206372

About the Contributors

Nur Atikah A. Rahman is currently the Deputy Dean of Academic, Career and Internationl as well as a senior lecturer at the School of Communication, Universiti Sains Malaysia. She holds a PhD in Mass Communication from Universiti Putra Malaysia. She has obtained her Master of Arts Communication (Advertising Strategy) and Bachelor of Communication (Persuasive Communication) in Universiti Sains Malaysia. In June 2020, she received a Foundation Certificate from the Institute of Practitioners in Advertising (IPA), Incorporated by Royal Charter, UK, funded by the Association of Accredited Advertising Agents Malaysia (4As). Prior to pursuing as an academic, she was a copywriter for several advertising and branding agencies in the private sector. Her research expertise include advertising, self-branding, social media influencer, creative content ideation, and brand loyalty.

Rani Ann Balaraman is a senior lecturer in the School of Communication, Universiti Sains Malaysia. She earned her PhD from Universiti Kebangsaan Malaysia in 2013 and Master of Publishing Studies from Universiti Malaya in 2003. Aside from that, she has obtained her Bachelor in Media Studies in Universiti Malaya in 2001. Before joining the academia, she was a reporter at several news agencies. Currently, she is actively involved in research areas such as citizen journalism, online journalism, media studies, new media and creative writing.

Carl Christian Capon is a committed researcher and academic specializing in Business Technology Management, with a strong focus on aligning emerging technologies with strategic business processes. His expertise centers on understanding how digital innovations can enhance organizational performance, streamline operations, and support data-driven decision-making. His research interests cover a broad spectrum within the computing discipline, including Information Systems, Computer Systems Organization, and Computer Systems Applications. Through his work, Mr. Capon explores the design, structure, and practical implementation of computer systems that empower organizations to adapt to rapidly evolving technological landscapes. Driven by a passion for innovation and interdisciplinary collaboration, Mr. Capon continues to contribute to the advancement of technology-enabled business solutions, advocating for systems that are efficient, intelligent, and responsive to organizational needs.

Anik Dwiastuti is an Asistant Professor in the Department of Mechanical and Industrial Engineering

Jipson Joseph is a research scholar of Law at CHRIST University, Bangalore, India. His research interests are in Constitutional Law, Human Rights, Global Poverty, Human Security, and Ethics.

Aisyah Larasati is an Associate Professor in the Department of Mechanical and Industrial Engineering - State University of Malang. She received her doctoral degree from the Department of Industrial Engineering and Management - Oklahoma State University. Her research interests include system engineering, data analytics, statistics, and service management.

Achyuta Nanda Mishra is a Professor at School of Law, Christ University, Bangalore. He has 23 years of teaching experience. He has his research interests in the areas of Constitutional law, Legal theory, Democracy and Globalization. He has supervised a Postdoctoral research scholar and is currently guiding Ph.D. scholars under his supervision.

Abdul Muid is an Assistant Professor in the Department of Mechanical and Industrial Engineering.

Izni Azrein Noor Azalie is a human geographer who graduated with an MSc in Global Transformations from Loughborough University UK and is currently in the final stages of his PhD at University College London, researching halal industrial governing and its effects on Brunei agri-food producers. He has been a lecturer at Universiti Brunei Darussalam (UBD) for 14 years. He has been involved in professional consultancies involving environmental and communal advisories relating to oil and gas explorations, environmental monitoring and impact assessments on urban development projects, and socio-economic costs of industrial development towards coastal fisheries and communities in Brunei Darussalam. His research specialisation covers industrial production networks, urban economy and development and industrial development in general. His research has expanded to include studies on creative industrial development, heritage industry conservation and poverty alleviation within the old urban centres. As Brunei embarked on a path of leveraging the development of the blue economy as part of its economic diversification strategies, it became imperative to understand the dynamics between policymakers and governmental strategies and how they are translated into actual practices. This sphere is currently of interest to the researcher.

Ananya Pandey is a Research Scholar in School of Law at Christ University, Bangalore. She has her research interests in the field of Constitutional Law, Environment Law, Human Rights, Food Security, Intellectual Property Law and Jurisprudence.

Leah Pelias is a dedicated scholar and practitioner in the field of Business Management, with a specialized focus on Information Systems. With a strong academic foundation and extensive research engagement, Dr. Pelias has established expertise across several interdisciplinary domains. Her field of specialization spans Multimedia, Design and Development, Identity Management, Recommender Systems, and Business Technology Management. Through this diverse technical scope, she integrates business strategies with innovative digital solutions, enabling organizations to navigate modern technological environments. Dr. Pelias's research interests include Information Systems, Computer Systems Organization, and Computer Systems Applications. Her work focuses on advancing system efficiency, enhancing user-centered technologies, and exploring intelligent computational models that support informed decision-making and improved organizational performance. Committed to both academic growth and practical innovation, Dr. Pelias continues to contribute to the development of emerging technologies that bridge business needs with cutting-edge information systems.

Neha Sah, Assistant Professor at Lovely Professional University, specializes in textiles and fashion design with over eight years of academic and research experience. She holds a Ph.D. in Clothing and Textiles from Govind Ballabh Pant University, with research focusing on technical textiles, including nonwovens and composites derived from chicken feathers and jute fibers. Her expertise includes eco-friendly dyeing, motif adaptation, and innovative textile applications. Dr. Sah has secured research funding under the National Technical Textiles Mission, supervises Ph.D. scholars on topics such as handloom textiles and adaptive garment design, and holds a patent grant for her Ph.D. thesis. She is dedicated to advancing textile education through impactful research, mentoring, and academic leadership.

Francis Sale is a committed researcher and academic specializing in Business Technology Management, with a strong focus on aligning emerging technologies with strategic business processes. His expertise centers on understanding how digital innovations can enhance organizational performance, streamline operations, and support data-driven decision-making. His research interests cover a broad spectrum within the computing discipline, including Information Systems, Computer Systems Organization, and Computer Systems Applications. Through his work, Mr. Sale explores the design, structure, and practical implementation of computer systems that empower organizations to adapt to rapidly evolving technological landscapes. Driven by a passion for innovation and interdisciplinary collaboration, Mr. Sale continues to contribute to the advancement of technology-enabled business solutions, advocating for systems that are efficient, intelligent, and responsive to organizational needs.

Sharifah Nadiah Syed Mukhir is currently a senior lecturer at the School of Communication, Universiti Sains Malaysia where she teaches persuasive communication and marketing. She obtained her PhD in Mass Communication at Ohio University, USA and received her MA in Communication from Universiti Sains Malaysia. She has obtained her Bachelor in Information Technology (Information Systems Engineering) from Multimedia University. She has also received a Foundation Certificate from the Institute of Practitioners in Advertising (IPA), Incorporated by Royal Charter, UK, funded by the Association of Accredited Advertising Agents Malaysia (4As) in 2020. Her research specialisation include consumer culture, advertising, integrated marketing communication and audience research.

Ahmad D. Ubaidillah is an alumna from the Department of Mechanical and Industrial Engineering at State University of Malang

Jing Yi Yong is a Senior Lecturer in the School of Management and Marketing at Taylor's University. She earned her Doctorate degree from Universiti Sains Malaysia, where she delved deep into her passion for exploring the antecedents and outcomes of green human resource management, unearthing invaluable insights into sustainable organizational practices. She has been published in esteemed scholarly journals such as the Journal of Cleaner Production, Business Strategy and Environment, Benchmarking: An International Journal, Industrial and Commercial Training, Journal of Management Development, and the International Journal of Engineering & Technology. Dr. Yong's contributions extend beyond publication, as she actively participates as a reviewer for international journals and conferences. Her research interests span a wide spectrum, including green human resource management, intellectual capital, environmental, social, and governance practices, sustainability, and family business dynamics.

Index

A

Aggregate Risk Potential 319, 323, 326
AI in Journalism 232, 239
Automated Scheduling 241, 272

B

Barro 277, 288, 309
Becker-Schultz 277
Biopiracy 69, 70, 74, 79, 81

C

Charles Jones 277
Conservation 61, 62, 67, 71, 74, 77, 81, 86, 101, 103, 105, 110, 111, 112, 117, 118, 119, 121, 122, 125, 126, 128
Corporate Monopoly 59, 69
Cultural Industry 108, 125

D

Digital Immunization Records 241
Digital Transformation 132

E

Economic benefits 209, 214, 285
Economic Growth 52, 85, 94, 101, 103, 110, 112, 178, 179, 191, 197, 198, 199, 201, 203, 205, 206, 207, 209, 210, 212, 213, 214, 215, 217, 218, 219, 221, 222, 277, 278, 279, 280, 281, 282, 283, 284, 285, 286, 287, 288, 289, 290, 298, 303, 304, 305, 306, 307, 308, 309
employability 33, 34, 35, 37, 42, 43, 45, 49, 50, 51, 52, 53, 54, 179, 181, 182, 190, 191, 192
Environmental Protection 178, 199, 205, 206, 210, 212, 214, 217, 221

F

Future-ready Talent 177, 182, 191
Fuzzy Rules 324, 329, 340

G

Generation Z 3, 6, 11, 12, 20, 21, 23, 25, 26, 31, 83, 84, 96, 97, 98
Genetic Resources 57, 60, 61, 62, 63, 67, 70, 71, 73, 75, 76, 77, 78, 79, 80, 81
goal-setting 33, 34, 35, 36, 50, 54
Governance 68, 83, 84, 85, 86, 87, 90, 91, 92, 93, 95, 96, 97, 104, 129, 203, 204, 211, 219
Growth Models 277, 278, 279

I

Inequality 178, 193, 197, 198, 199, 207, 208, 209, 210, 213, 217, 218, 220, 222, 223, 288, 311
Institutional 35, 58, 59, 62, 69, 71, 72, 292
Intended Exposure 136, 141, 145

J

Job Pursuit Intention 88, 94, 98
Job Search 83, 86, 88, 94, 95

L

Livelihood 61, 67, 73, 76, 112, 211, 213
Lucas 277, 299, 302, 303, 306, 307, 310

M

Malay 102, 112, 113, 117, 118, 123, 125, 128
Mankiw-Romer-Weil 277
Multidimensionality 105, 198, 200, 202, 214

N

Neo-Classical Growth 277

P

Personal Branding 181, 182, 183, 192, 194, 195
Physical Capital 204, 277, 278, 279, 281, 283, 288, 289
Plant Variety Protection 58, 63, 64, 68, 71, 79
Poverty-trap 209
Preventive Action 318, 321, 322, 333, 334, 340

R

RAD 253, 254, 258, 259, 261, 262, 271, 275
Recruitment 42, 91, 92, 178, 179, 180, 182, 183, 184, 190, 191, 193, 195
Rewards System 242, 248, 251, 253, 254, 271
Risk Agent 318, 319, 320, 321, 322, 323, 324, 326, 328, 330, 331, 333, 340
Risk Event 318, 319, 320, 321, 322, 328, 329, 330, 331, 340

S

SDGs 85, 101, 103, 178, 196, 197, 198, 204, 206, 207, 216
Sexual Content 131, 132, 133, 135, 136, 138, 140, 141, 143, 145, 146, 147, 148, 151
Signaling Theory 83, 96
SMS Reminders 241, 249, 270, 271, 272
Social Identity Theory 83, 86, 91, 92
Social Media 2, 3, 4, 6, 7, 11, 19, 20, 21, 22, 23, 25, 26, 29, 38, 39, 50, 84, 122, 138, 148, 149, 153, 154, 155, 156, 157, 158, 159, 160, 161, 162, 163, 164, 165, 166, 168, 169, 170, 171, 173, 174, 176, 177, 179, 180, 181, 182, 183, 184, 185, 186, 187, 188, 189, 190, 191, 193, 194, 195, 196, 217, 226, 228, 231, 232, 233, 234, 235, 239, 240
sport content 160
Sport media 171
Sugar-Free Drinks 1, 3, 4, 7, 8, 9, 10, 11, 17, 21, 23, 27, 28
Sugar Production Company 321
Supply Chain Management 315, 316, 317, 323, 337, 339, 340
Supply Chain Risk Analysis 313
Sustainable Development 59, 61, 62, 73, 74, 80, 85, 86, 88, 91, 98, 101, 102, 103, 104, 118, 178, 196, 197, 198, 199, 205, 206, 210, 211, 214, 216, 218, 219, 220, 222
Sustainable Development Goals 80, 85, 101, 103, 178, 196, 197, 198, 206, 220, 222
Sustainable Digital Persona 179

T

Technology Acceptance Model (TAM) 153, 156, 157, 162, 170, 171, 173, 175, 176
Theory of Reasoned Action 1, 5, 6, 18, 22, 24

U

Unintended Exposure 135, 136, 141, 143, 145, 148, 151
Uses and Gratifications Theory (UGT) 153, 158, 170, 173

V

Vaccine Program 275
Vietnamese Students 1, 19, 34, 35, 39, 52, 131
Voucher 241, 242, 244, 248, 251, 252, 253, 254, 260, 261, 262, 266, 267, 270, 271, 272

www.ingramcontent.com/pod-product-compliance
Lightning Source LLC
LaVergne TN
LVHW080907300926
849162LV00003B/590